'Mark Ledwidge has written an important book on African Americans and US foreign policy. Based on his meticulous research Dr Ledwidge has produced an original and incisive analysis of how African Americans engaged with the development of US foreign policy in the twentieth century and were often thwarted in the process. His cases include the Italian Ethiopian invasion in the 1930s, World War II and the influence of leading African American activists and intellectuals at the foundation of the United Nations. He shows the extent to which African American aims and engagements faced a state dominated by an (often unthinking) white ideology. By focusing so clearly on this one dimension of African American and US politics, Dr Ledwidge builds up an impressive portrait of this key aspect of American political development. The book will be valuable to students and scholars of US history, foreign policy race and politics, and international relations.'

Desmond King, *University of Oxford*, UK

'Mark Ledwidge has broken new ground with this book. Not only has he established that African Americans were interested and active in US foreign affairs, he has also shown, with the most meticulous and painstaking research in American archives, that they were often far more influential than was thought, and that the American state was deeply interested in their activities. Indeed, he shows that unless African American activists and intellectuals were completely 'bought in' to dominant white establishment foreign policy mindsets, they were placed under surveillance, denied basic rights to travel abroad, or faced imprisonment. This book is also timely – with Barack Obama, America's first black head of state. Yet, its message may well be quite bleak in regard to President Obama's chances of transforming America as African Americans who 'succeed' in US politics tend to be thoroughly assimilated into the 'mainstream'. The virtue of Mark Ledwidge's study is that he shows precisely how the processes of white foreign policy elites' engagement with, or marginalisation and repression of, African Americans, actually works.'

Inderjeet Parmar, *University of Manchester*, UK

'Books can be insightful; and sometimes they address underdeveloped areas of knowledge. Rarely do they do both. Ledwidge's book does in exceptional clarity and detail. Through his examination of the role of the African American Foreign Affairs Network, Ledwidge illuminates the complex set of issues connecting race and foreign policy. The book tells us a great deal about that network; still more about the nature of the US; and crucially, still more about the interaction of race and international politics.'

Stuart Croft, *University of Warwick*, UK

Race and US Foreign Policy

African-Americans' analysis of, and interest in, foreign affairs represents a rich and dynamic legacy, and this work provides a cutting-edge insight into this neglected aspect of US foreign affairs.

In addition to extending the parameters of US foreign policy literature to include race and ethnicity, the book documents case-specific analyses of the evolutionary development of the African-American Foreign Affairs Network (AAFAN). Whilst the examination of race in regard to the construction of US foreign policy is significant, this book also provides a cross-disciplinary approach which utilises historical and political science methods to paint a more realistic appraisal of US foreign policy. Including analysis of original archival evidence, this theoretically informed work seeks to transcend the standard mono-disciplinary approach which overestimates the separation between domestic and foreign affairs.

The unique approach of this work will add an important dimension to a newly emerging field and will be of interest to scholars in ethnic and racial studies, American politics, US foreign policy and US history.

Mark Ledwidge is an Honorary Research Fellow in the Department of Politics, University of Manchester, UK.

Routledge Studies in US Foreign Policy

Edited by Inderjeet Parmar, *University of Manchester*
and John Dumbrell, *University of Durham*

This new series sets out to publish high-quality works by leading and emerging scholars critically engaging with United States Foreign Policy. The series welcomes a variety of approaches to the subject and draws on scholarship from international relations, security studies, international political economy, foreign policy analysis and contemporary international history.

Subjects covered include the role of administrations and institutions, the media, think tanks, ideologues and intellectuals, elites, transnational corporations, public opinion, and pressure groups in shaping foreign policy, US relations with individual nations, with global regions and global institutions and America's evolving strategic and military policies.

The series aims to provide a range of books – from individual research monographs and edited collections to textbooks and supplemental reading for scholars, researchers, policy analysts, and students.

Race and US Foreign Policy

The African-American Foreign Affairs Network

Mark Ledwidge

Routledge
Taylor & Francis Group

LONDON AND NEW YORK

First published 2012
by Routledge
2 Park Square, Milton Park, Abingdon, Oxon, OX14 4RN

Simultaneously published in the USA and Canada
by Routledge
711 Third Avenue, New York, NY 10017

Routledge is an imprint of the Taylor & Francis Group, an informa business

British Library Cataloguing in Publication Data
A catalogue record for this book is available from the British Library

Library of Congress Cataloging-in-Publication Data
Ledwidge, Mark.
Race and US foreign policy: the African-American foreign affairs network /
Mark Ledwidge.
p. cm.
Includes bibliographical references and index.
1. United States--Foreign relations--20th century--Citizen
participation. 2. African Americans--Politics and government--
20th century. I. Title.
E744.L425 2011
323.1196'073--dc22
2011005718

ISBN: 978-0-415-48211-0 (hbk)
ISBN: 978-0-203-80618-0 (ebk)

Typeset in Times by Taylor & Francis Books

For all those people whose voices were silenced

Contents

Abbreviations

AAFAN	African-American Foreign Affairs Network
ANC	African National Congress
AUN	Association for the United Nations, Inc.
CAA	Council of African Affairs
CDAAA	Committee to Defend America by Aiding the Allies
CFR	Council on Foreign Relations
CJC	Chicago's Joint Committee
ERC	Ethiopian Research Council
FFF	Fight For Freedom
ICFE	International Council of Friends of Ethiopia
IEW	Italo-Ethiopian War
LON	League of Nations
MOWM	March on Washington Movement
NAACP	National Association for the Advancement of Colored People
NCNW	National Council of Negro Women
NGO	Non-Governmental Organisations
PAC	Pan-African Congress
PARA	Pan-African Reconstruction Association
PCDE	Provisional Committee for the Defence of Ethiopia
RACON	(Survey of) Racial Conditions in the United States
UN	United Nations
UNCIO	United Nations Conference on International Organisation
UNIA	Universal Negro Improvement Association
WASP	White Anglo-Saxon Protestant

1   Introduction

African-Americans' analysis of, and interest in, foreign affairs represents a rich and dynamic legacy dating back to the Haitian Revolution (22 August 1791),[1] and includes the Berlin Conference (1884–85), Belgium's colonisation of the Congo (1885),[2] the Versailles Peace Conference of 1919,[3] the formation of the United Nations Organisation in 1945[4] and the African independence struggle. African-Americans' analysis and engagement with foreign affairs has been largely obscured, because of the assumption that African-Americans have almost exclusively directed their activities towards obtaining domestic equality.[5] According to Benjamin Bowser, 'Black writers and leaders have always made the association between their domestic circumstances and foreign affairs, especially regarding Africa and the Caribbean. This tradition has been developing since World War One as a by-product of black urbanisation and increasing knowledge and awareness of Africa and African issues.'[6]

This book seeks to establish five claims: first, African-Americans were interested in international affairs and US foreign policy; second, African-Americans conceptualised and organised around their view of international relations; third, African-Americans' conception of international relations was not solely derived from white America's conception of foreign affairs nor the government's conception of foreign affairs; fourth, African-Americans' unique political position in US society as a racially oppressed group defined their approach to foreign policy issues; finally, the American state's response to the African-American Foreign Affairs Network (AAFAN) reflected the marginalised status of African-Americans. This book argues that a small group of African-Americans formed foreign affairs networks prior to the First World War (WWI) dedicated to the liberation of African people worldwide. It highlights the evolution of the African-American Foreign Affairs Network between 1900 and 1968 by examining the origins, rise and influence of AAFAN through in-depth case studies, ranging from the discussions surrounding the formation of the League of Nations in Paris (1919–20) to African-Americans' attempts to promote their interests in relation to the formation of the United Nations (1944–45). It also provides insight into the decline of AAFAN (1947–68), and examines its strategies and tactics as well as its internal divisions. There will also be discussion of AAFAN's success in gaining increased access to the foreign affairs establishment and diversifying traditional conceptions of foreign affairs.

This book aims to enhance our knowledge of American political development regarding how power is distributed in a racialised political system. Its priority is the study and analysis of AAFAN in order to establish its membership, ideological parameters, foreign policy proposals and success in achieving its aims. There will be no historical insight into the activities of the US foreign policy establishment as a whole, except where they relate to the activities of AAFAN. This book explains the relationship between rigid structures, such as racial inequality and the maintenance of Anglo-American political hegemony, within the domestic and international arenas. It also extends the parameters of foreign policy to include race and ethnicity within the nucleus of US foreign policy scholarship and consequently expands our knowledge of AAFAN's attempts to move from the political margins (before 1919) in order to promote the interests of African-Americans.[7] The study will assess the degree of elasticity of Western democracy by determining whether a subordinate racial group was provided adequate opportunities to meet its interests. It also indicates that a small cadre of African-Americans demonstrated their commitment to the redemption of African people by attending the 1900 Pan-African Conference in London.[8]

This project demonstrates that African-Americans' fight for political freedom was not exclusively focused on attaining racial equality within the domestic arena.[9]

Benjamin Bowser argued: 'since the turn of the century, there have been over 100,000 books, magazine and newspaper articles published in the US alone on issues related to race.'[10] Indeed, 'virtually every institution in American life has been widely covered – described, criticized, defended and analysed ... [however] ... there is one area in which the impact of racial assumptions has not been widely discussed – foreign policy.'[11] Indeed, despite the recent scholarship of Dudziak, Layton, Plummer and Von Eschen, African-Americans foreign affairs activities are still relatively unknown in mainstream academia. This book examines a (still) neglected topic, i.e. African-Americans' interest in foreign affairs.[12]

This book provides insight into the political behaviour of a racially marginalised group by demonstrating African-Americans' interest 'in global issues ... [as] ... social scientists and the general public have ... underestimated the scope and discounted the richness of this aspect of the Black experience.'[13] W. E. B. Du Bois envisaged the colour-line as the main problem of the twentieth century.[14] This book examines the role of the colour-line in the formation of US foreign policy. Like Plummer, it

> does not place official policy makers at the centre of its narrative. Some ... [scholars] ... will read that displacement as, at worst, an indication that the work lacks legitimacy as a study of the history of foreign relations ... Part of the difficulty lies in the field's tendency to ground

itself in the world view of policy makers, to conflate its own authorial voices with those of official Washington, and see as both normative and neutral the clearly ethnocentric commitments of elite national leadership.[15]

Michael Hunt, Michael Krenn and Thomas McCarthy argue that US foreign policy has endorsed a form of white hegemony.[16] Roediger's racial thesis[17] like Hacker's suggests that America is 'inherently a white country: in character, in structure, in culture ... black Americans create lives of their own. Yet, as a people, they face boundaries ... set by the white majority.'[18] Given the historical evidence, we would expect whites to dominate the formation and execution of US foreign policy. Certainly, US academics have overwhelmingly focused on the activities of elite Euro-Americans or produced research from their perspective.[19] While the twentieth century witnessed the rise of a US foreign policy establishment,[20] less widely recognised has been the rise of the AAFAN.[21]

Structure of the book

Chapter 1 provides an introductory overview of the book by mapping its structure, form and substance. It contains a brief summary of each case study. The aim of each sumary is to identify the existing level of knowledge about AAFAN from 1900 to the late 1960s. In addition to mentioning the methodological approach used in this book, there is a discussion of the four theoretical models that have been selected for testing in relation to the historical evidence.

Chapter 2 focuses on the activities and evolution of AAFAN between 1900 and the early 1920s, examining the Pan-African Conference (1900), the Pan-African Congress (1919) and the Universal Negro Improvement Association's (UNIA) conventions (1920s). It highlights the actions and activities of early Pan-Africanist's such as H. Sylvester Williams, Marcus Garvey and W. E. B. Du Bois.

Chapter 3 provides a detailed account of African-Americans' activities relating to the Italo-Ethiopian War[22] (1935–37), which catapulted foreign affairs to the forefront of the minds of African-Americans and set the stage for successive mobilisations in relation to foreign affairs.[23] Chapter 4 examines the role and the views of the AAFAN and America's entry into the Second World War (WWII). Chapter 5 examines African-Americans attempts to fashion and use the United Nations Organisation (UNO) to highlight domestic and international racial inequalities 1944–45. Chapter 6 address AAFAN's activities during the early Cold War period and the impact of anticommunism on their transnational activities. Chapter 7 explores Malcolm X and Martin Luther King's efforts to influence US foreign policy during the 1960s. Chapter 8 examines the theoretical implications of the historical evidence and considers which theory best explains that evidence.

Chapter 2: The forging of the African-American Foreign Affairs Community

This chapter addresses the formation of the AAFAN and identifies the gaps in the existing knowledge regarding the development of AAFAN[24] from 1900 through the1920s. African-Americans interest in foreign affairs in 1900 was derived from an earlier interest in Africa.[25] For example, the Berlin Conference and Europe's assault on African sovereignty disturbed some African-Americans and prompted them to see racism as a global phenomenon.[26] Significantly the great migration (1915–25) from the South to the North provided African-Americans with increased freedoms which enabled greater participation in political activities.[27] By the early 1900s, African-Americans established a number of significant interest groups,[28] including the Niagara Movement, the National Association for the Advancement of Colored People (NAACP) and the Universal Negro Improvement Association (UNIA).[29] These organisations were dedicated to reforming domestic and international race relations,[30] they championed a multiplicity of views and agendas[31] before proceeding with the examination of AAFAN's ideological and structural parameters. This section considers what principles assisted in the birth of the AAFAN.

African-Americans tendency to view international events though a racial lens was a result of white America's oppressive colour-line, plus their disdain for racial inequality. Indeed, African-Americans' racial consciousness was shaped by the brutal system of enslavement that consigned all Africans to a subordinate role within US society.[32] The alleged inferiority of Africans provided the basis and justification for Euro-Americans' enslavement of African people.[33] Racism justified the post-slavery system of segregation enacted in the American South and the de facto segregation that existed in the North. In short, American racism forced African-Americans to live separate and unequal lives in relation to white America. Hence race assumed a primary basis for black organisational activities; although inter-racial organisations existed prior to the 1960s civil rights struggle in America, this was the exception rather than the rule.

In brief, African-Americans' racial consciousness was a product of American history that had been shaped by a rigid and hierarchical colour-line[34] founded on Euro-American hegemony.

Ideological diversity of AAFAN

The structural parameters of AAFAN reflected the complexities facing a marginal group attempting to effect changes from below whilst operating in a hostile socio-political and economic environment dedicated to maintaining the status quo. The AAFAN was not a structured organisation like the Council on Foreign Relations (CFR).[35] As AAFAN was not a formal organisation,[36] the activities of individual African-Americans and their organisations regarding foreign affairs were stimulated on a case-by-case basis by particular international issues. In short, the marginal status of black America hampered their organisational capacity. Regarding the composition of the AAFAN, Plummer indicates that 'the black foreign policy audience initially sprang from a core of politicians, clergy, press, intellectuals, and cadres from Christian, social welfare and peace organisations. It was later joined by conventional civil rights groups and organisations.'[37] Although Plummer utilises the word 'audience' regarding African-Americans' interest in foreign affairs, this book utilises the term 'network'. This book argues that between 1900 and 1945 African-Americans evolved from the audience phase by increasing their participation in foreign affairs. Consequently network[38] is better suited to describing African-Americans' involvement in international issues. In short, African-Americans' foreign affairs activities created a network dedicated to influencing global events rather than observing them (as an audience might). AAFAN transcended its audience phase when it attempted to shape foreign affairs. Finally the term 'network' transcends national boundaries and reflects the Pan-African ethos of Du Bois, Garvey and Malcolm X who sought to mobilise people of African descent (on a global basis) in their fight for racial liberation.[39]

This book suggests that AAFAN began as a small network of loosely organised black activists who were ideologically heterogeneous and whose organisational sophistication developed relative to their increased exposure and activities in relation to foreign affairs. Although Plummer provides no specific date for the emergence of AAFAN, her research indicates that the twentieth century witnessed the rise of AAFAN. Certainly, the 1900 Pan-African Conference, organised by H. Sylvester Williams and W. E. B. Du Bois, indicates diasporean Africans' desire to form foreign affairs interest groups.[40] Additionally the Niagara Movement and the UNIA formulated long-range programmes designed to effect changes in the international arena.[41] The limited success of these African-American interest groups attests to the structural impediments that hampered the efforts of black organisations during the early part of the twentieth century. Plummer challenged the view that African-Americans ignored foreign affairs as 'the density of organisational networks ... question(s) the literature on political participation which maintained that blacks were isolationists and lacked the resources to participate in a wide spectrum of social and political activities.'[42] AAFAN's activities between 1900 and the 1960s involved an array of African-American leaders and their (respective) organisations with representatives from the grass roots and the 'talented tenth'.[43]

Members of the AAFAN employed multi-faceted ideologies[44] to advance their goals. For example, the NAACP was formed to promote domestic racial equality and it actively engaged in foreign affairs.[45] The evidence indicates that the NAACP's involvement in international issues was pioneered by W. E. B. Du Bois,[46] a central figure within the NAACP and the Pan-Africanist movement.[47]

Du Bois exemplified African-Americans' dual commitment to fighting domestic and international white supremacy.[48] However, Du Bois' two-pronged strategy was not unique. Indeed, whilst campaigning to win 'Africa for the Africans,'[49] Garvey and the UNIA promoted the national development of African-Americans and people of African descent[50] wherever they were in the world. One of the major differences between Garvey and Du Bois' liberal Pan-Africanism was the latter's relationship with white people. While Garvey avoided contact with the white establishment, Du Bois and Robert Moton, the heir to Booker T. Washington's Tuskegee Institute, actively sought and ultimately established links with the US foreign policy establishment.[51] The degree of black interaction with the white establishment (later) became a significant factor regarding which strategy African-Americans endorsed whilst in pursuit of their interests.[52]

Historical and ideological continuity

The issue of race featured heavily in the literature reviewed, especially in the work of black writers. The literature reviewed referred to the integrationist and nationalist ideologies. According to James Cone, the integrationist and nationalist philosophies are the primary theoretical frameworks utilised by African-Americans in their fight for black liberation.[53] Integrationists desire to enter into the American mainstream,[54] while black nationalists favour the formation of a separate black nation in an attempt to avoid contact and coalitions with white people.[55] The integrationist and nationalist theories represent divergent schools of thought championed by African-American activists within the domestic context. However, the assimilationist and separatist ideologies influenced African-Americans conception and implementation of their international agenda. The liberal wing of AAFAN was more inclined to pursue coalitions with the white majority, while nationalists favoured organising on a racial basis. Consequently, AAFAN's appeal to white or predominantly white institutions was determined by the relative strength of the integrationist and nationalist philosophies at that time. Therefore, researchers should acknowledge how the political ideology of members of AAFAN influenced the strategies they adopted in pursuit of their aims. The evidence suggests African-Americans utilised variants of the nationalist and integrationist theories that were more commonly associated with domestic race relations to conceptualise foreign affairs.

The literature examined fell into two distinct categories. Generally the mainstream foreign policy literature ignores the possibility that US foreign policy has had a racial orientation. One could argue that the all-encompassing nature of the American colour-line is not adequately reflected in many researchers' analysis of US foreign policy.[56] W. E. B. Du Bois maintained that American 'foreign policy … [is] … a mirror image of [its] domestic policy. [Thus] a nation whose … white citizens could not treat with equity, justice and equality, Black neighbours and citizens living in the same … nation could not develop a foreign policy involving international relationships reflecting equality and justice with two-thirds of the people of the world who are of colour.'[57]

Ledwidge argues that America's racial worldview shaped its foreign policy.[58] Hunt's examination of the 'Black legend',[59] regarding America's perception of Latin-American states, illustrates the foreign policy establishment's utilisation of racial stereotypes to inform its policies. Hunt indicates that the racism of the White Anglo-Saxon Protestant (WASP) elite in tandem with US national interests justified and promoted American domination of people of colour.[60] Thus American imperialism was racial in character.[61] America's racial worldview was utilitarian in nature as it helped to establish and maintain white domination domestically and internationally.[62] For some African-Americans the idea of a race neutral brand of US foreign policy is absurd given that the foreign policy establishment and Americans in general have failed to establish racial equality domestically.[63] For example, Parmar points to the alleged racism of Council on Foreign Relations member Elihu Root.[64] Given that the CFR claimed to be motivated by scientific and rational deliberations,[65] evidence of CFR racism suggests that US foreign policy should be examined from a racial perspective.[66]

Although Hunt's thesis is cogent and important, his thesis regarding race and foreign affairs needs to be expanded because Hunt's argument only examined how WASP racism shaped US foreign policy. Hunt's thesis needs to be examined in conjunction with the worldview or activities of non-white groups in order to ascertain what role they or their ideas played in relation to the construction of US foreign policy. The examination of AAFAN's activities extends Hunt's (WASP) thesis and examines African-Americans' worldview in addition to views of the WASP elite. Interestingly black writers such as Clarke concur with Hunt's theory regarding racism's impact on US foreign policy. Clarke argues that Europeans and Euro-Americans have conducted international relations from a racial perspective in order to support their national interests.[67] Indeed, Du Bois argued that the 'Negro problem in America ... [was] ... a local phase of a world problem.'[68] The Pan-African Conference of 1900 and succeeding Pan-African Congresses thought white supremacy was global in nature and therefore required the coordinated efforts of all people of African descent to defeat it.[69]

Given black writer's concern about US foreign policy[70] the absence of in-depth studies pertaining to African-Americans' activities in relation to foreign policy is problematic.[71] The fact that mainstream foreign affairs literature has not been systematically explored, AAFAN's internationalism (within the context of American history) is problematic as African-Americans articulated their foreign policy positions to the US government. It could be argued that African-Americans' views on foreign affairs were of little interest to the American state, but this contention is negated by the interest of the US State Department and that of domestic intelligence agencies in African-Americans' international outlook.[72] However, the State Department and the

General Intelligence Department of the Federal Bureau of Investigation[73] were primarily concerned with neutralising or containing African-American activists involved in foreign policy advocacy,[74] at least until WWII. The state's campaign to neutralise the nationalist and Pan-Africanist wing of the African-American liberation movement necessitates an in-depth study regarding the alleged threat they posed to domestic race relations. Black Nationalism and Pan-Africanism will be examined in order to ascertain their relevance to the formation of the AAFAN and their attempts to direct US foreign policy.

Case study method

The use of case studies in this book relates to the following factors. Ultimately, case studies are an acceptable means of conducting research in a wide array of academic disciplines.[75] According to Yin, use of historical, sociological and political science methods in addition to archival data complements the use of case studies.[76]

Yin's contention justifies the use of political science theories and the case study method to ascertain why AAFAN's foreign affairs preferences were peripheral to the construction of US foreign policy. The utilisation of three historical case studies provides greater scope to assess for continuities via the case studies. The three case studies plus Chapters 2, 7 and 8 allow for a balanced account of the subject matter. Likewise, the theoretical models add additional weight to the final conclusions. This book's cross-disciplinary approach has incorporated data from history, sociology, political science, black studies' international relations and primary data from archives in Britain and America.

The case studies

The empirical component of this thesis will focus on the case studies. The first three were constructed to test the theories used in this thesis.

Chapter 3: A case study of the Italo-Ethiopian War 1934–36

This case study examines the role of the AAFAN during the Italo-Ethiopian War (IEW) (1934–36) and specifically focuses on the objectives, activities and accomplishments of the AAFAN. It, like the additional case studies, facilitates the utilisation of racial and political science theories to draw insightful conclusions from the empirical data. This case study ascertains whether there were any formal links between the AAFAN and the wider foreign policy community during the IEW, which will aid in tracking the evolutionary development of the AAFAN.

Although researchers have examined the Italo-Ethiopian War (IEW) few have provided a systematic account of the war's impact on domestic race relations or acknowledged how America's racial worldview shaped its orientation towards Italy and Ethiopia, and whether the respective racial status of Italian and African-Americans affected the administration's response to both groups.

In addition, the varied perspectives of the authors must be contextualised within America's domestic arena and within the global context. Also the significant data concerning continental and diasporean Africans' efforts to aid Ethiopia, which substantiate their desire to maintain Ethiopian sovereignty,[77] must be highlighted in order to construct an accurate account of their views regarding the war.

Given America's isolationist policies prior to and especially after WWI, one could argue that the US government's isolationist policies were a familiar response to international conflicts. However, most authors fail to acknowledge the significance of race in relation to America's orientation to the IEW.

African-Americans' efforts to aid Ethiopia raises the question of why their anti-colonialist stance (during the IEW) has not been linked with the anti-colonialist tendencies espoused by continental and diasporean Africans after (and during) WWII. That white people, especially WASPs, have dominated US foreign policy[78] could be extended in regard to Western academia's tendency to focus their research on issues geared to their own interests.[79] The relative absence of African-American academics (historically) has led to an absence of literature outlining the black experience in America. The lack of African-American academics is a direct consequence of America's institutional racism which has insulated the white population from competing on a level playing field with African-Americans, as white people have assumed the dominant position over black people within US society.[80] The Italo-Ethiopian War lent credence to the black nationalist contention that white nations were bent on the racial subordination of black people everywhere;[81] As a result, black nationalism became the dominant political ideology among African-Americans[82] between 1934 and 1936. The war also led to African-Americans' wider appreciation of and ideological adherence to Pan-Africanism. Martin Delany's maxim, 'Africa for the Africans at home and abroad' was reflected in African-Americans' response to the IEW which explains why the remnants of the UNIA were central to the campaign to aid Ethiopia.[83] Indeed, Marcus Garvey, whose deportation from America had stripped him of much of his influence, rallied behind Ethiopia in articles printed in his official organisational paper, the *Black Man Magazine*.[84] American racism, and black people's desire for self-determination, encouraged them to form separate organisations despite attempts to establish a popular front that was ideologically and racially diverse.[85]

The IEW clarified the relationship between African-Americans and people of African descent worlwide and encouraged African-Americans to evaluate US foreign policy and international relations. The war propelled the black nationalists' thesis regarding the colonial status of African-Americans to the forefront of the black struggle.

Chapter 4: From isolationism to globalism: African-Americans' response to US entry into the Second World War (1939–41)

This case study examines the AAFAN's response to America's intervention into World War II. The case study highlights the US administration and allied nation's claims that the fight for freedom against the Axis Powers (Germany, Italy, Japan) was a fight to defend democracy. However, for African-Americans who were effectively second-class citizens on the fringes of US society, America's fight for democracy did not guarantee the democratic rights of its black population. In addition, African-Americans recognised that America's support for the Allies would ultimately result in the maintenance of those countries colonial possessions.[86] For example, A. Philip Randolph, the 'leader of the ... March on Washington Movement, declared that his organisation ... [would] ... link the interests of ... [black Americans to] ... the interests of ... [blacks globally. Randolph asked] ... Are we fighting ... [WWII] ... to restore Singapore, Malaya and Burma to ... Britain? [he also asked] Must Africa continue to live in the slavery of the mandated colonialism of white powers.'[87] Randolph's statement indicates his partial acceptance of the Pan-Africanist model of international relations advanced by Du Bois and Garvey, still Randolph would not have considered himself a Pan-Africanist. This case study examines African-Americans' divided loyalties stemming from the contradictions of supporting a war against fascism abroad, which meant supporting a racialised colonial system, whilst fighting for and being denied domestic racial equality. This case study highlights the debate within the African-American community concerning fighting in what many initially considered a 'white man's war'.[88] African-American journalist George Schuyler maintained: 'so far as the coloured peoples of the earth are concerned, it is a toss-up between the democracies and the dictatorships ... what is there to choose between the rule of the British in Africa and the rule of the Germans in Austria?'[89] Consequently, this case study examines AAFAN's response to America's interventionist policies between 1939 and 1941, when the US abandoned its isolationist foreign policy.[90]

America's entry into the war was significant for African-Americans for the following reasons. Despite the fact America entered WWII to defend its national interests, the propaganda used to justify America's entry into WWII focused on the illegitimacy of the Axis Powers' non-democratic character.[91] Despite allied rhetoric concerning the four freedoms, their claims were contravened by allied colonialism and American racism.[92] Despite the 'widespread indifference, even hostility, on the part of the Negro community to the war',[93] African-Americans did not support Hitler or Germany.[94]

While the allied powers highlighted the racial extremism of Nazi Germany,[95] It has been suggested that Hitler's doctrine of white supremacy shared some similarities with America's racial colour-line.[96] Britain and France's foreign affairs record was also marred by racism as black people recognised:

the lie that Belgium, France, and America will fight any war for liberty and civilisation. For it is in Africa that Negroes ... suffered ... the vilest tortures ... Germany hasn't an inch in Africa. That is one of the things this war is about, the partition of Africa. Hitler wants some of Africa ... Japan has not an inch in Africa ... Mussolini controls a small number of Africans. Who is it then that has sixty million slaves, and France, with another forty million Negroes under its control? These democracies are the thieves.[97]

African-Americans and diasporean Africans recognised that Nazi propaganda was a logical out-growth of white racism in general. Consequently, some African-Americans maintained that WWII was a fight between white nations[98] bent on achieving international supremacy. Du Bois stated: 'if Hitler wins, down with the blacks! If the democracies win, the blacks are already down.'[99]

Blacks argued that their service in the armed forces should be conditional upon the desegregation of the armed forces and the dismantling of the 'Jim Crow' system in general. African-Americans recognised that they were combatants within the domestic and international arena. Therefore, African-Americans engaged in a two pronged attack: 'the Double V slogan ... victory for democracy abroad and at home was the American Negro's battle cry. Victory meant ... victory over the Axis. To American Negroes victory also meant independence for colonized peoples.'[100] A. Philip Randolph called for a march on Washington in order to embarrass the US administration into giving African-Americans access to government employment, significantly, African-Americans recognised that the war provided the political leverage for African-Americans to engage in a pre-1960s civil rights struggle that challenged America to promote domestic reforms in order to align its alleged foreign policy objectives[101] with its domestic political practice.[102]

The assumption that African-Americans would blindly support the Allies' (alleged) war on fascism is problematic given the nature of American race relations. Many scholars have overlooked the fact that some African-Americans perceived WWII as a struggle (excluding Japan) between white imperialist nations competing over the resources of the colonialised world.

Chapter 5: African-Americans and the formation of the United Nations Organisation 1944–47

This case study examines America's post-war foreign policy dilemmas: how it could reconcile the idealistic foreign policy propaganda, such as the 'Atlantic Charter' that proclaimed democratic freedom despite the existence of British and French colonialism; and how it could reconcile domestic racism while an ascendant Soviet Union called for the end of colonialism.

American racism was challenged by AAFAN's proposed resolutions that were designed to realign domestic and international race relations.

The creation of the UN laid the basis for the reconstruction of American and international race relations, as African-Americans attempted to utilise the human rights issue to promote domestic racial reforms. In addition, people of African descent in the Caribbean and Africa mobilised to promote international racial equality and subsequently organised a Pan-African congress in 1945. This case study focuses on the efforts of a politically marginalised group to win power by connecting its domestic agenda to international issues and thereby laying the basis for the 1960s civil rights struggle and African de-colonisation.

The formation of the UN was finalised at the San Francisco conference in 1945.[103] The aim of the UN was to establish, maintain and promote international order. The UN was designed to establish international peace and to prevent another world war, by providing 'collective security' within the international arena.[104]

This case study explores AAFAN's efforts to lobby the UN on behalf of African-Americans and people of African descent in order to secure five demands: first, granting basic human rights and political freedom to colonial subjects; second, the right of self-government for colonised people; third, eliminating the system of racial exploitation in the international arena; fourth, undermining the colonial powers' capitalist exploitation of the colonised territories; finally, granting independence to the colonialised territories in order to end colonial rule.

It explores how America's colour line threatened its foreign policy goals, i.e., the propagation of American political ideals to a global audience.[105] According to Mary L. Dudziak, the US State Department's attempt to demonstrate the superiority of the democratic political system, vis-à-vis the challenge posed by the Soviet Union, was undermined by its treatment of African-Americans.[106]

The UN case study illustrates African-Americans' utilisation of the anti-racist and pro-freedom principles espoused by the Allies during WWII[107] to reconstruct domestic and international race relations in order to increase the political power of people of colour after the war.[108] This case study reveals the friction caused by the attempts of African-Americans such as Walter White to end colonialism and (what they defined as) a racially based system of white domination both domestically and internationally throughout the colonies.

It shows that the activism of Walter White was linked to the internationalism advocated by Garvey and Du Bois, which had highlighted the transnational character of the colour-line. By the end of WWII 'black American intellectuals were united in believing that the battle against white racism in their own country could not be won without a larger international battle against colonial imperialism in Africa.'[109] By 1945 the NAACP, the National Urban League, and the Council on African Affairs believed that the status of African-Americans was intimately connected to the fate of Africa.[110] The link between the pre- and post-WWII internationalism needs to be highlighted, especially since Du Bois was an active participant in early Pan-Africanism as well as post-war internationalism.

African-Americans involvement in the UN conference justifies the examination of this case study as three African-Americans were granted consultant status at the San Francisco Conference by the US Administration.[111] Given Hunt's racial thesis, the inclusion of three African-Americans by the state in US foreign affairs needs to be explained, especially since all three were representatives of the NAACP.[112] Although Carol Anderson suggests that African-Americans' anti-colonial foreign policy was 'diametrically opposed to that of the Western powers',[113] Solomon maintains that as late as December 1944 the US Department of State articulated its concern for the plight of the African colonies.[114] Significantly Solomon's contention suggests AAFAN's foreign affairs agenda was compatible with the Truman administration's foreign policy aims (in 1945). Alternatively, Harris maintains that post-1944 through to the UN conference the 'State Department laboured under the notion of preserving the status quo for African colonies.'[115] The contradictory assertions of Anderson and Harris regarding the State Department's orientation towards colonialism raised questions regarding the orientation of the Truman administration as a whole to colonialism, and raised complex issues in relation to the US government's desire to gain new economic markets and its orientation towards British imperial preference, whilst attempting to contain the Soviet Union.

The case study illustrates that African-Americans desired to win greater political power for themselves and people of colour (globally), to the extent that major African-American organisations generally subordinated their ideological differences to their common attempt to re-order race relations within the domestic and international context. As a result, members of AAFAN held preparatory meetings prior to the UN conference and although African-Americans presented a united front to the US Administration, issues pertaining to wider representation did arise. The next chapter examines the aftermath of the struggle to insert a racial clause in the UN charter by detailing African-American efforts to petition the UN to encourage America to reconfigure its domestic colour line and outlines the negative impact of America's cold war politics on African-Americans global consciousness.

Chapter 6: Human rights, racial reconstruction and the Cold War 1950–60

This chapter foregrounds the 1950s as being the historical conduit which witnessed the formation and mobilisation of the conservative and progressive forces that precipitated the monumental clashes of the 1960s. This chapter establishes the link between the fight to maintain or end white hegemony within America and; the struggle to maintain or end white hegemony in the global context. The chapter follows AAFAN's attempt to support African independence whilst adhering to the narrow confines of McCarthyite politics, increased political repression and their efforts to overturn Jim Crow without been labeled as communist agitators. Alternatively the chapter illustrates how

American racism hampered her efforts to contain communism and win the support of the developing world.

Chapter 7: Malcolm and Martin and the shadow of US Foreign Policy

This chapter examines two of the most controversial and acclaimed leaders of the African-American liberation struggle. This chapter departs from academic orthodoxy as it highlights King and Malcolm's orientation to foreign affairs. The chapter broadly suggests that the civil rights legislation of 1964 and 1965 resulted from the mass mobilisation of African-Americans; in addition to the requirements of US foreign policy. The primary thesis of the chapter maintains that while sections of the US establishment recognized the need to eradicate the overt aspects of US racial oppression the liberalisation of American race relations did not extend to the arena of foreign policy.

Consequently the chapter contends that in regard to King and Malcolm's foray into foreign affairs that there was a qualitative difference in the states response to issues related to the domestic sphere; while criticism of foreign affairs received swift and decisive condemnation from both the executive branch and the intelligence apparatus of the state. The chapter will highlight Malcolm X's attempt to petition the UN to charge the United States for violating the human rights of African-Americans in addition to Kings criticism of US involvement in the war in Vietnam.

Theoretical approaches and methodology

This section discusses the four theoretical models selected for testing and explains the methodology utilised in this book. It examines the theoretical models and is followed by a brief discussion of US foreign policy. Each theory will be discussed in relation to its utilisation. The section will provide the justification for the use of theories in this book. Any valid theoretical model should explain AAFAN's political status within the American context. The four theoretical models – pluralism, statism, Marxist Theory and racialism– will be assessed relative to their predictions concerning AAFAN's efforts to influence US foreign policy. This will be compared to the empirical evidence to determine if the evidence supports their conclusions. The theory, or theories, that accords with AAFAN's status in relation to US foreign policy will be validated. The theory, or theories, that do not explain AAFAN's role in relation to US foreign policy will be invalidated.

The theories provide an analytical framework designed to draw conclusions when applied to the empirical data. They will explain AAFAN's standing in relation to US foreign policy and assist in the examination of the empirical data in order to generate and answer the questions derived from the theories. One goal of this research is to assess how AAFAN sought to win power from below. Therefore the methodological and theoretical approaches explain the origin, rise and influence of the AAFAN in relation to US foreign policy.

US foreign policy

Although domestic and foreign policy issues are often studied in isolation from each other, a nation's foreign policy is ultimately connected to its domestic political, social and economic configuration.[116] While the dynamics of conducting foreign and domestic policy are different, a nation's domestic context cannot be neatly separated from its foreign policy. Indeed, some authors claim that US foreign policy has conformed to America's overall conceptions of race[117] whereby Euro-Americans have sought to maintain their dominance over people of colour.[118] Other authors claim that African-Americans' conception of and interest in foreign affairs has been marginal to the construction of US foreign policy.[119] Still the idea that African-Americans have played a marginal role in foreign policy must take into account that foreign policy[120] is generally insulated from public participation.[121]

Theories to be tested

This section examines the four theories by describing them briefly, and highlighting testable propositions designed to explain/predict the substance of the empirical data derived from the case studies.

Pluralism

'[M]ost Western students of politics tend to start ... with the assumption that power in Western societies is competitive, fragmented and diffused; [i.e. pluralist] everybody, directly or through organized groups, has some form of power and nobody has or can have too much of it'.[122] Pluralism suggests that power within modern political systems should be, and perhaps is (in America), dispersed between organised or potentially organised groups.[123] It prioritises a dispersal of socio-political and economic power in order to prevent the concentration of power. However, pluralism 'does not mean that all citizens are included in the political process. Dahl ... [maintains] ... that many citizens are inactive, that income and wealth and political resources are unequally distributed.'[124]

Pluralism credits America's separation of powers in the government[125] and the federal system, which guarantees state rights, with preventing a concentration of power in the US political system.[126]

Pressure group pluralism

This book emphasises pressure group pluralism. Although, Bentley notes the centrality of pressure group pluralism, the question is how do interests groups correct power inequalities, since 'Pluralists do not see all pressure groups as having equal resources, access or influence.'[127] This study assesses the AAFAN's relative power regarding foreign policy by observing the relative correlation between their policies, aims and the substance of US foreign policy. Pluralists underestimate the impact of ideology[128] and institutional hegemony pertaining to group representation in the decision-making process as 'the influence of pressure groups does not derive [only] from their resources but also from the institutional, historical and ideological context within which decisions are made.'[129] Given African-Americans historical exclusion from voting, it is feasible that the preconditions for a pluralist political system did not exist for generations of African-Americans. In short, pluralism fails to account for the color-line.[130] The melting pot thesis, which assumes that marginal groups can be incorporated into the political mainstream (which is dominated by the WASP contingent) is also suspect because[131] despite the assimilation of white ethnics,[132] African-Americans phenotype has been a visual barrier to their incorporation into mainstream America. In short, 'Nathan Glazer, Milton Gordon, and Talcott Parsons ... [belief in the] ... egalitarianism of U.S intuitions and. ... [the] ... progressive emancipation of non-European groups'[133] ignores white America's aversion to African-Americans.

Pluralism *argues that in the US competitive groups are presented with broadly equal opportunities to vie for their interests.*[134] *Thus, if a group accepts American values they can assimilate into American political culture. In short, pluralists would contend that 'racial and ethnic factors ... [would] ... play no role at all in the distributive process, either positive or negative. Therefore, pluralists would argue that African-Americans' exclusion from the 'foreign policy establishment' was based on their organisational weakness or lack of proven intellectual ability, not their racial identity. Pluralism would predict that one group would not dominate foreign policy.*

Statism

Statists argue the state author's and executes policies geared to its own agenda.[135] The state's ability/inability to operate independently is important given the state's central role domestically and internationally. Statists refute claims that the state is a benevolent, impartial entity that provides equal protection for all social groups.[136] 'Indeed, autonomous state actions often take forms designed to reinforce the authority, political longevity, and control of the state organisations whose incumbents generated the relevant policies or policy ideas. In short, one hidden or overt feature of all autonomous state actions will be the reinforcement of the prerogatives of collectivities of state officials'.[137] That is, 'the top decision makers [in the state] formulate policy according to their own values and interests, without taking account of the values and interests of the general public.'[138] In brief, 'The special position of the state in foreign policy consists. ... in the formal and informal obligations that the President and state Department in particular, are charged with to further the "national interest." The President and state Department are highly insulated ... "from specific societal pressures," and therefore ... enjoy a high level of autonomy in establishing goals and promoting policies for their realisation.'[139]

Evidently the state possesses a level of autonomy; hence state officials do operate outside the boundaries of popular democracy.[140] The ability of powerful interests to contravene democratic mechanisms was addressed by C. Wright Mills who pointed to a power elite within US society, with 'psychological and social unity'.[141] Still Mills ignored the racial and gender characteristics of America's power elite.[142] Discussions concerning state policies and state autonomy must view the state and US democracy as a contested arena which has reflected America's racial bias.[143] In short, Statists have failed to highlight the racial orientation of US policies in regard to domestic and international politics.[144] However, Des King acknowledges the overt racial orientation of the US state prior to the 1960's.[145] Still the American state has undermined selective white interests' by advancing policies, which reconfigured the colour-line in defence of national interests.[146]

In short, 'foreign policy has to be understood as being made in certain domestic and international contexts';[147] whereby domestic racism has facilitated a racial brand of foreign affairs.[148] In short, the US state has endorsed the colour-line in foreign and domestic policies.[149]

The state has acted as an interdependent entity, which maintained racial conventions[150] but also reconfigured race relations as required.

Statist Theory *contends that state interests would be the dominant factor*[151] *in AAFAN's inclusion or exclusion from the US 'foreign policy establishment'. To validate statism the empirical data should confirm that the state arbitrated participation in US foreign policy, resulting in the state's domination of group interests and the control of foreign policy by state officials. The statist model would be falsified if the data indicated that foreign policy was defined by competing interest groups or that private interests directed the state's foreign policy and determined which groups were represented in US foreign policy. However, if African-Americans achieved their foreign policy goals despite state opposition, their influence in US foreign policy, in relation to the specified case studies, would be validated.*

Marxist Theory

Marx and Engels presented an economic account of human history.[152] Marx saw socio-political conflicts as symptoms of class conflict within the economic sphere. Marx argued that economic competition generated distinct classes which desired 'ownership and control over the means of production and the distribution of the fruits of the productive process.'[153] Marx defined capitalism as a system of exploitation where the bourgeoisie dominate the proletariat.[154] Marx defined the proletariat and bourgeoisie,[155] as the principal classes in industrialised states[156] and argued that capitalist exploitation would cause a class war thus destroying capitalism and creating a communist state, which would outlaw private ownership.[157]

The state

According to Marxism the state upholds the bourgeoisie's control over the proletariat,[158] since economic dominance does not equate to political dominance, Marx suggests that economic dominance is augmented via the ruling class's production of ideas and culture, which is predicated on producing ideas that reinforce the status quo.

While, Marx and Engels accepted the possibility of state autonomy, they defined it as temporary[159] suggesting that the bourgeoisie's economic power facilitated their control over the state.[160] Despite revisionists re-interpretations, most Marxists still accord the economic arena a central position in their conceptual worldview.[161]

Marxism was selected because its revolutionary character appealed to a small cadre of African-American communists who believed it could rectify their subordinate status in America,[162] and because the economic exploitation of African-Americans' could be explained by class as opposed to a racial analysis.

Marxism *contends that the capitalist class controls the state.*[163] *Given African-Americans' inferior economic or class status,*[164] *Marxists would predict that their role in relation to foreign policy decisions would be minimal. Marxism would be validated if AAFAN's involvement in US foreign policy was marginal in relation to the substance of its policies. Marxism would be invalidated if AAFAN was able to incorporate their interests into US foreign policy and if AAFAN's racial status led to the marginalisation of their foreign affairs goals, as Marxism contends that class not race is the primary determinant of a group's political dominance or marginality.*

The racialized state

In domestic politics interest groups compete to direct state policies.[165] Thus the state is a contested arena through which interest groups seek to advance their interests. The presumption is that the identity of state executives affects the substance of state policies.[166] Despite the election of Obama (2008), WASP's are still a predominant force in US politics.[167] In short, the WASP elite have dominated US society,[168] in government and in the private sector in America.[169] Overall, the white population have had unequal access/entry into the state.[170] For most of US history, the state's main objective in its racial policy was repression and exclusion.[171] In addition, the US state has advanced racialised foreign policies'.[172] Thus America's foreign policy should be assessed in regard to racial bias.

Racial Colony

The central premise of the racial colony thesis is derived from the claims of numerous authors who argue that white America has deliberately oppressed African-Americans. This thesis accepts the premise of Des King in relation to the US state's institutionalised racism, indeed the federal government is assumed to have played a significant role in the construction of the colour-line. In short, white America, including the federal government, is conceived primarily as a socio-political and economic construct whereby African-American's marginalised racial status is relative to the historical cultural and political context. The fundamental premise of the Racial Colony thesis is that Euro-Americans have dominated America's political and economic institutions from the inception of that nation. Indeed, according to Wilson, white America strictly and stringently controls entry and naturalisation of outsiders within its bounds. This is especially the case in regard to black Americans. Memberships and naturalised citizenship within the white nation are carefully scrutinised, given long consideration (especially for non-Europeans) and is grudgingly and tentatively tendered.[173]

Wilson's emphasis revolves around white people's ability to exclude non-white people from positions of power, authority and legitimacy within important US institutions. Given that exclusion, one would expect that African-Americans' foreign policy goals to be marginalised due to the relative power inequalities that exist between African and Euro-Americans. However, Wilson acknowledges the possibility of group assimilation within the US as

> any group which achieves substantial economic surplus combined with cohesive economic-political organization and distinctive group consciousness and identity, can and does exert power and influence beyond their actual numbers in the general population. An economically enriched, articulated tribe can use its leverage to significantly influence the actions and attitudes of the dominant White American nation and perhaps make deep inroads into its social, economic and political infrastructure. Ultimately, some of these tribal groups may be truly assimilated into the White American nation.[174]

While many authors maintain that American society is essentially a meritocracy, the historical experiences of African-Americans challenge and negate that contention.[175] Essentially, the oppressed status of African-Americans is assumed to be derived from their racial designation as black people or Africans. Significantly, there is no evidence that the immigrant model of assimilation applies to African-Americans, especially since most US immigrants have come from Europe. Therefore, irrespective of their ethnicity, the majority of immigrants were essentially white, which facilitated their incorporation within the domestic context. Indeed,

> No group, in the history of the United States has ever sustained the high level of residential segregation that has been imposed on blacks in large American cities for the past fifty years. This extreme racial isolation did not just happen; it was manufactured by whites through a series of

self-conscious actions and purposeful institutional arrangement that continue today. Not only is the depth of black segregation unprecedented and utterly unique compared with any other groups, but it shows little sign of change with the passage of time or improvements in socio-economic status.[176]

In addition to the racial aspect of this theory, other authors maintain that African-Americans have been colonised by the white majority.[177] Although there are some problems with this analogy,[178] 'one ... is unavoidably struck by the political oppression and economic exploitation of the Black community which stand at the heart of any form of colonialism.'[179] The racialised colony model suggests that African-Americans would not generally attain positions of power within the US administration. The essential characteristics of a colonised African population would be replicated within the American context, whereby the political goals of African-Americans would be secondary to the desires of the white majority. 'Colonial subjects have their political decisions made for them by the colonial masters, and those decisions are handed down directly or through a process of "indirect rule".'[180] Just as British colonialists ruled the African masses through a specially selected cadre of Africans loyal to the colonial establishment,[181] Ture argues that 'the white power structure rules the black community through local blacks who are responsive to the white leaders.'[182] Of course, history has shown that the colonised population would generally attempt to define and execute its own interests, in addition to developing its own organic cadre of leaders dedicated to challenging the colonial power. The aforementioned theme is clearly evident in African-American history, as African-Americans have both colluded with and challenged the white establishment. In short, this theory will demonstrate that African-Americans had a varied response to their marginal racial status in relation to their attempts to influence US foreign policy.

Racialized Colony

This theory suggests that white racism is a central characteristic of US society,[183] which determines the relative power of African-Americans in relation to white America.[184] This theory maintains that white people's racial dominance has facilitated their institutional control over the decision-making apparatus in America.[185] The US state is viewed as an instrument of white power, which generally promoted and protected white interests.[186] This theory argues that African-Americans have been politically and economically colonised by whites.[187] In short, the economic and political dominance of white America over black America is assumed to constitute white colonial dominance over black people 'on the basis of the division and separateness of the black and white American communities as well as the gross political and economic inequalities which inhere between them, we believe that the relationship of the white to the black community can be more accurately and productively described as that between an imperial nation and its economically dependent colony ... '[188] *where black interests and black people are defined and determined by elite white people who either cajole or force black people into accepting their dictates. However, this theory acknowledges African-Americans ability to counteract white hegemony thus their relative success would also depend on their own actions.*

Racialized Colony methodology

The methodology employed to validate or invalidate the race-based analysis of US foreign policy is varied. It suggests that the state's actions fluctuate due to the complexities of domestic and foreign affairs. It examines AAFAN's ideological worldview in relation to US foreign policy and by comparing it to the substance of US foreign policy, we can compare the state's and AAFAN's conception of foreign affairs. If AAFAN and the US state held different conceptions of foreign affairs, then the question is, 'why were AAFAN's policy recommendations marginalised/ignored?' The methodology does not require that the US state or state officials made overt statements that AAFAN's marginal status was race based, instead the following factors will be used to determine if race factored into AAFAN's marginalisation: Euro-American hegemony in the higher echelons of the state and corporate arenas;[189] formal or informal exclusion of African-Americans from the US polity prior to the 1964 and 1965 Civil and Voting Right Acts suggests US foreign policy was unrepresentative of the American population, since African-American's were second-class citizens US foreign policy did not formally address the interests of African-Americans; the degree of similarity between the US state's and white America's foreign policy, with AAFAN's conception of foreign affairs; the US state's and white America's attempts (or otherwise) to include or consult African-Americans in relation to foreign policy decisions.

These four factors will help validate or invalidate whether race was a significant factor in AAFAN's marginal position regarding the formation of US foreign policy. While documentary evidence should be a pertinent factor in determining AAFAN's marginalisation, it is conceivable that state officials conceal institutional racism in order to avoid being linked with controversial issues.[190]

Positivist methods

This book utilises positivist methods and the empirical data is compiled from archives and case studies with primary and secondary sources. AAFAN's foreign affairs activities are accessed in several case studies which utilise qualitative evidence to highlight the degree of similarity or divergence between AAFAN's and the US 'foreign policy establishment's' conception of foreign affairs. The case studies will validate or invalidate the theories by analysing the empirical data from private and public sources pertaining to the US 'foreign policy establishment', and the personal correspondences and policy papers of AAFAN.

Due to the existing gaps within secondary sources, this book has mined the papers of eminent African-Americans and black organisations and Anglo-American organisations and individuals to contrast their roles and ideas with African-Americans to determine the degree of overlap and interconnection between both communities.

The empirical data from each case study will be assessed in the following chapters via the four theories in order to draw conclusions and determine which theory provides the best explanation of the three case studies. The use of sociological and political science theories are designed to provide rigorous methods of evaluation regarding how race, class and power impacted on AAFAN's efforts to promote their international agenda within a racialised political context.

The Academy

Despite the liberal tendencies of Western academia, it has not been immune to both racial and cultural imperialism.[191] Indeed, Somit and Tanenhaus argue: 'In the leading study of the profession [political science] ... [that] the role and status of Black academics is ignored completely'.[192] The truth is 'International Relations and political science have a considerable distance to go in achieving a routine and regular accommodation of scholars of colour in the field[193] which has constrained their ability to propagate their views to mainstream audiences. Secondly, given academics' tendency to focus on their personal interests the interests of funding bodies and the academy, the relative absence of non-whites in the academy could affect the subject preferences'.[194] One can only hope that African-American history and marginal perspectives would receive the attention they deserve. Equally problematic are political science theorists' (such as Dunleavy and O'Leary's *'Theories of the state: Politics of Liberal Democracy'*; Birch's *'Concept & Theories of Modern Democracy'*; and Marsh and Stoker's *'Theory and Methods in Political Science'*) who omit substantive coverage of racial theories in their analysis of American history and American political culture, especially since contemporary sociologists Omi and Winant have demonstrated the importance of racial issues.

Conclusion

The following chapters elaborate the themes briefly introduced in this chapter. Chapter 2 describes the emergence of AAFAN and the role of Du Bois and Garvey in shaping the ideological basis of AAFAN's early foray into international relation; Chapters 3, 4 and 5 examine and assess the three case studies with a view to utilising the theoretical models employed in this thesis to explain the historical outcomes in relation to each specific case study; Chapters 6 and 7 provide extended coverage of the books hypothesis in regard to the seminal events of the 1950s and 1960s. Chapter 8, the concluding chapter, summarises the findings of each chapter and examines their respective conclusions in order to construct an inclusive framework, which can contextualise the activities of AAFAN throughout the specified period. The conclusions derived from the three case studies will be central to the construction of the theoretical framework designed to contextualise and explain the ideological worldview of AAFAN and its corresponding activities in relation to international affairs. The final chapter also assesses AAFAN's ability/inability to meet its interests by utilising the conclusions derived from the case studies, to formulate a definitive theoretical conclusion.

2 The forging of the African-American Foreign Affairs Community

This chapter will examine the evolutionary construction of AAFAN by highlighting the activities of a small cadre of African-American intellectuals and activists who sought to increase African-Americans' interest in and awareness of foreign affairs. The chapter provides a brief summary of the Pan-African Conference (1900), the Pan-African Congress (1919) and the Universal Negro Improvement Association's (UNIA) conventions (1920s) in recognition of their centrality to the development of AAFAN. In addition, the chapter demonstrates the link between domestic race relations and the international struggle for racial equality by drawing attention to the often overlooked internationalism that pervaded the Niagara Movement, the black organisation that preceded the National Association for the Advancement of Colored People (NAACP).[1]

The dawn of the twentieth century ushered in a new phase of struggle for African-Americans. Although the 14th (1868) and 15th (1870) amendments to the Constitution had appeared to herald in a new age of American race relations, the optimism of the period was quickly dampened by the imposition of white racial supremacy in the South which utilised Jim Crow laws to politically and economically disenfranchise African-Americans.[2] Ultimately the vast majority of African-Americans were deprived of the vote along with the other political rights possessed by white Americans. Although the northern states were less oppressive, African-Americans were still second-class citizens, separate from and subordinate to the white majority. Given that American race relations in the early part of the twentieth century were marked by African-Americans' desire to reconfigure the racial status quo and the majority of white Americans' desire to maintain their racial supremacy, American race relations were far from tranquil.[3] Therefore, as African-Americans were unable to secure any powerful allies within the domestic arena, some of them sought to mobilise the oppressed masses of the black world. In the nineteenth century, European and North American nations had practically colonised the whole world. The sophisticated ideology of the Euro-American world, which was backed by military power combined with the notion of cultural and biological supremacy, created the required orientation to justify their predominance in the international arena. While many African-Americans aspired to become Americans, some sought to reconnect to their historical origins in Africa and called for the construction of a Pan-African movement designed to unite people of African descent around the world. The interest in Pan-Africanism culminated in the convening of the Pan-African Conference in London (1900).

The origins of Pan-Africanism

The historical circumstances that led to the genesis of Pan-Africanism stem from the triangular system of enslavement, which forcibly deposited Africans in the Americas and the Caribbean. Tony Martin argues that Pan-Africanism was the brainchild of the descendants of enslaved Africans often referred to in the literature as American Negroes and West Indians.[4] Thus Pan-Africanism owes its origins and conceptual framework to the descendants of enslaved Africans in the western hemisphere whose, disconnection from their national and cultural identities, ignited their efforts to reconstitute their African identity. West Indians and black Americans attempts to reconnect with their African heritage is significant as Africans, black Americans and West Indians have been portrayed as separate and distinct groups. Indeed, Cornel West argues that 'Black Americans ... are hybrid in blood, colour and cultural creations.'[5] Other authors suggest that black people in America have always maintained aspects of their original identity despite slavery as a

> lingering memory [remained] in the minds of American slaves. That memory enabled them to go back to the sense of community in the traditional African setting and to include all Africans in their common experience of oppression in North America ... during the process of their becoming a single people, Yorubas, Akans, Ibos, Angolans, and others were present on slave ships to America and experienced a common horror – unearthly moans and piercing shrieks, the smell of filth and the stench of death, all during the violent rhythms and quiet coursings of ships at sea. As such, slave ships were the first real incubators of slave unity across cultural lines, cruelly revealing irreducible links from one ethnic group, fostering resistance thousands of miles before the shores of the new land appeared on the horizon – before there was mention of natural rights in North America.[6]

John Hendrik Clarke maintains that the relationship between black people in America, the Caribbean and Africa was derived from their common historical experiences and racial designation.[7] However, some scholars suggest there is little or no connection between black people in America and the Caribbean and Africa 'until very recent times, few black Americans have regarded the African connection as a major theme in their lives.'[8] Paul Marc Henry in his essay, 'Pan-Africanism: A Dream Come True',[9] maintains that the structural position of black people in America was not comparable to the position of Africans in Africa. Tony Martin defines Pan-Africanism as a methodological structure designed to unify people of African descent. The implication is that the black populations in America and the Caribbean maintained a historical and psychological link to the continent of Africa.[10] Indeed, George Padmore suggests that 'the idea of Pan-Africanism ... arose as a manifestation of fraternal solidarity among Africans and peoples of African descent.'[11] The modern version of Pan-Africanism was developed by diasporian Africans[12] as 'the three great Pan-Africanists came from Trinidad: H. Sylvester Williams, George Padmore and C.L.R. James.'[13] The thrust of Pan-Africanism is that people of African descent should unify in order to counter European imperialism and to defend their own interests. The implicit assumptions derived from the Pan-African position are that race and historical origins have shaped international affairs and by extension the formation of US foreign policy. The contention that US foreign policy has been shaped by its domestic racial context[14] may extend to the behaviour and ideological assumptions of black and white Americans. For some African-Americans the idea of a race-neutral brand of US foreign policy is absurd given that the architects of US foreign policy – i.e. the US state, the foreign policy establishment and Americans in general – have failed to establish racial equality domestically. For example, Parmar points to the alleged racism of a Council on Foreign Relations member, Elihu Root.[15] Since the CFR claimed to be motivated by scientific and rational deliberations,[16] evidence of CFR racism suggests that US foreign policy should be examined from a racial perspective.[17]

One would expect that race would be a determining factor in US foreign policy. Mainstream foreign affairs literature's failure to systematically appraise US foreign policy from a racial perspective is problematic because,

> As Americans came into closer contact with an ever-widening circle of foreign peoples in the last decade of the nineteenth century, racial assumptions continued to guide their response. Those crying for a strenuous foreign policy invoked the need to enhance the racial vitality of the Anglo-Saxon stock and to honour the tutelary obligations superior race owed lesser ones, while those sceptical about foreign crusades and colonies either laboured to repel charges that they were traitors to their kind or recoiled in horror from races they considered irredeemably backward. Accepted by the turn of the century as an important ingredient in a demonstrably successful foreign policy no less than in the established domestic order, race would pass to subsequent generations as a well-nigh irresistible legacy.[18]

This contrasts with African-American writers'/scholars' and activists' emphasis on the importance of race and race relations domestically and internationally. Clearly some African-Americans were prepared to examine international relations from a racial perspective as their Pan-Africanism was designed to unite and uplift the black race from the yoke of white domination.

In 1897, H. Sylvester Williams' concern for African people throughout the world prompted him to begin organising a conference.[19] In 1898 Williams visited Birmingham, Manchester, Liverpool, Edinburgh, Stirling, Dundee, Glasgow, Belfast, Dublin, and numerous places in ... London, with the result that a council of several representative members of the race present in London was held, and an association was formed with the object: to encourage a feeling of unity; to facilitate friendly intercourse among Africans in general; to promote and protect the interests of all subjects claiming African descent, wholly or in part, in British Colonies and other places, especially in Africa, by circulating accurate information on all subjects affecting their rights and privileges.[20]

Consequently, an African Association (AFA) was formed[21] on 19 November 1898 to promote the interests and draw attention to the plight of African people. The association informed the British and German governments that they intended to call a Pan-African Conference in 1900 'in order to take steps to influence public opinion on existing proceedings and conditions affecting the welfare of the natives in the various parts of the world viz. South Africa, West Africa, West Indies, and United States of America.'[22] The intention of the AFA was to form an international organisation designed to end the racial subjugation of African people.

The Pan-African Conference

The Pan-African Conference was organised by H. Sylvester Williams from Trinidad, who was a barrister in London,[23] and the African-American Bishop Alexander Walters of 'the AME Zion Church.'[24] The conference was held at Westminster Town Hall in London;[25] the thirty participants at the conference were drawn from the educated elite from 'the United States, Haiti, Abyssinia, Liberia, the British West Indies and West Africa.'[26] The conference represented the talented tenth of what Du Bois called the African World and set the stage for a Pan-African movement, which had no mass appeal[27] until the later founding of Marcus Garvey's UNIA.[28] In fact, the Pan-African Conference popularised the term Pan-Africanism,[29] which had previously been described by Du Bois as 'Pan-Negroism.'[30] Penny Von Eschen argues correctly that the Pan-Africanists were fighting against the colonial dominance of European nations[31] whilst seeking independence and self-determination for African people. Although the delegates sought to counter the effects of global white dominance, they were not opposed to white participation as Du Bois stated in his report 'there are good friends in England yet, and though we wade through the mire of the evil curses of civilisation in the colonies, their voices will blend with ours, that righteousness and justice be the ruling word of British civilisation.'[32]

Thus on 23 July 1900, people of African descent opened the Pan-African Conference,[33] which was attended by the following Americans: 'Bishop Alexander Walters of the Zion Church; Hon. Henry F. Downing, ex-consul at Luanda; Miss Anna Jones, educator from Kansas City; Mrs. Anna J. Cooper and Miss Barier from Washington; Professor Burghardt du Bois; Thomas Calloway; Augustus Straker, former judge in Michigan.'[34]

The delegates of African descent were also joined by English and American patrons and the Bishop of London who opened and blessed the conference, while Bishop Walters, assumed the presidency.[35] The conference drafted five resolutions:

That a general association comprising the intellectual elite of civilised Blacks would be established under the name Pan-African Association, to centralise or control the activities of all organisations, whether in independent countries or colonies, which have as their objective the protection and education of peoples of African origins.

That a Pan-African Congress would be organised every two years, either in a major European or American city or in the capital of a Black independent State.

That the 1902 Congress would take place in the United States, and that of 1904 in Haiti, in order to add lustre to the celebration of Haiti's one hundredth anniversary as an independent nation.

That a manifesto would be drawn up, appealing to the justice, political wisdom and humanity of Christian nations; and that a special address signed by Congress members who are British subjects would be sent to Her Britannic Majesty protesting the cruel treatment inflicted upon the indigenous people of the South African colonies.

A memorial would be addressed to the Emperor Menelik and to the Presidents of the Republics of Haiti and Liberia, proclaiming them Grand Protectors of the Pan-African Association in order to direct their attention to the urgent necessity of consolidating and harmonising their diplomatic efforts, with a view to reacting against the policy of extermination and degradation, which prevails in Europe in regard to Black and coloured people.[36]

Overall the conference sought to address the inequalities stemming from the international colour-line encompassing the Caribbean 'Imperialism in Africa ... Jim Crow and the disfranchisement movement [in America].'[37] Indeed, an African-American 'participant ... Alexander Walters, declared that "in matters of race there were no geographic or national limitation" to racial consciousness.'[38] Hence the Pan-African Conference participants believed that race was an important factor in international relations.

The role of African-Americans

Although only eight African-Americans attended the 1900 conference, the centrality of African-Americans in the Pan-African Conference is reflected in the fact that Bishop Alexander Walters assisted H. Sylvester in the organisation of the conference and was president of the Pan-African Association while Henry F. Downing and Mrs Anna J. Cooper served on the executive committee.[39]

W.E.B. Du Bois served as Chairman of the Committee on Address.[40] Due to the AFA's/Pan-African association's desire 'to influence public opinion and to make ... authentic representation to the authorities on matters affecting the welfare of our race all over the globe,'[41] they decided conferences should be held biennially (the first in America in 1902). The location of the first conference in London, the centre of the British Empire, and the desire to convene the second conference in America indicate Britain's importance in foreign affairs and the recognition of the increasing importance of the United States in world affairs. Consequently, the conference appealed to Britain and America to alleviate the oppression of all African people

> Therefore, in view of the past and present history of friends, both in Great Britain and the United States, this Conference, the first of its kind ever assembled in London, unanimously hope that in the acute period of transition the race is experiencing from prejudice, greed and self, the society will not relinquish its influential aid to us in efforts put forth to assert our manhood and become loyal and true citizens of the various countries represented, but will continue to extend that encouragement, which has characterised the very life of the society, from the early founders to the present.[42]

The delegates at the conference established a permanent headquarters in London and nominally created eighteen branches of the Pan-African Association,[43] the first of which was in America and was headed by Dr Du Bois and T. J. Calloway.[44] Each branch was simultaneously designed to lobby on behalf of black people domestically and internationally. This dual agenda indicates that a small number of African-Americans were sufficiently aware of the link between domestic race relations and international race relations, i.e., that racism was in fact a global phenomenon and that the subjugation of Africa and Africans helped to facilitate their own subjugation in America. The delegates of the 1900 Pan-African Conference's recognition of the problems in Southern Africa, especially Rhodesia, signposted issues of racial strife that are still unresolved in the twenty-first century.[45] One of the most celebrated aspects of the Pan-African Conference was Du Bois' 'Address to the Nations of the World', which highlighted both Du Bois' and the conference's concern over the apparent correlation between a group's racial identity and their standing in domestic and international affairs.

> In the metropolis of the modern world, in this the closing year of the nineteenth century, there has been assembled a congress of men and women of African blood, to deliberate solemnly upon the present situation and outlook of the darker races of mankind. The problem of the twentieth century is the problem of the colour-line, the question as to how far differences of race, which show themselves chiefly in the colour of the skin and the texture of the hair, are going to be made, hereafter, the basis of

denying to over half the world the right of sharing to their utmost ability the opportunities and privileges of modern civilisation.[46]

Du Bois clearly recognised in 1900 that a clash of cultures was inevitable and that race would play an important role in future international events

the modern world must needs remember that in this age, when the ends of the world are being brought so near together, the millions of black men in Africa, America and the Islands of the Sea, not to speak of the brown and yellow myriads elsewhere, are bound to have great influence upon the world in the future, by reason of sheer numbers and physical contact. If now the world of culture bends itself towards giving the Negroes and other dark men the largest and broadest opportunity for education and self-development, then this contact and influence is bound to have a beneficial effect upon the world and hasten human progress. But if, by reason of carelessness, prejudice, greed and injustice, the black world is to be exploited and ravished and degraded, the results must be deplorable, if not fatal.[47]

The Pan-African Conference called for reform and the internationalisation of racial equality and the redistribution of wealth from the Western world to the colonised masses of what became known as the Third World. In addition, African-Americans also called for domestic political equality.[48]

Let not the spirit of Garrison, Phillips, and Douglas wholly die out in America; may the conscience of a great nation rise and rebuke all dishonesty and unrighteous oppression toward the American Negro, and grant to him the right of franchise, security of person and property, and generous recognition of the great work he has accomplished in a generation toward raising nine millions of human beings from slavery to manhood.[49]

The Pan-African Conference foresaw the tumultuous struggles of the late 1950s and 1960s in both America and the colonised countries of Africa and the Caribbean, where black people sought to engage in an international struggle against Western hegemony.

The significance of the Pan-African Conference

If the Pan-African Conference is judged on the basis of its intention to create an international organisation designed to lobby on behalf of people of African descent, then it clearly failed since there were no additional conferences. The significance of the Pan-African Conference stems from its influence on the intellectual development of its participants, principally Dr Du Bois, as it was this conference that laid the basis for Du Bois' interest in and activities relating to foreign affairs, which led to his involvement in the subsequent Pan-African congresses that were undoubtedly inspired by the vision of H. Sylvester

Williams. In fact, Du Bois' initial foray into the Pan-African movement in 1900 launched his illustrious career in that movement, which led to his being called the father of Pan-Africanism and culminated in his residency and death in (1963) in Kwame Nkrumah's Ghana.[50] In addition, despite the small number of African-American participants, it demonstrates their commitment to the struggle for the international liberation of people of African descent. The spirit of the Pan-African movement re-surfaced within the African-American Civil Rights Movement, which began in the early part of the twentieth century.[51]

The Niagara movement (1905)

The link between African-American domestic organisations and foreign affairs was verified by the Niagara Movement, a democratic black organisation comprising an executive committee and ten additional subcommittees. The organisation was established on 11 July 1905, in Buffalo NY,[52] by Du Bois and William Monroe Trotter, 'the Niagara movement ... [included a] ... broad spectrum of black professionals and intelligentsia who demanded full equality for black people in contrast to the Booker T. Washington program of acquiescence in second-class citizenship.'[53]

Despite its brief existence, the Niagara Movement was significant. First, its democratic structure, contradicted American racial conventions suggesting African-Americans lacked the intellectual ability to engage in complex political activity. Second, it illustrated African-Americans' desire to eradicate white America's political and economic supremacy. Additionally, the Niagara Movement demonstrated that African-Americans sought to challenge the international dimension of the colour-line whilst campaigning to obtain their (full) civil and human rights within the domestic arena. In short, the political aims of the Niagara Movement sought to enable African-American participation in all political issues as, 'First we would vote; with the right to vote goes everything.'[54] Herbert Aptheker claims the Niagara Movement[55] also addressed the foreign affairs agenda of its members: 'The concept of Pan-Africanism was present in the original calls written by Du Bois at the 1906 annual meeting of this movement. The constitution was amended to add among its fourteen standing committees one called the Pan-African department.'[56] The promotion of African and African-American Unity was not unprecedented as Aptheker maintains that 'possibilities of African and Afro-American co-operation, in religious, educational, and commercial endeavours, were projected by black people in the United States from the eighteenth century onwards.'[57] The Niagara Movement demonstrates that some African-Americans felt that their struggle for domestic political and civil rights was directly related to the international struggles of all African people. This is why Du Bois highlighted the plight of other African people in *The Horizon*, a publication of the Niagara Movement, in which he pointed to, 'The shameful exploitation of African peoples by Western capital, including, he added, some from the United States, especially Rockefeller, and warned: 'The day of reckoning is coming.'[58] Finally, the Niagara Movement's

Pan-African department clearly[59] demonstrates Du Bois' and the organisations commitment to their evolving conception of international network. Despite the fact that the African-American internationalists were a small vanguard movement, they paved the way for the evolution and development of an African-American foreign affairs community (AAFAN).

National Association for the Advancement of Coloured People

The short-lived Niagara Movement's led to the development of a robust and politically defiant African-American leadership cadre.[60] According to Padmore, 'Never before had Negroes spoken so defiantly to white folk. The whole nation sat up and took notice. For Du Bois and his friends posed in uncompromising terms a challenge to white America.'[61] In short, the Niagara Movement attacked the accommodationist Booker T. Washington 'In sharp language, [and] placed full responsibility for the race problem squarely on the whites.'[62] The strident challenge of the Niagara Movement led to the formation of the NAACP in 1910[63] in response to a race riot that occurred in 1908 in Springfield, Illinois.[64] However, unlike the Niagara Movement, the NAACP was an inter-racial organisation, which included white liberals from the North as well as some former members of the Niagara Movement.[65] According to Logan, the demise of the Niagara Movement stemmed from a 'lack of funds ... because its membership was confined to Negroes.'[66] Significantly, the NAACP did not adopt the programme of the Niagara Organisation. Indeed the inter-racial makeup of the NAACP led to the defection of Harvard-educated William Monroe Trotter and Ida B. Wells Barnet. 'In the end Trotter, the most radical Negro leader, and Mrs. Ida Wells Barnett who was leading an anti-lynching crusade, refused to join the new organisation, being distrustful of white leadership.'[67] Clearly the transition from the Niagara Movement to the NAACP was problematic as 'whites dominated the leadership of the new organisation; as Du Bois was the only black officer.'[68] In brief, the NAACP did not explicitly endorse the Niagara Movement's earlier Pan-Africanism (which I will discuss later). Padmore correctly observed that the NAACP became the staunch advocate of African-American political empowerment within the domestic sphere. The NAACP's inaugural meeting was overwhelmingly dominated by white people[69] some of whom believed 'no civil rights organisation could be credible if led by radicals, which meant excluding African-Americans like Trotter and Wells-Barnett from leadership positions and minimising the damage that could be done by Du Bois.'[70] The dissociation of black leadership from the NAACP suggests that the white liberals in the NAACP were still adhering to the racial colour-line. Indeed, after the NAACP's founding conference, Oswald Villard offered his assessment of the colored leaders he assembled. 'All of the speeches from the floor were by colored people – how they do love to talk! – and hardly one relevant, while not one contributed anything of value. Truly they are a child race still.'[71]

Given the paternalistic attitude of some NAACP leaders, it is not surprising that the Niagara Movement's Pan-Africanism was not central to the goals of the NAACP. Indeed, Du Bois was the catalyst of the NAACP's internationalism.[72] Did the NAACP seek to curtail or neutralise the evolving internationalism of Du Bois?[73] Clearly Du Bois' internationalism was enhanced by his membership within the NAACP

> as during his tenure as editor of *The Crisis* (1910–32) and ... *The Crisis* ... became the most widely read and politically influential journal among the Negroes in America [in fact] its influence extended far beyond the shores of America, and it was extensively read in all Foreign lands peopled by coloured folk. By the end of the First World War, the name of William Edward Burghart Du Bois was highly respected and esteemed among Africans and peoples of African descent throughout the world.[74]

Du Bois' domestic and international prominence placed him at the centre of the Pan-African movement. Thus from the turn of the century he led the liberal wing of the Pan-African movement, which he defined as the organised protection of the 'Negro World', led by American Negroes.[75] However, Du Bois' race-based Pan-Africanism received little support from African-Americans or the African-American leadership class. Indeed, Roark contends that during Du Bois' editorship of the NAACP's *The Crisis*, 'he struggled to nurture racial pride among American Negroes and to stimulate antagonism toward colonialism abroad.'[76] Indeed, Padmore informs us that Du Bois' efforts to promote Pan-Africanism among African-Americans were less than successful.[77] Despite Du Bois' stature as an international advocate of black liberation, the premier black leader of the early twentieth century was Marcus Garvey, the author of an alternative Pan-Africanism.

Marcus Garvey and the Universal Negro Improvement Association

Although Marcus Garvey was born (17 August 1887) and reared in Jamaica,[78] his Universal Negro Improvement Association and African Communities League (established 1 August 1914[79]) found its greatest success in America.[80] Thus one cannot adequately examine African-American foreign affairs activities during the 1920s[81] and 1930s without examining the internationalism of Marcus Garvey. The impetus for Garvey's activism originated in London where

> Garvey ... [read] along with numerous other books, Booker T. Washington's autobiography, 'Up From Slavery'. It impacted Garvey profoundly and fuelled his clarion call, which birthed the UNIA. ... Its text had welled in Garvey the imperative questions: 'Where is the Black man's government? Where is his King and Kingdom? Where is his President, his country, and his ambassador, his army, navy, his men of big affairs?' And not finding them, true to his resolve he declared, 'I shall create them.'[82]

In contrast to the elite-led internationalism of Du Bois, Garvey's UNIA was a mass-based movement with international appeal among people of African descent.[83] The UNIA rejected the appeal of Du Bois and the liberal wing of AAFAN to Western nations and the US government for assistance. Garvey 'argued that Black people had long been oppressed because of their race ... they should ... put their own racial self-interest first in everything they did.'[84] In 1916, Garvey visited America in response to an invitation from Booker T. Washington,[85] who died before his arrival. Garvey met Dr Robert R. Moton, the successor to Washington at Tuskegee, and Du Bois at the NAACP office in order to express his desire to aid African-Americans.[86]

> Despite receiving no help from Tuskegee or the NAACP, in 1917 Garvey established the Harlem branch of the UNIA, which boasted a growth of two thousand members in two months ... 1918 saw the incorporation of the African Communities League, the business arm of the UNIA. That year also saw the birth of the *Negro World*, a well written ... Pan-African news and nationalist propaganda vehicle which became the most widely read Black weekly in the world ... The ... paper was published in three languages, namely English, Spanish and French.[87]

The circulation of the UNIA paper indicates the international prominence of the UNIA and Marcus Garvey. By 1919 Garvey was known worldwide.[88] The UNIA's activities were impacting both (US) domestic and international race relations. Martin contends that the US government objected to Garvey's activities. Consequently in '1917, undercover police began watching his movements ... [Garvey] ... said that George Tyler, the man who tried to kill him in 1919, announced that he had been sent by Edwin P. Kilroe, an assistant district attorney who had given Marcus some trouble. From 1919, US officials began looking for a way to deport him, but they needed a suitable pretext, and it was a few more years before they found one.'[89]

Garvey's international impact is also reflected in Britain's hostility towards his activities, as

> millions of the people ... [Garvey] ... organized ... were the colonized subjects of Britain. And it was not in Britain's interest to encourage people who desired to be free of colonialism ... British governors and their agents banned the 'Negro World' in their African and West Indian colonies, jailed and deported Garveyites and denied them entry into some countries. Even in independent countries like Costa Rica, South Africa, Panama, Liberia and the United States, British diplomats spied on the UNIA and sometimes encouraged the local authorities to move against it. In New York, for example, the British consul general in 1923 got together with some anti-Garvey West Indians to publish the *British West Indian Review*. The purpose of this magazine was to counteract Garvey's message and stimulate loyalty to the British king and country.[90]

Clearly the UNIA's activities were not welcomed by the American and colonial governments.[91] Although the UNIA represented an organised foreign affairs group, the US state did not accommodate said constituency. Garvey claimed that by 1919 the UNIA

> had over 300 branches in America and abroad. It was at this time that we launched the idea of the Black Star Line Steamship Corporation. The Black Star Line Steamship Corporation that I organised in 1919, under charter from the State of Delaware, was the great attraction that brought to the Universal Negro Improvement Association millions of supporters from Central America, South America, Africa and the West Indies.[92]

While Garvey's mobilisation of the global African community was impressive, his real success occurred with the opening of his international convention in 1920. In 1919, however, Dr Du Bois took centre stage with the organisation of the Pan-African Congress.

1919 Pan-African Congress

The aftermath of the First World War left a defeated and broken Germany and a war-weary world. Undoubtedly, the war had drained the vitality of the Western world. Consequently Du Bois and other black leaders sought to exploit the weakness of the West by petitioning G. S. Clemenceau, the French prime minister, to

> take up with the Great Powers, looking to an exchange of views, regarding the establishing of a great Independent State of Africa, to be settled and governed by Negroes. This State is to embrace, very largely, the free states already established, but to the larger and affording more means for support and general government, or the establishing of an Independent Negro Central African State, composed of the Belgian Congo, German East Africa, and if possible, Uganda, French Equatorial Africa, German Southwest Africa and the Portuguese territories of Angola and Mozambique; such a state to be under International guarantees and control.[93]

In addition, in a letter to George Foster Peabody, Du Bois pointed to the comments of (British CABINET Minister) Lord Robert Cecil who called for the confiscation of Germany's colonies.[94] For Du Bois, the question of Germany's colonies revolved around African people's rights to govern themselves; thus he sought to convince the Western nations and especially the British Labour Party to honour the rights of black people.[95] Du Bois' appealed to the British Labour Party and Clemenceau spoke to the realisation that AAFAN's international objectives would 'receive no adequate attention'[96] from President Woodrow Wilson and US Secretary of State Robert Lansing. The fact that AAFAN's appeals received inadequate attention alludes to the marginality of AAFAN and Du Bois in regard to determining US foreign policy. In short, African-Americans activists from the UNIA[97] to the NAACP were determined to defend the rights of African people at the peace conference in Versailles, and Du Bois stood at the forefront of that movement. According to a letter dated 31 October 1919 from the acting Secretary of State, the US Department of State was concerned about the activities of AAFAN and Du Bois, as it stated:

> The department has received your letter of 27 November, enclosing a memorandum on the future of Africa, and asking whether there would be any objection to granting passports to six representatives American Negroes to attend a Pan-African Conference to be held in Paris at the time of the Peace Conference. Before rendering a final decision concerning your request, I should be grateful if you could find a convenient time to come to Washington to discuss the question more fully.[98]

The fate of the delegation assembled by the UNIA and Monroe Trotter's National Equal Rights League, which included A. Philip Randolph and Ida. B. Wells Barnet, indicates the US state's response to the actions of AAFAN. The 'visa applications of Garvey's and Trotter's would-be emissaries were summarily rejected; their letters and petitions [were] ignored.'[99] Garvey's attempts to petition the League of Nations demonstrate that the UNIA recognised the inter-relationship between the redemption of Africa and the redistribution of territory that took place after the First World War. The fact that the UNIA's goals were ignored by Woodrow Wilson[100] and the League of Nations confirms the marginal status of the AAFAN.

Significantly

> Garvey sent several delegations to the League. Germany's African colonies had been taken ... by the victorious nations after ... World War ... [one] ... and Garvey ... [felt] ... the colonies should be handed over to black rule. A UNIA representative had first (unsuccessfully) lobbied for this at the Paris Peace Conference which followed the war in 1919. UNIA delegations put this and other requests to the League of Nations in 1922, 1923, 1928 and 1931. Garvey himself was the UNIA representative on the last two occasions. The League never agreed to these requests.[101]

or the UNIA's commitment to and understanding of the diplomatic requirements of international relations.

Although the UNIA communicated its goals to US officials, its agenda was ignored; in contrast, Du Bois and Robert Moton were being heralded as representatives of their race. Significantly the NAACP was instructed 'to urge the claims of the Negro race upon the delegates of the Entente Powers at the Peace Conference ... in session at Versailles',[102] by the National Association of Loyal Negroes, who called for the formation of a centralised African state comprising territory from British, Portuguese, French and Belgian colonial possessions and a Pan-African Conference.[103] While the NAACP commissioned Du Bois to sail to Paris, he maintained that Moton was sent 'by the President and the Secretary of War to talk to colored troops before they embark and possibly to be consulted during the peace conference.'[104] Evidently some African-Americans were utilised for formal or informal roles by the American state. Du Bois' and Moton's presence on board the *Orizaba* provided them with the opportunity to lecture to the 'fifty-two correspondents'[105] to the peace conference about AAFAN's views. According to *The Crisis* magazine, Du Bois sailed to Paris with three objectives: 'He goes as special representative of *The Crisis* at the Peace Conference; to collect first-hand material to go into a History of the American Negro in the Great War; and finally as the representative of the National Association for the Advancement of Colored People, for the purpose of bringing to bear all pressure possible on delegates at the Peace Table in the interest of Colored peoples of the United States and of the World.'[106]

In short, Du Bois apparently represented the interests of the NAACP, which had announced its backing of the twelve-point programme established by Du Bois.[107]

Evidently Du Bois' internationalism was supported by the NAACP, which demonstrated its commitment to international affairs by dedicating their yearly meeting 'at Carnegie Hall, New York City ... 6 January ... [to] institute the Pan-African Movement in the United States. This will be one of the most important meetings the Association has ever held. The speakers are not yet announced; but they will represent colored and white leaders of liberal thought.'[108]

The importance of the meeting, which included discussions by Dr William Sheppard, Harvard professor Horace Meyer Kallen, NAACP Field Secretary James Weldon Johnson and Colonel William Jay Schieffelin, who had been invited to attend the peace conference,[109] stems from the NAACP's involvement in international affairs despite its commitment to reforming domestic race relations. Indeed, Weldon Johnson launched a two-pronged attack on domestic and international race relations as he explained why the NAACP is interested in the discussion of the African question.

1. Because no other nation is likely to bring it up.
2. Because this is really an international question. Africa was at the bottom of the war. If this question is not settled, war will continue.
3. Because the NAACP is interested in questions concerning the Negro everywhere.
4. Mr Johnson then left the subject of Africa and launched upon a magnificent plea for the establishment of the rights of the Negroes in America. The American Negro problem is not going to be settled at Versailles. This is a domestic trouble and our fight must be at close quarters.[110]

The importance of the aforementioned meeting is that it demonstrates that the NAACP believed that international affairs were ultimately connected to domestic circumstances pertaining to race. Indeed, the NAACP's commitment to the reconstruction of international relations and for a League of Nations was clearly articulated in their meeting's resolutions.[111]

The 1919 Conference

The Pan-African Congress of 1919 brought together delegates of African descent in Paris (including African-Americans).[112] The Congress was sanctioned after Du Bois lobbied

> black French politician Blaise Diagne [who] ... persuaded Premier Georges Clemenceau to permit the Pan-African Congress to meet in Paris, February 19–21, 1919. Fifty-seven persons attended the congress, widely if thinly representing Africa and the diaspora. They came from France's African colonies, including Algeria; the British African colonies' Portuguese Africa; South Africa; the Belgian Congo; Egypt; Ethiopia; Liberia; the French Antilles; Haiti; and the Dominican Republic. Few attended from the British Caribbean because of Britain's refusal to grant such subjects passports.[113]

The thrust of the congress was to promote the political welfare of African people. However, the Western nations did not respond favourably to African people's attempts to apply the principle of self-rule and racial and economic equality to themselves. According to Clarke, the American government's response to the Pan-African Congress was articulated on 19 February 1919 when Acting Secretary Polk stated that the 'State Department had been officially advised by the French Government that no such Conference would be held. It was announced recently that no passports would be issued for American delegates desiring to attend the meeting. But at the very time that Polk was assuring American Negroes that no Congress would be held, the Congress actually assembled in Paris.'[114]

Similarly Britain withheld passports from potential black participants under its jurisdiction.[115] Also Du Bois revealed that while he was organising the 1919 congress in Paris, he was observed by American Secret Service operatives.[116] Levering Lewis maintains that Clemenceau's motives in granting Du Bois permission for the 1919 congress, via Blaise Diagne a member of the French chamber of deputies elected from Senegal[117] who convinced Clemenceau to permit the Congress on Du Bois' behalf, was politically motivated to enhance France's international image pertaining to race and therefore strengthening its bid to acquire Germany's colonies. Clearly France was not advocating racial equality between black and white people; however, it did expose the extreme character of American race relations.[118] The significance of the 1919 Pan-African Congress was its symbolic value as a demonstration of a vanguard movement's attempt to promote the interests of African people worldwide. The stimulus for the twentieth-century Pan-African movement clearly emanated from the work of H. Sylvester Williams, Dr Du Bois and Marcus Garvey, as these diasporian Africans highlighted the existence of an international racial awareness among people of African descent. In addition, the 1919 Congress, which included sixteen African-Americans (the largest delegation), confirmed the existence of an AAFAN; the involvement of the UNIA and the NAACP pertaining to international relations and the British and American governments' awareness and unsympathetic view of an internationalist cadre seeking racial equality indicated Britain's and America's desire to thwart the efforts of the racially subordinate populations under their jurisdiction proved that Du Bois and members of AAFAN were capable of discussing international issues and constructing their own view of international relations via their resolutions; that Woodrow Wilson and Colonel House recognised the political capital obtained from entertaining the notion that the views of Du Bois and Moton were worth hearing.

While the events surrounding the 1919 PAC are important for validating the existence of an AAFAN, the activities of the UNIA demonstrate that AAFAN was able to mobilise a sizable foreign affairs contingent within the United States and beyond. This is important, as it refutes the contention that African-Americans were only concerned with domestic civil rights issues. By far the most convincing evidence of the UNIA's large international constituency were the 'eight international conventions, five of which took place in the United States (1920, 1921, 1922, 1924 and 1926), two in Kingston, Jamaica (1929 and 1934), and the last one in Toronto, Canada, in 1938.[119] The first of these conventions was held in New York City in 1920. According to Robert Hill and a number of authors

> 1 August 1920, was the red-letter day for the Negro peoples of the world, in that on that day at 9:30 a.m. there assembled in Liberty Hall, New York, 120–40 W. 138th street, 25,000 representatives of the race from … [throughout] … the world … from Nigeria, the Gold Coast, Sierra Leone, Liberia, West Africa, from Cape Town and Johannesburg, South Africa, and from East and Central Africa, from every known island in the West Indies … They came from South and Central America, from Europe and from Asia. Contingents of thousands came from Philadelphia, Detroit, Chicago, Cincinnati, in the United States, and from every other nook and corner of the republic.[120]

The 1920 convention demonstrated the organisational ability of the UNIA and both the domestic and the international support of the organisation.

> After the morning display at Liberty Hall there was the parade and review throughout the streets of Harlem, in which 50,000 members of the organisation, along with the legionary and uniform ranks, including Black Cross nurse[s,] motor corps, Juvenile [divisions] and African Guards marched. The military spectacle of these auxiliaries was wonderful. Eighteen bands of music were in line and marched. Fully, 30,000 people

saw the parade from the streets and homes in Harlem. The demonstration was of such as never seen in Harlem before and probably not to be seen again. The parade started at 1 o'clock and ended at 4 o'clock.[121]

The inaugural meeting at Madison Square Gardens was both well attended and enthusiastically greeted by African-Americans, who clearly welcomed and embraced the Pan-Africanism of Marcus Garvey, as

> 25,000 delegates packed the arena with crowds spilling into the streets outside. Present were delegates from every corner of the globe. The impact of the convention's many resolutions and declarations are still with us. Termed the Black Bill of Rights, the numerous resolutions included: that Black history be taught in schools; that lynching and racial discrimination be brought to an end [in America]; that Africa belonged to the Africans; and that Tricolours of Africa, the Red, the Black, the Green be adopted as the standard of the race. The assembly also elected Garvey as the President General of the UNIA, and the Provisional President of Africa. The last day of the Convention was declared a national holiday for Blacks. Such was the magnitude of the UNIA that a parallel convention lasting the same 31 days occurred in Port of Spain, Trinidad, attended by delegates unable to attend the one in New York.[122]

Clearly the UNIA was not just a back-to-Africa movement, since it sought to combat racial oppression in America and throughout the African diaspora; indeed, the Bill of Rights, endorsed at the convention, points to the domestic and international concerns of the UNIA.[123]

The fact that five of the UNIA conventions were held in the United States validates the existence of a foreign affairs community in America that discussed and analysed international issues. However, the US state's response to the Garvey movement was to engineer its destruction rather than incorporate its views into US foreign policy. While the UNIA had a sufficiently large organisational base to command the attention of the American state, it did not seriously consider its foreign policy goals. Indeed, the goals of the UNIA were incompatible with the goals of the US state and incompatible with white America's racial worldview. Consequently, Marcus Garvey's UNIA was targeted for destruction by the US state as no black organisation 'drew more investigation and surveillance by the Military Intelligence Division, State Department, and Bureau of Investigation in the Red Scare years than Marcus Garvey ... Garvey worried guardians of the racial status quo both in and outside of government ... primarily because his flamboyant nationalism and assertions of racial pride drew hundreds of thousands of followers to his movement.'[124] Indeed, J. Edgar Hoover, a known racist, launched a prototype of the Cointelpro programme of the 1960s against Marcus Garvey and the UNIA.[125] According to Ward Churchill, Hoover prompted the Justice Department to manufacture false charges against Marcus Garvey by recommending to … Justice Department officials that the federal government devote its vast legal resources to contriving a case, any case, against Garvey, to make him appear guilty of a crime. In this way, the black dissident's eventual imprisonment could be made to seem a simple 'criminal matter' rather than the act of political repression it actually was. The key to understanding what really happened in the Garvey case lies squarely in appreciation of the fact that the decision to bring about his elimination had been made at the highest level of the Bureau long before any hint of criminal conduct could be attached to him.[126]

Hoover's actions demonstrate the link and impact of America's domestic racism with AAFAN's ability to influence or shape international relations. In short, the UNIA's self-help philosophy, if implemented, would allow African-Americans and African people in general to compete with the corporate interests of America/European nations, which would clearly disturb the international status quo. Indeed, the Garvey movement, through investing by its worldwide membership, acquired hotels, restaurants, factories, universities of higher learning, printing plant, publishing companies, newspapers, trans-oceanic steamship lines, to name but a few. In addition, it established civil services (employment offices, job training, courts, passport services), health-care services (under the Black Cross nurses), regiments (the African Legions), all as foundational springboards necessary to the construction of the new continental African nation and homeland. The UNIA in fact entered into negotiations and even sent supplies to the emerging Republic of Liberia, West Africa, as the beachhead for the establishing of the Pan-African vision on the continent, only to be thwarted by a coalition of Firestone Rubber Company, the US and colonial government's pressure on Liberia.[127] In short, the internationalism of the UNIA, challenged the racial and economic status quo by attempting to undermine international white supremacy.[128] Consequently, the programme of the UNIA was subversive to white Americans such as J. Edgar Hoover because it sought to reconstruct race relations within the domestic and international arena.[129] The pluralist notion that organised interest groups provide an opportunity to secure interests is invalidated in relation to the UNIA and African-Americans, as

> by 1919, the UNIA had branches in thirty States, while others sprang up in Central and South America, the Spanish and English-speaking Caribbean and blossomed on the Mother continent, Africa, where it skipped down the coast to influence the young founders of the African National Congress in far off South Africa. Before the dawn of 1920 the organizations' ranks had swelled to over a million members, and would in subsequent years rise to well over 6 million … which has not be equalled since by any Black mass organization. … [However the UNIA experienced] hostility [from] … capitalist interests within Europe (Britain especially) and the United States [which is logical given that] … it was their ill-gotten gains

that a triumphant UNIA would attempt to reclaim. [Consequently] US authorities conspired to bar Garvey's re-entry from the Caribbean when on company business acquiring funds for the Black Star Line steamship company.[130]

However, despite the UNIA's organised popular support it was neither ignored nor incorporated into the US foreign policy establishment. Instead, the UNIA was targeted for destruction by the US state as white America elected to maintain a monopoly over the decision-making capacity in America. In addition to white America's desire to maintain their economic and political dominance over African-Americans and the US Administration's desire to profit from the (global) economic status quo, which would be jeopardised if the Pan-Africanist vision was realised.

In short, the demise of Marcus Garvey and the UNIA in the 1920s was facilitated by conservative forces in the US state apparatus and also by members of the liberal wing of the civil rights struggle including members of the NAACP, whose 'Garvey must go' campaign ironically aided US officials' assault on the UNIA. Ironically, the reformist policies of the NAACP were also too radical for some US officials as Garvey [was not] alone in being accorded

'special attention' by the Bureau. For instance, during the massive railroad strikes in 1920s, the FBI – as part of its much broader anti-labor and anti-black endeavors – went out of its way to topple A. Philip Randolph, black head of the Brotherhood of Sleeping Car Porters Union. About the same time, Hoover's agent initiated a 'close surveillance' (a term usually associated with infiltration) of W. E. B. Du Bois' National Association for the Advancement of Colored People (NAACP) in the name of knowing 'what every radical organization in the country was doing'.[131]

In conclusion, the forging of AAFAN is a story of fire and water where the strident militancy of the (mass orientated) UNIA's Pan-Africanism was doused by a combination of factors, such as AAFAN's internal rivalry between Du Bois' liberal Pan-Africanism[132] and Garvey's 'race first' internationalism. The rivalry of the UNIA and NAACP assumed domestic and international dimensions as Du Bois and Garvey sought to promote their own brand of racial upliftment. In addition, the UNIA was undermined by the British and US governments, whose campaign was headed by J. Edgar Hoover and the General Intelligence Division who, with the assistance of NAACP members and others black leaders, secured the conviction and deportation of Garvey. While Garvey had a worldwide following of millions, Du Bois' internationalism lacked any real organisational foundation or popular appeal. Clearly the NAACP aided Du Bois' efforts to convince the great powers that Germany's colonies should be handed back to Africans.[133]

However, the NAACP did not provide the seven hundred and fifty dollars for the Pan-African Congress. Du Bois was informed 'Mr Dill has not paid the 750 dollars and that matter was not taken up yesterday ... [indeed] Mr. Grimke and Mr. Lous were opposed to more expenditure abroad.'[134] The NAACP board had misgivings about Du Bois' objectives in Paris despite claims that they supported his actions. Du Bois wrote in April 1919:

> I wish to express to the Board my disappointment at the apparent attitude towards my trip to France. I did not first suggest this trip nor did I suggest the war history. The Board voted $2,000 to compile historical material. It is distinctly understood in the debate that a trip to Europe might be necessary, and certainly no one dreamed that $2,000 would be sufficient to compile and publish an historical work of the size and completeness contemplated. From the foundation of the Association it has been contemplated that funds for research would be given to my department ... A journey to France was not only clearly within the terms of the vote of the Board, but also my decision was reinforced by the action of the board in regard to African program ... So far as the Pan-African Congress was concerned the Board had, of course, a right to refuse its support because while it had adopted my general program, it had never voted an appropriation. At the same time, would it have been sensible for me to have gone to Paris at this time and taken no action of the sort? I want, therefore, to present on the minutes of this meeting my earnest protest against the attitude of the Board of Directors.[135]

The NAACP's internationalism had been lit by Du Bois but the flame could not be sustained without the support of African-Americans in general, which Du Bois (unlike Garvey) had failed to mobilise. Nevertheless Du Bois' domestic and international liberalism triumphed over Garvey's 'race first' approach to American domestic issues and international affairs and Du Bois went on to build/lead an elitist Pan-African movement that held Pan-African congresses in 1921, 1923, 1927, 1945. However, Du Bois' victory over Garvey was a hollow one at best. Despite their ideological differences, Garvey's and Du Bois' international aims were deemed subversive by the British and American governments because their aims sought to reshape international race relations. The issue was not how close members of AAFAN came to executing their reality, the real problem lay in the idea that blacks had a right to determine foreign policy itself. The pluralist notion that organised interest groups' ideas or interests will receive a variable degree of government interest is correct. However, although the UNIA and Du Bois' Pan-African movement sought to remedy the legitimate grievances of Africans and African-Americans, the response of some state officials was to target the UNIA for destruction and inhibit the participation of African-Americans in the 1919 congress. In brief, the US state's wishes were of greater importance than the aims of AAFAN and African-American's struggle for racial equality was tantamount to political heresy. Ironically, Du Bois' was forced to resign from the NAACP in 1934 due to his advocacy of black 'segregation for economic defence [in America]',[136] which Garvey had argued for in the 1920s. Subsequently Du Bois, like Garvey, was politically targeted, prosecuted and indicted by the federal government,[137] in the same way as his organisation had helped destroy Marcus Garvey. In essence, the liberal and radical approach to international relations (of Du Bois and Garvey) were rejected by the US government. However, the ghost of Garvey's 'race first' internationalism resurfaced in the racially explosive atmosphere surrounding the Italo-Ethiopian War, which will be examined in the next chapter. In the final analysis, the evidence demonstrates that African-Americans struggled to erase the colour-line both domestically and internationally (in this case study), which is consistent with the fact that their struggle against racism was an ongoing theme in relation to their status in America.

3 A case study of the Italo-Ethiopian War 1934–36

The hands of Destiny pulled back history's curtain in 1935 and let the world's black peoples see the sources from whence they sprang. It allowed them to see beyond the shame of slavery into that distant era when their ships plied the seas, laden with the spices and gold of ancient commerce and the turreted and spired cities of their birth.[1]

This case study examines the role of AAFAN during the Italo-Ethiopian War (IEW) from 1934 to 1936. The chapter highlights the impact the AAFAN's mobilisation had on US foreign policy regarding the IEW. Second, the chapter explains the relevance of the IEW in relation to the historical construction of AAFAN and compares African and Italian-Americans success in aiding Ethiopia and Italy. The chapter briefly explores African-Americans interaction with the Communist Party USA (CPUSA). Finally the chapter discusses the theoretical implications of the historical evidence. This case study is significant because it utilises political science theories to assess AAFAN's foreign affairs activities which remedies mainstream academia's failure to use racial theories to examine US foreign policy in addition to highlighting the difficulties encountered by a subordinate racial group attempting to shape US foreign policy from below.

Prior to considering AAFAN's domestic activism, we will examine the historical context of the IEW in relation to international affairs. Although the IEW began at Wal Wal on 5 December 1934, the roots of the IEW and Italy's presence in East Africa stemmed from Europe's scramble for Africa and the Berlin Conference (1884–85) which granted Italy colonies in Libya, Somalia and Eritrea.[2] Italy's attack on Ethiopia in 1934 was designed to avenge its humiliating defeat at the hands of Emperor Menelik II at Adowa[3] (Ethiopia) in 1896 in addition to Mussolini's[4] colonial ambition.[5] However, Italian imperialism ultimately stemmed from European power politics,[6] as Italy's alliance with Britain and France during WWI was secured by their pledges, that she would receive territory from Germany's African colonies at the peace conference.[7] However, America's refusal to redistribute German colonies caused Britain and France to abandon their pledges thereby increasing Italian imperialist zeal.[8] Thus, the machinations of European and American foreign policy prior to and during the 1930s created the context for the IEW and arguably led to WWII.

Italy's pursuit of Ethiopian territory provoked a response from black America. African-American interest in Ethiopia stemmed from two factors: one racial,[9] the other derived from their cultural and historical identification with Africa. Contrary to the claim that Ethiopians are not black Africans, the historical evidence states that

> Classical historians and geographers called the entire region from Egypt to India, both countries inclusive, by the name of Ethiopia, and hence regarded all of the dusky inhabitants of the region as Ethiopians. The ancient Greek scholars referred to the founders of civilisation as the wonderful Ethiopians and credited them with profound knowledge of astronomy and mathematics. The African origin of this culture was for a long time denied, but now the evidence is so compelling as to be undeniable.[10]

Given African-Americans African ancestry and the global dimensions of the colour-line which characterised Africans as the lowest branch of the human family, African-Americans empathy with Ethiopia was logical. Especially since Ethiopia acquired a religious and cultural significance among African-Americans as a symbol of racial pride as Ethiopia was a major centre in the biblical world, along with Jordan, Syria, Palestine and Egypt, and for centuries Europeans referred to the whole of the continent of Africa as Ethiopia, while the region which today bears the name 'Ethiopia' was formerly the kingdom of Abyssinia. The biblical references to Ethiopia were cherished by black people, and when the Abyssinians defeated the Italians at Idowa in 1896, the black people in the United States took the words of the psalm 'Princes come out of Egypt, Ethiopia stretches forth her hands unto God', to mean that the redemption of Africa was near at hand.[11] Martin maintains that Ethiopia's importance resonated throughout the entire African diaspora.[12] Given, that Ethiopia was one of the three remaining independent black nations after Europe's scramble for Africa, continental and diasporan Africans saw Ethiopia as a beacon of hope and a symbol of racial pride.[13]

A complex web of racial, historical and political pragmatism laid the basis for African-Americans' support for Ethiopian independence in 1935 because African-Americans drew parallels between their domestic oppression and global white supremacy. Black America's adherence to Ethiopianism, an African-centred approach to the Christian faith, which placed Ethiopia at the centre of a black theology designed to counter the Eurocentric version of Christianity,[14] demonstrates the importance of Ethiopia to black people.

The position of AAFAN on the Italo-Ethiopian War

AAFAN's commitment to the maintenance of Ethiopian sovereignty[15] stimulated AAFAN to raise funds to aid Ethiopia's war effort in addition to purchasing medical supplies and recruiting African-Americans to fight on Ethiopia's behalf. Although most African-Americans supported Ethiopia's effort to defend its sovereignty,[16] African-American activists dedicated to the defence of Abyssinia, adhered to divergent ideological perspectives.

The actions of AAFAN

While African-American visits to Abyssinia were infrequent prior to the IEW, some African-Americans established a political relationship with Ethiopia. Significantly Ethiopia's invitation to African-Americans to migrate there[17] concerned Addison Southard the US consul to Ethiopia.[18] Subsequently, the US State Department began monitoring the activities of black nationalists, as it felt their activities undermined US prestige abroad.[19] Evidently the US state sought to inhibit the spread of global Pan-Africanism and the existence of a political relationship between African-Americans and Ethiopians. Indeed, 'when Italy invaded Ethiopia … [Afro-Americans] protested with all the means at their command. Almost overnight even the most provincial among the American Negroes became internationally minded. Ethiopia [was regarded as] a Negro nation and its destruction would symbolise the final victory of the white man over the Negro.'[20] The following initiatives will be briefly examined to confirm African-Americans' commitment to Ethiopia: petitions to the League of Nations, the creation of new organisations, fund-raising drives, demonstrations, recruitment drives and rallies, articles within the Black Press, an economic boycott and the Popular Front.

Petitions to the League of Nations

Although African-Americans believed the IEW was a result of European racial imperialism, AAFAN still petitioned the League of Nations on Ethiopia's behalf. A petition was submitted to the league[21] by Dr Willis Huggins, a reporter for *The Chicago Defender*,[22] on behalf of 'the International Council of Friends of Ethiopia [and the Provisional Committee for the Defence of Ethiopia or PCDE] to inform the League of its position [in August 1935].'[23]

The NAACP extended its domestic mandate into the international arena by criticising Italian foreign policy.[24] The NAACP telegraphed the league and the US State Department in March 1935.[25] The 'Committee for Ethiopia [New York City] … petition[ed] … President Roosevelt – urging that he remind Italy of her obligations under the Pact of Paris to forever renounce war as a instrument of national policy.'[26] Ethiopia's and AAFAN's petitions challenged the league to uphold its primary objective – the peaceful resolution of international conflicts. African-Americans failed to induce league action since their policies lacked official backing from the US state. In addition, Ethiopia failed to secure international assistance. Perhaps the league's principles were compromised by Britain's and France's foreign policy, as both were imperialist, racist and self-interested.[27] In short, British and French colonialism and their desire to appease Italy ensured their limited response to Italian colonialism in Ethiopia.[28] For Marcus Garvey, the league was a vehicle of white Western imperialism, which was validated by its rejection of the rights of colonised nations when it refused to ratify the Japanese proposal to the 1919 peace conference, which demanded that 'The equality of nations ... [become] ... a basic principle of the League of Nations, the High Contracting Parties agree to accord, as soon as possible, to all alien nationals of state's members of the League, equal and just treatment in every respect, making no distinction, either in law or in fact, on account of their race or nationality.'[29]

The league adopted a conservative agenda that maintained the racial status quo internationally i.e. global white hegemony.[30] African-American support for Ethiopia permeated both secular and religious organisations as the National Baptist Convention with three million members sent a telegram to Cordell Hull, the secretary of state, calling for Ethiopia's right to maintain its sovereignty.[31] The action of the National Baptist Convention confirm that African-American activism in support of Ethiopia was not confined to the Garveyite Black Nationalists in Harlem. Blacks from diverse backgrounds and religious affiliations identified with their Ethiopian brethren, resulting in an African-American call to arms in defence of Ethiopia. Consequently, recruitment drives were held to enlist volunteers, evidently African-American support for Ethiopia was significant enough for individuals to offer their lives to defend its sovereignty.

The creation of new organisations

AAFAN mobilised the wider black community in organisations dedicated to supporting Ethiopia, which indicates AAFAN successfully constructed an organic organisational base, which incorporated the diverse ideological strands within the African-American community. AAFAN also formed alliances with white activists and communist groups.[32] When the war began, a number of African-American intellectuals formed the Provisional Committee for the Defence of Ethiopia (PCDE) in Harlem, comprising delegates from twenty organisations with a combined membership of 15,000 black people.[33] Asante's assertion indicates a organisational network was employed in order to facilitate a broad coalition of organisations which suggests AAFAN was equipped to lobby state agencies in order to support Ethiopia.

Another example of AAFAN's organisational ability was the International Council of Friends of Ethiopia (ICFE), which was established in Harlem in 1935 in order to build a national campaign in America to aid Ethiopia. The founding members of this organisation were Azaj Workneh Martin, the Ethiopian minister to Great Britain, and Dr Willis N. Huggins, 'a prominent Negro educator and director of the Board of Research on African Civilisation.'[34] Significantly the ICFE was headed by an official representative of the Ethiopian government, who granted Huggins official recognition from his government[35] to raise funds for Ethiopia in the US.[36] Evidently Dr Huggins had developed a Pan-African union between himself and other Africans, as Huggins was introduced to

Ajaz Martin in London by Amy Jacques Garvey (the second wife of Marcus Garvey) and C. L. R. James.[37] Huggins' association with two prominent black activists in London indicates that African-American activism in support of Ethiopia was internationally recognised by other Africans. Huggins' return to America witnessed the creation of the 'Friends of Ethiopia which sought to mobilise on a national scale. By December 1935, the organisation was reported to have had 106 branches in operation'.[38] It also affiliated itself with mostly black organisations.[39]

The existence of the PCDE and the ICFE indicates that the AAFAN successfully mobilised African-Americans. AAFAN also consisted of grassroots black nationalists and Pan-Africanists, such as the Pan-African Reconstruction Association (PARA) established in Harlem (in 1934) by Samuel Daniels.[40] PARA's remit was to promote a Pan-African agenda 'to strive for the economic uplift of the Negro people of the World'[41] along with a plethora of Garveyite organisations based in Harlem. In addition to the talented tenth of the African-American community, which was represented by the Ethiopian Research Council (ERC), established in December 1934[42] by Leo Hansberry, 'the Howard University Africanist ... Malaku Bayen, the cousin of Haile Selassie, Ralph Bunche a political science professor, also at Howard University and two unnamed Ethiopian students',[43] the ERC provided historical and cultural data on Ethiopia. The existence of the ERC, identifies that the Pan-Africanist ethos was evident in AAFAN's support of Ethiopia and permeated the black community. The ERC was significant because it became a source of information for Ethiopia in America in the absence of official Ethiopian (diplomatic) representation in Washington, DC.[44] Although the existence of organisations in itself does not necessarily indicate that the AAFAN grasped the complexities of international relations. However, the remit of the committee for Ethiopia, which was formed on 18 July 1935 in Harlem,[45] 'to raise funds to force the United States to act in the Ethiopian situation under the Kellogg-Briand Peace pact,'[46] demonstrates African-Americans' comprehension of the relevant international treaties pertaining to the IEW. Given AAFAN's ability to apply international treaties to the plight of Ethiopia, one wonders why African-Americans were not considered as potential candidates for incorporation into the Council on Foreign Relations (CFR) since 'the CFR was convinced of its own objectivity, impartiality and of the scientific nature of its studies', one would think that the CFR would make its membership more representative of US society.[47] However, given the CFR's racialised Anglo-Saxon worldview,[48] it is not surprising African-Americans were not invited into the CFR.

Fund-raising drives

AAFAN's concern for Ethiopia was evident in its fund-raising efforts, despite the deprivation of the depression and African-Americans' economic weakness.[49] Prior to the war, African-American 'religious leaders of different denominations throughout the United States, held special services at which collections were taken to support Ethiopia should Mussolini attack it.'[50] African-Americans' economic aid was also sought by the Ethiopian minister to Britain, Dr Ajaz Martin, who wrote to black people in America (7 August 1935) asking them 'to come and help Ethiopia.'[51] In March 1935, the PCDE held a rally at the Abyssinian Baptist Church (Harlem) in conjunction with its Minister Adam Clayton Powell Senior, attended by 3,000 people, in order to secure funds and arms for Ethiopia and to plan a March (in New York) of 50,000, and lodge their protests with Mussolini, the US secretary of state, the league and New York's mayor.[52] African-Americans (especially in Harlem, the nucleus of AAFAN's activities to aid Ethiopia) demonstrated a willingness to secure funds for Ethiopia. African-Americans' inability to raise substantial funds for Ethiopia could be interpreted as a failure to sufficiently organise, which supports pluralist notions that ineffective organisation decreases an interest group's capacity to meet their interests. Although African-Americans' marginal economic status undoubtedly hampered their efforts to economically aid Ethiopia.[53] Additional factors undermined AAFAN's efforts to raise funds: first, the historical legacy of a racialised colour-line undermined African-Americans' economic capacity as did the economic hardship of the Depression; second, the activities of black fraudsters who solicited funds for Ethiopia for their own benefit; third, the Ethiopian government failed to provide official agents to collect funds on its behalf and also to provide a central location in the US where funds could be collected; finally, African-Americans' were reluctant to co-operate with and to seek financial assistance from white Americans.

Demonstrations

While African-Americans experienced problems raising funds to aid Ethiopia, their dedication to Ethiopia was a national phenomenon.[54] Harlem became the centre of the campaign to aid Ethiopia and as a result hosted the most significant demonstrations.[55] For example, in August 1935 Harlem hosted two demonstrations in Harlem where twenty thousand participants protested Italy's invasion of Ethiopia.[56] The attendance at this demonstration indicates black America's concern for Ethiopia. The activities on the east coast were complemented in the mid-west[57] as members of Chicago's Joint Committee (CJC) 'marched outside the Italian consulate [in Chicago]'[58] and sponsored a rally on the south-side of Chicago on 14 August, which was attended by two thousand people.[59] On the 31st August, the CJC organised 'a March and petition drive to urge congress to invoke the Kellogg-Briand Pact and impose an embargo on Italy.'[60] The CJC's attempt to apply the 1928 Kellogg-Briand Pact, which was designed to 'outlaw war',[61] provides further evidence of AAFAN's attempts to utilise international agreements to safeguard their interests. However, African-Americans organisational abilities were not exclusively confined to America: 'On the 18th August, the [bi-racial] Committee for Ethiopia [which was founded during the War] held a day of prayer observed by over 3,000 congregations in the US and the Caribbean'.[62] The 18 August observance demonstrated AAFAN's concern for Ethiopia and reflected the views of people of African descent in the Caribbean and indicated that AAFAN possessed the organisational ability to establish operational unity with groups outside of America. In addition, the AAFAN utilised the Pan-African model of racial unity in their campaign to lobby on behalf of Ethiopia's national interests.

Recruitment drives and rallies

Asante maintains the PARA was the foremost organisation involved in the recruitment of African-Americans. Samuel Daniels (the head of PARA) called a meeting on 14 July 1935 to recruit African-Americans to fight to defend Ethiopia:[63] 'Daniels claimed that 850 men from New York were ready to go to Ethiopia; he also claimed PARA had 22 branches in US cities with 30,000 members.'[64] Another militant group, the Black Legion, reportedly 3,000 strong, 'inaugurated a training camp in up-state New York with instructions for 500 aviation students and for two full regiments of infantry.'[65] Daniels preached the 'race first' philosophy of Marcus Garvey as he exhorted African people to fight for their motherland.[66] Evidently, African-Americans were prepared to fight the IEW on a racial basis. Daniels' activities were part of a wider movement, as 'Boston, Philadelphia, Chicago, Detroit and Kansas City all witnessed extensive efforts to recruit black American volunteers for combat duty in East Africa.'[67] Indeed, a report appeared in the black press (21 July) that nearly a thousand black volunteers from New York had answered PARA's call to serve Ethiopia in addition to thousands from other cities including Chicago (8,000), Detroit (5,000), Kansas City (2,000) and Philadelphia (1,500).[68]

The black press

The importance of the war was demonstrated in the black press, which carried almost daily coverage and demanded that Europe, Italy and the league respect Ethiopia's sovereignty.[69] The *Pittsburgh Courier* issued an article that stated 'Ethiopia is on the spot. Three of the World's principal Robber Nations have turned thumbs down on her. The league of bandits misnamed the League of Nations will do nothing to save her just in the same way as it did not prevent the Japanese from appropriating Chinese Real Estate.'[70] The *Amsterdam News* attacked Italy's aggression whilst the *Pittsburgh Courier* argued the IEW was 'A conspiracy on the part of the major European powers to advance their own interests at the expense of that African Nation Ethiopia, and the black man. White imperialism was seen as the real enemy for it was representing a united front against the coloured people.'[71] The black press maintained that the IEW was a race war.[72] Even established black organisations such as the NAACP and the Urban League joined the campaign to aid Ethiopia.[73] 'In an article in

The Crisis, Harold Preece stated ... that the Rape of Ethiopia is the rape of the Negro Race.'[74] Clarke implies that the reporting of the war was racially biased as he argues that J. A. Rogers was the 'only reporter on the scene who was looking at the conflict from a black perspective',[75] which implies the Western media's reporting was unsatisfactory to people of African descent. The fact that J. A. Rogers was sent to report on the war by Robert Vann, the publisher of the *Pittsburgh Courier* and assistant to the US Attorney General,[76] was significant, as Rogers was the only correspondent sent by a black news-paper. In addition, it demonstrates the *Courier*'s commitment to reporting on the IEW and Vann's personal interest in the conflict. The *Courier*'s interest in this subject was shared by the public as the interest generated by the conflict led to increased sales of the *Courier* (by 25,000).[77]

The increased sales of the *Courier* verify black interest in the IEW. The centrality of the *Pittsburgh Courier* in relation to the coverage of the war was confirmed by their declaration 'On 13 July 1935 ... that the Ethiopians ... [were] ... willing to accept Afro-American volunteers into its armed forces.'[78] Evidently, the black press articulated its support for Ethiopia and cited race as a significant factor in the war.[79] In short, writers linked Ethiopia's plight to the welfare of African people worldwide.[80]

Economic boycott

The zeal whipped up by the black press and the campaign to aid Ethiopia, heightened existing ethnic tensions between black and white communities. As a result, African-Americans initiated economic boycotts aimed at white merchants. African-Americans' economic campaign demonstrates the complex interplay between foreign affairs and domestic race relations. The motivation for these boycotts was twofold: 'Black nationalists organised campaigns against Jewish and Italian businesses in Harlem, as they believed these ethnic groups exploited the black community economically, by failing to hire black employees and siphoning funds from the black community.'[81] However, 'Adam Clayton Powell Jr. reminded ... [African-Americans] ... that putting Italian shopkeepers out of business would not restore the crown to the emperor of Ethiopia, and above all, it would not help Harlem.'[82] Nevertheless local boycotts led to calls for a 'national black boycott of Italian-American stores. Left wing and moderate black leaders, most notably Congressman Arthur Mitchell of Chicago, attempted to calm the explosive situation by suggesting Italian-Americans were not responsible for fascist aggression.'[83] The congressman's argument failed to persuade many black people, as black activists continued to call for a national boycott of Italian-owned businesses.[84] For example, Ira Kemp's and Arthur Reid's African Patriotic League con-tinued to push for boycotts specifically aimed at Italian-Americans.[85] These boycotts revealed the racial and ethnic cleavages that existed within America's cities and began to undermine the inter-racial alliance between black and white activists.

Popular Front[86]

Although many African-Americans maintained that the IEW was caused by Italy's white supremacist views, they still formed political alliances with ideologically and racially diverse groups.[87] The PCDE which represented 'an umbrella structure of some twenty organisations with a claimed membership in excess of 15,000 persons was one such group. It consisted of elements from virtually every stratum of black Manhattan ... educators, communists and nationalists were included in the organisations, all dedicated to the one purpose of providing aid to our brothers in Ethiopia.'[88] The members of the popular front were clearly committed to the defence of Ethiopia and sought to transcend their ideological differences to achieve their common interests.[89] Even Black Nationalists and Pan-Africanists joined the popular front, led by the PCDE, which was 'the most significant popular front group [supporters of the PCDE came] from the League of Struggle for Negro Rights [also a popular front group] and the Benevolent Paternal Order of Elks and the Universal Negro Improvement Association (UNIA) still the strongest Pan-African organisation although significantly reduced.'[90]

However, despite the popular front, African and Italian-Americans engaged in several violent confrontations on the east coast of America. On 11 August 1935 in Jersey City, New Jersey, a riot between African and Italian-Americans occurred.[91] On 4 October, African-Americans and Italians clashed in Brooklyn and Harlem following Italy's invasion of Ethiopia.[92] The severity of the attacks between Italian and African-Americans is reflected in the fact that 'over a thousand policemen ... [were deployed to] suppress the fighting'. The altercations indicate that (some) African and Italian-Americans were sufficiently motivated to fight in the streets in defence of the respective countries, which indicates that their racial and ethnic identities were significant enough to transcend their alleged commonality as American citizens.

The evidence substantiates that African-Americans' defence of Ethiopia was based on racial considerations and their comparative status in relation to the white world. In short, the IEW led to the adoption of an international racial worldview,[93] which stimulated a revival of Black nationalism.[94] Felix H. Bretton from New Orleans expressed his support for Ethiopia in nationalistic terms stating that African-Americans should 'Begin to look for the higher things in life – a flag of his own, a government of his own and complete liberty.' Even black denominations supported a racial worldview 'tinged with nationalistic creed and ... the belief that Ethiopia had been predestined by biblical prophecy to redeem the black race from white rule'.[95] In August 1935, Dr L. K. Williams, president of the National Baptist Convention working to aid Ethiopia, stated:

> Americans of African descent are deeply stirred in their attitude and sympathies for Ethiopia, a Negroid people who represent almost the only remaining example of independent government by the black race on the

continent of Africa. While ... we are Americans to the core we cannot be deaf to the cry that comes from a menaced nation in the land of our fathers.[96]

William's racial orientation to the war was not unique, as the Fraternal Council of Negro Churches, comprising leaders from nine denominations, stated that 'Black churches felt betrayed by white Christianity.'[97] This indicates that African-Americans indictment of white people was extended to their westernised version of Christianity, which was considered a vehicle of white supremacy.

The centrality of race was evident in the views of W. E. B. Du Bois, who was, at that time, teaching at Atlanta University. Du Bois pointed to the racial roots of the war 'Benito Mussolini had killed the faith of all black folk in white men.'[98] Other black intellectuals also adopted the nationalistic stance of the black community as 'Black intellectuals from the Urban League and the NAACP were also spouting militant rhetoric pertaining to the war.'[99] In addition, Elmer A. Carter of the Urban League claimed 'Ethiopia was the spiritual fatherland of Negroes and that its invasion by Italy might create that unity of colored races ... the prophets of Nordic supremacy have so long feared.'[100] The aforementioned indicates that the AAFAN had the overwhelming support of the black community.

However, there were ideological differences among members of AAFAN as (black) left-wing intellectuals and communists argued that class and economics/imperialism were the fundamental shaping factors responsible for the IEW, while nationalists and Pan-Africanists believed that racism and Western imperialism were the primary factors responsible for the war. While intellectuals from the left felt the war was an example of Italian imperialism[101] nationalists, Garveyites and the black masses saw it as 'a war of black against white. This nationalistic attitude was prevalent in black America, permeating every geographical section of the nation.'[102]

The re-emergence of black nationalism

The IEW led to the re-emergence of the black nationalist philosophy initiated by Marcus Garvey during the 1920s.[103] Despite the decline of the UNIA, Marcus Garvey was at the forefront of black opposition to Mussolini's invasion of Ethiopia.[104] Consequently, the remaining local chapters of the UNIA, especially in Harlem, were at the vanguard of the movement to aid Ethiopia. Mainstream academia has overlooked the importance of both Pan-Africanism and Black nationalism in relation to the African-American liberation struggle. Regarding the IEW, *The New York Times* stated, 'not since the days of Marcus Garvey ... had black nationalists won so large a following on the streets of Harlem.'[105]

African-Americans' activism on behalf of Ethiopia did not compel the government to intercede on Ethiopia's behalf nor halt Italy's invasion of

Ethiopia.[106] In brief, African-Americans failed to aid Ethiopia due to their subordinate political and economic status[107] domestically. For example, the Friends of Ethiopia did not raise significant funds to contribute to Selassie's government.[108] The Committee for Ethiopia's financial contribution to Ethiopia was also limited. However, 'the white led relief organisations with close ties to the Philanthropic world such as American Aid for Ethiopia, were more successful than the Friends and other black groups in providing direct aid to the embattled Ethiopians, but few blacks were willing to join these groups.'[109]

African-Americans did achieve some success. The Medical Committee for the Defence of Ethiopia stated: 'a New York based group of thirty black physicians, nurses, dentists, and pharmacists launched a fund-raising drive ... In November, they sent two tons of bandages and a portable field hospital.'[110] In general, white Americans did not utilise their political and economic resources to aid Ethiopia. One could argue that America's failure to support Ethiopia was a consequence of white racism as, 'the government of the United States was hardly in the mood to rescue Ethiopia, in view of its own economic recession, its isolation, and its racialist tendencies.'[111] In addition, American racism undermined AAFAN's efforts to promote their foreign policy goals, as white racism generally ensured that AAFAN's policy recommendations would be considered marginal to white views. Indeed, the *Inter-Racial Review*, which was published periodically on behalf of the Catholic Inter-Racial Council in New York, maintained 'that Africans were not capable of self development. It called for a humane colonialism in Africa as a bulwark against communism and Islam.'[112] Interestingly, the logic of the Catholic Inter-Racial Council in New York, regarding the necessity of Western/white leadership in Africa, mirrors the logic and outcome of US race relations between African and European Americans.[113]

The position of the US administration

The Roosevelt administration's orientation to the IEW was harder to decipher than that of the Catholic Inter-Racial Council. As despite Hunts' racial thesis regarding US foreign policy's racial orientation, the Roosevelt administration's actions were consistent with America's isolationist policies. Therefore US non-engagement with the IEW could have stemmed from their desire to avoid American involvement in international wars.[114] Although the isolationist ethos was dominant in US foreign policy, some government officials argued that isolationism was an antiquated policy, which needed to be replaced by a pragmatic form of interventionism. Thus,

Secretary (Cordell) Hull, in an address on 16 February 1935 at New York, said that the enormous speeding up of trade and communications made futile any endeavour to induce the United States again to withdraw into 'splendid isolation'. Our policies must of necessity be those of a great power; we could not, even if we would, 'fail profoundly to affect international relations'. The Secretary said that there had been a time when the ocean meant, or could mean, a certain degree of isolation; but that modern communication had ended this forever.[115]

Hull's suggestion that America should review its foreign affairs policies was shared by others

> as speaking over WOR [radio] ... Thomas Jesse Jones, educational director of the Phelps-Stokes Fund, declared that 'the paramount responsibility of the American people ... is to support our State Department in all efforts to win the Italian government and Premier Mussolini to the way of peaceful negotiations ... [Jones maintained that] ... Americans are vitally interested in the safety and progress of Abyssinia and Liberia, the only native governments on the whole continent of Africa.'[116]

In short, the mid-1930s found US foreign policy in an ideological battle between the isolationist old guard and the interventionists.[117]

Neutrality legislation

Nevertheless despite Cordell Hull's critique of isolationist foreign policy, the US government opted to remain neutral during the IEW. Of course, America's non-engagement policy during the IEW was clearly an euphemism for isolationism, as

> in 1935 there developed considerable public support in the United States for an embargo on the export of arms to belligerents as a means of keeping the United States out of war ... Under the influence of this concept and with the shadow of a new European war on the horizon the Congress passed a joint resolution in August 1935 providing that upon the outbreak or during the progress of war between or among two or more foreign states 'the President shall proclaim such fact, and it shall thereafter be unlawful to export arms, ammunition, or implements of war' from the United States to any belligerent country. This legislation contained provisions for the licensing of arms export, the prohibition of the carriage by United States vessels of arms to belligerent states, and the restriction of travel by United States citizens on vessels of belligerent states. This joint resolution, known as the Neutrality Act was signed by President Roosevelt on 31 August 1935.[118]

In signing it, the president said he had done so 'because it was intended as an expression of the fixed desire of the Government and the people of the United States to avoid any action which might involve us in war'. However, he said that the 'inflexible' arms-embargo provisions "might drag us into war instead of keeping us out": that no Congress and no Executive could foresee all possible future situations.'[119] Clearly, the US government desired to avoid participating in foreign wars, irrespective of the racial context. Of course, given that the US government was reasonably informed that Italy was planning to attack Ethiopia in September 1934,[120] it is significant that America failed to warn Ethiopia or the league of the impending attack, especially since Ambassador Breckinridge Long (at Rome) informed Cordell Hull that Italy's planned aggression would be detrimental to world peace.[121] While the ambassador's stated concern pertaining to Italy and Ethiopia was the maintenance of world peace not race, interestingly 'during [the] period [of the war] there was an increase in the export from the United States to Italy of War materials which did not come within the category of arms, ammunition, and implements of war.'[122] The increase of war exports to Italy contradicts America's alleged desire to maintain international peace. Again America's actions aided Italy's war effort.

Following Italy's invasion of Ethiopia on 3 October 1935, President Roosevelt acting

> in accordance with provisions of the Neutrality Act, issued proclamations putting into effect an embargo on the export of arms, ammunition, and implements of war to the two belligerent nations and restrictions on travel by United States citizens on vessels of the belligerents ... [however] the president stated any of our people ... who engage in transactions of any character with either of the belligerents do so at their own risk.[123]

Evidently, economic transactions between US citizens and the combatants were not prohibited, which, given Italy's superior economic status and trading capacity, contradicts the US government's claim of 'contribut[ing] to the cause of peace in every practical way.'[124] The US government's, and the secretary of state's (Cordell Hull's), belief that the war should be resolved by the league[125] was in reality a death blow to Ethiopia given the racial and cultural orientation of the league and its members.

The actions of the Roosevelt administration

The US government's goal regarding the IEW was to keep America and American citizens out of the war.[126] Therefore African-Americans intending to fight for Ethiopia were advised of the government's legal position by Robert L. Vann, the black assistant to the attorney general (and owner of the *Pittsburgh Courier*): 'Vann advised the [African-Americans and AAFAN] newspapers that Americans who enlisted in either the Italian or Ethiopian military would be in violation of a federal law equally of 1818 governing the enlistment of U.S citizens in a foreign army.'[127] The government's prohibition against Italian and African-American enlistment in foreign armies suggests the law applied equally to both groups. In addition, it demonstrates the US government's knowledge of black recruitment activities, which explains the utilisation of Robert Vann to prohibit them.[128]

The government's reaction to AAFAN's domestic activities illustrates that international issues can directly affect domestic relations. The State Department and secretary of state's actions indicate that African-American activism affected America's domestic context, as 'Cordell Hull brought military recruitment to a halt, declaring volunteer efforts on behalf of Ethiopia a violation of the Neutrality Act.'[129] The government's response shows how seriously they took AAFAN actions.[130] The US government's investigation of AAFAN's organisational efforts is indicative of its punitive orientation towards AAFAN's campaign to aid Ethiopia.[131] This is validated by the government's efforts to curtail the recruitment activities of AAFAN, which is reasonable given they were illegal. However, there is no evidence that the government supported or acknowledged AAFAN's legal activities in a constructive manner.

The administration reoriented AAFAN's actions.[132] In brief, the state realigned AAFAN's agenda to suit its foreign policies rather than adopting AAFAN's agenda.[133] The evidence here contravenes the depiction of the state as a passive institution moved by interest groups.[134] Although given the superior economic and political status of Italian-Americans and Italy, the black agenda would be offset by other factors, notwithstanding Hunt's thesis regarding the Anglo-American elite's racist worldview.[135]

Neutrality

Although the Roosevelt administration's foreign policy was reportedly neutral regarding the IEW, Marcus Garvey maintained: 'the country [America] is neutral. Yet not neutral. It is neutral for those who will take advantage of the loopholes.'[136] Garvey claimed the US government's neutrality worked against the interests of African-Americans and Ethiopia. Plummer also maintains that American neutrality aided Italy.[137] The US government was ambivalent about Ethiopia's plight as US neutrality did not compel America to cease trading with Italy. America's reluctance to aid Ethiopia is demonstrated by the Standard Oil incident where Haile Selassie's government made economic overtures to

> the Standard Vacuum Oil Company, which received a seventy-five year extensive exploratory contract. The deal was an effort to involve the United States as a principal in Ethiopian affairs by means of a corporate lever and to obtain badly needed funds. The State Department pressured the oil company into cancelling the contract, however, because no one had consulted the government.[138]

This incident contradicts the Shoup and Minter thesis that the US state is bound to respond to the wishes of capitalists as the state bypassed economic opportunities to safeguard their foreign policy. The fact that the US government forced Standard Oil to withdraw from its deal with the Ethiopian government while continuing to trade with Italy indicates the American state was not beholden to the capitalist class, as Standard Oil's profits were secondary to the state's foreign policy requirements pertaining to Ethiopia.[139]

The Roosevelt administration doubtlessly knew that its actions and Ethiopia's comparative weakness in relation to Italy would aid Italy. American indifference to Ethiopia reinforced and legitimised Britain's and France's in action pertaining to Ethiopia.[140] The failure of America, Britain and France to aid Ethiopia is explained by the following reasons. Italy's strategic importance in Europe in light of Germany's growing threat took precedence over Ethiopia's plight. Therefore, British and French strategic interests necessitated their lack of action on behalf of Ethiopia as 'both France and England needed the friendship of Italy, in order to curb the Hitler menace.'[141] In addition, those nations' diplomatic and economic relations with Italy were of greater significance and ultimately more profitable than their diplomatic and economic relations with Ethiopia. Finally, given those nations' belief in and adherence to white supremacy coupled with the military threat posed by Italy, Britain, France and America chose to avoid a military conflict with an industrialised white nation in defence of Ethiopia.

Additionally, American isolationism may have determined the US states' response to Ethiopia as

> Moral embargo aside, the 1936 presidential campaign strengthened FDR's reservations about Ethiopia. He didn't want to lose potentially isolationist votes. The internal State Department discussion of a proposed visit by the Ethiopian emperor focuses on probable reactions of Afro-Americans and Italian-Americans, and the difficulties that would ensue if Haile Selassie made fund raising a focus of his tour. After some debate, some officials tabled the emperor's tour. Roosevelt remained cool to Ethiopian solicitations throughout his second government.[142]

One must acknowledge America's isolationist disposition, as determining American inaction pertaining to Ethiopia. The question is: how significant a factor was Ethiopia's racial identity? Marcus Garvey's evaluation of the US government's actions suggested that race and domestic power politics were paramount. Garvey argued that African-Americans' political naïveté was causing them to be tricked whilst 'the Italian-American cannot be fooled, and ... by his usual systematic organisation he is using the peculiar neutrality to help Mussolini and Italy.'[143] In short, Garvey maintained that America had indirectly aided Italy and opposed AAFAN's and African-Americans' agenda. Garvey's contention supports Hunt's and Bowser's racial theories, which argue that US foreign policy has been racially biased.[144] In addition, Garvey argued that the electoral process was integral to African-Americans efforts to influence foreign policy.[145] Garvey's claims raise key questions regarding whether African-Americans' marginal racial status hindered their efforts to shape US foreign policy, given Seaburys' contention that the vote has significantly aided minority groups to influence foreign policy.[146] In short,

Italian-Americans' superior racial and economic status combined with their voting power aided Italy, as Garvey claimed

> President [Roosevelt] found it difficult to stop the American oil supply to Italy, a stoppage which would have immediately handicapped the Italians in Abyssinia. Italian finance in America and Italian political power have combined to influence American businessmen to break through the neutrality to assist Italy, whilst the Negroes in America cannot bring a similar pressure to prevent the Italians getting the advantage.[147]

In short, Italian-Americans' superior organisational and political-economic power-base placed them in a superior position relative to African-Americans in terms of meeting their interests.[148] Essentially, American neutrality favoured Italy who, according to the league, caused the IEW.

The position of Italian-Americans

Gaetano Salvemini maintains that Italian-Americans largely supported Italian Fascism.[149] Indeed, Americans generally held Mussolini's fascist government in high regard during the early 1930s.[150] The affiliation between Italian-Americans and the fascist government allowed the Italian government to encourage 'Italian-Americans to lobby President Roosevelt and congressmen elected in districts with a strong Italian constituency against support for the League's embargo.'[151] Indeed, some Italian-Americans became active agents of Italian foreign policy,[152] although other Italian-Americans opposed the Fascist regime and the war in East Africa.[153] However 'after a few months ... [the] ... antifascist vision scarcely reflected reality. The majority of Italian-Americans became enthusiastic supporters of Italy's colonial venture.'[154]

The actions of Italian-Americans

According to Salvemini, when the war commenced,

> in October 1935 ... demonstrations were ... [held across] ... United States to show that all Italians were siding with Mussolini. The Federation of War Veterans donated a field hospital, with doctors and nurses. The local branches of the War Veterans Federations publicly recruited volunteers for the fighting front, not only among the Italians resident in the United States, but also among American citizens of Italian origin, without the federal government taking any steps to discourage such a movement or to denationalise those who enrolled.[155]

Italian-Americans in New York campaigned on behalf of the fascist forces and 'innumerable meetings ... took place in New York from the autumn of 1935 to the summer of 1936,[156] including the mass meeting

on 14 December 1935 ... held at Madison Square Garden, with the aim
of launching a drive on behalf of the Italian Red Cross. Mayor LaGuardia
attended, stating that he 'exclusively' meant to help the campaign for the
benefit of the Italian Red Cross, that noble institution functioning independently from every political or religious creed. But [Generoso] Pope,
Judge Ferdinand Pecora, Judge Cotillo, and Consul Vecchiotti assailed
Great Britain and the League and upheld Italy's right to civilise Ethiopia.[157]

The New York Italian-Americans' orientation to the war was demonstrated
after the

victory of the Italian army and the proclamation of the empire were
celebrated on the evening of 13 June 1936, in ... Madison Square Garden.
This gathering was officially summoned by Consul Vecchiotti in person ...
The American authorities never dreamed of calling him to order, as they
had once done with Rolandi-Ricci [the former Italian ambassador] and
Thaon di Revel [fascist agent active in America in the 1920s]. If they had
such an idea, they didn't take any action in view of the coming presidential elections of November 1936. In this rally G. Pope handed over
to the consul a cheque for one hundred thousand dollars, this being the
seventh cheque for the same amount. The money had been collected
through his two dailies (newspapers). Joseph Gerli offered 100,000 lire.
The sums collected in New York by the consulate and Pope's papers
amount to $741,862, without taking into account the money sent to the
Italian government directly, without intermediaries.[158]

The Italian-American clergy also glorified Italian imperialism declaring their
support for the fascist regime according to *L' Indipendente*, an Italian-American
publication in New Haven, Connecticut.[159]

Evidently, Italian-Americans' racial and historical origins encouraged their
support of Italian fascism as their loyalty to Italy ensured their opposition to
the AAFAN,[160] although some participated in popular front demonstrations
with African-Americans.[161] Nevertheless racial tensions fractured the popular
front's inter-racial character, as African-Americans grew hostile to white
people in general and Italian-Americans specifically. Indeed, Nadia Venturini
maintains that 'although Harlem is half-a-world away from the horn of
Africa, the Italian-Ethiopian War was ... fought on the streets of New York
City. The War brought Italian Americans and African Americans into intense
confrontations for the first time.'[162] The violent episodes attest to Italian-
Americans support of Italy and the racialised hostility between them and
African-Americans. For example, black people in Birmingham, Alabama,
boycotted Italian businesses and were arrested by the police,[163] and Italian-
Americans in Boston hung a figurine of Haile Sellassie.[164] Clearly both communities supported their own racial/ethnic group irrespective of their supposed
commonalties as Americans. The fact that 'the New York metropolitan

area ... contributed $500,000 to the Italian Red Cross,'[165] indicates Italian-Americans donated funds on behalf of their fatherland.[166] The evidence indicates that Italian-Americans aided the Italian war-effort financially.[167] In terms of Italian-Americans' capacity to aid Italian foreign policy,

> Mario Orsini Ratto, who acted as Italian consul in Baltimore and Philadelphia ... [stated in 1933 in his book *The Future of Italo-Americans*] ... thanks to the Italo-Americans, Italy has been able to lay the demands of fascism before the United States in a much favourable light. [He continues] ... Italo-Americans can, in a ten year period of serious organisation, become a formidable electoral and financial force and offer unprecedented opportunities for intellectual and economic influence ... The masses of emigrants have a[n] ... American mentality, but they are sensitive to the ... encouragement's and provisions which the Italian Government devises in their favour.[168]

In brief, the evidence indicates that Italian-Americans generally supported Mussolini's action against Ethiopia[169] in addition to apparently influencing US foreign policy towards Italy.[170]

In this case, international affairs directly affected US race relations. Significantly, Italian-Americans' ethnic identity may have inhibited their integration into the WASP-dominated foreign policy establishment. However, their marginal status pertaining to the WASP elite was offset by their assimilation into the white hierarchy in America,[171] which elevated them above the African-American community.

The US Communist Party

Penny Von Eschen's claim that US communists, Pan-Africanists and black nationalists held common ideological ground during the early part of the century[172] is validated by the formation of interracial, popular front organisations[173] that incorporated diverse ideological persuasions. However, the conflicting views of black people and communists regarding the cause of the IEW and African-Americans' belief that white racism caused the war, undermined the inter-racial popular front.[174] In short, communists in the (PCDE) in Harlem were forced 'to redirect anti-white sentiment toward a critique of fascism.'[175] Despite James Ford leader of the Harlem section of the Communist Party (speech at the Seventh Congress of the Communist Internationalist in Moscow) on behalf of Ethiopia, C. L. R. James (and others) attacked the Soviet Union stating 'Stalin who claims to be a friend of Negroes, sold oil to Italy all though the Italian campaign.'[176] African-American mistrust of communists increased as former black communists revealed the contradictions between communist ideology and communists' actions. AAFAN observed that the Soviet state, like its US counterpart, was willing to profit from the activities of Italian fascism.[177] Nonetheless, the Soviet Union had to review its policies towards Italy 'on 14 September (1935), responding to mounting protests and continuing Italian encroachments on Ethiopian soil, the USSR banned arms sales to Italy. It nullified this gesture ... by selling the Italians larger shares of oil, coal, grain, and lumber. Indeed, Soviet imports consisted of 25 per cent of the total Italian petroleum inventory.'[178]

In brief, the realities of the war undermined the popular front due to racial and ideological differences.[179] Black people questioned the sincerity of the Soviet Union and the CPUSA. George Padmore, 'a former executive secretary of the international trade union Committee of Negro Workers, charged ... [in] ... May 1935 that the Soviet Union would ... sacrifice Ethiopia to Italy if Soviet interests might be saved.'[180] Padmore's statement is significant as he was at one time 'the most trusted Negro leader in the Comintern apparatus.'[181] Black people recognised that communist ideology denunciations of imperialism were less convincing in practice.[182]

Black dissatisfaction with communism and the Soviet Union led to black defections from the Communist Party. In August 1935,

> Herman Mackawain ... leader ... [of] ... the Harlem section, resigned ... from the Party ... Mackawain ... accused Russia of abandoning revolutionary activities in Africa and Asia to appease its European allies ... [according to Naison] ... A 'New York Times' story in ... September, reporting Soviet sales of coal tar, wheat, and oil to Italy at below market price, added fuel to Mackawain's charges. Although the Soviets ... [denounced] ... Italian aggression at ... the League, Harlem newspapers seized upon their trade policies as yet another sign that 'the Soviet Union cannot be counted on to stand steadfast as far as Negroes are concerned.[183]

Given that white people have dominated the Soviet state[184] and its actions (during the IEW), AAFAN's race-based analysis was plausible. Consequently, many black communists in Harlem left CPUSA[185] perhaps they sympathised with the Pan-Africanists and black nationalists who believed the war was caused by white nations' racism.[186] The popular front collapsed because of the conflicting interpretations of nationalists and communists regarding the role of the Soviet Union in the IEW and the importance of the colour-line internationally[187] and domestically.[188] In brief, African-Americans believed the domestic colour-line extended into the international arena.[189]

Although African-Americans believed the Soviet Union sacrificed Ethiopia, due to white racism, the Soviet Union's response may have been motivated by strategic foreign policy considerations; since the Soviet Union joined the league to protect itself from Germany and it 'had no desire to antagonize Rome, which had not yet allied itself with Berlin.'[190] One could argue 'The Soviet Union['s] ... [failure to] ... openly rebuk[e] Italy during the 1935 League sessions'[191] may have stemmed from political not racial considerations. Nonetheless, the NAACP criticised Soviet foreign policy and attributed Soviet in action to Soviet racism.[192]

The League

As required by its remit, the league sought a diplomatic solution[193] to the conflict between Italy and Ethiopia.[194] Although the formal declarations of the league suggest it was committed to defending Ethiopia,[195] the league, like Britain and France, sacrificed Ethiopia in the interests of *realpolitik* and highlighted its inadequacy regarding the resolution of international conflicts. The league's actions suggest the member states were not committed to preventing the war, despite their efforts to mediate between the two combatants, as it failed to protect Ethiopia despite declaring Italy to be the aggressor and swearing 'to defend' Ethiopia.[196]

W. E. B. Du Bois indicted Europe as a whole[197] and noted that the league would not defend African interests against European imperialism. Italy's actions were significant given that the Kellogg-Briand Pact forbade league members from waging war against each other.[198] The league's in action led African-Americans to conclude that it was an instrument of white supremacy.[199]

The IEW re-ignited the racial awareness of people of African descent within America and colonised territories.[200] The American ambassador correctly observed that Italy's victory over Ethiopia would 'continue on ... for a generation as an ... irritation to European politics and an additional menace to world peace.'[201]

The evidence substantiates African-Americans' commitment to Ethiopia, demonstrated by their mobilisation on Ethiopia's behalf, which included fund-raising drives, petitions to the league, demonstrations, recruitment drives, as well as the (attempted) economic boycott and the creation and mobilisation of (African-American) organisations and the press campaign. The evidence indicates that US foreign policy conflicted with Africans-Americans' campaign to aid Ethiopia. The evidence indicates that African-Americans backed Ethiopia, and proves that their political activism was not confined to domestic issues.[202]

The Chicago Defender claimed

> the ... Italo-Ethiopian conflict ... crystallis[ed] the interests of the black people of the world. The violation of Ethiopia's sovereignty provided the blacks with the much needed platform of racial solidarity on which all may stand ... [the desire to aid Ethiopia] ... resounded in the hearts of millions of blacks scattered throughout the four corners of the world ... many would have ... answered the call had not geographical difficulties ... [and] ... international red tape prohibited their participation.[203]

The US government's neutrality policy regarding the IEW was successful because it encountered no domestic opposition from powerful political or economic groups within the private or public sphere. The Roosevelt administration recognised that white people would not willingly assist Ethiopia.[204]

Given US racism, white Americans would incline towards assessing Ethiopia from a racial perspective. Hunt's thesis would also suggest that the state's racial orientation would prevent it from aiding Ethiopia.

Italian-Americans on the east coast supported Italy by funding its war effort and fighting African-Americans in the streets. Italy's superior economic and military standing (in relation to Ethiopia) ensured Italian-Americans' and Italy's success relative to their respective combatants. It has been argued that Italian-Americans possession of the vote forced Roosevelt to take greater account of the views of Italian-Americans due to their greater potential to punish him at the polling booth. Undoubtedly the possession of the franchise and Italian-Americans superior political and economic power lent more weight to their actions in relation to African-American efforts.

Despite African-Americans efforts to aid Ethiopia, the following factors contributed to their failure to influence US foreign policy to safeguard Ethiopian sovereignty: their inability to raise (substantial) funds or send medical supplies and teams of African-American medical personnel,[205] the US government's threat of legal sanctions against African-Americans who desired to fight for Ethiopia, in addition to the confusion caused by white people regarding Ethiopia's racial designation and orientation towards African-Americans.[206] While black people's failure to build inter-racial alliances could be construed as a factor in their failure to meet their goals, it is doubtful that white Americans were committed to saving Ethiopia.

African-Americans lacked the political power to successfully lobby the US foreign policy establishment. In addition, black people's inability to utilise the vote reduced their ability to shape US foreign policy. In brief, African-Americans' domestic status, which was derived from their racial status, prevented them from aiding Ethiopia.

The significance of the Italo-Ethiopian War from AAFAN's perspective

The IEW was significant because it revitalised[207] the black nationalist and Pan-African philosophies that had dominated the black struggle in the 1920s. The war fostered the belief that Italian imperialism epitomised white nations' desire to subjugate Africa. The contention that white nations facilitated Italian imperialism is significant as

> Before the ... [war] ... Great Britain ... [was aware of] ... Italian aims in Ethiopia. Through diplomatic contacts and in 1935 at the Stresa Conference, Italy had made it clear it wanted a protectorate over Ethiopia, and that it would use force to get it ... [indeed] before Great Britain decided on what action to take, it commissioned John Maffey, former governor of the Sudan, to assess the impact that the Italian occupation of Ethiopia would have on British interests. The summary report concluded that Britain's interests were compatible with Italian domination of Ethiopia.[208]

The war led to the operational utilisation of Pan-Africanism.

The adoption of the nationalist position explains why African-Americans made few demands of the US government. The existence of white supremacy made it unlikely that white people would fight to defend Ethiopia or fight a white nation on behalf of Africans. As a result, African-Americans organised themselves on a racial basis despite the creation of the popular front. The IEW forced the African-American community to exam US foreign policy and the character of international relations and to clarify their relationship to African people worldwide. The colonisation of black countries by European nations fostered the view that US race relations were a form of racial colonialism.[209] The IEW stimulated African-American recognition of the international aspect of Western imperialism and its use of racism to promote its actions.

The IEW provides insight into the American political system between 1934 and 1936. Whether it provides a basis to draw long-term conclusions regarding US foreign policy in relation to African-Americans is yet to be determined. In brief, the colour-line was the key factor in AAFAN's failure to meet its goals in relation to the IEW. The power inequalities between European and African-Americans caused the under-development of black America which negated their political power in America and institutionalised their marginal role in relation to the decision-making apparatus in American politics. The marginal status of African-Americans created the basis of the state's dismissal of their foreign policy goals, in addition to there being no pragmatic reason for the state to support black interests.

Pluralism suggests that in the US, competitive groups are presented with (broadly) equal opportunities to vie for their interests[210] and if a group accepts American values they could, if sufficiently organised, assimilate into American political culture. Consequently, African-Americans' failure to influence US foreign policy could be attributed to their organisational or intellectual incompetence, not white racism. Pluralism suggests that one group can not dominate foreign policy. However, pluralism fails to adequately acknowledge the historically inequalities between African and Euro-Americans. African-Americans second-class citizenship and inability to vote hampered their efforts on Ethiopia's behalf. Although some African-Americans could vote in the North, their voting power was limited due to the restrictions placed on the majority of African-Americans. Ironically, black people concluded that their demands would be rejected by the US government because of white racism. Finally, African-American economic subordination to white America and the opposition of government agencies such as the Federal Bureau of Investigation hampered their efforts to aid Ethiopia.

The US foreign policy establishment has not historically been representative of American society.[211] Consequently, African-Americans' marginal status pertaining to the foreign policy establishment during the IEW does not necessarily support a race-based analysis. However, the WASP elites domination of the foreign policy establishment and its exclusion of black people[212] from government exemplifies white exclusion of black people from foreign affairs issues. African-Americans could not compete with governmental and private actors because of their racial identity. Hunt's claim that US foreign policy has been shaped by WASPS[213] corroborates with the evidence. Hunt claims the domestic racial hierarchy is reflected in the making of US foreign policy.[214] Although the US State Department prevented African-American recruitment, thirty-seven Italian-Americans 'of the Association of Italians Abroad (Manhattan, New York) enlisted as volunteers and served under the Italian flag in the IEW'.[215] While Hunt acknowledges WASP dominance of foreign affairs, he does not highlight the activities of African-Americans.

Statism would argue that state interests would determine whether AAFAN was included or excluded from the foreign policy establishment. The US state maintained its (allegedly) neutrality policies pertaining to the IEW irrespective of African-Americans activities. The legal ruling preventing US citizens from enlisting in foreign armies was directed at all Americans. However, the US State and Justice Department was more successful in undermining African-American activities.[216] Despite the state's neutrality policies, Italian-Americans provided substantial financial assistance to Italy. Consequently, the state either failed to halt Italian-American support of Mussolini or it only desired to inhibit their enlistment in the Italian army, although the state maintained its neutral status. Statism fails to acknowledge the actions and activities of AAFAN, which is indicative of statism's narrow focus and its tendency not to acknowledge the actions of marginal groups from below. Statism is partially validated given the state's success in meeting its foreign policy goals; however, statism fails to account for the existence of institutionalised racism within the state[217] and the foreign policy establishment.

The **Marxist** contention that capitalist control of the US state[218] would orientate it to prioritise capitalist interests is invalidated, although America maintained trade relations with Italy (unopposed by the state) irrespective of Neutrality legislation state. However, when Standard Oil and the Ethiopian government brokered a deal that interfered with the US foreign policy, the Roosevelt administration compelled Standard Oil to withdraw from the deal with the Ethiopian government. In this instance, capitalist interests were undermined by the state's foreign policy goals. However, the Marxist contention that the interests of the subordinate classes are secondary to the interests of the ruling class is convincing. As African-Americans' marginal economic and class status hampered their efforts to aid Ethiopia. Marxism partially explains black people's failure to advance their interests and their foreign policy goals because Marxism acknowledges their marginal economic status. However, African-Americans' racial identity has determined their political status, more than their economic status. In short, the colour-line has taken greater precedence over African-Americans' class or economic status within the US context. For example, for a rich African-American living in the post-reconstruction South, economic wealth might secure various concessions from white people. Nevertheless, southern racial conventions might still prohibit that individual from voting.

The Marxist theory fails to highlight the significance of race as a determining factor in the formation, execution and general worldview of the US foreign policy establishment. Marxism also underestimates the power of the state to determine and execute national policies despite resistance from sections of the capitalist class.

Racialised Colony defines the state/foreign policy establishment as a hegemonic colonial power that would orientate AAFAN to comply with its foreign policy goals.[219] This theory suggests that an organic leadership class would challenge the hegemony of the foreign policy establishment and promote its own foreign affairs policies, which AAFAN did during the IEW. Conversely, Robert Vann, the (black) assistant to the US attorney general, facilitated state policies by ensuring that AAFAN complied with the state's dictates. Given that hegemonic groups are frequently challenged by organic interests from below, the racialised colony thesis accounts for AAFAN's use of organic ideologies such as Pan-Africanism and black nationalism to promote black interests. AAFAN's failure to meet its interests resulted from black dependence on the state to protect their interests. However, since the state did not require African-Americans assistance during the IEW and there were no compelling external factors to encourage the state to advance black interests, AAFAN was unable to compel US foreign policy to defend Ethiopia. The racialised colony thesis provides the best explanation of the evidence examined in this case study. African-Americans views on the IEW were addressed in the *Chicago Defender* by Metz T. P. Lochard in 'Black Races Profit from the Italian-Ethiopian Conflict': seeing

> Africa through the prism of its white detractors, the Negro had come to regard it with disdain and disaffection, evincing little or no concern in its people, its history past, or future. Today, however, he has an absorbing interest in both Africa and the Africans; he is beginning to be proud of the history of his ancestral land as the film of prejudice is gradually removed from his field of vision. He no longer subscribes to the distorted version of biased historians who have described Africa not as the cradle of civilisation, but as the birthplace of ignorance, superstition and savagery.[220]

The IEW stimulated African-American mass participation in a single foreign policy issue[221] and catapulted black nationalism to the forefront of the black struggle. The nationalist position elucidated the racial aspect of Italian and European imperialism and highlighted the connection between domestic and foreign affairs for African-Americans. AAFAN's ideological conception of the IEW was significant as 'Pan-Africanism and Garveyism (which) represented pinnacles of Black Nationalist achievement ... provided ways of framing ... (foreign and domestic race relations) issues for subsequent generations of activists.'[222] Significantly 'the consciousness that developed during the Ethiopian crisis forewarned African-Americans of the dangers involved in Fascist and Nazi expansionism.'[223] As a result, African-Americans foresaw the dangers of fascist extremism prior to WWII. African-Americans dislike of Western racial imperialism will also be demonstrated in Chapter 4.

4   From isolationism to globalism

African-Americans' response to US entry into the Second World War 1939–41

This new war is a fight not to preserve democracy or to blot out 'evil things', but to guard the empires of England and France from Hitler.[1]

This case study explores African-Americans' responses to the international crisis that ensued at the outbreak of WWII, particularly their views of US foreign policy, 1939–41. Although this case study encompasses African-Americans' views concerning the validity or invalidity of the isolationist and interventionist doctrines in relation to the war in Europe, the chapter will address African-Americans' response to WWII and the accompanying propaganda in favour of US intervention in defence of democracy at home and abroad.[2] US propaganda, which increasingly framed its opposition to the Axis Powers in moral terms, was significantly compromised by domestic race relations[3] and the Allies' colonial subordination of people of colour within the international arena. One of the chief aims of Chapter 5 will be to highlight the marginalised views and activities of AAFAN, which grappled with notions of patriotism and dissent in the light of America's domestic racial inequalities, which members of AAFAN contended were part of the international system of white racial supremacy. The examination of the interventionist and isolationist blocs' efforts to shape African-American opinions is vital to this chapter given their initial indifference to WWII, in addition to the fact that it verifies the plurality of America's competing interests (in this case) but also highlights the disparity in power between the groups presented in this case study. While the allied nations alleged commitment to democracy and the four freedoms[4] drew a sharp contrast between themselves and the Axis Powers, AAFAN was more cautious when assessing the character of the Allies and the Axis Powers.

The central themes of this chapter will be preceded by a brief historical context of the events leading up to WWII. The causal factors that culminated in WWII are related to the collapse of the league and the international consensus (established at Versailles) it was commissioned to promote. The league's inability to decisively intervene and halt Japan's invasion of Manchuria in 1931 demonstrated that state's could engage in international aggression despite the existence of the league and the great powers.[5] When coupled with Mussolini's invasion and conquest of Abyssinia, which, 'because of the failure of the League of Nations' leading members to halt Mussolini's aggression in 1935–36, the League was ... discredited [subsequently]; it played little or no role ... in the Spanish Civil war or in Japan's open assault upon China in 1937'.[6] The warnings issued by Haile Selassie and other black people such as 'the Haitian delegate to the League of Nations ... [who stated] ... let us never forget that one day we may all be somebody's Ethiopia', were ignored. The warnings issued by Haile Selassie and the Haitian delegate were prophetic as 'within a few years, most European nations [became] victims of Hitler's aggression in World War Two.'[7] The evidence points to the significance of the Italo-Ethiopian War as a gateway event leading to WWII and the centrality of the league in the collapse of the international order.[8]

The Axis Powers' territorial expansionism provoked WWII because they threatened British and French interests internationally and in Europe. The question is: why did America depart from the isolationist policies, which had under-girded the Neutrality legislation enforced during the Italo-Ethiopian War?[9] American non-interventionism, which remained the dominant ideology up to 1939,[10] did not suddenly die on 7 December 1941, which is validated by the Roosevelt administration's progressive trend towards an interventionist foreign policy, which culminated in the 'bases for destroyers' deal in 1940 and the 'lend-lease' agreement Roosevelt pushed through Congress in 1941.[11] Roosevelt repealed US neutrality legislation in order to safeguard British sovereignty[12] despite America's refusal to safeguard Ethiopian sovereignty in the face of Italian aggression during the 1930s.[13] Given the strong cultural, political and economic ties between the US and Britain and the strategic importance of Britain within global politics, America's defence of Britain appears quite logical. Of course, American intervention on Britain's behalf could have demonstrated its commitment to maintaining the trans-Atlantic Anglo-Saxon status quo[14] while the defeat of Ethiopia by a (so-called) 'civilised' white nation was of little concern.

The notion that America entered the war to save Britain, based on their racial or cultural ties, fails to explain America's entry into WWII, especially since US interventionists received 'considerable isolationist opposition'[15] from Charles Lindbergh and the America First Organisation (AFO) whose 'supporters [were overwhelmingly] from the upper Midwest and from non-Anglo ethnics nation-wide.'[16] That the AFO overwhelmingly comprised dissenting white ethnics[17] opposed to US intervention and WASP foreign policy, demonstrates the existence of ideological cleavages amongst white people and alludes to the importance of ethnicity in determining the views/actions of white people pertaining to foreign affairs.[18] Indeed, the role of ethnicity in determining the ethnic composition of the isolationist and interventionist movements may require further research. In summation, the idea that America entered the war because of its close ties with Britain oversimplifies the complexities of international politics since many white Americans opposed aiding Britain.[19] While the special relationship thesis based on WASP cultural and racial affinity is compelling, it does have its limits in fully explaining America's entry into the war, as does the contention that America has historically been wholly opposed to interventionism as it has intervened regularly within the Americas and the Pacific when it served its national interest.[20] Clearly, American isolationism was confined to Europe and beyond.[21] Essentially, one could argue that US economic protectionism facilitated its entry into the war, since Japan's desire for an economic empire in the Pacific triggered Japanese and US economic hostilities,[22] which resulted in American 'economic sanctions against Japan ... [which] were widely recognised in Washington as carrying grave risks of war.'[23] And it was the United State's 'embargo on Japanese assets, which forced Japan to take action'[24] that climaxed with the attack on Pearl Harbour. Thus, Zinn argues that Japanese disruption of 'potential US markets',[25] followed by US sanctions, ultimately led to US intervention in the war.

The position of African-Americans

The IEW stimulated African-Americans' wider appreciation, interest and recognition of foreign affairs,[26] which placed them at the cutting edge of a grass-roots foreign affairs community, which led to some African-Americans' military involvement in the Spanish civil war, where they fought against fascism. Evidently African-Americans' interest in foreign affairs encompassed more than one foreign affairs issue. African-Americans' desire to fight on behalf of Ethiopia and the anti-fascist forces in Spain[27] indicates that (some) African-Americans embraced the concept of interventionism, which only received mainstream support after Japan's bombing of Pearl Harbour. Clearly, AAFAN and African-Americans in general recognised the danger that Italian fascism posed to world peace, in terms of the dangerous precedent set by Italy, that military action in order to facilitate a state's expansionist goals was permissible, while America and Europe chose to ignore Italy's actions. Padmore highlighted British hypocrisy by stating 'is it strange that [the British prime minister] Mr. Chamberlain denounces the wrongdoings of Hitler but remains silent about Mussolini's brute force, bad faith, injustice and oppression' towards Abyssinians and Albanians.[28] The precedent set by both Mussolini's aggression and America's and Europe's failure to respond collectively and decisively (perhaps) fuelled German expansionism, which ultimately caused the war in Europe, while European nations (and to a lesser degree America) could tolerate Japanese aggression against China, and Italy's invasion of Ethiopia; they evidently felt that the sovereignty of European nations was worth fighting for. While African-American activities during the IEW favoured interventionism, their initial response to WWII reflected the complexity of their domestic context[29] and international race relations. African-Americans' response to the plight of Britain and France in the face of German aggression was affected by both nations' failure to aid Ethiopia and their perception of British and French imperialism, which subjugated millions of people of African descent worldwide.

While Nazi ideology hailed the alleged superiority of the white race, African-Americans felt that European and white American views on race were not altogether dissimilar to those of the Nazis.[30] Although African-Americans acknowledged that allied racism was less pronounced than Nazi extremism, they recognised that 'the world of the 1940s was still by and large a Western white-dominated world. The long-established patterns of white power and non-white powerlessness were still the generally accepted order of things.'[31] Given Britain and France's enslavement and colonisation of African people, African-Americans and AAFAN viewed the struggle between the Allies and Axis Powers as an internal fight between white imperialists, with both sides intent on dictating the affairs of people of African descent and people of colour.[32] Thus, Max Yergan stated to Du Bois: 'the present war is the central fact in the world today. In my opinion, it is a conflict waged, among other purposes, to enable powerful [white] administrations to continue and extend their control over colonies and their inhabitants. This is true whether the victors are imperialist Britain and France or Nazi Germany.'[33]

Consequently, many African-Americans initially argued that the war in Europe was a white man's war.[34] Given the history of black participation in wars fought on behalf of white people, some African-Americans suggested observing the war from the sidelines.[35] The fact that the British and French colonisers had sacrificed Ethiopia in an attempt to maintain the balance of power in Europe, intensified African-American apathy to their plight. Even Frank Crosswaith, a vigorous supporter of the allied cause, stated: 'one cannot overlook the fact ... that ... if the ... rulers of Britain, of France and the other powerful democracies had not permitted their economic interests to ... smother their social thinking, those countries would have effectively halted the axis powers when Ethiopia and the other small, peaceful and defenceless nations were being crucified on the rugged cross of dictatorship.'[36]

In brief, African-Americans'/AAFAN's anti-colonialist stance was the root cause of their reluctance to support Britain and France's fight against Germany. Significantly, AAFAN's indifference to the plight of European nations was derived from their adoption of the Pan-African worldview which called for racial solidarity against those nations that oppressed African people specifically and people of colour in general. Ultimately, however, AAFAN's ideological commitment to remaining neutral in regard to (specific) white nations' attempts to determine which nation or nations would lead the white world proved to be impossible.[37]

As Germany's military victories increased, so did African-American awareness of the all-encompassing nature of Nazi racism, which forced African-Americans to come to terms with the fact that German fascism might pose more problems for black people than the racism practised by the allied nations. Consequently, AAFAN and African-Americans were forced to adopt a pragmatic response to the war that differentiated between allied racial imperialism and the racial totalitarianism championed by the Axis Powers. Increasingly, AAFAN and African-Americans argued that despite the abysmal record of the allied nations, supporting them against Germany was the lesser of two evils.[38] The role of Japan during the early 1940s challenged African-Americans' racial worldview that characterised European nations as the principal cause of international conflicts.[39] While Japan had won the admiration of many African-Americans in its attempt to enshrine the principle of racial equality at the League of Nations and its symbolic commitment to the plight of Ethiopia,[40] Japanese imperialism in Asia contradicted the notion that the principal enemy of the coloured world was (white) western supremacy still. Some African-Americans were not opposed to a Japanese attack on America[41] because they believed that the Japanese would liberate African-Americans from racial oppression.

African-Americans' opinions concerning the war ranged from indifference to enthusiasm, as some felt the war would weaken the grasp of European nations on the black world,[42] while others supported the war out of a sense of patriotism.[43] Some African-Americans utilised allied propaganda, which claimed to be fighting in defence of democracy, to call for the extension of democracy to the colonies and the eradication of the colour-line internationally and within America.[44] Some African-Americans argued that their support of the war should be used to gain political and economic leverage within the domestic context, whereby American democracy would extend full political freedom to the black population.[45] African-Americans' orientation towards WWII was significant because the US government and private organisations examined and attempted to shape African-Americans' opinions towards the war.[46]

The actions of AAFAN between 1939 and 1940

Despite AAFAN's reservations concerning the war, it and the majority of African-Americans generally endorsed President Roosevelt's foreign policy,[47] which increasingly pursued interventionist policies designed to aid Britain and France, irrespective of the strong isolationist contingent in Congress and private organisations dedicated to keeping America out of the war. Although the AAFAN, African-Americans and diasporean Africans despised the allied nations' colonialist domination of African people, they still rallied in defence of democracy.[48] Consequently, African-Americans supported the US efforts to safeguard democracy in Europe by helping to preserve the political status quo in Europe in order to prevent the rise of a New World Order under the leadership of the Axis Powers. However, remaining true to their tradition of radical activism, African-Americans mounted a domestic campaign utilising allied and US propaganda regarding the virtues of democratic freedoms, which were denied to black people in America and in the colonies.[49]

Although some African-Americans and white people argued, prior to and after US entry into the war, that it was inappropriate to mount a civil rights campaign during a national crisis, the overwhelming majority of African-Americans supported the 'Double V' campaign, which represented victory abroad and at home.[50] Apparently the black press played a significant role in

WWII activism as 'by linking segregation with fascism, the black press found a rationale for its Double V campaign which called for a victory at home as well as abroad. One implication was clear enough; without the first, the second would be worthless. Another implication was less obvious but no less significant: whites would have to pay a price for black support of the war.'[51]

The domestic civil rights campaign received widespread support from established organisations such as the NAACP,[52] which endorsed the March on Washington Committee and the civil rights campaign. In short, the 'Double V' campaign along with the MOWM demonstrated AAFAN's political maturity as AAFAN recognised that the requirements of US foreign policy would compel the Roosevelt administration to reform domestic race relations. Essentially, the domestic campaign was designed to pressure the state to meet black interests in return for their support for its foreign policy. Essentially African-American support for the war in Europe and America's war effort was a pragmatic act as opposed to a genuine desire to save Europe;[53] however African-Americans' patriotism really blossomed in 1941 as they manifested their desire to fight on behalf of America.[54] Nevertheless, a small number of African-Americans maintained their opposition to participating in the war, not because they were isolationists, but because they wanted to end Western supremacy;[55] indeed, some African-Americans believed Japan would help to neutralise white supremacy.[56] It is easy to dismiss the importance of African-American opposition or support for US entry into the war, but President Roosevelt was sufficiently concerned about African-American allegiance to commission the FBI to compile a national report on African-American views on the war.[57] In addition, white organisations representing both isolationist and interventionist positions attempted to influence African-Americans' opinions in line with their respective ideologies[58] and German and Japanese agents highlighted US racial inequalities to encourage the formation of a racial fifth column in America.[59]

Generally, the actions of AAFAN between 1939 and 1940 suggest an over-whelming dissatisfaction with race relations domestically and internationally. This dissatisfaction is indicated by African-Americans' initial reluctance to differentiate between the racism of the Allies and the Axis powers, hence the assertion that WWII was 'a white man's war'.[60] African-Americans' orientation to the war, shifted during 1940. Neither AAFAN's nor African-Americans' support for the allied nations was derived from a radical shift in the Allies' treatment of black people. Rather, African-Americans' pragmatic reorientation was a calculated plan to transform American race relations. Certainly, African-American awareness of Hitler's and Mussolini's racist ideologies (and practices) caused them to reject those regimes. However, Congress' failure to enact anti-lynching legislation, white America's reluctance to desegregate the armed forces, racial attacks on black soldiers and the discrimination faced by blacks on a daily basis[61] highlighted the similarities between the racism of white America and Nazi Germany.[62] A comparative analysis of the Allies' and Axis Powers' views on race failed to convince African-Americans of the moral superiority of the allied nations on the issue of race. However, African-Americans' support of the Roosevelt administration's foreign policy was advantageous as allied propaganda and specifically the American creed was relatively more liberal than the totalitarianism of the Axis Powers. African-American patriotism and their belief in the adaptability of US democracy and the shifts in US race relations encouraged them to re-evaluate their position on the war. In reality, African-Americans' activism between 1939 and 1940 was limited because of black apathy towards what was perceived as a European war. In essence, African-American support for the war was more pronounced from 1941 onwards.[63] As a result of African-American apathy and their eventual adherence to Roosevelt's interventionist policies, the black community did not lobby for specific foreign policies designed to meet their goals. African-Americans challenged the domestic colour-line and supported the war effort because they could not dismiss the Axis Powers as being another variant of white supremacy, given the intensity of the Nazis' racial hatred towards black people. Subsequently, AAFAN elected to strategically undermine domestic racial inequalities in exchange for their support for the war. Indeed 'a delegation led by Walter F. White, executive secretary of the ... [NAACP] ... called on President Roosevelt to inquire what ... African-Americans might expect from the administration';[64] despite the president's promises, it became clear that black people would have to fight for their civil rights.

The impact of AAFAN's actions

The AAFAN's opinions and activities before Pearl Harbour did little to affect the course of US foreign policy because African-Americans' apathy towards the war prevented them from challenging President Roosevelt's foreign policy. As the shadow of war loomed, most African-Americans, including black leaders, pledged their support for the Roosevelt administration's policy of aiding the allied war effort.

Despite African-Americans initial contention that the war in Europe was a white man's war, most African-Americans supported America's interventionist policies. After Japan's attack on Pearl Harbour, despite many African-Americans' admiration for Japan there were few dissenting voices among black Americans regarding America's entry into the war.[65] In short, there was no significant internal dissent among black people on an organisational level, nor a press campaign opposed to US intervention as between '1941 to 1945 ... the majority of national black leaders patriotically backed the war effort.'[66] Interestingly, the black press supported Roosevelt's interventionist foreign policy[67] whilst AAFAN utilised US foreign policy's promotion of democracy and the four freedoms expressed within the Atlantic Charter to advance black interests. Anticipating the coming conflict, the NAACP's Annual Conference (28 June 1941) formally requested 'that Negroes be admitted to all departments of military service the Navy, the Army, Marine and Air Corps with emphasis placed upon all types of promotion ... that Negroes be given a fair share in employment in industries holding defence contracts, whether these industries are private or administrational.'[68] Despite African-Americans' and diasporean Africans' commitment to securing the freedom of all African people, AAFAN seized the moment to launch a domestic campaign against the colour-line within the United States. In short, the fight for democracy abroad facilitated a domestic civil rights struggle, which called for the political and economic emancipation of black people in America. African-Americans' response to America's foreign and domestic policies during the war was the initiation of a domestic civil rights campaign, which called for the extension of democratic freedom domestically and internationally,[69] i.e. the 'Double V' campaign.

Interestingly, the 'Double V' campaign may have been established to steer African-Americans away from more militant actions. Indeed, Verney claims:

> From 1941 ... heightened black assertiveness was expressed in a variety of ways. If most black newspapers backed the war effort, support was not unconditional. In a phrase coined by the 'Pittsburgh Courier', blacks were urged to fight a 'double V' campaign in a war against Hitler abroad and discrimination at home ... [this] ... slogan, may have been the product of conservative black opinion makers during the Second World war. The historian Lee Finkle has argued that black newspaper editors aware of the militancy of their leaders sought to use the phrase to unite blacks in support of the war.[70]

The campaign demonstrates how a major national and foreign policy crisis became a conduit for a change in race relations.[71] AAFAN's and African-Americans' domestic campaign highlighted the contradictions between American foreign policy, which championed democracy and political freedoms abroad, whilst refusing to establish racial equality at home.[72] In addition, African-Americans specifically extended the promotion of political freedom beyond Europe, as they called for the emancipation of their colonised kith and kin in Africa and the Caribbean.[73] African-Americans' had evidently embraced a moderate form of Pan-Africanism in addition to the 'race first' doctrine championed by Marcus Garvey. However, given AAFAN's inability to effect progressive changes in the colour-line internationally, their immediate goal involved securing black employment in the defence industry and desegregating the armed forces, as the African-American population was deliberately marginalised in both these arenas. Under the leadership of the five most influential African-American organisations, AAFAN, the African-American community and Philip Randolph formed the March on Washington Movement (MOWM), which intended to march on the capital to force the administration to address African-American concerns.[74] Although one could argue that the MOWM was a domestic phenomenon unrelated to foreign affairs, WWII caused the disparate factions of the African-American leadership cadre to unite around both domestic and foreign affairs issues. African-Americans recognised that WWII provided a window of opportunity to reform American race relations,[75] because WWII increased the value of anti-racist propaganda. WWII facilitated change within the American context, as the oppression of blacks undermined America's moral critique of Nazi Germany thereby tainting America's international image and forcing the US to address domestic race relations.

Indeed, the MOWM's threat of bringing 100,000 African-Americans to Washington to lobby for defence jobs gained the attention of President Roosevelt[76] who, after consultation with his wife, formed a special committee[77] to persuade Randolph and the African-American leadership to abort the march. Significantly, African-Americans' domestic activism during the 1940s led to the 'protest movements of the 1950s and 1960s' Charles Silberman observes; 'the seeds were sown by the March on Washington.'[78] As a result, Roosevelt responded to AAFAN by making several high-profile appointments of African-Americans[79] and by issuing Executive Order 8802.[80] The *Chicago Defender*'s editorial argued that 'A. Philip Randolph ... scored again when his recommendation for the appointment of two Negroes to the committee on Fair Employment Practice was approved by President Roosevelt ... [In addition] ... the issuance of the executive order and the appointment of two Negroes on the committee on Fair Employment Practices are two signal victories ... [that] ... extends far beyond the period of national emergency.'[81]

In short, AAFAN's actions and the state's efforts to win the propaganda war against the Axis Powers forced America to curtail its own civil and human rights violations against blacks.[82] Evidently, African-Americans exploited US rhetoric and won concessions from the Roosevelt administration.[83] African-Americans charged that American and allied racism was comparable to the racism espoused by the Axis Powers, which forced the US government to reform US race relations, whereby the state appeared to promote racial equality; however, white racism continued unabated during the war, which is verified by the continuation of racial attacks on the black population, black soldiers and the armed forces' resistance to desegregation.[84] Roosevelt's reforms helped facilitate the civil rights struggle that took place in the 1960s by demonstrating that the threat of mass action could stimulate racial reforms.[85] In short, African-Americans recognised that America's international image could be undermined by the domestic colour-line and negatively affect US foreign policy (this tactic was utilised by African-American activists during the 1960s Cold War climate to aid their quest for domestic reforms).

The position of the Roosevelt administration

Between 1939 and 1941 American foreign policy was marked by the conflicting ideologies of isolationism and interventionism.[86] Although Americans sympathised with the plight of Britain and France, many were reluctant to become embroiled in another European conflict. Indeed, American scepticism regarding US involvement in Europe stemmed from belief that America was tricked into WWI by the Allies, especially the British, and the collective greed of arms manufacturers and international bankers.[87] This view gained enough political currency to discourage American involvement in foreign wars. Thus, America retreated into its isolationist posture although military and technological advances and the slow ascendancy of an interventionist cadre threatened the conventional wisdom that relied on avoiding European entanglements and on the security provided by the Atlantic Ocean.[88] Nevertheless, isolationism was still dominant within the US Congress as 'isolationists in Congress obtained passage [of] ... strict neutrality legislation ... between 1935 and 1937',[89] which apparently reflected national sentiment. Indeed, as late as December 1940, President Roosevelt was still arguing in favour of keeping America out of the war.[90] Although the Roosevelt administration apparently opposed American participation in a war during the mid-1930s, President Roosevelt and Secretary of State Cordell Hull had opposed the enactment of rigid neutrality legislation because it restricted the executive branch from pursuing flexible foreign policies. While the Roosevelt administration's foreign policy was ambiguous, the deepening crisis in Europe forced America to re-evaluate its foreign policy and ultimately aid the Allies.[91]

The actions of the Roosevelt administration

During the build-up to the war, American isolationists successfully hampered the Roosevelt administration's efforts to assist Britain prior to and during the early stages of the war in Europe, but by 1939 the president 'urged Congress to repeal the embargo and permit ... [America] to sell arms on a cash-and-carry basis to Britain and France.'[92] Consequently, by March 1939 the president succeeded in supplying arms to the Allies despite the opposition of isolationists.[93] Regarding the sale of arms to Britain and France, President Roosevelt's actions demonstrated his support for the Allies and the political status quo in Europe, without wishing to fight in the war.[94] While the administration's interventionist policies were hampered by the activities of isolationists, Roosevelt's speech urging America to become the 'arsenal of democracy' in 1940 and the emergence of the lend-lease programme[95] in 1941 point to the desire of some state officials to reject its isolationist policies.[96]

Consequently, by 13 June 1940 'the administration of the United States was doing everything in its power to make available to the allied administrations the material they urgently required ... because of ... [its] [belief] ... in ... the ideals ... the allies were fighting for.'[97] Evidently the isolationists had lost ground to President Roosevelt's foreign policy agenda. Indeed, President Roosevelt's foreign policy became increasingly interventionist as during the late 1930s, 'Hitler's aggression in Europe and Japanese expansionism in the Pacific, [Roosevelt] ... moved the United State's back towards engagement in World affairs.'[98] Arguably, Roosevelt's foreign policy became progressively more interventionist due to Germany's successful advance in Europe, whereby forcing America to begin its mobilisation for war.[99] However, Japan's assault on Pearl Harbour catapulted the Roosevelt administration and the American people into WWII.[100] Du Bois' significance in promoting the interventionist cause is exemplified in Henry Stimson's letter (24 January 1940) which stated

> On 26 January, the commercial treaty between ... [America] ... and Japan will ... end ... prompt measures should ... be taken by our administration to restrict ... the ... substantial aid that Japan is receiving through the procurement of essential war materials from the United State's. What action can and will be taken must depend in large measure upon the extent to which the people as a whole are informed upon this question and alive to the far-reaching consequences involved in our present position. I consented, a year ago, to become Honorary Chairman of The American Committee for Non-Participation in Japanese Aggression because I felt that the members of this Committee were endeavouring, intelligently and honestly, to place before the American people one of the most significant issues that we must face in our foreign policy during this critical period in our own history and that of all nations. Subsequent experience has confirmed that confidence. I am glad to beseech for the Committee such co-operation and support as you may be able to give for its important work.[101]

The administration's campaign to aid the Allies forced it to address the issue of domestic race relations in order to ensure the support of African-Americans. Therefore US foreign policy pertaining to the war followed an evolutionary path towards the adoption of interventionist policies due to America's desire to aid the allied nations. Consequently, the Roosevelt administration embarked on a propaganda campaign that successfully won the backing of Americans (including black Americans)[102] to protect American interests in the Pacific.[103]

While America had begun to mobilise for war prior to Japan's attack on Pearl Harbour, the administration had not definitively committed itself to entering the war in Europe. Despite America's concern for the allied nations in Europe, its most decisive action in regard to foreign policy occurred in the Pacific where America defended its interests from Japan's challenge to America's economic dominance in the region.[104] In fact, some authors maintain that America's foreign policy in relation to Japan was significantly antagonistic to make war between both nations inevitable. Du Bois argued:

> It is clear as day that the United State's Minister Grew returned from America to Japan with distinct orders to go as far as possible by public threats toward stirring up war between America and Japan. It looks to certain Americans today as a wise move for helping England; but America should remember that when it, Canada and Australia broke the alliance between England and Japan, it threw Japan into the arms of Germany and Italy.[105]

The Roosevelt administration's actions laid the basis for America's entry into WWII by creating the ideological justification for US aid to the Allies and mobilising American industry to defend American interests by force if and when required.[106] The administration's symbiotic relationship with the East Coast WASP elite was instrumental in spearheading America's interventionist ethos and preparing America for the possibility of war. The introduction of racial reforms within the defence industry facilitated the increased support of African-Americans for the Roosevelt administration's domestic and foreign affairs agenda, and unintentionally established a political precedent, which would be utilised in the future civil rights struggle that relied on US foreign policy concerns to win domestic concessions pertaining to race relations.

The position of non-State actors

The dilemma initiated by the events between 1939 and 1941 is reflected in the fact that private groups, such as the Council on Foreign Relations (CFR), a bastion of the US East Coast foreign policy establishment, actively encouraged African-Americans' to endorse aid to the allied nations. CFR's efforts to mobilise African-Americans to aid the Allies is indicative of African-American's growing importance to the interventionist cause. Clearly the defeat of the isolationist doctrine required the assistance of the most marginalised group in US society. It also indicates the recognition of interventionists' that the war effort required the assistance of the entire population. The CFR's effort to recruit black people into the interventionist cause identifies its awareness that African-Americans were largely indifferent to the plight of the allied nations.

The overall objectives of the CFR and the foreign policy establishment were to aid the allied nations whilst defeating the isolationist forces within the public and political spheres. Therefore, the CFR embarked on a propaganda campaign to win support for theirs and the Roosevelt administration's foreign policy aims. Interestingly, members of the East Coast foreign policy establishment championed the eradication of the colour-line both internationally and domestically which clearly appealed to AAFAN's and African-Americans' interests, as African-Americans' argued that their support for the Allies required the reformation of race relations domestically and internationally. However, 'it is important to note that this was a new-found interest in racial matters for the CFR',[107] which, given the extreme character of US race relations, could be construed as a self-serving attempt to win black support for CFR objectives.

The interventionist bloc's efforts to construct a broad-based coalition supporting their foreign policy prompted them to establish political and organisational links with the African-American community. The CFR's propaganda to the African-American community was co-ordinated by the Committee to Defend America by Aiding the Allies (CDAAA) established in 1940 and Fight For Freedom (FFF) formed in April 1941. The historical legacy of racial separation between white and black people in America (North and South) and the elitist character of the CFR hindered its efforts among black people because the white foreign policy establishment had not cultivated a prior relationship with African-Americans concerning foreign affairs. The CFR's sudden interest in African-Americans' foreign affairs activities was arguably designed to win AAFAN's allegiance to its views as opposed to forming a coalition of equals. Therefore the CFR only enlisted the support of (so-called) responsible black leaders willing to accept the ideology sanctioned by the foreign policy establishment. These leaders worked to convince African-Americans that the 'members of the Fight for Freedom Committee or of the Committee to Defend America by aiding the Allies were advocates of domestic reform'.[108] Crosswaith states: 'It is encouraging that men of such character should be active in movements to convince the American people that we must defeat Hitlerism. For it means that America's struggle to protect democracy abroad will be in the hands of men whose record on an important domestic issue prove that they are genuine believers in democracy.'[109] Members of the African-American reformist leadership cadre willingly adopted the language and views endorsed by the interventionist bloc even when it contradicted their previous opinions; clearly, they expected to derive personal and collective benefits by following the establishment's preferred line. Realising that American racism was undermining black support and damaging the perception of US democracy, the American state and the foreign policy establishment began reordering domestic race relations because the US colour-line contradicted America's democratic ideals.[110] Clearly, the existence and character of American racism was well known to the Roosevelt administration and the CFR prior to 1939. The president's and especially the CFR's interest in racial issues (given its almost complete WASP membership) was perhaps dictated by the necessities of mobilising for war rather than a conversion to the cause of racial equality. Significantly the October 1939 *Crisis* editorial remarked on the

> sudden concern of the Country over current threats to democracy abroad and the expressed desire to defend it ... has surprised ... colored Americans. Not since the world war has so much been said about fighting for the rights of oppressed minorities ... never before has vicious racialism been so ridiculed and denounced ... the sincerity of this new affection for democracy will be established beyond doubt when the restrictions on Negro suffrage are removed ... in short we shall have more confidence in the sincerity of these loud advocates of war for democracy abroad when they show more willingness to fight for it at home.[111]

Nonetheless, the racial reforms facilitated by state officials and the interventionist bloc were significant events in American history. Importantly, the CDAAA and the FFF not only called for racial reforms but also actively lobbied to promote reform in the public sphere. The bigger question is whether the CFR's sudden concern for racial equality stemmed from authentic concerns for African-Americans, as opposed to a means to ensure their interventionist policies received the necessary support to overcome the isolationism and aid the Allies.

The actions of CDAAA and FFF

The CDAAA and FFF supported the Roosevelt administration's interventionist policy to aid the Allies; however, it is less well known that the CDAAA and FFF facilitated the recruitment of black leaders into the interventionist movement and within the state. One might assume the CDAAA's and FFF's actions illustrate a classic example of pluralist interest group politics; however, the centrality of the CFR within the US State Department, and its commitment to advance official US foreign policy, begs the question of whether the CFR and the FFF were extensions of the US state. The state's and CFR's commitment to mobilising African-American support for the war possibly explains the importance of ensuring black involvement in interventionist organisations and the state. The recruitment of moderate black leaders and the distribution of CFR propaganda highlighting the Hitler regime's clear and present danger to African-Americans' future were designed to facilitate the CFR's and the state's construction of a politically diverse coalition to support America's entry into the war.

The CDAAA and the FFF and the WASP elite employed a multifaceted approach to assimilate African-Americans into the interventionist bloc by 'engaging in the politics of race, from organizing petitions, meetings, sports events, and newspaper and other campaigns, in attempting to win a sceptical black elite and mass opinion for aid to the Allies and for war.'[112] Evidently the CDAAA and the FFF recognised that their efforts to gain black support for their policies required that they address the following issues:

Domestic racial oppression, because it contradicted allied discourse regarding the virtues of democracy and the four freedoms embodied within the Atlantic Charter. Hence the 'CDAAA/FFF black mobilization campaign focused on the need to fight racism at home and abroad, to link the fight against Hitlerism with the struggle against domestic racial discrimination and inequality.'[113] As a result, the interventionist bloc campaigned to end black exclusion from the defence industry and the armed forces.

The recruitment of African-American leaders who publicly endorsed aid to the Allies as the African-American population would respond negatively to a movement headed exclusively by WASPs from the state or from the East Coast establishment. Therefore, the WASP establishment organised black chapters in Harlem and utilised black leaders, such as A. Philip Randolph, Frank R. Crosswaith,[114] Adam Clayton Powell, Ralph Bunche and newspaper editors, a key grouping in the construction of black opinion,[115] to propagate its views.

Mobilising the black press to include the editorials of pro-intervention leaders such as A. Philip Randolph and Frank Crosswaith, to convince African-Americans of the merits of the interventionism position,[116] in addition to the CDAAA's development of pro-Allied, pro-interventionist and anti-Nazi advertisements in black newspapers. For example, academics Ralph

Bunche and Abram L. Harris wrote an article, 'Stop Hitler Now! The Negro Must Help' in June 1940. In this article, which was sent to around seventy black newspapers, Bunche and Harris outlined the undemocratic, aggressive and totalitarian nature of the Nazi threat in the wake of the fall of France.[117]

The marginalisation of the isolationist doctrine within the black community the CDAAA and FFF worked to undermine isolationist sentiments amongst African-Americans by combating the propaganda of the isolationist America First Organisation. The FFF highlighted the white supremacist views of Charles A. Lindbergh, a leader of America First who believed white people should construct an international white front,[118] despite his organisation's political overtures to African-Americans requesting their political support. Additionally, Frank Crosswaith argued that 'the reactionary character of the leaders of the America First Committee (AFC) shows that ... Hitler has had some success in the United State's too.'[119] Clearly associating the AFC with Hitler would undermine African-American support of its policies.

The CDAAAs' call for the extension of Executive Order 8802. The CDAAA, largely reacting to black pressures, was also part of a broader-based delegation in late June 1941. After the Executive Order 8802 had been issued, it met with war and navy department officials to suggest 'the enlargement of opportunities for Negroes in the army and navy and to make clear our sympathy with the Negro demand for equal opportunities.'[120]

The CDAAA, in a subsequent press release, called for President Roosevelt to extend his Executive Order banning racist employment practices to the armed services, as 'anti-Negro discrimination was inconsistent with the democratic principles which the American people as a whole are being called upon to defend'.[121] The actions of the CDAAA and the FFF pertaining to African-Americans were designed to convince African-Americans to support the interventionist movement (authored by the East Coast foreign policy establishment) and the Roosevelt administration's foreign policy, which, the evidence suggests, were intimately linked. Interestingly, the East Coast foreign policy establishment/CFR was reluctant to highlight its involvement in the CDAAA and the FFF, as it realised that the elitist and racially exclusive CFR would struggle to rally black support for a WASP initiative. This explains why the CDAAA and the FFF employees were trained to hide their links with the East Coast power elite.[122] It is likely that the average African-American was unaware that their decision (which may or may not have been influenced by the CFR) to advocate aid to the Allies, might have been affected by the CFR, an organisation that had done little or nothing to support or assess African-Americans interests in foreign affairs.

It is difficult to ascertain the impact of the CDAAA's and FFF's campaign to persuade African-Americans to aid the Allies; however, black attitudes towards WWII shifted from 1940 onwards. Mainstream black leaders altered their perception of the war, as a conflict between white imperialists all dedicated to the continuation of global white supremacy; this shift probably stemmed from the belief that the Axis Powers' racial ideology presented more danger to the welfare of black people than the racism practised by the Allies. The character of German and Italian racism forced African-Americans to reappraise their orientation to the war. Nevertheless, the administration's campaign to neutralise black opposition to WWII, the survey of Racial Conditions in the United States (RACON) and the CFR's campaign to acquire African-American support for the war must be considered as important factors in determining African-Americans' eventual support of the war. For example, the black press' support for the allied cause and its criticism of the Axis Powers' racism are important, given that the CFR and its black and white supporters produced and distributed pro-interventionist propaganda to the black press highlighting German and Italian racism,[123] and the need for US racial reforms, all of which became central features in African-Americans' 'Double V' campaign. Of course, there were noticeable criticism of the Allies, especially from W. E. B. Du Bois' column (in the *Amsterdam News*) 'As the Crow Flies', but generally, black people urged the Allies to adopt racial and political reforms in their colonies, to encourage their cause among people of African descent. Du Bois maintained that African-Americans should encourage the Allies to aid Africa and specifically Ethiopia.[124] Du Bois argued that African-Americans

> ought to make it known to the administration that our ... generous help to England is predicated upon ordinary decency in its treatment of Africa after the war and that the United State's will not stand by and see Ethiopia transferred from Italy to England in the face of the conscience of the world. We ought to let it be known that this is the price of our loyalty and co-operation.[125]

In addition, there is evidence of the black press' continuity regarding the dangers of Nazi Germany and Italian fascism, as the black press and black leaders domestically and internationally had maintained, during the Italo-Ethiopian War, that Italian militarism/fascism and the Western world's tacit collusion would ultimately lead to an international crisis; additionally, African-Americans also criticised the Nazi regime.[126] While it is likely that the CFR campaign affected African-American views on the war, African-Americans were aware of Nazi racism prior to WWII; the fundamental difference lies in the fact that after 1940 black apathy towards the war and the Allied cause gave way to increasing support for the aforementioned.[127] One could argue that the East Coast elite helped re-orientate African-American views on foreign affairs. The CFR's uncharacteristic venture into pressure group politics is indicative of its recognition that African-Americans already possessed their own organically shaped views. The warhawk organisation's and the state's solicitation of African-American support was simultaneously paired with the issue of racial reform, which many African-Americans demanded in exchange for their support of the war. The evidence suggests African-Americans/leaders won concessions from the state and the interventionist bloc by lobbying the administration to adopt domestic reforms. Roosevelt's Executive Order 8802 and the CDAAA's and FFF's call for racial equality in the defence industry was arguably designed to guarantee African-American support for US intervention. Although the evidence points to the existence of a two-way relationship (albeit unequal in terms of power), the CDAAA and FFF only promoted limited racial reforms, which is not surprising, since the issue of 'race' made Northern elites distinctly uncomfortable, as noted by many council members and leaders.[128] The racial policies of CDAAA and FFF were a limited response to an issue requiring their attention to safeguard their wider agenda. Indeed, some black leaders questioned the sincerity of pro-interventionist organisations affiliated with segregationist politicians such as Senator Carter Glass.[129] Chadwin indicates that Glass actively discouraged, through the threat of resignation, any southern FFF chapters from challenging the use of the racist poll tax of black people to disfranchise African-Americans.[130]

The CDAAA's commitment to black people is highlighted by the fact that pro-war southern segregationists were infrequently challenged by their liberal northern pro-war counterparts. For example, the committee's secretary objected to a specific piece of propaganda 'referring to the right of colored citizens to vote in the South'. It did not 'object personally; she simply,' it was reported, 'says that our committees in the South with which she is working cannot use it'.[131] Evidently the principal aim of the pro-war groups was mobilisation for war, and racial reform was a tactic to further their primary goal. The evidence does not definitively validate the contention that the CFR's recruitment of moderate black leaders and its various campaigns to influence African-American opinion were major factors behind the shift in African-American opinion. It is likely that the CFR's actions combined with the administration's limited racial reforms encouraged African-American support for US interventionism.

Isolationism

The CFR and the Roosevelt administration were not the only ones seeking to influence African-Americans' views on international relations. America First, one of the chief opponents of the Roosevelt administration[132] and the CFR, sought to ensure that America would maintain its isolationist foreign policy by resisting US Anglophiles' desire to aid Britain. America First argued that German hegemony in Europe would not damage US interests.[133] In contrast to the WASP East Coast elite, the America First Organisation was composed of 'supporters from the upper Midwest and from non-Anglo ethnics nation-wide'[134] who were obviously less concerned with supporting Britain on the basis of protecting a shared heritage.

Like the CFR, America First sought to convince African-Americans of the merits of the isolationist position, which brought it into direct conflict with the FFF organisation. It 'took on America First's black supporters by identifying and writing to them, advising them of the 'errors' of their ways. America First, which had its own 'Charles Young (Colored) Division', was actively courting the black press and needed to be counteracted, according to Edward W. White.[135] FFF's efforts to neutralise America First's campaign to recruit the African-American community suggest that it felt the America First had or could influence the thinking of the black community.[136]

The impact of the isolationist movement was clearly curtailed by the overtly racist ideas and its affiliation with the Nazi leadership of Charles Lindbergh,[137] one of its foremost leaders, who believed America should cooperate with the 'extremely intelligent and able people' of Germany in preparing against the Bolshevik onslaught and in rectifying the injustices of the post-war settlement. Encouraging Britain in its opposition to Germany was a profoundly mistaken policy. 'It is time to turn from our quarrels and to build our white ramparts again.' If, however, Europe proved bent on self-destruction, then the United States had no choice but to stand aloof.[138] Lindbergh's racial views proved to be a liability, and FFF used them to undermine his organisation's efforts to court the black community.[139] There is no evidence to suggest that America First significantly influenced the black community. America First's effort to win black support was (probably) curtailed by its overwhelmingly white membership and its tenuous links to the African-American community. The Roosevelt administration's[140] hostility to America First and FFF portrayal of America First as a racist organisation may have undermined America First's efforts within the black community.

The AAFAN

African-Americans inability to influence international relations was linked to their marginal status in US society. African-American orientation to the war on Europe may have altered by the white establishment, given that AAFAN and African-American civil rights leaders were slow to champion the cause of Britain and France due to their colonial holdings in Africa and the Caribbean. Nevertheless, African-American apathy concerning WWII gave way to black advocacy of the war, which occurred within the context of the state receiving popular support from the American population.

The US government

The US government's interventionist policies were successful because it utilised its power and authority to secure state interests whilst neutralising alternative conceptions of US foreign policy. In short, the state department's links with the WASP elite facilitated the (indirect) promotion of its interventionist policies thus shaping public opinion along interventionist lines. In short, the state's power and authority enabled it to marginalise alternative foreign policies in the name of national and international interests. Ultimately, US public opinion (overwhelmingly) supported aid to the Allies and Roosevelt's foreign policy, which enhanced the administration's position on foreign affairs.

The CFR

CFR's advocacy of aid to the Allies complemented the administration's foreign policy objectives, thereby providing the CFR with a powerful ally in its mission to secure its objectives. Consequently, the CFR's compatibility with the state and its links with the State Department provided obvious advantages over other interest groups in securing the administration's support for its agenda and in neutralising its isolationist rivals. The elite status of the CFR and its financial and political status were decisive factors in the CFR's efforts to secure support for the allied cause.

The isolationist bloc

The isolationists' policies were undermined by two factors: first, the ascendancy of the interventionist bloc, which acquired the support of the state apparatus; second, isolationist politicians and their supporters failed to gain widespread support for their political goals, which were decisively undermined by the president and the state. The isolationist doctrine, which prevented US intervention in the Italo-Ethiopian War, failed to construct a sufficient argument to justify the maintenance of American neutrality given the Axis Powers' assault on Europe. America's 'destroyers for bases' deal with Britain sought to protect US strategic interests,[141] evidently America accepted the violation of Chinese and Ethiopian sovereignty,[142] but it did not countenance Germany's violation of British and French sovereignty.[143] Hunt's contention that US foreign policy is racially biased suggests that America would be more predisposed to maintaining the sovereignty of European nations, than protecting non-white nations.

The **Pluralist** contention that US society is comprised competitive interest groups organised to promote their interests is apparently borne out by the empirical data, as the WASP elite within the CFR and the state apparatus in addition to the America First Organisation mounted ideological campaigns designed to win public support for their foreign policy goals. The propaganda campaign conducted by the Roosevelt administration and the CFR in order to neutralise the isolationists demonstrates the competitive nature of the struggle as opposed to the dominance of a single group. The evidence validates the existence of a competitive struggle for ideological hegemony between the isolationist and interventionist blocs as each group pursued their interests. The case pertaining to AAFAN is arguably different. Although some scholars define pluralism as the existence of equal opportunities to pursue group interests, US racial conventions inhibited African-Americans from meeting their interests. The racial preferences bestowed on white people pertaining to politics and foreign policy prevented African-Americans from influencing international relations because black people lacked the political legitimacy to define and direct the state's actions. While the Roosevelt administration recruited African-Americans into administrative positions, there is no evidence that these appointees' positions enabled them to make decisions on US foreign policy in accordance with the views of the African-American population.[144] In short, the CDAAA's and FFF's recruitment of black leaders represented WASP paternalism and utilisation of African-American leaders to serve their interests, as no black people were recruited to positions within the CFR or the State Department where they could directly impact on US foreign policy decisions. For example, the CDAA and FFF did nothing to promote AAFAN's and African-Americans' concerns regarding European colonialism and the reformation of international race relations. Rather, CDAAA and FFF strategically confined and perhaps redefined[145] AAFAN's agenda to focus on domestic reforms. AAFAN did influence the Roosevelt administration; however, their influence was only able to win domestic reforms rather than reshaping US foreign policy or undermining Western imperialism. Although AAFAN and African-Americans initially defined WWII as a white man's war,[146] they altered their position and adopted the interventionist policies endorsed by the white foreign policy establishment. While African-Americans organisational efforts did win them some domestic reforms, their marginal status, resulting from their subordinate racial designation and the historical dominance of the WASP elite in relation to US foreign policy, prevented them from competing on an equal basis. In brief, pluralism provides a partial explanation of the evidence assessed in this case study because it does not acknowledge the structural impediments placed on the AAFAN due to institutional racism within the public and political arenas in regard to the construction of US foreign policy. The State Department and CFR were successful in executing their desired goals, i.e., mobilising a broad-based coalition to aid the Allies. The close relationship between the CFR and state also undermines pluralism. The racial and class status of the CFR clearly aided its interaction and assimilation into a state managed by individuals from similar backgrounds.

Statism provides an adequate explanation of the events surrounding African-Americans' activities pertaining to US foreign policy. The expectation that AAFAN and African-Americans' perspective on US foreign policy would be subordinated to the state's is substantiated by the empirical evidence. African-Americans initial apathy concerning WWII stemmed from the belief that it was a war between white imperialists dedicated to global white supremacy. What factors influenced African-Americans to embrace the case for intervention? The idea that African-Americans embraced interventionism (between 1939 and 1941) because they were alerted to Nazi racial doctrines is compelling, but it does not explain their rejection of the isolationist doctrine. African-American awareness of the dangers posed by the militaristic and racial totalitarianism espoused by Italy and Germany was verified by their efforts to warn white nations that Italy's assault on Ethiopia would encourage additional international conflicts. People of African descent were aware of Italian, German and American racism and they recognised that Britain and France practised and believed in racial doctrines not completely indistinct from those espoused by Germany and Italy. In short, African-Americans orientation to WWII did not change because they were suddenly alerted to Nazi racism in 1939. The Roosevelt administration, which had maintained US neutrality during the IEW, sponsored interventionist policies to aid the Allies and CFR members were assimilated into the State Department to formulate US foreign policy.

Indeed, the CFR propaganda campaign, which sought to neutralise isolationist propaganda and mobilise American aid for the Allies was allowed to work in tandem with the State Department. The CFR also engineered the creation of the CDAAA and the FFF in order to influence African-Americans to support aid to the Allies, which was clearly a State Department objective. One wonders whether A. Philip Randolph[147] and Frank Crosswaith, who were indirectly recruited by the CFR through the CDAAA and CFR to propagate the interventionist doctrines amongst African-Americans, were aware of the connections between the interventionist organisations and the US state. The CFR's integration into the State Department, and its creation of organisations dedicated to winning African-American support for US intervention, enabled the Roosevelt administration to win African-American support whilst insulating it from additional black demands. Given the relative power differentials between the state, the CFR and African-Americans, one could argue that the CDAAA and the FFF pursued and facilitated the CFR's and the state's foreign policy goals. The recruitment of African-Americans to state jobs via the Executive Order 8802 and the CDAAA and FFF utilisation of black leaders to advance their interests indicates that the state and WASPs directed the opinions of leaders such as Frank Crosswaith, who utilised the president's domestic reforms to promote black support for the Allies.

In short, African-Americans joined the WASP-led interventionist movement, in fact the stimulus for their support of the allied cause may have originated from the CFR and the State Department. Essentially, the state's and the CFR's focus on racial equality, whether sincere or politically expedient, and African-Americans' aversion to Nazi racism facilitated the state's campaign to integrate African-Americans into the interventionist camp despite blacks initial apathy for the plight of the Allies. African-Americans were obliged to support the Allies and preserve British and French imperialism despite the maintenance of domestic and global white supremacy. In addition, state-sponsored surveillance (RACON), the prosecution of black individuals and organisations who advocated an anti-war stance indicates that the state utilised a stick and the carrot to align African-Americans with state goals. The state shaped black opinion due to the absence of credible opposition and incorporated African-Americans into the interventionist bloc which facilitated America's support for the Allies and its preparation for war. Finally, African-Americans' marginal racial status in relation to white America and the state hampered AAFAN's efforts to influence US foreign policy to aid people of African descents' fight against imperialism.

The **Marxist** contention that capitalists control and direct the state is significant given that some authors maintain that the CFR is a representative of the capitalist class. However, there is no definitive evidence that the CFR convinced the state to adopt interventionist policies, although, given the similarities between the CFR's and the state's policies, their goals were apparently mutually compatible. Nevertheless the Marxist assertion that economically subordinate classes don't (generally) determine the states' foreign policy is validated in regard to African-Americans, as the state and the foreign policy establishment determined US foreign policy. African-Americans marginal economic and political status hampered their efforts to author and execute their foreign policy goals. The fact that black people won domestic concessions was based on their own efforts and the fact that the state needed to mobilise the entire population to aid the Allies and mobilise for war, which granted African-Americans the leverage to facilitate their domestic agenda. Nonetheless, in the arena of foreign policy, the blueprint for America's actions came from a specific section of the (East Coast WASP) capitalist elite. It is feasible that the East Coast elite's power was derived from their superior organisation; and conceivably, if other groups were sufficiently organised, they could have directed state policy. Perhaps the classical Marxist notion of a homogeneous ruling class should focus on the existence of competitive elite groups jockeying for dominant status, who can be influenced, neutralised or replaced by competent mass pressure groups or even the state. While Marxism accounts for African-Americans' and AAFAN's marginal position in relation to the construction and execution of US foreign policy, it does not acknowledge the additional impediments placed on African-Americans due to their racial identity.

Racialised Colony: the framing and execution of US foreign policy between 1939 and 1941 was determined by the white WASP elite; furthermore, African-Americans' anti-imperialist conception of international relations, which focused on the racialisation of European imperialism, was ignored by the US state and the foreign policy establishment, which did not address the issue of white racial supremacy (internationally). For white America, US foreign policy revolved around whether to continue US isolationism, or to engage in an interventionist form of foreign policy. In fact, white America's indifference to the plight of people of African descent pertaining to Britain and France's exploitation of continental and diasporean Africans arguably led to AAFAN's and African-Americans' belief that WWII was a white man's war,[148] which, irrespective of who won global white supremacy, would remain intact. Hence the necessity of the WASP elite's campaign to convince African-Americans to back aid to the Allies. The actions of the state and the CFR, given their historical neglect of African-Americans' opinions regarding foreign affairs, were self-serving as the main objective was to persuade African-Americans to accept their conception of foreign affairs. Although the state and the WASP elite addressed the issue of race, the call for domestic reforms was a practical necessity (although not inevitable as many white Americans argued against any racial reforms) because America needed to mobilise its whole population for war. Given allied propaganda concerning the extreme content of the Axis Powers' racial worldview, America was bound to reform American race relations.

The state and the foreign policy establishment's actions towards African-Americans were designed to orientate them to support the state's interventionist policies. While it is difficult to assess the impact of the foreign policy establishment's and state's efforts to influence African-Americans, it is evident that between 1940 and 1941, African-Americans increased their support for the Allies and America's entry into WWII. With regard to the United States' harassment and prosecution of African-Americans who opposed the war via RACON,[149] coupled with its recruitment of African-American leaders who accepted their foreign policy agenda and its provision of jobs for them, it could be argued that the state co-opted those black leaders in order to meet its interests.[150] In addition, the CFR's use of the CDAAA and the FFF to propagate the WASP elite's foreign affairs agenda augmented the state's actions, because it suggested that private (white) citizens were prepared to incorporate black people in their movement and call for racial reforms. In brief, the state and the CFR affected the formation of AAFAN's and the black population's opinions on foreign affairs, due to their superior organisational resources and their institutional and political dominance, which was arguably derived from their racial designation. The AAFAN and African-Americans generally adopted the state's and the foreign policy establishment's international agendas out of their desire to appear patriotic and to improve their status in America by fighting on America's behalf and significantly to avoid prosecution for so-called subversive activity. African-Americans' racially marginalised status and their desire to assimilate into America's political mainstream in addition to their disdain for Hitler's regime prompted their support of the state's and the foreign policy establishments' interventionist policies. Furthermore, the African-American community's relative weakness in relation to powerful and organised white interest groups allowed the state's and the CFR to orientate black views on foreign policy in order to support their interests, which suggests that race and the institutional power of white America was able to dominate and colonise the views and opinions of African-Americans in relation to the war.

The period between 1939 and 1941 demonstrates that African-Americans' forged greater links with the state and the US foreign policy establishment, although the WASP elite was responsible for cementing the relationship between AAFAN and the black community in general. Nevertheless, it is evident that AAFAN's connection with the foreign policy establishment increased relative to their limited interaction with state officials, or associates of the CFR pertaining to the IEW, as black leaders were recruited to aid the

CFR propaganda campaign to persuade black support for aid to the Allies. The evidence indicates that the black community did affect changes in the policies of the US government, by applying collective pressure in order to secure their goals at a critical juncture when the state needed African-American assistance. However, African-Americans did not affect the direction of US foreign policy (in regard to promoting the interests of the global black constituency), just as it failed to do so in relation to the IEW and the Versailles Peace Conference in 1919. Indeed, African-Americans' success was limited to the arena of domestic policies, where they gained concessions from the administration and vocal support from the WASP elite in favour of the concept of racial equality, but not substantial reforms in US race relations, as the CDAAA and the FFF were loathe to assault the bastion of white privilege in the South and nation-wide. Overall, the reforms championed by the administration and the CFR were self-serving because they resulted in the greater utilisation of the African-American population in the defence industries, which was not really a concession so much as a necessity. The WASP elite's courtship of the African-American community was a political necessity given its desire to defeat the isolationist bloc's efforts to maintain American neutrality in relation to WWII, which required the mobilisation and support of diverse sections of the US population to counteract German and Japanese propaganda pertaining to American race relations and the racialised character of US democracy.[151] In addition, the WASP elite needed to persuade the black community that it had a political stake in aiding the Allies, due to the extreme character of Nazi racism,[152] and to give the appearance that the Atlantic Charter's four freedoms existed in US society.

Nevertheless, the actions of the WASP elite were not solely a response to their political needs, as African-American protest pertaining to domestic circumstances embarrassed the state and the WASP elite, which helped win concessions from both parties. Indeed, the African-Americans' MOWM demonstrated their ability to organise to meet black interests, as did the 'Double V' campaign, which championed democracy at home and abroad.[153] This case study validates the contention that interest group politics can and did affect changes in American politics. However, the changes that occurred were not in the arena of foreign policy, which suggests that in this case the arena of foreign policy was the preserve of an almost exclusively white anglophile elite, which possessed powerful connections in the state and the foreign policy establishment that allowed it to author and execute foreign policy, which met their interests despite the existence of well organised white opposition from the Isolationist bloc. The interventionist bloc successfully persuaded an apathetic black community that aiding the Allies would benefit black people despite their reservations regarding allied racial imperialism and American racism.[154] The actions of AAFAN coincided with African-Americans' domestic agenda to obtain their full civil rights,[155] as it demonstrated that US foreign policy goals could be adversely affected by domestic race relations, which laid the basis for the tactics employed during the civil rights struggle, which was conducted during the Cold War which also provided African-Americans with additional leverage in order to push domestic reforms. This chapter's analysis of AAFAN's activities and ideological orientation during WWII revolves around African-Americans desire to challenge the racial colour-line both internationally and domestically. The following chapter will examine African-Americans' attempts to infuse the UN's organisation with an anti-racist clause, in order to resolve the issue of racial oppression both domestically and internationally.

5 African-Americans and the formation of the United Nations Organisation 1944–47

The determination of policies relative to colonial and dependant areas in the post-war period will be the criterion by which millions of people will judge the moral, political and economic principles of the major members of the United Nations.[1]

Mary Dudziak argues that post-WWII America was embroiled in the 'intersection of race, cold war, and foreign relations.'[2] This chapter will highlight AAFAN's activities in relation to the following issues, exploring the activities of AAFAN between 1944 and 1945 by examining their efforts to ensure the United Nations (UN) charter authorised de-colonisation and guaranteed that UN members practise domestic and international racial equality within their subject territories.[3] In short, AAFAN sought to utilise the principles defined in the Dumbarton Oaks proposals (7 October 1944), which established the purpose of the United Nations Organisation[4] (Pillars of Peace Pamphlet No. 4, 1 May 1946) to pursue their own international agenda. This case study chronicles the development of AAFAN in relation to the racial and political changes occasioned by WWII: that war amplified AAFAN's fight for racial reforms internationally[5] within a racially stratified society, that despite US propaganda had failed to eradicate racism, which forced blacks to seek new allies in their quest for liberation.[6]

This chapter is structured as follows: first, a brief historical overview concerning the formation of the UN; followed by an account of AAFAN's foreign affairs goals and activities in conjunction with the US administration and finally an assessment of AAFAN's impact on US foreign policy in relation to the formation of the UN Charter. Significantly, this chapter invalidates mainstream literature, which, according to Plummer, defined African-Americans as disinterested isolationists indifferent to foreign affairs.[7] The format will be duplicated (in less depth) in relation to the US administration.

UN formation

The call for an international organisation dedicated to world peace developed during the Second World War[8] as the allied nations endured the horrors of war. The Allies' aim was to construct an organisation that enshrined and extended the principles expressed in the Atlantic Charter, i.e. democracy and political freedom.[9] The allied nations established the blueprint for the UN at a series of conferences starting with Dumbarton Oaks, 7 October 1944, which established the aims and principles of the UN;[10] the Yalta Conference outlined the conclusions of the allied powers.[11] While the stated goals of the allied nations[12] were commendable, the continuing legacies of racialised colonialism contravened the Allies' rhetoric in defence of political equality.[13] African-Americans, such as James Farmer, had earlier highlighted the contradictions of the imperialist and racist allied nations fighting a war of liberation on the basis of democratic freedom.[14] African-Americans' initial scepticism was confirmed when it became apparent that the chief concern of the Allies was the restoration of 'free elections, democratic governments, and constitutional safeguards of freedom throughout ... Europe'[15] while failing to endorse the promotion of self-government in Africa, Asia or the Caribbean. However African-American leaders such as Mary McLeod Bethune, a leading member of the NAACP and head of the National Council of Negro Women NCNW, who supported the allied cause in Europe, planned to convince America and the West that the domestic and international colour-line was no longer acceptable in the post-war world.[16] Farer maintains: 'At its inception, the United Nations seemed destined to be the engine of human rights'[17] despite evidence which indicates that enforceable human rights were not really championed by the sponsoring states.[18] In fact, the cry for equality and human rights was particularly strong among African-Americans and not the states who met at San Francisco.

The position of AAFAN

AAFAN's post-war foreign affairs activities stemmed from WWII, during African-Americans' struggle for domestic and international racial equality via the 'Double V' campaign and the March on Washington Movement (MOWM),[19] in addition to challenging the Allies to end colonialism.[20] During the mid-1940s, African-Americans believed that their marginal status paralleled the status of the colonised masses of African people worldwide.[21]

While African-Americans' supported America's entry into the war after Pearl Harbour, African-American leaders were also committed to the erasure of the domestic colour-line.[22] Consequently, the five major African-American organisations (NAACP, the National Urban League, the National Negro Congress, the National Council of Negro Women, the March on Washington Movement) proclaimed their support for de-colonisation[23] and pursued their own agenda regarding post-war race relations. As a result, African-Americans engaged in post-war negotiations[24] in regard to the construction of a new world order dedicated to racial and political equality between the West and the world of colour.[25] As early as 1941, the NAACP began to organise a committee which would enable African-Americans to present their views at any future peace conference.[26] In 1943, the NAACP Board requested Du Bois' aid in 'the formation of a committee to present the cause of the Negro, not only of America but of the West Indies and Africa at the next Peace Conference.'[27]

AAFAN's/African-Americans' desire to promote global racial equality and African independence became their primary objective during the early post-war years.[28] Even the NAACP[29] remained active in post-war foreign affairs, as it supported Du Bois' interest in global Pan-Africanism,[30] and participated in the proceedings pertaining to the ratification of the UN Charter at San Francisco.[31]

African-American interest in foreign affairs was exemplified by the founding of the Council of African Affairs (CAA)[32] in 1939 by Max Yergan[33] and Paul Robeson and its involvement in highlighting the plight of colonised Africans.[34] The CAA disseminated current and historical data regarding the struggle of African people within *New Africa*, its official monthly bulletin, and emphasised the similarities between racial oppression in Africa and America.[35]

The formation of CAA, the most active African-American organisation in relation to foreign affairs in the post-war period,[36] suggests that some of the African-American intelligentsia had accepted Du Bois' and Garvey's contention that racialised oppression in Africa was inextricably linked to the oppression of diasporean Africans. Given AAFAN's global agenda, some African-Americans ended their wartime alliance with the American state and the West in order to pursue the interests of the black world. The CAA reminded America that 'President Roosevelt ha[d] said that the Atlantic Charter applies not only to the part of the world that borders the Atlantic but to the whole world.'[37] African-Americans formed other organisations such as the Federated Organisations of Coloured Peoples (which consisted of sixteen black organisations) that were specifically formed 'for the purpose of seeking to have provisions made in the Charter of the United Nations that would protect the rights of coloured peoples and minorities generally.'[38]

One of the chief areas of interest and ideological contestation for African-Americans' was the Dumbarton Oaks Conference, which contrasted with the events surrounding the 1919 Peace Conference and the Italo-Ethiopian War (1934–37) as African-Americans were now in a position to openly confer with US officials. For example, Ralph Bunche attended the Dumbarton Oaks Conference and assisted the construction of 'US policy in the colonies'.[39] In addition, Henry S. Villard, head of the State Department's Division of African Affairs, promised to consider carefully the CAA's recommendations to the Dumbarton Oaks Conference in relation to Africa.[40] African-Americans' response to the Dumbarton Oaks proposals ranged from the cautiously optimistic to the extremely critical.[41] Nevertheless AAFAN was willing to petition the state to meet their objectives,[42] for example the CAA's attempt to influence State Department officials (such as Henry S. Villard) to support an African development plan prior to Dumbarton Oaks.[43] African-Americans' cooperation with state officials[44] points to their belief that the government would seriously consider their international agenda. For example, the National

Council of Negro Women (NCNW) headed by Mary McLeod Bethune (who was a national member of Americans United for World Organisation[45]) attended regional meetings sponsored by the State Department to discuss the Dumbarton Oaks propositions.[46] The NCNW also initiated educational programmes to inform African-Americans, and specifically black women, on foreign affairs. The NCNW organised its own event on 8 April 1945 at Washington DC's Asbury Church (featuring) Assistant Secretary of State Archibald MacLeish, who lectured on Dumbarton Oaks as a 'Guide to World Security'.[47] Significantly in 1945, the US state provided AAFAN the opportunity to engage in foreign affairs in a manner uncommon before WWII.[48] For example, Dr Du Bois voiced his opposition to the proposed framework of the UN at the highest levels of government when he attended the Washington Conference[49] chaired by 'Edward Stettinius the under secretary of state, [who] assembled representatives of ninety-six social organisations to discuss the Dumbarton Oaks proposals'. Du Bois was not alone in his opposition to the Dumbarton Oaks accords as Bethune, A. Philip Randolph, MOWM and the Council of African Affair'[50] all criticised the proposals for failing to tackle colonialism. Du Bois argued that Security Council regulations would only accept petitions from sovereign states, thus preventing representatives from the colonies from securing their own interests via the Security Council[51] and confining[52] their protests to their colonial overlords whose interests were served by maintaining the status quo. Du Bois noted that the proposed Security Council's procedures would stifle African-American appeals for UN intervention to halt their domestic subordination as the Security Council would only recognise the rights of sovereign states.[53] This is important, given his future activities in this regard. Not all black groups advocated race-orientated policy recommendations; the National Negro Congress argued that the allied nations would secure Negro interests.[54] However, the allied nation's discussions and proposals at Dumbarton Oaks did nothing substantial to liberate the colonised masses of the world nor to merit the faith bestowed on them by African-American organisations.[55] The logic of the Dumbarton Oaks accords was to ensure the international balance of power between the Soviet Union, America and their co-convenors.[56] Accordingly, the CAA suggestion of US advocacy of a lend-lease programme for Ethiopia and Liberia and China's lukewarm advocacy of establishing a racial and national equality clause in the UN Charter was ignored by the allied nations.[57] The Dumbarton Oaks accords neither supported the liberation of the colonised masses of Africa and Asia nor removed the spectre of Western racial imperialism.[58] Rather, Dumbarton Oaks enshrined the power of the major allied nations. A *Time Magazine* article claimed the Dumbarton Oaks proposals represented an 'invitation to imperialism to any big power so minded [i.e. Soviet Union, America or Britain]. However shocked the other big powers may be, they will look the other way a long time before risking a breach of big-power unity.'[59] Evidently African-Americans were not alone in recognising the shortcomings in the Dumbarton Oaks proposals.[60]

The actions of AAFAN

> When the ... United Nations (conference) opened on 25 April 1945, Metz
> T. P. Lochard, editor-in-chief of *The Chicago Defender*, declared that the
> World Security Conference in San Francisco has but one meaning to the
> Negro people – that is, how far democratic principles shall be stretched to
> embrace the rights of our brothers in the colonies and to what extent the
> American Negro's own security at home shall be guaranteed.[61]

The AAFAN's main objective at the UN conference was to ensure that the
UN Charter adopted enforceable human rights principles.[62] The ideological
basis of AAFAN's actions at the conference stemmed from the following
assertions: first, the status of the colonised masses of African people was
linked to the marginal status of African-Americans';[63] second, the global black
communities' support of the Allies during the war entitled them to post-war
domestic and international reforms;[64] third, the Allies' condemnation of Nazi
racism required them to abandon the doctrine of white supremacy and to
champion racial reforms within all states;[65] fourth, the Roosevelt administration had committed America to the extension of the Atlantic charter and the
four freedoms to all people;[66] finally, war-torn Europe would be compelled to
relinquish its hold on the black world.[67]

African-Americans believed that their sacrifices during the war entitled
them to a place at the peace table.[68] In addition, in 1944, the CAA 'asked that
[black] organisations and their members write to newspapers, government officials, church bodies, and trade unions "voicing the stake of colonial peoples
in the post-war international security plans."'[69] African-Americans, including
politician Rev. Archibald Carey, held a series of meetings dedicated to foreign
affairs and the formation of the UN.[70] In addition, African-Americans held a
series of conferences which exemplified black commitment to post-war foreign
affairs. At the vanguard of this multifaceted movement was the NAACP,
which organised a (black) organisational front[71] and assisted Dr Du Bois[72] in
hosting the colonial conference on Friday, 6 April 1945 in Harlem, where
African-Americans and foreign delegates (of colour) advanced their conception
of international relations independent of the Western nations.[73] The colonial
conference indicated AAFAN's ability to engage in discussions pertaining to
international relations.[74] Also the presence of foreign nationals at the conference suggests that foreign delegates were sufficiently motivated to liaise
with AAFAN, which suggests that they possessed enough credibility to gain
international support for their conference. It also suggests that people of
colour believed they needed to formulate their own agenda prior to the San
Francisco conference in order to promote their own interests.

A conference organised by Mary Mcleod Bethune was held in Chicago[75]
'ninety delegates from eighteen cities and thirteen states call[ed] for black
representation at the San Francisco conference ... [along with] its avowed
intention to unite the World of Color in order to establish international racial

equality and its sponsorship of Benjamin F. McLaurin and A. Philip Randolph as appointees to the mantle of leadership.'[76]

Randolph and McLaurin were not central to African-American activism at San Francisco; that privilege was reserved for the three African-Americans approved by the US State Department.[77] The CAA organised the 'conference on "Africa new perspectives" ... (14 April) ... in attendance at the conference were approximately 150 Negro and white leaders ... [and numerous international] ... government officials' (although Henry S. Villard, head of the Division of African Affairs from the US State Department pulled out).[78] African-Americans' activities were not confined to the leadership cadre. Black students attended an inter-racial conference at the University of North Carolina which elected two representatives (one black) to observe the proceedings at San Francisco.[79] Given the racial context of the American South, the activities of the black students indicate the increased politicisation of African-Americans generally and the emergent role of black students in political struggles. The *Baltimore Afro-American* (newspaper) stated that the convention highlighted southern black interest in international affairs, which invalidates the view that southern African-Americans were exclusively preoccupied with domestic civil rights. The fact that Frank P. Graham, the president of the University of North Carolina, sanctioned and spoke at the convention[80] indicates that he recognised African-Americans' increasing willingness to challenge the status quo[81] domestically and internationally. AAFAN's interest in the San Francisco conference was apparently part of the wider black communities' interest in the peace conference. AAFAN's major obstacle in relation to securing their international agenda was the US administration who selected an all-white delegation to represent US interests at the UN.[82]

However, Ralph Bunche's attendance at Dumbarton Oaks and his assistance with the construction of 'US policy in the colonies'[83] indicates that 'acceptable' black people could play a role in formulating US foreign policy.[84] While Bunche held an official position 'as a technical expert on trusteeship', his ability to propose or acknowledge African-American interests was undermined by the realities of his professional career and his fear of been perceived as going native by his white colleagues, which distanced him from the African-American community.[85] Although AAFAN's views contravened those of the US State Department and Dean Acheson,[86] their campaign to secure a black presence at San Francisco led to the NAACP being asked to send representatives to the UN conference.[87] As a result, Dr Du Bois, Walter White and Mary Bethune were employed as consultants to the US delegation.[88] In addition, Du Bois was selected by the 'Association for the United Nations, Inc.' (AUN)[89] (letter 5 April 1945 Charlotte B. Mahon) to join its 'strategy committee (headed by Clark M. Eichelberger) to work in San Francisco during the ... United Nations conference ... [the letter states] ... it was felt advisable to form a core committee representing the interests of all of us ... for ... exchange of information, planning of strategy and mutual guidance ... for the benefit of all organisations and persons interested in our field.'[90]

The campaigns of African-Americans to promote the interests of their constituency encouraged the state to grant AAFAN limited access into an arena from which they had largely been excluded. Despite African-Americans' admission into the UN conference, internal rivalries threatened to destabilise their attempts to present a united front dedicated to racial equality internationally.[91] While black organisations like The Congress of Colored Parents and Teachers, enthusiastically supported NAACP leadership at San Francisco,[92] some African-Americans' felt the NAACP monopolised AAFAN's efforts to define black interests at the UN.[93] Evidently some African-Americans believed the multiracial character of the NAACP hampered its ability to define black interests. In addition, the fact that the NAACP's leading official was Euro-American[94] tended to reinforce the notion that even organisations dedicated to black empowerment required white leadership, which symbolised black dependence on liberal white leadership to advance black interests.

Consequently, some African-Americans argued that there were no official representatives from independent black organisations.[95] While African-Americans were an integral part of the NAACP leadership, some African-Americans were concerned that a white man was the official leader of a organisation that was predominantly black. Although this apathy was (apparently) less pronounced than during the IEW, it caused the AAFAN to question whether a white-led organisation would adequately advance or defend black interests. Indeed,

> black groups challenged the NAACP designation as consultant to the American delegation on the grounds that it was not a truly representative Afro-American organisation. The Fraternal Council of Negro Churches wired the State Department to the effect that no purely Afro-American group was among the forty-two designated to advise the American delegation; there were some inter-racial organisations, but none that represented the sovereign will of black Americans.[96]

Nevertheless, the participation of Du Bois and White in regular meetings with the numerous black organisational representatives covering the proceedings at San Francisco, and Walter White's appeal to Stettinius to 'endorse the extension of charter human rights to minorities and colonized populations',[97] points to their promotion of black interests. African-American distrust of white leadership indicates their inclination towards conceiving their struggle in racial terms. Although the NAACP's advocacy of an international bill of rights and its call for domestic and international racial equality drew the support of the African-American community,[98] AAFAN's commitment to black issues[99] and their increasing relationship with state officials created legitimate concerns about whether black inclusion would lead to the co-option[100] of their leadership class. This concern is clearly reflected in African-Americans' efforts to ensure that the NAACP consultants were primarily concerned with black issues.[101] It also highlights the fact that the state and wider society's inclusion of African-Americans in institutions or activities dominated by white people can subvert African-American commitment to their interests. It also explains African-Americans' hostility to the State Department's exclusive promotion of the NAACP as the foremost black organisation, although it was headed by white people.[102] Essentially, the evidence could validate the contention that African-Americans' organic agenda was hijacked by the state, which utilised the limited distribution of impressive titles in order to co-opt black leaders and thereby secure state/white interests.[103] The colonial status of black leaders was alluded to by *The Chicago Defender* in 1945 as it stated, 'Today the status and standing of Negro America ... is part and parcel of the color problem of the world, known as the colonial question. The Negro is the colonial of America, exploited and robbed of the fruits of his labor just as men of colour in the Congo or India or the South seas.'[104]

Ironically, Plummer maintains that the NAACP's model of black advocacy, which was criticised by black organisations, also failed to win real support from mainstream non-government organisations which did little to facilitate erasing the colour-line domestically or internationally.[105] While African-Americans campaigned for black liberation, the quasi-free black republics, with the exception of Haiti,[106] failed to address the issues of racial equality, de-colonisation and global white supremacy. The failure of Haiti, Ethiopia and Liberia[107] to address black issues mirrored the silence of Ralph Bunche, whose status-anxiety compelled him to avoid outward support of black issues,[108] and those black people whose views were not sanctioned by white people (liberal or conservative). The silence of the *independent* black republics may have stemmed from their political and economic dependency on the Western nations. In brief, the actions of AAFAN entailed beseeching the international community to facilitate their agenda for international racial equality and black liberation. AAFAN/African-Americans felt that their domestic status paralleled the position of colonised diasporean Africans and people of colour in general. Although the AAFAN's conception of foreign affairs incorporated a racial worldview, they elected to work in conjunction with government officials and white organisations, which represented a departure from the black nationalist ethos utilised during the Italo-Ethiopian War. Whilst the nationalist wing of the black liberation struggle led African-American activism in the 1930s (drawing on the Garveyite 'race first' tradition), black leaders in the 1940s included a new generation of leaders whose commitment to Africa was less pronounced than that of Du Bois or Garvey.[109] The new leaders accepted American values and called for domestic and international reforms as opposed to promoting Pan-Africanism.[110]

Impact

AAFAN failed to be incorporated into the foreign policy establishment or to achieve their established goals. The US delegation rejected AAFAN's proposals concerning de-colonisation and racial equality as part of its UN Charter recommendations. However, African-American leaders did engage in constructive dialogue with government and State Department officials, enabling them to critique state foreign policy and highlight their agenda, which state officials did at least acknowledge. In addition, the consultants impacted on the US delegations policies.

> The weight of public opinion ... [forced] ... the American delegation ... to take a more progressive stance on human rights and trusteeship ... Stettinius admitted that the American delegation would support amendments to the Dumbarton Oaks proposals that guaranteed freedom from discrimination on account of 'race, language, religion, or sex' ... [However] the NAACP consultants were disappointed by a further amendment that 'nothing in this Charter shall authorize the Organisation to intervene in matters, which are essentially within the domestic jurisdiction of the state concerned.' They held that this language severely limited the functions and powers of the General Assembly as well as the Commission to Promote Human Rights.[111]

AAFAN's access to the US foreign policy establishment was clearly facilitated by the domestic reforms produced by WWII as a consequence of the Allies' efforts to erase the (blatantly) overt aspects of European and American racism. In brief, America's efforts to realign domestic race relations, in addition to African-American activism,[112] softened American racism and provided the political leverage for AAFAN to ensure their inclusion in the proceedings at San Francisco. In short, AAFAN's or African-Americans' activities at San Francisco resulted in the following outcomes: they liaised with members of the US foreign policy establishment on an organisational and personal level in a manner previously denied them, and their presence at San Francisco allowed African-Americans to gain a greater awareness of international relations. African-Americans' participation at the UN conference gave them direct contact with progressive people of colour, struggling against colonialism whilst their participation in international politics at state level honed their organisational skills, enhanced their image and challenged the myth that they could not engage in foreign affairs at the highest level. Indeed, African-Americans and other interest groups compelled the American delegation to adopt a more progressive agenda. African-Americans' efforts (regarding the delegation) assisted in creating a moral framework that substantiated AAFAN's call for racial equality and the right of self-government for the colonised masses. According to Harris, Ralph Bunche 'in his role as expert on dependent areas for the American delegation to the San Francisco Conference on International organisation, was in large measure responsible for the trusteeship provisions of the United Nations charter [which] ... marked a breakthrough in protecting the interests of colonial subjects.'[113]

Nonetheless, America and the Western nations ensured that the UN Charter, irrespective of the efforts of the Soviet Union[114] did not sanction the UN to intervene to end colonialism or black oppression in America. In reality, neither the Soviet Union nor the other major nations campaigned to authorise the UN Charter to undermine state sovereignty in the name of human rights. State sovereignty was generally protected by the UN Charter,[115] which safeguarded the international status quo by safeguarding Western hegemony.[116] Nevertheless, AAFAN's involvement in the UN conference helped create an alternative conception of the UN that in time would allow people of colour to challenge Western racial hegemony and colonialism.[117] African-Americans petitioned the UN twice on behalf of their human rights (much to the dismay of the US administration).[118] In addition, in 1965 Minister Malcolm X was in the process of petitioning the UN to intercede on behalf of African-Americans[119] before he was assassinated. Significantly, Roark's contention that African-Americans' interest in international relations flourished briefly after WWII but ended abruptly in 1947 is invalidated as the evidence suggests that the radical wing of the black struggle continued to pursue a foreign affairs agenda. Mainstream black leaders led by the NAACP and Walter White accepted the dictates of Truman's foreign policy in return for domestic reforms.[120] The mainstream cadre's support for Cold War policies did not preclude them from critiquing Euro-American foreign policy or supporting black liberation in the developing world. Nevertheless they did support anti-communism.[121] AAFAN's involvement in the San Francisco conference augmented African-American interest in foreign affairs and increased their, commitment to eradicating white hegemony at home and abroad.

The position of the US administration

The US administration post-WWII foreign policy was aligned with its wartime rhetoric in support of the Atlantic Charter and the four freedoms championed by the Allies.[122] The unity of the Allies was undermined by the death of President Roosevelt,[123] who 'refused to become a staunch anti-Soviet',[124] and the realities of post-war power politics. Some authors suggest that the Roosevelt administration was committed to maintaining good relations with the Soviet Union[125] in addition to campaigning for the extension of political freedom for all subject people,[126] which was in itself controversial because it raised questions regarding the legitimacy of European colonialism.[127] In brief, the evidence indicates 'that [President] Roosevelt was committed to de-colonisation as a means to preserve peace after the war by forestalling independence struggles ... his plan was not altogether altruistic; it would also enable the United States to acquire post-war air and naval bases that were deemed vital to American security.'[128] The direction of US foreign policy was clearly contested, not least by Britain who desired to maintain its empire.[129] Indeed, Edward Stettinius, the secretary of state, alluded to the divergent views of government officials and leaders of the armed forces in relation to the Roosevelt administration's foreign policy objectives.[130] The US state was experiencing additional pressures as the wartime sacrifices of the Allies' colonial subjects prompted calls from them, and the AAFAN, for the extension of the four freedoms and the principles of the Atlantic Charter to all peoples. Given America's desire to weaken the European colonialists' economic control of their colonies (i.e. imperial preference)[131] and the Soviet Union's desire to curtail French and British political dominance, the Cold War between Soviet Union and America was not necessarily inevitable. In this regard, the National Council of American-Soviet Friendship, Inc. (NCASF) stated that 'it [was] universally acknowledged that the cornerstone of any effective world organisation must be the continued unity of the Anglo-American-Soviet coalition.'[132] African-Americans' desire for an enlightened form of foreign policy, which embraced universal democracy for all[133] was exemplified in the CAA's call for an African Charter whereby the US would sponsor African development. However, the African-American agenda appeared to be losing ground due to the state's increasing tendency to protect European interests within the international arena.[134] In retrospect, black optimism during the late 1940s was understandable given their unprecedented access to the state and the foreign policy establishment. In addition, the government appeared to be actively interested in colonial matters. This is exemplified by the creation of the 'Division of Dependant Areas Affairs (within the Department of state on 20 December 1944) ... [which was responsible] ... for the formulation and co-ordination of policy and action regarding activities of the proposed United Nations organisation affecting dependant areas.'[135] Indeed, on 5 January 1944 Stettinius informed Paul Robeson and the CAA that the US government 'realizes that the problems of the dependent peoples are of a unique nature, requiring special consideration and treatment. The appropriate divisions and committees of the Department of state are devoting serious attention to those problems ... [to] ... ensure the greatest tangible advancement possible ... based on the principles of equitable and just treatment for all peoples.'[136]

Although some state officials favoured a more liberal brand of foreign policy, the US administration opted to protect the status quo,[137] as the government, accepting the advice of the military, decided to safeguard European colonialism on the grounds that it was essential to maintaining international stability and the containment of Soviet Union.[138] US strategic/economic interests in the Pacific sidelined its anti-imperialist stance[139] because US foreign policy elevated its national interests over and above the promotion of international freedom. The pursuit of US economic interests was evident in America's incursions into Africa, which were facilitated by the Marshall Plan, which guaranteed American access/investment in Africa as 'in exchange for Yankee dollars, an impoverished Europe ... allowed America a wedge in Africa.'[140] In addition, US corporations' heavy investment in South Africa,[141] irrespective of its extreme racial doctrines, is indicative of US capital's commitment to increased profits. Essentially the wartime rhetoric concerning the four freedoms did not extend to the colonised world of colour.

The US administration's actions[142] at San Francisco reflected the complexity of post-war politics as they pursued both progressive and conservative policies.[143] For example, the US administration's massive propaganda campaign designed to increase public interest, regarding international politics and the UN, was clearly progressive,[144] as was the state's incorporation of numerous civic and political organisations, some of which had no prior involvement in foreign affairs issues. This ensured that America, while focused on international relations, did not revert to domestic issues as it did after WWI.[145] Numerous conferences, including those organised by the State Department, stimulated discussions of foreign affairs and raised questions pertaining to America's post-war policies. Especially striking was the state's recruitment of Ralph Bunche into the foreign policy establishment and discussions with black organisations in regard to the substance of US foreign policy. Given that US foreign policy has historically been shaped by the educated WASP elite, even to the exclusion of other white ethnic groups, the government's liaisons with the African-American community were a significant departure from the conventions of state foreign policy. Evidently the WWII[146] context forced the US administration to re-orientate race relations to secure black support in order to construct a strong and diverse domestic consensus to ensure America would not abandon its interventionist policies after the war. Large numbers of individuals/organisations were encouraged to observe the proceedings at San Francisco, including the African-American consultants to the American delegation.[147] However, the state's populist/liberal approach regarding diverse public participation at the UN proceedings was undermined by the composition of the US delegation,[148] which was ideologically inclined to the right. The delegation's conservative ideological makeup naturally inclined it towards supporting the status quo, i.e. colonialism and the Anglo-American alliance, in addition to undermining US and Soviet relations. The secretary of state's announcement that the delegations agenda would not be altered by the consultants or by other external bodies elucidates the government's intent to insulate the delegation's status quo agenda[149] from competing models of foreign affairs. The delegation's commitment to ending racial oppression or colonialism[150] was bound to be limited, because of its conservative orientation. The delegation demonstrated its cautious approach to foreign affairs

> at the first meeting of delegates and consultants, Secretary of State Stettinius announced that the American delegation would not introduce or support a human rights declaration for the proposed charter and that questions relating to colonies should be taken up sometime in the future after San Francisco. At their 1 May meeting, numerous consultants requested that the American delegation take the lead on difficult issues before the conference and act on principle. Du Bois read a statement on behalf of the NAACP consultants in which he defended the idea of racial equality. All people were entitled to such fundamental rights as freedom of thought, expression and movement.[151]

Nonetheless 'the NAACP's lobbying, together with pressure from other groups in San Francisco, began to bear fruit ... if they did not succeed in achieving ... decolonization, they did secure statements in the Charter that the United Nations would function "without distinction as to race, sex, language, or religion." '[152]

However, the state's desire to obtain strategic raw materials in Africa[153] and Asia, and to establish military bases in areas deemed vital to America's national interests, directed its foreign policy.[154] Nevertheless characterising the Truman administration foreign policy as purely conservative oversimplifies his administration's objectives, as American foreign policy was not conservative in all regards. Roosevelt's and Truman's foreign policy sought to exploit wartime and post-war conditions in order to advance American interests.[155] America's lend-lease agreements and its 'destroyers for bases' deals provided strategic gains for America as did Roosevelt's[156] anti-imperialist rhetoric, which facilitated American overtures to the mineral-rich colonies in the hope of capturing their markets from their European rivals.

Overall, the Truman administration's post-war objectives dictated the American delegation's policy recommendations at San Francisco, while Roosevelt's wartime emphasis on democratic rights and the four freedoms, gave way to the realities of American *realpolitik*.[157] US officials such as John Foster Dulles worried that UN proposals could undermine the interests of the Anglo-American alliance by criticising British colonialism and American segregation, which would be unfortunate for both governments.[158] Nonetheless, divisions did exist amongst the US delegation pertaining to America's position on European colonialism, as

> Mr Stassen ... [asked in regard to independence] ... whether it would be better ... for the United states to support the Soviet Union and Chinese position [who favoured independence] ... for the following reasons: (1) Independence as a goal for all peoples who aspire to and are capable of it has been the traditional and sacred policy of this government. It has been ... our policy in the Philippines, and it has been reiterated on numerous occasions by President Roosevelt and former Secretary of State Cordell Hull. (2) An excellent opportunity is afforded to make a profitable gesture on behalf of the peoples of the orient as well as those in Africa and the Caribbean.[159]

The Truman administration and delegation, accepting the logic of the US military,[160] sought to protect US strategic interests by maintaining European colonialism.[161] Evidently the location of US military bases could facilitate the infiltration of US capital in those designated areas, in 1945/1946. It is plausible that (as early as 1945/1946) Truman's foreign policy was committed to the expansion of American capital and the maintenance of colonialism, in addition to the containment of the Soviet Union.[162] Despite Roark's contention that US anti-colonialism stemmed from the negative impact imperial preference had on US trade, he argued that by January 1945 anti-communism was the state's major priority.[163] In brief, the proceedings at San Francisco witnessed America's descent into the Cold War and the demise of policies advocating democracy for all or to end colonialism and racial inequality.[164] The American delegation, whilst professing the importance of political freedom, ignored the cause of the oppressed and pursued the status quo formula African-Americans had critiqued at Dumbarton Oaks. Ultimately, the composition of the American delegation ensured that the agenda adopted by the delegation would support the status quo given the absence of white liberals or African-Americans in the delegation. The US delegation avoided the submission of proposals, which impinged on domestic race relations, citing that UN intervention to safeguard African-American human rights would violate state's rights.[165] Interestingly, the delegation's failure to promote the welfare of African-Americans mirrored the circumstances of black people throughout the diaspora and Africa, whose freedoms were neglected by the Western nations. The US delegations support of the status quo was exemplified by its objection to the sole female delegate Dean Gildersleeve's call for gender equality clauses in the UN Charter. The delegation rejected Gildersleeve's proposals because they would encourage the calls for racial equality clauses in the Charter.[166] Nevertheless, the activities of the numerous NGOs/individuals at the UN summit, including Walter White, Du Bois and Bethune, forced the US delegation to liberalise their Charter proposals.[167] Given America's standing in the UN, the US delegation's liberalised agenda may have facilitated the centrality of the UN in the battles between the progressive and conservative forces within the international arena, which began in the late 1940s.[168] Although the US delegation stifled the assault from below, the secretary of state admitted that the government bowed to interest group pressure, which resulted in a re-orientating of their agenda at San Francisco.[169] Ironically, the state's campaign to court public interest in the proceedings at San Francisco provided the leverage for interest groups to influence American foreign policy. The state's populist approach regarding its UN policies facilitated non-state actor's efforts to redefine US foreign policy, which is indicative of how the granting of concessions can inadvertently re-orientate state policies.[170] Nevertheless, the (emerging) Cold War climate encouraged the return to state-directed foreign policy, as the Truman administration initiated and led the fight against communism. Ultimately, the state-sanctioned fight against communism stifled AAFAN's progressive internationalism and stimulated the NAACP to reign in their foreign affairs activism, which apparently led to the sacking of Du Bois by the NAACP leadership. In addition, the African-American mainstream leadership later abandoned their international agenda[171] for racial equality, and lined up behind state policies whilst pursuing domestic reforms.[172] Truman's racial reforms and anti-Soviet propaganda, which led to McCarthyism, undermined Walter White's and African-Americans' support for the Soviet Union and their efforts to challenge racial and colonial oppression.[173] Consequently, African-Americans restricted their activism to domestic civil rights and paid less attention to international affairs. This explains Penny Von Eschen's contention that African-American internationalism peaked between

1946 and 1947[174] when government pressure discouraged African-American interest in foreign affairs.

In brief the AAFAN achieved greater and more productive links with the foreign policy establishment, which enabled African-Americans to disseminate their views to a more influential constituency comprising domestic/international groups, organisations and diplomatic officials. AAFAN's pressure group tactics and the state's populist agenda to ensure US involvement in the UN resulted in AAFAN's increased access to the foreign policy establishment. American officials recognised that US racism was damaging their international image and aided the AAFAN's efforts to establish a role in foreign affairs. Unfortunately, the AAFAN's marginal status did not allow them to compel the US delegation to adopt measures to end colonialism and sanction global racial equality.[175] One sympathises with Du Bois' claim that 'the conclusions at San Francisco were to mention human rights and close the door to every practical possibility of realising them'.[176] Du Bois' contention is unsurprising given the delegations' rejection of his proposals to end race discrimination.[177] In brief, African-Americans' marginal status confined them to being the moral conscience of the US delegation without the power to execute their agenda.[178] The fact that African-Americans' policy recommendations were overlooked is not unique. Yet African-American exceptionalism within the domestic context (in relation to other interest groups) is unique, given their political exclusion from exercising full democratic rights. Black America's call for a racial equality clause in the UN Charter was a direct response to their marginal status in America[179] and related to their circumstances. Unfortunately, African-Americans, and their colonised counterparts in the Caribbean and Africa, depended on the US WASP elite and their European equivalent to champion racial reforms.

The Truman administration's realignment of US foreign policy, from its wartime emphasis on allied co-operation to its anti-Soviet containment policies whilst maintaining its interventionist brand of foreign policy, is not surprising given the power of the state to shape the national agenda, especially since American economic and military ascendancy encouraged widespread support for adventurous foreign policy goals. Essentially, the post-war international context, which left a decimated Europe[180] reliant on US aid, assisted the US administration in extending their influence further afield and securing US interests.[181] In short, state military and corporate interests were all served by US (strategic) expansionism.[182] Coupled with the exaltation of victory and congressional support, this guaranteed that the Truman administration could execute its foreign policy.[183] The Truman administration's redefinition of US post-war foreign policy was indicative of the invasive character of state ideology (in this case), which successfully utilised anti-Soviet propaganda under the guise of national interests to ensure state hegemony pertaining to foreign policy.[184]

The American delegation's position on the Soviet Union was summed up by 'Representative [Charles] Eaton [who] felt that the basic problem was, who was going to be masters of the world. He said he did not want to vote in this delegation in any way that would put Soviet Union in control of the World. It was as he saw it a struggle as to whose ideas were going to dominate.'[185] The ideological basis of the Truman doctrine was already evident at San Francisco. AAFAN's support of the Soviet Union's foreign policy at San Francisco had no bearing on the state's orientation to its former ally, as powerful US interests[186] took precedence over AAFAN's marginal point of view.

Theoretical implications

Pluralists contend that interest group politics is an essential ingredient in an organised constituency's efforts to secure their political goals. Although the US political system claims to provide checks and balances which prevent vast political inequalities, the racial inequalities, which deprived much of the black population from full voting rights, undoubtedly limited African-Americans' ability to direct foreign affairs. In short, African-Americans' racial status hindered their efforts to utilise the interest group method. In brief, African-Americans' inability to utilise the full spectrum of political methods stifled their attempts to engage in the political process via the pluralist method.

Numerous interest groups participated at the proceedings in San Francisco, engaging in competitive and co-operative efforts to promote their international agendas. The facts suggest that despite African-Americans' increased role in the formation of US foreign policy (barring Ralph Bunche), they did not participate in the decision-making process. The observer status conferred on Du Bois, White and Bethune symbolised the general role of AAFAN at San Francisco. Race had a bearing on the marginal status of black people at the UN. The disproportionate absence of African-Americans within the state apparatus demonstrated the scale of US political apartheid.[187] While other US interest groups could demonstrate their disapproval of the Truman administration's foreign policy fully at the next presidential election, the colour-line prevented the majority of African-Americans from doing so. The fact that politicians and the Truman administration knew black people had a limited ability to hurt them at the polls undermined their utilisation of the interest group method.

In short, AAFAN'S racial identity, political marginality and US racial conventions weakened their efforts to utilise the interest group method. The existence of diverse interest groups validates the (partial) existence of pluralism; however, the theory fails to account for the realities of US race relations and fails to adequately explain what occurred at San Francisco.

In **Statism**, the idea that AAFAN's foreign policy goals would be subordinate to the state's is validated by the evidence, as African-Americans received no practical support from the state or the US delegation[188] for their de-colonisation[189] proposals or their desire to insert a racial equality clause in the UN Charter. Although AAFAN initially maintained its conception of foreign affairs, despite State Department indifference, the liberal wing of AAFAN eventually abandoned their focus on de-colonisation and international affairs after the UN conference. African-Americans retreated from foreign affairs because of the state's racial reforms[190] and its efforts to limit black activism to the arena of domestic politics; consequently, black dissatisfaction was generally contained[191] until the 1950s and 1960s. State power and AAFAN's dependence on the state to protect their interests hindered AAFAN's efforts to mount an independent campaign designed to meet their goals. Although the AAFAN did partially alter the American delegation and the State Department's conception of the UN's international role, it could not prevent American support for European colonialism. AAFAN also failed to prevent American alienation from the Soviet Union, which was aggravated by European and British power politics.[192] AAFAN also failed to compel the state to propose measures to empower the UN to campaign for African and Asian independence.

The state-orientated US foreign policy to ensure Anglo-American and Western (global) hegemony[193] which eventually reoriented all but the most committed African-Americans' (such as Du Bois' and Robeson's) positions on international relations. Black marginality relative to white America and the state inhibited their efforts to aid diasporean and continental African's fight against racism and colonialism.[194] African-Americans could not compel the US delegation to sanction a racial equality clause that would resolve their domestic oppression.[195]

Statism fails to account for the impact of race in regard to US foreign policy outcomes at San Francisco.[196]

The **Marxist** contention that capitalists direct state actions is compelling. The evidence indicates the state directed US foreign policy in relation to the UN conference. Given the Truman administration's efforts to secure America's national interests by strategically locating American military outposts throughout the globe, the impetus for US foreign policy came from the state and the military, whose representatives formed an integral part of the US delegation.[197] Arguably the state's collaboration with the military facilitated the access of American corporations to new markets. The evidence indicates the state played the central role in defining America's post-war international agenda. The state facilitated America's strategic interests[198] to ensure America's expansionist thrust. The state determined US foreign policy at San Francisco, because it provided the ideological justification for US foreign policy and engineered the political context for US military and economic penetration into the international arena. Still, Cheng argues that the US Congress supported Truman's foreign policy in terms of providing the money to rebuild Europe, on the basis of anti-communism not on the expansion of American capitalism, which suggests at least that the state determined the ideological basis for US foreign policy.[199]

Marxism fails to account for the state's ability to determine US foreign policy independent of the capitalist class or in conjunction with other organised interest groups. In relation to African-Americans, the Marxist theory argues that the subordinate class (or classes) play a marginal role in the construction of US foreign policy. African-Americans were a subordinate class during the mid-1940s, thus they played a marginal role in the construction of US foreign policy at San Francisco.[200] Marxism correctly identifies the marginal role of subordinate classes in the construction of US foreign policy; however, it fails to account for the invasive nature of white racism.[201] Race, in addition to class conventions, relegated the African-American political class concerned with foreign affairs (given that the majority of Americans have never practically engaged in foreign affairs) to a role commensurate with their general status in America.

Racial Colony: The framing and execution of US foreign policy at San Francisco was determined by the WASP elite, although African-Americans' engaged in constructive dialogue with the US foreign policy establishment, it rejected their anti-imperialist agenda, in principle and practice as being too radical. AAFAN'S model of international relations recognised that their status in America (in relation to white people) was analogous to the position of colonised people (especially of African descent) throughout the world, as, despite African-Americans' role at San Francisco, they were (with the exception of Ralph Bunche) excluded from the US delegation regardless of their calls for inclusion.[202] The respective involvement of Bunche, Du Bois, White or Bethune (who were employed as consultants to the American delegation and invited to high-profile meetings with State Department officials) in the proceedings at San Francisco qualified them for inclusion in the delegation. A renowned scholar such as Dr Du Bois was clearly equipped to comprehend the complexities of international relations.[203] Indeed, the Americans United for World Organisation, Inc. speakers' bureau (which was chaired by Ernest Hopkins President of Dartmouth) requested that Du Bois 'speak occasionally for [them because] ... we feel sure of your own stature, we should be proud and grateful if you would join the speakers bureau.'[204] Despite the recognition of Du Bois' talent, the state assembled a delegation that would promote state and presidential policies,[205] which necessitated the exclusion of African-Americans such as Du Bois who desired to overthrow Western hegemony. The US delegation's failure to promote self-rule in the colonies was directly related to America's support of Western hegemony, which enabled developed nations to exploit the natural and human resources of Africa, Asia and the Caribbean.[206] Some foreign affairs specialists overlook the link between a nation's domestic configuration and its foreign policies;, however, the US delegation's rejection of a racial equality clause stemmed from their desire to prohibit the UN from intervening in American race relations.[207] The US state rejected the racial equality clause because it would have authorised the UN to insist that its members promote (domestic) racial equality whilst white America had a vested interest in maintaining black subordination, because it enhanced the status and wealth of the white majority in America.

Despite African-Americans' increased visibility within the foreign affairs community, their impact on the decision-making process was marginal. The foreign policy establishment mirrored American political and sociological trends as the white majority dictated, and defined the interests of African-Americans and people of colour worldwide. AAFAN's ability to win concessions from the state is indicative of their struggle to do so, and the increasing pressure for America to promote racial reforms in order to bolster its international image. Dean Acheson, secretary of state, argued that 'the existence of discrimination against minority groups in this country has an adverse effect upon our relations with other countries.'[208] In short, the racial colony theory provides the best explanation of what occurred at San Francisco.

Conclusion

The African-American role at San Francisco represented the zenith of their struggle during the war years[209] to improve the status of the black community within the American context.[210] Although AAFAN was unable to achieve its goals, its limited success stemmed from their increased access to the state, which enabled them to persuade state officials to legitimise their call for domestic and international racial equality.[211] Doubtlessly African-Americans' presence at the conference enhanced America's image as a democratic nation working to end racial oppression. The Soviet Union highlighted the contradictions between America's image and its foreign policy.[212] The US acting secretary of state's telegram to Stettinius (Washington, 8 May 1945) is indicative of America's dilemma regarding the Soviet Union as he maintained

> Molotov ... stated that Soviet Union will take the initiative in having the international Organization clothed with power ... to promote self-government for dependent people. Although this has been our historic role, the Soviet Union, I fear, may appear before the world as the champion of all dependant people. Molotov's move may confirm in the minds of people in Asia ... that the Anglo-American powers are not their real champions and will turn to Soviet Union as their more outspoken friend and spokesman.[213]

Of course, the Soviet Union's alleged support of self-government did not prevent them from eventually subordinating Eastern Europe and depriving those states of their sovereignty.

The state's recruitment of specific African-Americans into the foreign affairs community stemmed from three issues, i.e. propaganda, pragmatism[214] and AAFAN's efforts to influence US and global politics. Du Bois indicated his concerns to the editor of *The New York Times* (1 November 1946) regarding the proceedings at San Francisco, 'the six million people of Australia could talk to the World from the highest seats of publicity, but black Africa, save for two small areas, was silent.'[215] In brief, US foreign policy chose to uphold white hegemony and Anglo-Saxon supremacy, which was (later) validated by the Atlantic Pact.[216]

AAFAN's ability to meet its goals was aided and undermined by its interactions with the state.[217] Eventually, most African-American leaders accepted the position of the state and confined their activities to domestic civil rights.[218] Only Robeson and Du Bois continued the fight against US foreign policy, because individuals who continued to critique US foreign policy during the 1940s and 1950s were ostracised and punished.[219] Although the state instituted reforms in the 1940s, these reforms did not prevent the civil rights campaigns of the 1950s and 1960s, which culminated with Minister Malcolm X's attacks on US foreign policy and Dr King's attack on the Vietnam War,[220] which, in addition to their domestic activities, marked them out as enemies of the state. Significantly, AAFAN's activities at San Francisco may have helped to lay a foundation for the civil rights explosion of the 1960s.[221]

The state and white America have endeavoured to preserve white privilege domestically; however, African-American struggles have resulted in greater success domestically while black involvement in foreign policy appears to have moved at a slower pace.[222] AAFAN's activities at San Francisco demonstrated how interest groups can affect state policies, in addition to highlighting how Cold War politics hindered[223] and helped African-Americans' liberation struggle. AAFAN assumed the marginal status they had endured over the centuries, as white America and specifically the WASP elite determined the overall direction of US foreign policy at San Francisco.

6 Human rights, racial reconstruction and the Cold War 1950–60

This chapter identifies the 1950s as a pivotal decade which redefined the character of America's foreign and domestic policies. It is viewed through the lens of AAFAN's rise and fall. It identifies how sections of the African-American leadership cadre where co-opted or neutralised due to a state campaign to align America's domestic and foreign policies to Cold War requirements. The chapter demonstrates the similarities between African-Americans' struggle to attain their human rights and the global assault on Western hegemony in its colonial guise. It also reveals how identity politics, historical amnesia and state power impacted the politics of AAFAN and the liberal wing of the African-American leadership cadre, to the extent that AAFAN tempered its support for de-colonisation in Africa and select African-American leaders' activities were neutralised by the state whilst moderates were granted access to establishment circles. Ultimately, it establishes the link between the tactical objectives pursued by the emerging Civil Rights Movement and the reluctance to support the global struggle for racial equality, and indicates why the Truman administration and successive administrations were compelled by historical circumstances to dismantle the state-sanctioned racial apartheid practised in the Southern states. The chapter addresses diverse issues including the Cold War, the UN, apartheid in South Africa, the Mau Mau revolt in Kenya, the Montgomery Bus Boycott, desegregation in Little Rock Arkansas and the events related to Ghanaian independence.

The initial section addresses the role of identity in determining the scope of AAFAN's foreign affairs activities at the dawn of the American century.

The post-war context stimulated intense introspection and debate within the African-American population. The key socio-political and ideological questions concerned the political status of the American Negroes relationship to Africa and the black world.[1] Irrespective of propaganda and the varied identity modification techniques utilised on African-Americans, they are the descendants of captive Africans. Still, the contention that slavery neutered their African identity is plausible; indeed American history indicates that white America's rejection of the Negro was predicated on their African origins and their colour.

The post-war context brought the issue of identity to the centre stage of America's racial politics as African-Americans' identification or disconnection with the colonised masses of African descent raised questions about their own identity.[2] In time, the concern for continental Africans and the African diaspora fuelled a black nationalist and Pan-Africanist activism that influenced the American Negroes' political consciousness throughout the 1950s and was consolidated in the late 1960s.[3] The key issues were historical memory, political power and notions of national loyalty. In short, the 1950s presaged the wider conflict over identity that would frame the intellectual revolt that led the American Negro to collectively redefine their identity, first as black and eventually African.

The Cold War

The following section summarises the descent into the Cold War by the Truman administration, this is followed by a summary of AAFAN's actions between 1946 and 1950.

In the aftermath of the creation of the UN, the tensions between the Soviet Union (USSR) and the United States escalated. As early as 1946 (US diplomat) George Kennan's telegram from Moscow outlined the ideological parameters of what would become Truman's containment theory.[4] With the battle lines established, Truman had to sell his foreign policy approach to the political establishment and the American public.[5] His primary task was to convince Americans of the alleged enormity of the Soviet threat in order to justify the expense of containing Soviet power.[6] Truman articulated his strategy in a speech to the joint houses of Congress on 12 March 1947 where he requested aid for Greece and Turkey.[7] He outlined his plan to protect US interests by maintaining effective military deterrents and containing the geographical parameters of the Soviet Union in order to thwart the global ambitions of the USSR.[8]

Truman's doctrine created the rationale and provided the cash for the reconstruction of key European economies via the Marshall plan, which provided the US economy with the required markets to sustain its growth, in addition to ensuring European stability as a means of containing the political and military power of the Soviet Union.[9] Likewise, the creation of the North Atlantic Treaty Organization (NATO) in 1949 provided the means to augment Europe's defences whilst allowing the US to maintain a military presence in Europe.[10] Finally, the revelation that the Soviet Union had obtained Nuclear weapons (by 1949) during August 1950 and the revolutionary birth of 'the people's republic of China'[11] on 1 October set the stage for a bipolar conflict between the USA and the USSR.

Eventually Truman's approach was institutionalised by the National Security doctrines outlined in NSC-68 which placed the political, economic and military containment of the Soviet Union as the major priority of US foreign policy.[12] Through subsequent decades, American political culture would re-conceptualise the Cold War within a religious context that would inform Ronald Reagan's depiction of the USSR as the Evil Empire and lay the basis for George W. Bush's religious orientation to the war on terror.[13]

The Truman administration implemented a whole range of political, economic and military policies which established the ideological parameters which informed the Cold War for numerous decades.[14] Notwithstanding Soviet dominion over Eastern Europe and its appeal to revolutionary struggles and anti-colonial rhetoric presented a credible challenge to capitalism, American power and Western hegemony.[15] However, in accordance with the requirements of this chapter, the following section shall assess how the Cold War impacted on AAFAN in regard to the domestic and international context.

The events surrounding the formation of the UN found African-Americans in an interesting position as AAFAN's activism prompted the American delegation to the UN to support proposals that shaped the UN charter to disavow discrimination in regard to 'race, language, religion, or sex'. In the short term, despite the UN Charter's concern for human rights, America and her European allies were able to safeguard their sovereignty and maintain their colonial possessions.[16] Nonetheless, AAFAN emerged from the war with a strong commitment for de-colonisation and the struggle for international racial equality.[17]

While the Roosevelt administration had lent credence to de-colonisation, Truman's views on colonisation were hard to discern.[18] Hence, given the ambiguity of Truman's views on domestic and foreign affairs, some African-Americans sought to assert their post-war independence from the government.[19] Consequently, African-American leaders ranging from Walter White to Paul Robeson and Dubois overtly articulated a Pan-racial and Pan-Africanist ethos predicated on the dismantling of global white hegemony.[20] While many American's may have expected a return to the pre-war status quo, the war years had a tremendous impact on racial and gender relations.[21] For African-Americans the logic was simple, having waged a moral and physical campaign against the racial supremacy of Nazi Germany, they could not countenance submission to racial oppression in America or throughout the world.[22] Hence, Roark argues that African-American leaders 'emerged from ... [WWII] ... determined to battle for equal rights for ... [Black] ... citizens in America and for Nationhood for darker peoples abroad'.[23]

On the other hand, sensing the enormity of the problem, many African-Americans would confine their efforts to domestic race relations. Given the decline of the European powers and the Truman administration's ambiguity towards colonialism, AAFAN was uncertain how to proceed. Thus, between 1946 and 1950 AAFAN faced hard choices which would redefine African-American leadership for the foreseeable future. In the domestic context, African-Americans' desire to obtain racial equality was heightened due to the barbarity that southern whites inflicted on African-American WWII veterans.[24]

In a manner reminiscent of the violence inflicted on African-American soldiers after WWI, the South witnessed a wave of brutal terrorism in the form of lynchings and political assassinations.[25] While the hanging, burning and mutilation of African-American males and females was part of the South's political heritage, this overt barbarity became increasingly problematic. The fact that these acts of domestic terrorism were sanctioned by southern politicians and carried out by law enforcement personnel, and ignored by the federal government was a damming indictment on American democracy.[26]

It is unsurprising that battle-hardened African-American veterans would challenge southern terrorism.[27] In short, the brave men who had buried comrades and bled in defence of democracy found it demeaning and intolerable to comply with Jim Crow laws and the denial of voting rights.[28] Although southern racists believed they could stifle African-American discontent through violence and the maintenance of the status quo,[29] the trajectory of national and international history suggested otherwise.[30] Indeed, the South's overt racism would receive international criticism.[31]

AAFAN's use of interest group politics during WWII and the formation of the UN, in addition to the wartime rhetoric of de-colonisation, democracy, self-determination, human rights, racial equality and the UN Charter, helped facilitate their ideological assault on America's colour-line.[32] The increasing tensions between the Soviet Union and America at the time provided a bold but controversial opportunity to expose the racial fault line that undergirded American democracy.[33] The USA's and USSR's efforts to highlight the moral, political and economic supremacy of their respective political systems to a global audience meant that the UN became the centre of Cold War politics during the penultimate years of the 1940s.[34] The Soviets claimed that American-backed colonialism and racial oppression were indicative of US and Western duplicity, which resonated in the non-white world.[35] Sensing American vulnerability, African-Americans sought to expose America's dismal human rights record.[36]

The UN

The pivotal moment occurred in 1946 when the 'United Nations Commission on Human Rights was established'.[37] This led to a series of embarrassing challenges to America's international image; the first was orchestrated by the National Negro Congress (NNC), which was cofounded in 1936 by Ralph Bunche and John P. Davis.[38] The NNC had been established as a liberal organisation with links to the NAACP and key members of the black establishment.

The NNC had once listed A. Phillip Randolph as its president before he was ousted in 1940, due to its metamorphosis into a communist organisation under the direction of communist Max Yergan and John Davis, which triggered the resignation of Ralph Bunche and the NAACP's disassociation from the organisation.[39] Under the guidance of Du Bois,[40] the NNC exploited the weakness that the US State Department had hoped to nullify, i.e. the UN's Commission on Human Rights being utilised by 'individuals and groups throughout the world protesting against wrongs which might be righted by the Commission'.[41] State Department fears echoed the concerns of the foreign policy establishment that America's overt racism would provoke international scrutiny via the UN.[42] Evidently, the broader purview of the executive branch and experts on foreign affairs prompted their recognition that the illiberal character of US race relations was a liability for US foreign policy.[43]

Clearly, AAFAN understood what southern Dixiecrats and white supremacists had not, that US racism caused the non-white world to question the validity of America's liberal credentials, and provided the Soviets with damaging propaganda.[44] Accordingly, the NNC crafted a scholarly petition that identified the scandalous inequalities visited on African-Americans and professed:

> Profound regret that we, a section of the Negro people, having failed to find relief from oppression through constitutional appeal, find ourselves forced to bring this vital issue, which we have sought for almost a century since emancipation to solve within the boundary of our country, to the attention of this historic body.[45]

The petition was sent to Truman and the head of the UN, Secretary General Trygve Lie.[46] The petition received national and international support from African-American and continental African leaders such as Kwame Nkrumah, Jomo Kenyatta and Nnamdi Azikiwe.[47] Evidently, the seeds of Pan-Africanism were bearing fruit as key African leaders noted the similarities between American racism and the racial foundations of European colonialism. Likewise, the African-American press acknowledged its support for the petition.[48] According to Carol Anderson, much to the consternation of the FBI and the State Department, the petition received both support and wide circulation in the Middle East.[49] 'In addition groups in Bolivia and the West Indies ... [and] ... almost 20 organizations in the United States, including the NAACP and several locals of the Congress of Industrial Organizations (CIO), wrote to the UN in support of the NNC's petition.'[50]

Moreover, the Soviet Union used the petition and a spate of lynchings in the American South to discredit American democracy.[51] However, the Soviet Union's propaganda allowed critics to question AAFAN's judgement and characterise African-Americans as Soviet dupes, or potential fifth columnists.[52]

Despite the realities of African-Americans continued oppression at the hands of the US government and Euro-Americans, UN officials requested that the NNC prove that African-American rights were being violated in America.[53] Of course, the issue was less about the NNC provision of evidence and more to do with the great powers' desire to prevent subordinate groups from using the UN to undermine the principal of state sovereignty, which was an issue for both superpowers.

While the NNC petition petered out due to the lack of financial resources, it had struck a raw nerve, to the extent that the Indian government lodged a complaint to the UN regarding South Africa's discriminatory practices against Indian workers.[54] In short, the NNC had created a dangerous precedent in regard to the provocative issue of race within the global context.

While the NAACP had distanced itself from the NNC, it was not above adopting the tactics of the NNC by continuing to criticise European colonialism and the racial undercurrents of British and American foreign policy.[55] Since the return of Du Bois, the NAACP had resumed and extended its international lobbying and its Pan-Africanist outlook due to his tireless campaigning.[56] As early as February 1946, the NAACP and the black press had blasted both Churchill's reference to the 'iron curtain', which called for 'a fraternal association of the English speaking peoples',[57] and Truman's pledge to protect Greece and Turkey. AAFAN argued that the concern for European freedom should be reflected in America's treatment of African-Americans and people of colour.[58] In this regard, *The Chicago Defender* noted that the containment of Russia would facilitate the maintenance of colonialism and white supremacy.[59] The contradictions of the Truman doctrine's fixation with freedom and democracy was elucidated by Ralph Matthews in the Baltimore *Afro-American*, who argued that the Truman doctrine meant 'that America ... [had] ... been duped into carrying the imperialist load of the British Empire'.[60]

AAFAN's critique of colonialism was telling as Du Bois' petition to the UN, *An Appeal to the World*, submitted on 23 October 1947,[61] identified the links between colonialism and African-American's oppressed status.[62] AAFAN recognised that colonial conquest had been founded on notions of racial and Western supremacy.[63] That being the case, the petition garnered the support of Nnamdi Azikwe who saw the petition as integral to the struggle against colonialism and called for a strategic alliance between African-Americans and their black counterparts in Africa.[64] Unfortunately for Du Bois, while *An Appeal to the World* received support from abroad, erstwhile allies began to baulk at the controversy elicited from the publicity generated from the appeal.[65] Eleanor Roosevelt, a staunch ally of Walter White and a board member of the NAACP, and the UN Economic and Social Council, took exception to the petition,[66] viewing it 'as an embarrassment ... [that would aid] ... the Soviets in the emerging Cold War'. Therefore, she worked hard to prevent the petition from making any progress.[67]

With mounting criticism from the liberal establishment on both sides of the colour-line, the elder statesman's plans unravelled as the sympathies of some white liberals were not sufficient to place African-American interests above the white establishments. Likewise, whether out of friendship, fear, or loyalty to the Euro-American elite, Walter White, the NAACP and the black establishment reined in their support for the petition and the internationalist thrust championed by Du Bois, and sought both safety and favour by embracing the core precepts outlined in the Truman administration's National Security agenda.[68] Unsurprising, Du Bois was summarily dismissed from the NAACP, for his leftist leanings and his failure to embrace Walter White's and the NAACP's ties to the Truman administration.[69] Evidently, the politics of power, race and national security were converging on AAFAN and respectable African-American leaders who, coveting their insider status, deferred to their white allies and accepted the logic of Soviet containment.[70] Still, as future events would prove, AAFAN's interest or commentary on foreign affairs was not completely compatible with mainstream interests.

An alternative analysis of AAFAN's conformity with the Truman administration credits Truman's racial reforms for securing black loyalty.[71] As despite harbouring his own racial attitudes, President Truman articulated a message of hope that resonated with some African-Americans.[72] Significantly, that message found expression in a number of attempts to redress the racial imbalance.[73] Given the realities of Cold War politics, Truman's Paulian conversion to racial equality was indicative of his quest for votes in the 1948 presidential election and the propaganda value of championing racial liberalism to offset Soviet criticism.[74] With that in mind, African-Americans developed an allegiance to Truman based both on sentiment and on pragmatism. Therefore, the loyalty some African-American leaders displayed towards Truman was predicated on his efforts to address racism within the domestic context as opposed to an unquestioning adherence to his policies.

As the latter years of the 1940s progressed, African-Americans and AAFAN faced difficult choices as their efforts at internationalising their struggle drew negative publicity and scorn[75] but their calls for racial equality appeared to be reaping some benefits.[76] As the Cold War intensified, AAFAN's mainstream leaders were placed between a hammer and an anvil. The dilemma was twofold: should AAFAN provide uncritical support for US foreign policy given its efforts to maintain European colonialism? Since European colonialism implied that Europeans were best suited to governing non-white people, African-American leaders could not justify supporting colonialism. In short, AAFAN risked contravening the anti-colonial stance they championed throughout WWII. The road ahead appeared challenging. The NAACP's internationalism was still evident as it sent Walter White to Paris in September 1948 where 'he focused his efforts on establishing a powerful UN Trusteeship Council ... [and lobbied to obtain] ... a strong ... [and enforceable] ... UN Declaration on Human rights ... his specific efforts included getting the former Italian colonies and South West Africa placed under direct UN control'.[77] Albeit it a much more organic way, the CAA was pressing for independence for the African continent[78] while A. Phillip Randolph lobbied Dean Acheson, the US secretary of state, to prevent Italy from being granted access to her former colonies.[79] While AAFAN was still aligned with some of its core principles (in the late 1940s), the question was how long could it hold the line?

Despite African-Americans' relative ambivalence towards McCarthyism,[80] it is instructive to note that by 1950 sections of the black press and even the NAACP had caved into mainstream hysteria concerning anti-communism.[81] Indeed, for the majority of the liberal civil rights leadership, relative economic and socio-political advances and their desire to reflect mainstream views prompted them to conspicuously highlight their American identity.[82] Of course, the allegiance to America was encouraged by the fate that befell individual

African-Americans and organisations that dared to challenge 1950s conventions by criticising American foreign policy. The fates of Paul Robeson, Du Bois and William Paterson, the Civil Rights Congress (CRC), NNC and CAA were indicative of the peril of appealing to the global constituency or failing to denounce communism, much less support it.[83] Is it any wonder then that events in Africa would be accorded less importance by most American Negroes?

Apartheid

In short, African-Americans began to rein in their racial and global consciousness whilst highlighting their allegiance to white America.[84] As a result, AAFAN was less willing to support the struggle against apartheid.[85] In 1948, white peopele in South Africa elected Daniel Malan whose administration enacted a racial system akin to the Aryan supremacy championed by Hitler and the white supremist logic of America's Jim Crow laws.[86] It is ironic that scholars claim that WWII helped eradicate overt expressions of white supremacy when apartheid laws instituted extreme racial codes in 1948, a mere three years after the war.[87] Since, most scholars point to the West's post-WWII rejection of white supremacy, why did South Africa become an integral partner in the Western alliance? Obviously racial supremacy was not entirely incompatible with Western norms.[88]

Given the similarities between apartheid, Aryanism and Jim Crow, the events in Southern Africa should have elicited a major response from AAFAN and African-American's in general, especially since indigenous Southern Africans authored a prototypical non-violent civil rights campaign of their own from 1948 to 1953, which was aptly named the Defiance Campaigns.[89] Given AAFAN's prior internationalism, it would be difficult to ignore the impact of the Cold War[90] as the Malan regime increased 'the long-standing norms of White supremacy and racial segregation by solidifying their legal basis'.[91] In actuality, the reaction to events in South Africa exemplified African-Americans' connection and disconnection with Africa.

On the other hand, the Truman administration was deliberate in regards to taking an interest in South Africa.[92] The Truman administration's orientation to South Africa was based on three factors: America's National Security pertaining to South Africa's anti-communism, and her uranium and other mineral deposits, which solidified its significance to America's foreign policy elites.[93] In regard to South Africa, 'the US foreign policy establishment talked incessantly about the dangers of "premature independence" and the need to preserve White rule as long as possible'.[94] The point being, white rule chimed with the status quo and ensured US access to the required resources.[95]

This being the case, it is instructive that mainstream African-American leaders battled against American apartheid with scant reference to the Southern African variant and were conspicuous in their use of anti-communist arguments to denounce the Malan regime.[96] In short, while a young Nelson Mandela mobilised the African masses in a forerunner of the civil disobedience campaigns utilised by African-Americans, African-Americans' liberal establishment steered clear of articulating their support in Pan-Africanist or overtly racial terms.[97]

Obviously, the racial and global consciousness that empowered the African diaspora to wage war on apartheid in the latter part of the twentieth century[98] was deficient in the early 1950s. The problem was three-fold: most American Negroes had limited exposure to Pan-Africanism or black nationalism and lacked the racial and historical literacy to appreciate the grandeur of African history, and hence had no desire to be identified as an African.[99] In fact, the use of the term 'Negro' had circumvented an authentic identification with Africa.[100] Likewise, cultural and racial bigotry and the ethno-centric para-meters of American political culture coupled with anti-communism dis-couraged Negroes from acknowledging their hyphenated identity.[101] Henceforth, in the early 1950s, which were characterised by loyalty boards in both government and private institutions, most Negroes were quick to affirm their loyalties to America and America alone.[102] Consequently, the fragmented identity of the American Negro and the logic of integration and the Cold War tempered their activism in regard to the global dimensions of the colour-line.[103] Thus, for the time being, the domestic struggle and anti-communism occupied the Negro agenda.

Notwithstanding, after considerable encouragement, George Houser, Bayard Rustin and others established a working relationship with the ANC which led to the establishment of Americans for South African Resistance (AFSAR)[104] 'headed by the ministers Donald Harrington, George Houser and Charles Trigg ... [its membership included] ... notable black Americans such as Charles S. Johnson, Mordecai Johnson, Adam Clayton Powell Jr., A. Phillip Randolph, Rev James Robinson, Bayard Rustin, George Schuyler and William Sutherland'.[105] The CAA also authored a more aggressive campaign which AFSAR refused to join due to the CAA's communist sympathies which included a rally in Harlem and a picket line outside the 'South African consulate in New York City'.[106] While AAFAN's attempts to construct an African lobby were significant, the efforts at fundraising on behalf of Walter Sisulu and the ANC 'totaled less than half that raised for Ethiopia, and in much better economic times'.[107] Despite having an enlarged economic capacity, AAFAN's efforts were paltry.

As a result, the Negro establishment, including the Negro press, were pilloried by grass-root advocates of black unity, and NAACP efforts to halt American loans to South Africa were not sufficient for rank and file members of the NAACP, who demanded that the board establish a foreign affairs department and declare 'the problems of the colored peoples of the world are similar to the problems of Negroes in the United States'.[108] The irony being that Du Bois had been fired for his internationalist thrust and predictably the board rejected the members enlightened call to extend the NAACP's remit.[109] Although the ANC's defiance campaign ended in 1953 with limited results, it did inform some African-Americans' views on the global dynamics of white hegemony.[110]

Horace Cayton maintained that the events in South Africa 'might prove to be a lesson to people of color throughout the world' and noted that a variant of the defiance campaign might even work in the United States.[111]Alternatively, Max Yergan, the former CAA stalwart now a firm advocate of anti-communist zeal,[112] became an apologist for Western imperialism, and the Negro establishment touted the relative gentility of lobbying government officials and argued against the use of mass protests and confrontational tactics.[113] While the events in South Africa troubled some African-Americans, the events in Kenya would raise questions that would become central to the black struggle in the mid-1960s.[114]

Mau Mau

Controversy came in the form of the Mau Mau, a group prepared to spill blood to wage a war against British colonialism.[115] The Mau Mau had been conceived in the late 1940s[116] and for some would personify Africans waging a valiant struggle against white supremacy or the unbridled savagery of African militants.[117] Doubtlessly for some the fact that Mau Mau killed other Africans was less troubling than their willingness to kill white settlers.[118] From a Western perspective, the fact that the settler population had inherited stolen Kenyan lands from brutal imperialist wars was clouded by the horror of black violence against white people, in a manner not dissimilar to the actions of the war veterans in Zimbabwe at the dawn of the twenty-first century which were equally controversial.[119] During the 1950s and 1960s, mainstream African-American leaders had moral (and perhaps psychological)[120] misgivings about the use of violence in the struggle for racial equality.[121] Consequently, the Mau Mau raised questions regarding the appropriate response to white supremacy which would lead African-Americans to critique the ideological rigidity of the civil rights elite.[122] The fact that the British had engaged in warfare, banditry and racial oppression to obtain Kenya was lost on the moralists, who overlooked the fact that the Mau Mau were fighting to reclaim their ancestral lands.[123] Thus, while it was difficult to ignore the realities of colonial history, Western hegemony and a moral discourse hampered black liberals' ability to support an armed struggle.[124]

African-American support for the Mau Mau was also tempered by their willingness to kill other Africans despite the fact that the British had co-opted some Kenyan chiefs and created a class of pro-British Kenyans.[125] In short, some African-Americans found it difficult to accept the realities of revolutionary violence aimed at one's own group. Of course the problem lay in utilising a simplified racial schema without accounting for the complexities of political struggles. Nonetheless, most African-Americans condemned the arrest of Jomo Kenyata and the brutality of the British response to the Mau Mau, which was ruthless and somewhat undiscriminating against the African population in Kenya.[126] In regards to the four-year war between the Mau Mau and the British, the American government's reaction was predictable. As in the case of

South Africa, the US government was committed to the maintenance of white rule.[127] Obviously, America's viewpoint was antithetical to many Africans whose desire for freedom and Europe's post-war vulnerability fuelled and informed their struggle.[128] In actuality, America had no comprehensive foreign policy strategy for Africa South of the Sahara.[129] Despite the fact that a group of consultants, including Ralph Bunch and Tobias Channing, recommended that America denounce colonialism, the foreign policy establishment remained steadfast in support of their European allies.[130] Again, anti-communism Western hegemony and economics were responsible for America's continued support for colonialism.[131] Controversial as it may be, the racial world view of the foreign policy establishment was still a factor in US foreign policy. Still, one acknowledges that US officials recognised the need to walk a careful line which showed some empathy in regard to the demands of the African populations.[132] In this regard, the US State Department under Truman had a European contingent which argued that European colonialism would abate the rise of communism in Africa.[133] Alternatively, the opposing group suggested that overt white rule could propel Africans into the communist camp.[134] Nevertheless, both State Department factions saw black freedom as secondary to Western hegemony and anti-communism.[135] In truth, the Truman and Eisenhower administrations both adhered to Cold War logic by supporting colonialism.[136] Indeed, in the 1950s US officials generally regarded Africans as backward, to the extent that they supported colonial rule in Africa.[137]

For African-Americans, the Mau Mau created polar discourses that resonated beyond the events in Kenya. For example, the black press envisioned independence in Africa and characterised the British settlers as brutal land grabbers whose violence was compared to Adolf Hitler.[138] The black press also provided overt support for Jomo Kenyatta despite the fact that Kenyatta was not the author of the Mau Mau rebellion.[139] Still, anti-African propaganda encouraged American Negros to perceive the Mau Mau as embodying the pagan savagery that white Americans had fostered in the minds of the African population in America.[140] As a result, even the black press was goaded into reflecting the racial biases of the Western world to the extent that the Mau Mau was labelled as an anti-white cult.[141] The identification with the West's racial depiction of Africa was accompanied by Cold War logic which saw the struggle in Kenya from the stand point of America's struggle against communism.[142] For example, Max Yergen ridiculed the Mau Mau and labelled them as communists.[143] Members of the progressive intelligentsia and the CAA held a conference in support of the Mau Mau, whereby Du Bois decried African-Americans' lack of support for the struggle in Kenya.[144] Doubtlessly from Du Bois' perspective, aside from geography, the colour-line in Kenya was consistent with the racial status quo in America. Similarly, the CAA efforts to raise funds for the Kenyan struggle were as woeful as the efforts to aid the ANC.[145] True to form, African-Americans' liberal leadership class lobbied the US government to stem British violence which had no appreciable impact on the crisis in Kenya.[146] A. Phillip Randolph wrote to President Eisenhower denouncing colonialism and the Mau Mau's armed struggle, which Walter White also characterised as being evil.[147] The condemnation of the Mau Mau was not universal as the *Amsterdam News* was scolded by its grass-roots clientele for ignoring the international crisis in Kenya and forsaking the Pan-Africanist approach for local concerns.[148]

Evidently, the Mau Mau's armed struggle struck a chord with the racial consciousness of some African-American's who saw no contradiction in Africans and African-Americans fighting for their liberation.[149] Over time the Mau Mau's actions would assert greater influence on AAFAN as African-Americans began to formulate a tactical methodology which borrowed and recycled strategies used in Africa. In short, the ideological cleavages between integrationists and black nationalists were already present in the early 1950s to the extent that Dr King and others of his ilk gravitated to Kenyans, such as Tom Mboya who backed the creation of a Kenyan elite educated in American universities and identified with the socio-political norms of the West's liberal establishment.[150] Incidentally, it was Tom Mboya and African-American donors who brought 'eighty-one Kenyans, including (President) Obama's father, to study in the US'.[151]

Alternatively, Malcolm X and the black nationalist contingent perceived the Mau Mau as a positive example of an organic movement willing to end colonialism by any means necessary.[152] In short, the undercurrents of future battles were simmering as the non-white world was set to challenge the racial imperialism of the Western world.

Still, state repression played a significant role in African-Americans' failure to wholeheartedly back events in Africa.[153] As on the home front, as early as 1950, Du Bois was charged by the Justice Department as being 'an agent of a foreign government'[154] and arrested in this regard in 1951.[155] In brief, Du Bois was portrayed as an advocate of Soviet foreign policy.[156] Equally problematic was the NAACP leadership's failure to assist the scholar despite his innocence and overwhelming support from the African-American community.[157] While the case was unsuccessful, Du Bois' activism was slowed and his chastisement from a government agency served as an example to discerning Negro leaders such as Walter White.[158]

Paul Robeson and William Patterson, the civil rights attorney and the CRC were also subjected to racial repression disguised as anti-Communist patriotism[159] the 'Department of State revoked Robeson's passport in 1950 ... [due to his] ... frequent criticism of the mistreatment of African-Americans in the United States during his travels'.[160] In 1951, Patterson and Robeson struck a blow for freedom when Patterson presented a petition to the UN in Paris and Robeson presented their case to the UN in New York. The petition targeted the UN's Prevention and Punishment of the Crime of Genocide (which was established in 1948) to charge the US with committing Genocide against the African-American population.[161] The US State Department grudgingly admitted that the 'petition was well documented and carefully presented'.[162] 'The lengthy petition ... [highlighted] ... 153 killings, 344 crimes of violence against blacks ... [and numerous other abuses] ... between 1945 and 1951'.[163] Unsurprisingly, 'Robeson and Patterson were targeted for counterintelligence measures by the intelligence community'.[164]

True to recent form, the NAACP leadership worked to undermine the petition and rallied in defence of America's international image.[165]

The Truman administration countered Patterson and Robeson by using Walter White, Tobias Channing (a NAACP board member and alternate member to the US delegation) and black lawyer Edith Sampson, 'who had served on the US delegation' previously, to counteract the petition by refuting its claims to various audiences in Europe.[166] Still, such was the damage to American prestige that Paterson was placed under house arrest like Robeson and Du Bois.[167] In view of the NAACP's actions, Du Bois maintained that the NAACP 'had bleached its soul in a flood of white Americanism ... [in short by the early 1950s the NAACP's] ... quest for human rights was rapidly dissolving'.[168] Fortunately, the fight against racial repression was global and continued despite the limited engagement of AAFAN and the NAACP.[169]

For the time being, African-Americans focused their efforts on challenging the domestic strand of white hegemony. This was problematic as a thorough analysis of American history recognises the synergy between its domestic and international politics to the extent that domestic values have informed US foreign policy; consequently, America's ambivalence towards African independence would be reflected in the adherence to the racial status quo in America.[170] Nonetheless, the landmark 1954 Supreme Court ruling of Brown vs. the Board of Education represented a significant shift in America's racial consciousness.[171] This raises the question: why would the American state appear to favour the maintenance of white rule abroad while undermining it at home?

First, the separation of powers which sanctioned the creation of the Judicial, legislative and executive branch of government[172] was a key factor in the events of 1954. Especially given the power of the southern cohort in Congress and that President Eisenhower's segregationist sympathies made him reluctant to address the issue of racial reform.[173]

In short, the judicial branches' ability to rule on cases without direct interference from the presidency or the two houses of Congress[174] provided the autonomy to overrule the Plessy vs. Ferguson Supreme Court ruling of 1896, which had legally sanctioned segregation in the American South.[175] Again, why did the Supreme Court overturn a previous ruling? Of course the legal victories of the NAACP in regard to desegregating higher education played a key role in the 1954 ruling.[176] In addition, the insight of the Warren Court was a significant factor in the 1954 ruling.[177] Nonetheless, the Supreme Court Justices were aware of the realities of Cold War politics, especially since the Justice Department brief compiled prior to Eisenhower's (1953–61) inauguration emphasised the importance of the international context in regard to the Brown decision.[178] The point is desegregation was a soft power stratagem[179] to enhance America's global profile, and to counter Soviet propaganda and increase America's credentials in the non-white world.[180]

In accordance with the goals of America's foreign affairs establishment, the 1954 Supreme Court ruling was heralded as a major achievement in Africa and Asia, which enhanced the reputation of American democracy.[181]

Whilst traditional civil rights literature contextualises the Brown decision in the domestic context, the Truman administration and groupings within Eisenhower's foreign affairs contingent, such as 'Foster Dulles and the State Department, were enthusiastic about the benefits of the decision for America's foreign relations'.[182] Rather than viewing racial reform as a moral imperative, the strategic planners within the foreign affairs establishment used it as political leverage within Cold War politics in order to further America's national security priorities.[183] Thus the desire for racial reform among sections of America's elite was to stem domestic agitation and to obtain diplomatic kudos and enhance America's international standing. Unfortunately, America's propaganda victory from the Brown ruling was short due to the historic gathering at Bandung in Indonesia.

The proceedings at Bandung marked a turning point in world history:[184] first, by representing an overt recognition that non-whites were prepared to utilise their demographic superiority over the white world; second, that their numerical advantages should be wielded into a powerful bloc to counter Western hegemony; and third, that the developing world was willing to pursue a non-alignment strategy to avoid taking sides in the Cold War.[185] The Bandung conference recognised that despite the different variants of Western imperialism it was characterised by its adherence to a hierarchical racial structure.[186] That is, the 'representatives of the twenty-nine nations from Asia, Africa and the Middle East'[187] acknowledged that race had been used to justify their subordination to the West. Conversely, Europeans and the Eisenhower administration were dismayed that white nations had been excluded from the conference; consequently, the West viewed the conference as anti-white and pro-communist.[188] Henceforth, 'the Eisenhower administration sent no greetings to the conference and did its best to ignore or sabotage it ... [Indeed] ... Foster and Alan Dulles agreed in January 1955 that Bandung likely portended an aggressive new communist strategy in Africa'.[189] In reality, the presence of China and pro-communist elements was countered by pro-Western factions at the conference.[190] AAFAN's response to the events at Bandung reflected the complexities of Cold War politics. On the one hand, the 'African-American press widely hailed the conference as a turning point in history ... noting the clear challenge to White supremacy ... the *Defender* predicted that the Asian-African Conference would "undoubtedly pose a problem for the United States, Great Britain and anti-capitalist Russia".'[191]

Still, AAFAN had limited interaction with the conference due to the limitations imposed on African-American internationalism. For example, both Du Bois and Robeson were prevented from attending due to the travelling ban imposed on them by the US government arising from alleged communist sympathies and their criticism of US foreign policy.[192] A defiant Du Bois wrote to the conference and declared that because of my 50 years of service in the cause of the 25 million coloured peoples of America I venture of my own initiative to address you in their name, since the United States will not allow me to attend this meeting ... [while Robeson stated] ... the time has come when the coloured peoples of the world will no longer be exploited ... by the Western World.[193]

In addition, Du Bois and Robeson expressed their distaste for the West's racial imperialism within the floundering CAA's new newsletter *Spotlight on Africa* (created in 1952) as the organisation battled against government repression to maintain the fight to dismantle the global colour-line.[194] AAFAN's dilemma was characterised by the actions of Congressman Adam Clayton Powell, who had demonstrated a previous commitment to international relations and a willingness to challenge US foreign policy prior to the Cold War.[195]

Despite Powell's recommendation that the State Department send American delegates to the conference, it refused and sought to prevent him from attending Bandung.[196] Although Powell was critical of the Eisenhower administration's ambivalence towards Bandung,[197] his attacks on Chou En-Lai of China and Paul Robeson uncharacteristically cast him as a defender of US foreign policy and Western hegemony,[198] to the extent that the black press charged Powell with adopting the establishment line and neglecting African-American interests.[199] Max Yergan, a recipient of State Department funding to facilitate trips to South Africa, Nigeria, Liberia and Senegal did his best to downplay the significance of global white supremacy and colonial repression.[200]

Of course, the approach adopted by Powell and Yergan did not occur in a vacuum as both men embraced the conceptual framework crafted by America's Euro-American elite in order to avoid censor and undoubtedly to reap the rewards. Powell's defence of US race relations garnered support from the mainstream press and the political establishment.[201] Erstwhile maverick or not, Powell recognised the benefits of evoking the national security ethos.[202]

Overall, the conference identified the commonalities endured by people of colour, which, although tempered by ideological, cultural and political cleavages, would continue to factor in UN and world politics,[203] to the extent that shortly after the conference James L. Hicks argued that the UN General Assembly vote to 'include the question of freedom of Algeria on the agenda'[204] was a by-product of the solidarity forged at Bandung. Meanwhile, for the Nation of Islam and a relatively unknown Malcolm X, Bandung exemplified the racial awakening that would signify the end of white supremacy.[205] The global narrative concerning race was about to shake America as the Eisenhower administration and the US foreign policy establishment would be beset by the activities of Rosa Parks, Dr Martin Luther King and events in Alabama and Arkansas as race and Cold War politics converged on America.

Montgomery

The Montgomery Bus Boycott was a seminal moment in African-American history, not because it was an unprecedented act of defiance, rather Rosa Parks' refusal to give her seat to a white passenger[206] and her arrest represented a continuation of the struggle against the humiliation of Jim Crow. Likewise, the arrest of teenager Claudette Colvin had foregrounded the issue in Montgomery prior to the courageous actions of Rosa Parks, even the boycott itself which commenced 'on 5 December 1955 ... [and] ... lasted for 381 days and ended in a resounding victory'[207] was not a new tactical innovation within the context of the struggle to end Jim Crow.[208] A holistic appraisal of the events pertaining to Montgomery Alabama should posit them as part of a global struggle against white hegemony. Although the bus boycott received significant international attention,[209] its significance has been circumscribed by a domestic discourse that fails to link African-Americans' actions with the campaigns for racial justice in South Africa, Kenya, the Gold Coast and numerous battles against Western and racial domination. The boycott was important as it indelibly weaved the names of Rosa Parks and Dr Martin Luther King into the fabric of twentieth-century history.[210] In addition, the eventual desegregation of the Montgomery Bus line would help fuse the NAACP's legal approach to racial equality with the paradoxical confrontational tactics of King's strategic non-violence approach.[211] The fact that King's ideological and tactical conversion into the discipline of non-violence was facilitated by Bayard Rustin is noteworthy as he was doubtlessly familiar with the ANC's use of civil disobedience in their defiance campaign, which he had supported as a member of AFSAR. Needless to say, Dr King would utilise strategies that Indians and Africans used to discredit colonialism and racial apartheid, which attests to the global dimensions of the struggle against racism where the participants adopted tactics used within the international context.

The fact that AAFAN and civil rights leaders made scant reference to the international dimensions of the struggle accorded with Cold War norms, which, like mainstream versions of the war on terror discourse, deemed foreign influences as somewhat subversive.[212] This is substantiated by King's inaugural speech on assumption of leadership over the Montgomery Improvement Association as he disavowed any connection between African-American demands and communism.[213] While the courage and strategic genius of the leadership of the Montgomery fraternity were key, their victory corresponded to 'pressures for racial reform that ... [emanated from] ... the presidential and international level in the early Cold War years'.[214]

Despite being a revered war hero, President Eisenhower's personal and political convictions were opposed to enforced desegregation; in brief, his empathy for the South's racial norms was responsible for limiting his administration's involvement in the battle for desegregation.[215] Irrespective of appearances, many whites, both liberal and conservative, were troubled by the tenacity of African-Americans' fight for justice.[216] In the South, whites battled against civil rights in two distinct manners: one variant appeared respectably clothed in genteel defiance involving legal and other non-violent means to argue the case for the state's rights, this approach chimed with the views of 'Powerful US senators like Strom Thurmond and Richard Russell [who] believed that racial integration would subvert the fundamental social order of the United States'.[217] The underbelly of southern resistance relied on a long tradition of brutality and violence to thwart the aspirations of African-Americans.[218] One act of savagery involved the murder of fourteen-year-old Emmett Till in Mississippi who 'was pistol whipped ... before been driven to the Tallahatchie River ... shot ... in the head ... before tying a three-foot-wide cotton ginning fan around his neck with barbed wire ... [and then] ... thrown ... [into the river].[219] Evidently, white America and the federal government could tolerate the frequent murders of African-Americans[220] as the murder and mutilation of this young boy did not spur the Eisenhower administration into action against the South!

Little Rock

In brief, the events at Little Rock Arkansas became a pivotal test for American democracy in regard to the implementation of the Brown ruling. In relative terms, Arkansas' response to the Supreme Court's desegregation order seemed reasonably moderate.[221] Nonetheless, the events of 4 September 1957 pre-cipitated a major national and international crisis when nine African-American students sought to integrate 'Little Rock's Central High school ... their admission had been ordered by a federal district court. However, just two days earlier, Arkansas' Governor, Orval Faubus, declared that the students' enrolment threatened "imminent danger of tumult, riot and breach of peace and the danger and the doing of violence to persons and property"'.[222] Faubus mobilised the state's national guard to prevent the African-Americans' attendance. Unfortunately, Faubus, Eisenhower and the US foreign policy establishment had not reckoned with the power of television cameras to communicate the hatred and violence of white supremacy to the national and global audience.[223]

In a way, the events at Little Rock recalled civil war hostilities in regard to states' rights versus federal authority.[224] Rather than morality or a commitment to racial equality, scenes such as the television coverage of fifteen-year-old Elizabeth Eckford halted by 'armed soldiers and screaming whites bearing down on a black girl with books in her arms and incomparable courage'[225] caused Eisenhower to respond. These scenes rattled the world's conscience and questioned America's commitment to racial equality.[226] Given Eisenhower's failure to enforce a federal court order to admit Autherine Lucy into the 'University of Alabama'[227] and his basic ambivalence towards the Brown ruling, his lack of commitment to civil rights was predictable. In actuality Eisenhower's intervention at Little Rock reflected his desire to comply with federal law and to defend national interests.[228] Thus Eisenhower's decision to send in federal troops (on 24 September) was geared to upholding the law by complying with the desegregation order. Eisenhower's message to 'Faubus ... emphasize[d] that "when ... [he] ... became President ... [he] ... took an oath to support and defend the Constitution of the United States ... [he stated that] ... The only assurance I can give you is that the Federal Constitution will be upheld ... by every legal means at my command".'[229]

Furthermore, the president and the foreign policy establishment sought to counteract the damage that Little Rock was inflicting on America's international profile;[230] as the Soviet Union was able to exploit the crises by emphasising America's white supremist tendencies.[231] Similarly in the developing world and Europe, America bore the brunt of increasing criticism; given Europe's abysmal treatment of its colonial subjects, Little Rock highlighted US hypocrisy and provided leverage for the Europeans to discourage America's interference in European affairs.[232]

John Foster Dulles was adamant that 'the Little Rock crisis, along with school desegregation battles elsewhere in the South, "are not helpful to the influence of the United States abroad"'.[233] Dulles' views were verified by Layton who indicated that Africans and Asians capitalised on Little Rock in order to question US foreign policy and the policies of the Eisenhower administration.[234] Indeed, 'rejecting American warnings about communist influence in South Africa, Nelson Mandela declared that Africans "do not require any schooling from the USA, which ... should learn to put its own house in order before trying to teach anyone else"'.[235] In brief, the Eisenhower administration's resolution of the crisis was partly designed to impress a foreign audience.[236] Eisenhower indicated his core concerns regarding Little Rock by stating, 'it would be difficult to exaggerate the harm that is being done to the prestige and influence'[237] of the United States abroad.

Borstalmann illustrates the transnational character of the Eisenhower administration's racial bigotry by alluding to several incidents and statements such as the 'White House chief of protocol complain[ing] about having to invite "these Niggers" from Africa to receptions ... [and highlights that Eisenhower's] ... racial thinking influenced his evaluation ... of the two States he most feared, the Soviet Union and the People's Republic of China'.[238] The Eisenhower administration's perceptions of the Chinese consisted of antiquated racial stereotypes, while the Soviet Union's precise racial categorisation eluded the Americans.[239] Still, the Caucasian origins of the Soviet ruling class eased anxieties from a racial standpoint as America's chief rival was at least governed by white people. As the 1950s drew to a close, racial issues intensified as the struggle for independence gathered steam and the racial imperialism that had defined the nineteenth century was on the retreat. Although AAFAN's internationalist thrust had declined due to the Cold War paradigm and state-sanctioned repression, events in Africa help redefine African-Americans' racial, historical and international consciousness.

Ghana

The Pan-Africanism pioneered by H. Sylvester Williams in 1900 had reached beyond the hulls of slave ships to remind an assorted cadre of Negro intellectuals that they were the lost progeny of Africa. For most black people, esteem, self-loathing or indifference to Africa was triggered by exposure to limited but self-affirming histories and suggestions of a great African past or the negative associations that Western culture attributed to being black and African.[240] Since African-Americans had limited exposure to the writings of their own intellectual class, such as David Walker and Martin Delaney, and historians, such as J.A Rogers and Carter G. Woodson, their views on Africa where based on specific events and a fractured group consciousness. One such historical event involved the struggle to decolonise the Gold Coast. The Gold Coast tended to resonate with diasporean Africans because of the multitudes of forts built to house enslaved Africans[241] prior to the middle passage and due to the large numbers of Africans taken from the west coast of Africa.[242] In addition, the Gold Coast had been a beneficiary of the work of Marcus Garvey, W. E. B. Du Bois and a myriad of diasporean Africans whose racial consciousness had stirred West Africans' racial consciousness.[243] Given the centrality of Francis Nkrumah to the independence movement, it is noteworthy that Nkrumah and Nnamdi Azikiwe, who became Nigeria's first head of state, received a political awakening during his studies at Lincoln University in Pennsylvania,[244] a historic institution whose alumni helped reshape US race relations.

Nkrumah began his studies at Lincoln in 1935 and, 'it was in the USA that Nkrumah became politically active ... influenced by ... Garvey's UNIA ... [and] ... the Council on African Affairs'.[245] According to John Henrik Clarke, Nkrumah was tutored in racial and black consciousness via the black nationalists and street orators in Harlem (where he resided).[246] Nkrumah was active in a number of Africanist study groups such as the 'Blyden society, named after the great nationalist and benefactor of West Africa Edward Wilmot Blyden ... [indeed Clarke] ... remember[ed] Kwame Nkrumah attending several meetings of this society'.[247]

On his return to London in 1945, Nkrumah became acquainted with George Padmore and became an avid Pan-Africanist and cultural nationalist.[248] This is verified by his decision to reject his European name in favour of his African name, Kwame, in addition to his role in organising the 1945 Pan-African Congress.[249] Ironically, Nkrumah's immersion into the racial consciousness of diasporean and racially politicised continental Africans ignited his African consciousness, which influenced his decision to promote the value of an organic African identity. Similarly, Barack Obama underwent his own metamorphoses due to racism, dialogue with fellow African-Americans and the writings of Malcolm, Fanon and others of that ilk.[250] Ultimately, Obama's respect for his African heritage allowed him to embrace Barack and discard Barry which culminated in a life-changing trip to Kenya.[251]

On his return to Africa in 1947, Nkrumah re-contextualised the transnationalist theorems of Pan-Africanists from the West and used them to modify his political outlook when he returned to the Gold Coast in 1947.[252] Hence, while African-Americans were struggling against Euro-American racism in Montgomery and Little Rock, Ghanaians under the leadership of Nkrumah and the Convention Peoples Party (which he founded in 1949)[253] were fighting European hegemony in Africa. Still, the black press fluctuated between interest and ambivalence[254] due to centuries of conditioning which had furnished them with Western biases towards Africa. However, as British concessions to Ghanaians increased, African-Americans, noting the Africans' successes, heightened their interest in the Gold Coast to the extent that the black press highlighted Nkrumah's connection to Lincoln University and implied that his leadership had benefited from his inculcation in African-American culture.[255]

On 5 March 1957, Kwame Nkrumah presided over the formal independence of the Gold Coast, which was renamed in honour of the ancient African kingdom of Ghana.[256] The independence of Ghana had a profound impact on the political consciousness of continental and diasporean Africans.[257] The impact was both immediate and long term, as proceeding generations of African-Americans received both psychological and practical benefits from the momentous event.[258] In time, African-Americans and diaspora Africans would, like Malcolm X and Obama, make pilgrimages to Elmina[259] and Cape Coast Castle to connect with the experience of enslaved Africans.[260] During the ceremony, the black press was captivated by the meeting between Richard Nixon and Dr Martin Luther King and the event's significance to US foreign policy;[261] nonetheless, the black press conveyed a sense of pride and racial redemption in its tone and expression.[262] The fact that Dr King attended was indicative of his interest in Africa and international affairs and his racial pride.[263] Indeed,

> the independence of ... Gold Coast ... [was] ... a starting point for a greater interest and more sophisticated understanding of Africa on the part of African-Americans.
> Indeed ... independence ... prompted an outpouring of interest ... in Ghana ... Africa as a whole on the part of black Americans.[264]

However, some African-Americans insisted on contextualising the Ghanaians' victory within the context of the Cold War.[265] Despite the fact that George Padmore, Nkrumah's adviser and architect of Ghana's independence, endorsed policies designed to attract Western investment, The Defender argued that Russia saw it as 'a golden opportunity to secure a political foothold through a Marxist introduction of an economic, materialistic way of life for Africans'.[266]

The fact that African-American leaders travelled to Ghana was indicative of the pride derived from the event; they, like people of African descent throughout the world, rejoiced at Ghana's independence.[267] The number of African-American notables who attended the independence celebrations denotes the importance that they placed on Africa. Adam Clayton Powell Jr. commented,

Nothing in my public life of 27 years has attracted the attention and attendance of colored American leadership as has Ghana. Those who made the trip included Martin Luther King Jr., head of the Southern Christian Leadership Conference; Lester Granger, executive director of the National Urban League; A. Phillip Randolph, president of the Brotherhood of Sleeping Car Porters and vice president of the American Federation of Labor; Ralph Bunche, United Nations undersecretary for special political affairs, representing Dag Hammarskold and the United Nations; Adam Clayton Powell Jr., congressman from New York; and Charles Diggs, congressman from Michigan; Horace Mann Bond, president of Lincoln University; John Johnson, president and owner of the Johnson Publishing Company; Dr C. B. Powell, editor and publisher of the *Amsterdam News*; John Sengstacke, editor and publisher of the *Defender*; Claude Barnett, head of the Associated Negro Press; Shirley Graham Du Bois, representing W.E.B Du Bois, whose passport had been revoked and not yet reinstated; William Sherrill, president of the Universal Negro Improvement Association; Rev. James H. Robinson, founder of Operation Crossroads Africa; and numerous religious dignitaries, representing the National Baptist Convention of the USA, Inc., the National Baptist Convention of America, the African Methodist Episcopal Church, the African Methodist Episcopal Zion Church, and the Christian Methodist Episcopal Church.[268]

Even the Eisenhower administration (1953–61) had to adjust to the new circumstances by recalibrating its position on colonisation;[269] in short, in light of America's reliance on African resources, the foreign affairs establishment had to feign support for African independence to secure allies at home and abroad.[270] Whether the executive branch formally acknowledged the linkages between African-Americans and Africans' quest for justice, racial equality was a global issue.[271] Hence, America could not ignore colonisation, especially when Dr King was already articulating the links between southern segregation and colonialism in Africa (which has largely been ignored) which were both predicated on racial supremacy.[272] According to an understudy to John Foster Dulles, who returned from Africa in 1958, Africans possessed a negative perception of white people ranging from ambivalence to hatred.[273] Essentially the United States was fighting a battle on two fronts, hence Richard Nixon's adoption of a liberal approach to racial equality during the Ghanaian independence ceremony.[274] Vice-president Nixon, who was not known for being racially liberal, recommended that America should create a bureau for African affairs in the State Department to accord with Africa's strategic importance.[275] In accordance with Nye's thesis,[276] Eisenhower, Nixon and a section of the foreign affairs establishment presented a pragmatic veneer of liberalism to advance US interests in Africa via the power of attraction.[277] This was crucial in regard to Ghana as Nkrumah was well acquainted with the realities of American racism. The immediate postscript of Ghanaian independence was a sense of hope and inspiration to leaders such as Dr King which helped them conceptualise an alternative identity outside of America and view the struggle in a broader historical context.[278] The nexus between the American Negroes' dual consciousness regarding being American and African prompted Richard Wright's exploration into his 'blackness' via the book *Black Power* where he fell short of accepting his African origins.[279] The *Afro-American* responded to Ghanaian independence in its editorial, 'proudly We Can Be Africans' the paper declared. 'We submit that it is time Americans took the designation "Negro" out of the shadow. With the increased importance of Africa in the world and the UN, those of us of African descent can take justifiable pride in the continent from which our forebears came. From now on we should refer to ourselves as Africans, rather than colored people or Afro-Americans or "Negros" when such designation becomes necessary'.[280]

Conclusion

Such was the fervour surrounding Ghana that AAFAN rekindled its interest in international issues. However, the McCarthyite purges and the dictates of US foreign policy had decimated the foreign affairs visionaries from the 1940s who had challenged Cold War policies. That is, the US government's targeting and neutralisation of select individuals including Du Bois, Paul Robeson, William Patterson and Josephine Baker had curtailed their activism and had the desired punitive effect of encouraging a neutered brand of internationalism.[281] In particular, the political assassinations of Du Bois and Robeson may have encouraged the new generation of black leaders to endorse a more state centric and rhetorical form of internationalism lacking any real practical engagement with transnational actors. Thus, while King's generation might touch on international issues, there was a narrower scope which gave precedence to domestic issues. Hence, King and the integrationist's wing of African-American leaders focused on desegregating the South and avoided an identity-based form of internationalism. To conclude, Walter White's and A. Phillip Randolf's pragmatic but costly decision to abandon the internationalism of WWII and the post-war period changed the character of African-Americans' struggle.[282] The NAACP's betrayal and dismissal of Du Bois and their retreat from the UN campaign on the behest of Mrs Roosevelt marked a turning point in AAFANs development. In short, access to the White House and the political establishment certainly bestowed benefits but it also tempered the politics of moderate African-American leaders, who basked in the reflected light of the establishment.

Still, the AAFAN did not completely abandon its anti-colonialist outlook, as the moderates tried to support the aspirations of Africa and Asia by applying Cold War rationales that suggested that European colonisation would propel Africans and Asians into the Soviet camp. Thus, moderate black leaders sought to encourage the Truman and Eisenhower administrations to refine its policies towards the developing world. On the domestic front, the NAACP's seminal victory in Brown vs. the Board of Education, the creation of SCLC, King's Campaign at Montgomery and Eisenhower's reluctant intervention at Little Rock amounted to major victories in domestic race relations. Overall the government's actions indicated that it was prepared to be more progressive in domestic politics.

Nonetheless, the prevailing winds of change that ushered in African-Americans courageous petitions to the UN and the ANC's defiance campaign, the Mau Mau rebellion in Kenya, Bandung and Ghanaian independence, represented a shift in American and international politics.

While the 1950s witnessed a conservative realignment of race relations, the 1960s would see a dramatic interplay between integrationists and black nationalist tendencies which would give birth to a new form of black consciousness. Though in reality, Elijah Muhammad and Malcolm X had already garnered a substantial following among the urban cohorts of black America which resonated with the global consciousness dedicated to the end of white supremacy. In the end, the ascension of Dr King and Malcolm X and a new crop of leaders would re-conceptualise and construct a mass movement in America that had a profound impact on America's domestic and foreign policy to the extent that assassination, non-violence, self-defence and war would become defining characteristics of AAFAN's experiences in the 1960s. On the one hand, the federal government would endorse a racial realignment while J. Edgar Hoover and government agencies would engage in a covert war on black leaders within the context of the Cold War and racial politics, which would eclipse the prior attacks on Marcus Garvey, Du Bois, Robeson and Elijah Muhammad.

7 Malcolm and Martin and the shadow of US foreign policy

This chapter provides insight into the international consciousness of two of the most controversial and acclaimed leaders of the African-American liberation struggle.[1] It departs from academic orthodoxy by highlighting Dr Martin Luther King and Minister Malcolm X's interest in foreign affairs. It also places Malcolm X's and Dr King's critique of US foreign policy within the context of America's Cold War politics and African-Americans' struggle for racial equality. While the chapter credits the mass mobilisation of African-Americans for precipitating the civil rights legislation of 1964 and 1965, it argues that desegregation was a foreign policy imperative and that the executive branch's support and sanction of a liberal racial agenda was part of America's national security strategy pertaining to the Cold War. The chapter illustrates that irrespective of the executive mandate to eradicate the legal aspects of racial oppression, the racial realignment did not extend to the arena of foreign policy. That is, the US government, foreign policy establishment and America's intelligence apparatus were generally unwilling to accommodate African-Americans' policy recommendations pertaining to foreign affairs. In short, the White Anglo-Saxon Protestant (WASP) elite desired to maintain their racial and ethnocentric hold over US foreign policy.

The exploration of the activities of King and Malcolm is significant as it highlights the state's response to both men and it demonstrates the state's failure to tolerate African-American criticism of US foreign policy, within a period of enhanced interest in racial issues. The examinations of the Kennedy and Lyndon Baines Johnson presidencies will indicate that the state's response to King's and Malcolm's forays into foreign affairs was generally belligerent, i.e., their criticism of foreign affairs was met by condemnation from the executive branch and counter intelligence measures. While the chapter acknowledges the state's preference for King's ideological standpoint and its differential treatment of both leaders, it indicates that the federal government sought to neutralise both King and Malcolm's efforts to transform international relations. Thus, despite the relative and clichéd association of militancy, self-defence and revolution with Malcolm X and moderation, non-violence and love ascribed to Dr King, both men drew the wrath of the Kennedy and Johnson administrations.

The chapter will focus on the latter part of each man's career, i.e., when foreign affairs assumed a greater priority in their respective activities. The core issues will include Malcolm X's Pan-Africanist approach to black liberation and his attempt to petition the UN to charge the United States for violating the human rights of African-Americans, and King's criticism of US involvement in the war in Vietnam and his calls for economic equality. King's activities will be interspersed with Malcolm's in relation to their increasing convergence and potential alliance, and end with King's post-1965 phase and his death in 1968, adopting a fluid approach that highlights the synergy between domestic and foreign affairs which will demonstrate the ideological and structural relationship between white hegemony at home and abroad. In this regard, the revolutionary trajectory of decolonisation in Africa is considered a key facet of King's and Malcolm's respective visions of a new world where people of colour could to determine their own destiny and redefine global politics.

The chapter will provide a short historical context which places Malcolm's organisational, ideological and respective activities within a broader international context, and is followed by an analysis of his and King's actions and the government's response. Given the goals of this text, it does not detail their respective assassinations or their domestic accomplishments, as, contrary to most (mainstream) literature on King and Malcolm, it places their activities within the broad context of a transnational movement against white hegemony.

The first section will contextualise the 1960s. This is followed by an analysis of Malcolm's early life which traces his political activism to his parents' political consciousness and covers his criminality and imprisonment, followed by his recruitment into the Lost Found Nation of Islam, and his eventual departure. This is followed by an exploration of Malcolm's articulation of revolutionary internationalism and his attempts to build organisational structures that reflected his black nationalist ideals, in addition to placing his assassination within the American and global context.

The 1960s

The 1960s was a pivotal decade in African-American history.[2] It was an era when the two main strategies of the African-American struggle, i.e. integration and black nationalism, fought for primacy in the black struggle.[3] With the independence of Ghana in 1957, the quest for freedom accelerated both in Africa and in the Caribbean as people of African descent struggled to end their racial oppression.[4] The trend continued as the United Nations declared 1960 to be 'The year of Africa'. No fewer than seventeen countries – Benin (Dahomey), Burkino Faso (Upper Volta), Cameroon, Central Africa Republic, Chad, Congo (Zaire), Gabon, Ivory Coast, Madagascar, Mali, Mauritania, Niger, Nigeria, Senegal, Somalia, and Togo – gained independence[5] that year. It is noteworthy then that during the 1960 presidential election, J. F. Kennedy (JFK) championed racial equality and African independence to attract black voters and win allies in the developing world.[6]

It was in the midst of this struggle that African-Americans' challenge to racial segregation and Euro-American hegemony would reach its greatest heights.[7] In the 1960s, the fundamental questions of civil rights, race, cultural and historical identity would be re-forged in the midst of a titanic national and international context[8] where success led to federal assistance, legal reprieve and interracial alliances and marches[9] but, according to Sam Yette, 'hope turned into hatred, dedication became disgust, and hands raised for help became clenched fists, and eyes searching for acceptance turned inward ... [*as*] ... Negroes turned Black ... [and] ... Blacks could see clearer what Negroes could not: If help would come, they, themselves would bring it'.[10]

Malcolm Little

During his tenure as an African-American leader, Malcolm X was referred to as America's angriest man;[11] however, given the historical context and his own personal history, Malcolm X like most African-Americans was subjected to the trauma of American racism.[12] Malcolm Little was born to Louise and Reverend Earl Little in Omaha Nebraska in 1925. 'Earl Little was ... president of the Omaha Branch of the UNIA, and Louise Little was responsible for sending news of Chapter activities to. ... the Negro World'.[13] According to Malcolm's eldest brother Wilfred, Little Malcolm and himself would travel to Detroit to UNIA meetings and bask in the glory of black history.[14] Hence Malcolm's black nationalist credo was ingrained in his youth as was his awareness of white racism as his house was firebombed when he was six by the Klan,[15] and the Little family accused the white supremacist Black Legion of murdering Reverend Little due to his promotion of Marcus Garvey.[16] Thus, Malcolm's conversion to the Nation of Islam's brand of black power was precipitated by his grounding in Garvey's Pan-Africanism, which even Elijah Muhammad had been influenced by.[17]

The death of Malcolm's father led to the mental breakdown of his mother and the break up of his family and his eventual drift into a life of crime first in Boston and then in New York.[18] While it is easy to write off Malcolm as a disaffected criminal, even in this phase in his life Malcolm showed glimpses of his conception of racial justice after being asked to report to the draft in 1943, as Malcolm informed the 'Army Psychiatrist ... Daddy-o, Now you and me, we're from up North here, so don't tell nobody ... I want to get sent down South. Organize them Niggers Soldiers, you dig? Steal us some guns, and kill us some crackers!'[19]

However, it was Malcolm's imprisonment in February 1946 at age 21 (for ten years on a burglary charge), of which he served six years at two facilities (the Charlestown State Prison and the Norfolk Prison Colony in 1948),[20] that altered his life, first under the tutelage of the jailhouse intellectual Bimbi who informed Malcolm of the power of the written word.[21] Malcolm had rejected education as a child when his white teacher, Mr Ostrowski, who, like his class mates, constantly referred to him as Nigger, destroyed his aspiration of being a lawyer by stating 'you've got to be realistic about being a Nigger. A Lawyer – that's no realistic goal for a Nigger'.[22] Given Malcolm's early baptism into the realities of US racism and his time to reflect in prison, although he was stunned when his younger sibling Reginald (a member of the Nation of Islam) told him that 'the white man is the devil ... [Malcolm maintains that his] ... mind was involuntarily flashing across the entire spectrum of White people ... [he] ... had ever known',[23] and this teaching permanently altered his life. Ultimately, Malcolm would embrace the teachings of the Nation of Islam (NOI) and utilise his time in prison to study and perfect his ability to propagate Elijah Muhammad's teachings.[24]

The NOI was formed in Detroit on 4 July 1930 by Fard Muhammad,[25] who preached a religious form of black nationalism with parallels with Garvey and Noble Drew Ali[26] which provided African-Americans with a transnational identity that called for the unification of people of colour and opposition to white supremacy.[27] In 1934, Elijah (formerly Poole) Muhammad assumed leadership after the departure of Fard and became the chief exponent of the organisation's teachings.[28] The NOI attracted intense state and federal scrutiny for hailing Japan's war effort, and advocacy of a race war led by Japan and encouraging blacks to evade the draft,[29] which Elijah 'served three years for in the Federal Correctional Institution at Milan, Michigan'.[30] Clegg indicates that the early history of the NOI was marked by the surveillance and counter-intelligence tactics of the FBI whose actions were dedicated to white hegemony domestically and internationally.[31] This trend continued to the extent that Malcolm X's prison letters, one of which he sent to President Truman in 1950,[32] were examined by the FBI in accordance to J. Edgar Hoover's desire to tie the NOI to (an imaginary)[33] communist plot against US democracy. Of course, Hoover's and the FBI's motives were also racial as he personally despised efforts to elevate the status of the American Negro and the organisation has a history of racial prejudice.[34]

Malcolm X

Still, what was anathema to Hoover attracted Malcolm as the NOI's religious and racial internationalism chimed with his Garveyite past. Once Malcolm was released from prison in August 1952,[35] he helped build the NOI at a feverish pace and after receiving personal tutelage from Elijah Muhammad, he became an assistant minister at Detroit's temple by the summer of 1953.[36] Subsequently, Malcolm helped to establish temples throughout America.[37] His organisational abilities, charisma and fiery intellectual caught the attention of the FBI and other US intelligence agencies, just as Elijah Muhammad had done previously.[38] However, unlike Elijah Muhammad, Malcolm's religious consciousness had a distinct and overt interest in Africa which accorded with his Garveyite roots.[39] In fact, Malcolm's African consciousness chimed with the anti-colonialist movement that was sweeping Africa, Asia and the Caribbean, which had increased steadily from the 1950s to the 1960s.[40] Essentially, Malcolm used the NOI's racial and religious paradigm to conceptualise international relations; as a result, his critique and condemnation of white America led to criticism of American and European foreign policy.[41] Such that while Malcolm was exhorting the so-called American Negro to unite against Euro-American hegemony, he made common cause with people of colour around the globe.[42]

The fact that Malcolm assumed leadership of Temple No 7 in Harlem, New York in June 1954,[43] in addition to becoming Elijah Muhammad's national representative, facilitated his interest in international relations, given New York's status as the UN headquarters and Harlem's reputation as the Mecca of the black world which had nurtured the ideological development of scores of black leaders.[44] In short, Harlem's black nationalist and Pan-Africanist ethos had helped shape the global consciousness that fired the revolutionary movements of the 1960s. Unsurprisingly, Malcolm embraced the spirit of Bandung which prompted liaisons with African and Asian Leaders.[45] As a result, Malcolm met Achmed Sukarno who was speaking at Adam Clayton Powell's Abyssinian Baptist Church in Harlem in addition to extending his personal and organisational networks with the Pan-Africanist and black nationalist contingent in New York.[46] Although mainstream white America discovered Malcolm and the NOI in 1959 via Mike Wallace and Louis Lomax's TV broadcast, entitled 'The Hate that Hate Produced', the nation was already on its way to expanding its global outreach.[47] Despite Elijah Muhammad's awareness that interactions with foreign governments would increase government attention, the NOI and Malcolm became the recipients of international attention.[48]

Indeed, the Eisenhower administration was clearly dismayed after receiving reports of Gamel Nasser's overtures to Elijah Muhammad[49] especially since, Nasser's Pan-Arabism and his criticism of the western world and his links to Nkrumah and other African revolutionaries did not endear him to America's foreign affairs elite.[50] Hence, fear of foreign sponsorship of the NOI from a hostile government and national interests prompted the US government to delay Elijah Muhammad's passport application in order to stifle the relationship between a foreign and domestic enemy.[51] As a result, Elijah Muhammad sent Malcolm on an ambassadorial mission to the East to meet with Nasser.[52] Malcolm was also hosted by Anwar Sadat,[53] another man who was destined for assassination, and travelled to various locales including Damascus, Jerusalem, Saudi Arabia and Jeddah; however, illness prevented his trips to Nigeria and Ethiopia. Although Malcolm was invited to make 'hajj', he declined preferring to reserve that privilege for his teacher.[54] Malcolm returned to New York on 22 July[55] with a greater appreciation of international relations and a renewed commitment to Pan-Africanism.

On 21 November 1959, Elijah Muhammad and two of his sons embarked on an extensive tour of North Africa and the Middle East which included Muhammad making the 'minor hajj' or 'umra'.[56] Nasser's rapport with Muhammad and his desire to recruit Muhammad to propagate Islam in West Africa was noted by the FBI as

During the leader's stay in Cairo, the FBI, through its office in Madrid, Spain, attempted to place stops on Visas of Muhammad and his sons ... [to prevent their entry into] ... Morocco and Algeria. The plan ... [was] ... designed to keep the Muslims from travelling to Senegal ... and discussing the American racial situation among ... [the Senegalese] ... [nonetheless] ... Muhammad and his sons did visit ... [West Africa] ... although they may have originally intended to do so.[57]

Unlike Malcolm, Elijah Muhammad was unimpressed with the realities of the East in terms of the extremes of wealth and poverty and the ethnic and cultural cleavages which undermined the racial unity so prized by the NOI.[58]

Although Elijah Muhammad greeted 1960 in Pakistan and his journey to the East consolidated his status as a Muslim leader in the West, his negative appraisal of Arab and African Muslims caused him to highlight his own teachings and put paid to ideas of a transnational Muslim alliance.[59] In short, Elijah Muhammad reasoned that flirtation with foreign affairs was one thing but a sustained commitment to foreign affairs would provoke more government surveillance, and in that he was right.[60] In brief, the understudy and his teacher would steer two different courses in regards to the pursuit of international alliances.[61]

Indeed, given the political climate, the foreign affairs and domestic activities of Malcolm X would draw increased interference from the US intelligence apparatus,[62] especially since the Eisenhower administration's final year was dominated by foreign affairs and race never strayed far from their concerns.[63] The Eisenhower administration had particular concerns with South Africa, Congo and Cuba.[64] The Sharpsville massacre lit the racial fuse in Southern Africa, then the independence struggle in Congo led by Patrice Lumumba and the communist challenge of Fidel Castro, and Castro's support of racial equality generated admiration from African-Americans and the non-white world.[65] African-American's quest for racial parity was apparent as they initiated the student sit-in movement 'in Greensboro, North Carolina ... [which] ... spread rapidly throughout the South'.[66] America's concern with Southern Africa and Congo involved securing their access to strategic minerals and Soviet containment which meant retaining the racial status quo.[67] Apparently, Eisenhower relied on the CIA to solve his foreign problems: 'in March 1960, according to former CIA agent David Atlee Phillips, the CIA decided to neutralise Castro ... who ... became one of three third world leaders ... that ... president Eisenhower and vice president Richard Nixon are alleged to have authorised the ... [CIA] ... to overthrow or assassinate in August 1960 (the others were Patrice Lumumba of the Congo and Rafael Trujillo of the Dominican Republic)'.[68]

Malcolm X compounded government concerns by supporting and interacting with Castro and Lumumba.[69] The Castro controversy involved problems with a midtown Manhattan hotel, however the African-American owner of the Theresa Hotel secured lodgings for Castro and the Cuban delegation to stay in

Harlem.[70] Castro invited NAACP officials including Robert F. Williams who had mobilised African-American self-defence units to repel Klan attacks in Monroe North Carolina and was allied with Minister Malcolm X and other Harlemites who supplied him with guns.[71] In a diplomatic Third World and racial coup on US soil, Castro met with 'Khrushchev ... Nasser ... Nehru ... [and] ... Malcolm X'[72] in Harlem.

Castro also visited the UN where Cuba and thirteen new African nations were admitted to the UN.[73] From a global perspective the spirit of Bandung was generating a serious threat to western interests. In New York, black nationalists and AAFAN were increasingly identifying with the interests of the new African nations as African diplomats 'turned to African-American leaders in Harlem for support ... [hence] ... Manhattan Borough President Hulan Jack, James Lawson ... Adam Clayton Powell, Jr., and Malcolm X – soon found themselves inundated with invitations to attend official embassy functions sponsored by Africans'.[74]

In addition to this, Kenneth Kaunda and speakers from Kenya, Liberia and the United Arab Republic participated in an anti-apartheid rally outside the Theresa Hotel on 16 April.[75] With Malcolm's open-air rallies denouncing US foreign policy and Pan-Africanist agitation and third world dignitaries, Harlem was a hive of foreign affairs intrigue.[76] Castro's invitation and meeting with Malcolm X on 20 September drew the displeasure of the CIA, the US State Department[77] and the FBI.[78] Not to mention Elijah Muhammad, who bore no love for godless communism and cautioned Malcolm to avoid entanglements with communists due to government repression.[79]

Malcolm's flirtation with revolutionaries elicited a response from the CIA as at '1:30 p.m. on 26 September, the CIA was notified that Malcolm X, in his capacity as a member of the twenty-eighth Precinct Community Council, was sponsoring "a large reception for Castro" on 2 October. A high level government official, the CIA memo said, had indicated a desire to discourage or prevent ... [the] ... reception from taking place'.[80] Nonetheless, the meeting took place.

However, it was the assassination of Patrice Lumumba that ignited the passion of Malcolm X[81] and the African-American leadership class including King.[82] Lumumba's short reign as head of state of the Congo, which began in 1960, was characterised by intense civil strife due to the secession of mineral-rich Katanga province under the leadership of Moise Tshombe.[83] Although Lumumba was brutally assassinated by Tshombe's forces on 17 January 1961, Tshombe was assisted by the Belgian and American governments.[84] Borstalmann argues that Lumumba's decision to obtain Soviet assistance to defeat Tshombe and his antipathy towards Belgian and Western hegemony sealed his fate. 'In late July Allen Dulles told Eisenhower that Lumumba was "a Castro or worse" who has been brought by the communists ... the president apparently granted permission to the CIA in late August to ... eliminate Lumumba'.[85] Kondo argues that the 'U.S. government orchestrated and aided Lumumba's murder, although its agents did not fire a bullet into his body.

The American intelligence community used' Congolese to secure their objectives.[86] Malcolm's single meeting with Lumumba and his racial loyality led to numerous speeches and interviews where he denounced America, Belgium and Tshombe for the murder of Lumumba.[87] Borstalmann alludes to the racial undertones of Western anger against the Congo as rumours of Congolese soldiers raping Caucasian women 'outraged the Belgian foreign minister ... [and became] ... the preoccupation of the White House and the State Department'.[88] Clearly rape is a despicable crime; however, white people seemed preoccupied with their mythical depiction of the black males' alleged fixation with white women, views which were cultivated in Europe and America as by-products of slavery and colonialism[89] and resonated with racial apartheid in South Africa and America.

Malcolm's concern over Lumumba's murder was reflected in a 1964 speech critical of the Johnson administration's dealings with Tshombe: 'the world knows Tshombe murdered Lumumba. And now he's a bed partner for Lyndon Baines Johnson ... the man you voted for ... [i.e. African-Americans] ... but I don't blame you, you were just tricked'.[90] In actuality, Malcolm's contempt for US foreign policy and domestic terrorism, such as the Los Angeles police officers' unwarranted assault on the NOI and the killing of Ronald Stokes (an official in the Los Angeles Mosque), and the murder of the four African-American girls in Birmingham, Alabama, contributed to his remarks about chickens coming home to roost after the assassination of JFK.[91]

Kennedy

The Kennedy administration (1961–63) encompassed a prolific period in regard to the domestic and international fight against racism.[92] During Kennedy's presidency, Elijah Muhammad, Malcolm X and Dr King were constantly making headlines. Indeed, from Pretoria to New York and Alabama, Africans and African-Americans worked to overturn the colour-line.[93] Despite Kennedy's messianic image, his presidency was dedicated to winning the Cold War not eradicating racism.[94] This is validated by his decision to retain Hoover and Allen Dulles as heads of the FBI and CIA, as both men were adherents to the racial status quo,[95] and the elevation of Europeanist George Ball to the post of under-secretary of state which facilitated the State Department's eurocentrism.[96] In actuality, Kennedy's orientation to race relations was concerned with global and domestic circumstances, including counteracting China's and the USSR's image as advocates of racial equality.[97] Kennedy, like Eisenhower, helped to sustain Pretoria's power, to the extent that the CIA was reputed to have helped capture Mandela,[98] whilst Hoover's FBI obsessed over fracturing the NOI leadership by separating Malcolm from Elijah Muhammad[99] and curtailing the popularity of Dr King.[100] Whether in South Africa or the American South, both the CIA and the FBI generally conformed to the maintenance of the racial status quo. Kennedy, like Eisenhower, used racial reform in conjunction with foreign affairs and domestic law and order.[101]

Malcolm rebuked Kennedy for failing to intervene in Birmingham, Alabama until black people abandoned non-violence and fought white people in the streets[102] Malcolm knew; Kennedy feared black people abandoning non-violence, plus the presence of television crews publicised southern racism which undermined America's image among new African nations,[103] the same African nations King used to exhort African-Americans to intensify the fight for freedom.[104] In 1961, James Reston's article in *The New York Times* had noted that African liberation was encouraging black America to increase their demands on white America.[105] The Kennedy administration tried to stunt civil rights activists' engagement with Africa. Hence JFK's and Dean Rusk's decision to convince 'King to cancel his scheduled UN testimony on apartheid in June 1963, to avoid "the danger that ... [America's] ... domestic racial policies will be made the focus of attention".'[106] Within the NOI, the FBI's counterintelligence schemes such as extensive phone tappings, surveillance, and the use of agent provocateurs, inflamed rivalries between Malcolm X and Elijah Muhammad's family.[107] In addition, the FBI used media sources to describe Malcolm as the heir apparent to an ailing Elijah Muhammad to intensify internal dissent.[108] Malcolm also chafed at civil rights activists and white critics who noted NOI inaction and its failure to retaliate against police brutality, which contravened its militant image.[109] Given existing tensions and the allegations of Elijah's adultery, Malcolm and his mentor's relationship faltered.[110] Still, Elijah Muhammad's conservatism regarding Malcolm's desire for retaliatory violence and his internationalism was designed to avoid government's repression.[111] In short, Malcolm's activism, sexual scandals and the fact that 'the CIA and the FBI ... [had] ... thoroughly infiltrated the Nation using ultrasensitive equipment'[112] allowed the state to destabilise Malcolm.

Malcolm contributed to his suspension by meeting with a number of the secretaries impregnated by Elijah Muhammad and by non-compliance with Muhammad's national directive that his ministers avoid any formal commentaries on Kennedy's assassination.[113] Of course, FBI files and NOI sources indicate that Elijah Muhammad was not upset over the death of Kennedy.[114] Indeed, even Dr King was recorded ridiculing the deceased president, which Hoover revealed to Robert F. Kennedy in addition to a request to increase the FBI's operations against King and Malcolm.[115] On 4 December 1963, Malcolm X, the NOI's national spokesman, was suspended by the Honourable Elijah Muhammad for commenting on the assassination President Kennedy.[116] The evidence suggests that (at minimum) government agencies including the FBI and the New York Police Department's (NYPD) Bureau of Special Services (BOSSI) instigated major counter-intelligence schemes which made Malcolm's suspension indefinite and help transform internal rivalries into a war between Malcolm and the NOI.[117] The FBI visited Malcolm during the suspension to solicit inside information and or recruit him with a view to reinstatement into the NOI as an asset.[118] Given Malcolm's status in the NOI and his leadership abilities, the government sought to neutralise his domestic influence. However, the intelligence apparatus increased its efforts to neutralise Malcolm after his suspension.[119]

Radical Pan-Africanism

In actuality, the US government saw Malcolm as a threat within the domestic and global context,[120] especially since Malcolm's departure from the NOI (after a string of death threats from the NOI) presaged a shift in his activities.[121] While the uninformed, including some academics, dismiss Malcolm X as a racist demagogue, few realise the threat he posed to US foreign policy in the mid-1960s.

On 8 March 1964, Malcolm announced his reluctant and permanent separation from the NOI.[122] Shortly afterwards he formed the Muslim Mosque, Inc (MMI), a black nationalist group which attracted a militant cohort of NOI defectors.[123] Malcolm called for African-Americans to control the economics and politics of the black community and to reconstruct their African identity.[124] Malcolm drew the attention of the 'FBI, Justice Department, State Department, Secret Service, CIA and Military intelligence'[125] by advocating that African-Americans should form armed self-defence units whenever the federal government failed to protect them.[126] Malcolm's statements prompted an FBI investigation of the MMI.[127] The goals of the MMI were also inimical to the US government, as Malcolm planned to elevate the black struggle from civil to human rights, thus creating the rationale to charge the US government with violating the human rights of African-Americans.[128] Malcolm adopted a transnational and racial worldview designed to convince African and Asian nations to petition the UN to intervene in America's domestic affairs.[129] With this in mind, Malcolm flew to Cairo on 13 April 1964 with the FBI monitoring his departure and the CIA tracking his movements abroad.[130] During his trip Malcolm was treated as a foreign dignitary in Saudi Arabia by King Faisal[131] and was welcomed by state officials in Nigeria, Ghana, Morocco and Algeria, and he received both acclaim and empathy for the plight of African-Americans.[132] During this trip Malcolm made 'hajj', which was a pragmatic and spiritual endeavour that aligned him with the Muslim world and, given his outward rejection of Muhammad's white devil thesis, helped ensure the possibility of an alliance with the civil rights leadership.[133]

On his return to the United States, Malcolm formed the Organisation of African-American Unity (OAAU) in June 1964.[134] The organisation was modelled on the OAU and was secular black nationalist and Pan-Africanist.[135] Malcolm hoped to get the organisation accepted in the OAU.[136] 'Moreover Malcolm claimed ... [the OAAU] ... was backed by new Afro-Asian states and refused to deny that Ghana—considered unfriendly by the State Department was one such state.'[137] The evidence is unequivocal: Malcolm was making waves and had made powerful enemies in the government and the NOI,[138] whose campaign to neutralise him was progressing and government agencies appeared unwilling to safeguard his life. On 9 July 1964, Malcolm flew to Africa for an (eighteen week) lobbying campaign to secure the UN petition.[139] He met with the following heads of state: Kenyatta, Nasser, Milton Obote of Uganda, Nmandi Azikiwe of Nigeria and Nkrumah.[140] The State Department's interest in Malcolm was political but also economic as the states that Malcolm visited had mineral resources which were critical to European and Western interests.[141] Equally, the said states were pivotal to Cold War interests, which was why 'military intelligence was constantly privy to State Department and FBI intelligence on Malcolm'.[142] Malcolm also attended the Second Cairo summit where Malcolm and fellow African-American Milton Henry allege they were monitored by a CIA agent.[143] Malcolm was granted observer status at the conference, and dialogued with the heads of states and revolutionaries and disseminated an eight-page memo which included these statements:

> we beseech the independent African states to help us bring our pro-blem before the United Nations, on the grounds that the United States government is morally incapable of protecting the lives and pro-perty of 22 million African-Americans ... in the interests of world peace and security, we beseech the heads of independent African states to recommend an immediate investigation into our problems by the United Nations Commission on Human Rights. ... We have been servants in America for over 300 years. We have a thorough knowledge of ... Uncle Sam. Therefore you must heed our warning: Don't escape European colonialism ... only to become enslaved by deceitful ... American colonialism.[144]

Malcolm's sense of peril was heightened by his hospitalisation after dinner, which doctors accredited to his consumption of a toxic substance inconsistent with food poisoning; hence, Malcolm concluded he was poisoned by CIA operatives.[145] Still, Malcolm's memo succeeded in getting the heads of state to pass a resolution that criticised the US government's tolerance of racial oppression at home despite lauding the 1964 Civil Rights Bill.[146]

Essentially, Malcolm had violated mainstream conventions by criticising America on foreign soil, in addition to promoting a Pan-African network capable of officially critiquing the United States.[147] Indeed, Malcolm was beginning to actualise his UN plan, which entailed encouraging the Afro-Asian bloc to use US racism to secure their own interests in regards to the United States.[148] More importantly, it was the first time African states had formally recognised their connection and kinship with the descendants of the enslaved Africans shipped to America.[149] Malcolm's efforts were not lost on the American press, who castigated him for trying to provoke a global race war and for flirting with communism[150] due to interviews with the Chinese media and meetings with Chinese officials in Ghana.[151] The press also alluded to NOI death threats[152] which the FBI and US officials failed to counteract.

Adding fuel to the fire, FBI claimed that Malcolm stated that he had received promises of support for his UN venture from African heads of state.[153] On 13 August 1964, M. S. Handler in *The New York Times* argued that the State and Justice Departments were concerned by Malcolm's UN campaign as they suggested it would be used in the Cold War context to discredit America.[154] *The Times* article elicited a response from one congressman who implored the State Department to counter Malcolm's activities.[155]

Shortly before the article, 'the Secretary of State's special assistant Ben Read asked a CIA executive to probe Malcolm's political and financial support. The executive had inhibitions because Malcolm was a US citizen and the CIA charter barred it from domestic functions. Read apparently dissolved the inhibitions by remarking Malcolm had for all practical purposes, renounced his US citizenship'.[156] Evidently two government officials were prepared to treat Malcolm as a foreign national.[157] Malcolm's actions caught the attention of Dean Rusk and President Johnson, and government officials who sought to ascertain whether he had been funded by China or Ghana to denounce US foreign policy.[158] Subsequently, the government unsuccessfully sought to charge the MMI and Malcolm under the 'Logan Act and the Foreign Agents Registration Act'.[159] The latter prevented Americans from fraternising with foreign governments while the other required that persons or organisations formally acknowledge employment by a foreign government. Kondo, Evanzz, and Carson provide credible evidence that government officials sought to contain Malcolm's assault on US foreign policy, to the extent that they contacted foreign governments in Africa and the Middle East soliciting information on Malcolm.[160] Alarmingly, US officials discovered Malcolm had informed an OAU official that he had initiated plans to raise recruits in Harlem to fight in the Congo.[161] Kondo maintains that 'he also began secretly meeting with African Leaders and Cuban Revolutionaries like Che Guevara to organize a continental army for service in the Congo'.[162]

The obvious rejoinder is: did Malcolm have the capacity to actualise his plans? Still, given the heightened tensions of US and global race relations and the Cold War, Malcolm's objectives were problematic as urban riots or uprisings and retaliatory violence were threatening to fracture US race relations.[163] In brief, Malcolm's Pan-Africanism had to be a concern as he organised cadres of the OAAU in America, Europe and Africa.[164] In addition, the rumours of foreign funding[165] had provoked a response and the fact that the Kenyan parliament voted in a resolution that voiced support for Malcolm and African-Americans' fight for freedom[166] was equally significant. In brief, the politics of Garvey, Robeson and Du Bois had found expression in a young charismatic leader[167] whose statements about the *Ballet or the Bullet, Message to the grassroots* and revolution and guerrilla warfare[168] had to have concerned the US government. Malcolm's characterisation of the United State's policies in Vietnam and the Congo as analogous with European imperialism[169] was problematic for the Johnson administration. In addition, appearances at Manchester University, Oxford,[170] the London School of Economics[171] and

Harvard[172] provided Malcolm with a grudging creditability amongst white people committed to an anti-establishment ethos.

Government repression

The US government grew increasingly concerned about Malcolm's impact on African governments who began to question America's commitment to protecting black people in the South.[173] George Breitman argues that 'the State Department ... blamed him, for a good part of the strong stand against US imperialism taken by African nations in the United Nations at the time of the latest atrocities in the Congo'.[174] Furthermore, Malcolm was a frequent guest in the delegate lounge at the UN where he conversed with African and Asian diplomats and solicited support for his UN campaign.[175] According to Jack Anderson in his article of 25 January 1965, Malcolm was 'expected to be a star attraction at the coming Afro-Asian Conference in Algiers'.[176] Given that this conference (held on 25 June) was stated to have around sixty rulers from African and Asian governments,[177] US officials would have balked at the idea of Malcolm having access to potential foreign backers. On the domestic front, Malcolm's offer to send men to train SNCC and SCLC in self-defence was cause for concern for government agencies, especially as he called for the formation of an African-American Mau Mau.[178]

Given the government's concerns, it is interesting that the FBI knew that the war between Malcolm and the NOI, which it had helped instigate, would in all likelihood lead to Malcolm's death, thus ending his direct impact on domestic and foreign affairs. This is important as Clegg argues that 'government agencies, such as the FBI ... [and the NYPD] ... that were in the best position to check the open hatred ... [between Malcolm and the NOI] ... watched from the side-lines. If anything, these forces silently delighted in the increasing destructiveness of the rivalry.'[179]

In addition to this, Evanzz and Cone suggest that Malcolm X and Dr Martin Luther King were heading towards a possible alliance that would join two of America's premier leaders;[180] since Malcolm had voiced his intent to radicalise the civil rights struggle, this posed problems for the US intelligence apparatus. In short, despite King's success during the iconic March on Washington, the bombing of the Sixteenth Street Church in Birmingham, Alabama on 15 September 1963 caused a crisis for King and the non-violent struggle as black leaders along with the masses began to question the wisdom of non-violence.[181] King's problems were escalating as by the 8 January 1964, the FBI had concocted a plan to encourage King to commit suicide or risk his extra-marital affairs been aired publicly.[182]

Malcolm and Martin

On 27 March 1964, King and Malcolm met in Washington as they observed the senatorial debate pertaining to the Civil Rights Act of 1964.[183] Both men answered questions from the press, shook hands and reportedly (privately) agreed the need for continued dialogue.[184] The meeting and photograph appeared in the *Washington Post* and increased the FBI's distrust and disdain for both leaders.[185] Furthermore, Evanzz suggests that the FBI discovered that Malcolm 'had ... formed a coalition of seventeen civil rights groups ... called "ACT"[186] ... the FBI encountered information indicating that Malcolm X and Dr. King might actually become partners in the civil rights struggle'.[187] Subsequently, the FBI discovered that Howard-educated Chicago lawyer William R. Ming had a professional relationship with Elijah Muhammad, Malcolm X and King, and in response to said connection 'Hoover, in conjunction with the CIA, initiated a new phase in the FBI's ... [campaigns] ... against Malcolm X and Dr. King.[188] This included a plan to instigate hostilities between King and the SCLC and Roy Wilkins and the NAACP.[189] One can only imagine the reaction of the FBI when on 27 June 1964 Clarence Jones, one of King's Lawyers called Malcolm X's office to arrange a meeting ... [as] ... King was interested in supporting Malcolm's proposed United Nations petition'.[190] Evidently King was willing to assist in internationalising the struggle, which he made clear in comments he made in Oslo where he referenced the Congo and maintained that African-Americans required international assistance in their struggle.[191]

While King was moving towards an internationalist stance, Malcolm's end was in sight and Malcolm knew it;[192] in early 1965 he spoke in Selma Alabama and reiterated his support for the SNCC and King (who was absent) publicly and privately to Coretta Scott King.[193] Subsequently, Malcolm's house was firebombed[194] and then on 21 February 1965, Malcolm's life was cut short under a hail of bullets reportedly directed by five NOI foot soldiers from Newark's Mosque No 25, all of whom except Talmadge Hayer evaded arrest.[195] Intriguingly, only three assailants were charged with the assassination. Talmadge Hayer was captured at the scene and confessed to the murder and denied the participation of his co-defendants; although Norman 3X Butler and Thomas 15X Johnson (two Mosque No 7 enforcers) were charged and imprisoned for the murder, there is evidence suggesting they were wrongly convicted.[196] In addition, BOSSI agent Eugene Roberts, who had infiltrated Malcolm's close protection security, informed his superiors that Malcolm was being set up for an assassination.[197] In short, the FBI, BOSSI, the press and government officials had forewarning that Malcolm X's life was in jeopardy; consequently, some authors' argue that the US intelligence apparatus deliberately inflamed the conflict to permanently neutralise Malcolm by indirectly causing his death.[198] In this regard, Clegg maintains that 'without question, the FBI and the NYPD share partial culpability for the Murder'.[199] The controversy will continue, but it is clear that the state viewed Malcolm as a threat both domestically and internationally.

Whilst America's political establishment shed no tears for Malcolm, the African and Asian world was disturbed by the violent death of a man it considered as a fellow revolutionary in the war against Western supremacy.[200]

Consequently, scores of newspaper articles praised Malcolm's efforts to challenge Western hegemony and white supremacy.[201] Closer to home the leadership of the NOI and Elijah Muhammad accused Malcolm of religious heresy and cast him as the chief opponent of Elijah Muhammad.[202] Despite the fact that the NOI would reach the height of its wealth and power in the early 1970s, it would and continues to be plagued with the stigma of Malcolm's murder.[203]

For Dr King, his private admiration for Malcolm was subsumed by his desire to condemn violence as an ineffective means of addressing political dissent,[204] characteristically King emphasised the tactical superiority of non-violence in regards to the black movement. In retrospect, the Civil Rights Act of 1964 coupled with the Voting Rights Act of 1965 represented the apex of the Civil Rights Movement in the South,[205] which had utilised mass mobilisation, television coverage and appeals to American ideals, in addition to the leverage obtained from the Cold War to redefine US race relations. In truth, Malcolm's death marked the emergence of a new paradigm in US race relations as the dismantling of racial apartheid did little to alleviate the poverty, unemployment and urban decay that characterised African-American life outside the South.[206] Consequently, 1965 witnessed intense racial eruptions in the urban enclaves such as in Watts in Los Angeles and in cities such as Detroit and Chicago.[207]

The riots unsettled King as the nightmarish conditions in the North including police brutality and de facto racism threatened to unseat the primacy of non-violence.[208] The absence of Malcolm the erstwhile champion of the North meant King would have to fill the vacuum left by his death as King recognised that without disciplined leadership the urban masses might strike at white injustice in a manner that could jeopardise the safety of the black community.

Like Malcolm, King's final years were controversial and have been under acknowledged due to the tendency to fore ground the popular narrative associated with King's *I have a Dream* ethos[209] which he dispensed with in his final evolutionary process.[210] In a way, King's final message resonated with aspects of Malcolm's critique of American power as it questioned the foundations of America's domestic and foreign power by conjoining race, class and the imperial tendencies of US capitalism into a cross-cutting system of oppression.[211] Although King derived no pleasure from denouncing America, from 1965 until his murder in 1968 his emphasis shifted from condemning the racist policies of city and state governments in the South to combating de facto racism in the North and questioning capitalism and American involvement in Vietnam.[212]

Capitalism, Vietnam and US Imperialism

Despite his liberal persona, JFK was directly responsible for deploying American military advisers in Vietnam, which pulled America into a brutal neo-colonist and Cold War conflict[213] between Vietnamese factions allied to the opposing super powers. After assuming the presidency in 1965, Lyndon B. Johnson (LBJ) increased America's military presence to the extent that Vietnam became a full-scale war.[214] Like Malcolm before them, many amongst the civil rights fraternity came to oppose the war,[215] not least for depleting the American Treasury and the black population as 'blacks ... [were drafted and died] ... in disproportionate numbers ... [and] ... civil rights workers were ... drafted to fight in a war they found repugnant; the government that condemned the violence of Watts, Newark, and Detroit was visiting death and destruction on a faraway country inhabited by people of a different race'.[216]

Muhammad Ali captured the sentiment of many African-Americans when he stated his reluctance to fight the 'Vietcong';[217] after all the Vietnamese had not oppressed African-Americans or 'called them niggers'. In short, African-Americans' anti-imperialism and their racial and global consciousness fuelled their reluctance to fight in defence of freedoms denied them at home.[218] Significantly, LBJ and the American military industrial complex siphoned millions into the war and impoverished his great society programmes to meet military expenditures.[219] Ultimately, the civil rights establishment splintered into two camps due to the Vietnam War. First, the NAACP and the older and more conservative wing of the movement took a state-centred approach which saw the Vietnam War as part of the Cold War;[220] hence, they limited their commentary on the war. Alternatively, the younger and more radical wing of the movement embraced anti-war politics[221] and black power, which was initiated by the SNCC's Willie Ricks and Stokely Carmichael who had became enamoured with Elijah Muhammad's black consciousness and Robert Williams' and Malcolm's doctrine of self-defence.[222]

King's decision to target the urban heartlands of the North began with the Chicago Freedom Movement[223] which he and SCLC initiated in 1966[224] in order to combat the racial hostilities that had flared in 1965.[225] In accordance with his new outlook and his respect for the elder statesman of the black movement, King met with Elijah Muhammad and is reported to have conceded that the northern ghettoes were akin to racialised colonies.[226] In retrospect, King had realised that the struggle against Jim Crow had done little to address the economic inequalities generated by centuries of racism both North and South, and that economic and racial oppression threatened to destabilise the urbanised North. Additionally, King's sojourn in Chicago convinced him that while white liberals had fought to eradicate segregation, they showed little inclination to support African-Americans' desires for economic parity.[227] In other words, while white liberals supported equality before the law, they were far from willing to countenance African-Americans' demands for better housing and good jobs.

King also noted that the intensity of the violence and abuse he experienced in Chicago surpassed the violence he had witnessed in the South;[228] consequently, King recognised that US racism was a endemic feature of US society. Due to the entrenched character of northern inequalities, King and SCLC experienced limited success in Chicago as a result of Mayor Daley's shrewd calculations and the black urbanites' refusal to adopt non-violence as a political strategy.[229] Whilst living and working in the Chicago ghetto, King began to voice his doubts about Vietnam and the inherent inequalities of American capitalism,[230] which led him to question whether a capitalist economy could eradicate poverty. In accord with his anti-war stance, in 1965 King announced plans to send letters to President Johnson, the Soviets and the Vietnamese combatants in the hope of ending the war. As a result, 'the US Ambassador to the United Nations, Arthur Goldberg, was ordered to meet with the SCLC Leader to bring him "on side". But when King appeared unconverted, a close ally of the President, Senator Thomas Dodd of Connecticut, lambasted King and warned that it was a criminal offence for private citizens to negotiate with foreign powers to influence US foreign policy.'[231]

Black power

King's troubles with the political establishment were matched by his decreasing popularity with white liberals who began to withdraw funding from the SCLC.[232] King and the movement received another blow due to the shooting of James Meredith in June 1966.[233] Meredith had initiated a Freedom March through Mississippi; after the shooting King, Stokely Carmichael, the SNCC and the Congress of Racial Equality CORE continued what would prove to be a controversial march.[234] The controversy erupted because 'SNCC' and a new black paramilitary force called the Deacons of Defence rejected non-violence and proclaimed their right to self-defence, which prompted the NAACP's Roy Wilkins and the National Urban League and Whitney Young to abandon the march.[235] The march injected the term 'black power' into America's political lexicon[236] and led the press, politicians, and government officials to recoil from the black struggle due to the black power mantra.

Although King accepted black power's emphasis on racial identity and ethnic pride, he rejected its association with self-defence and revolution.[237] Notwithstanding, King knew that revolutionary struggles in Africa and Asia, police brutality, and racial violence in America had primed some African-Americans to believe that pacifism was tantamount to racial suicide.[238] Hence with the creation of the Black Panthers (in 1967) and other paramilitary groups, self-defence and revolution became hallmarks of the post-1965 black movement.[239] Although King rejected self-defence stratagems, 1966 saw him forego his prior crisis of conscience in regard to his unwillingness to court controversy by condemning the war in Vietnam.[240] Thus, despite the misgivings of his colleagues, King brought his concerns about Vietnam and the failings of US capitalism to the forefront of his political discourse.[241] Predictably, King's status with the Johnson administration plummeted and would never recover.[242]

Indeed, by 1967 King's perceived radicalism had him publicly extolling the values of democratic socialism[243] and calling for a radical redistribution of economic and political power in America ... and ... [arguing] ... that the movement ... had to change from ... reform ... to a revolutionary movement ... King said, we are called upon to raise certain basic questions about the whole society ... We must see now that the evils of racism, economic exploitation, and militarism are all tied together, and your really can't get rid of one without getting rid of the others.[244]

Of course King's use of the word 'revolution' must be distinguished from its use by Malcolm X and the young revolutionaries who had embraced Malcolm's teachings. Nevertheless, King's strident rhetoric would have disturbed the political establishment not least for its ambiguity.

King verified his convergence with aspects of Malcolm's worldview as he concluded that black people in the ghetto represented a subject population and the 'vast majority of white Americans ... [were] ... racists'.[245]

Depending on one's perspective, King's post-1965 stance could be construed as foolhardy or courageous as views on Vietnam were antithetical to the economic interests of the American military industrial complex. King conveyed his concerns to the SCLC leadership regarding his quest to eradicate the ghetto as he felt it would make him powerful enemies as you are 'getting on dangerous ground because you are messing with Wall Street. You are messing with the captains of industry'.[246] Nevertheless, King's last year was replete with references to the war in Vietnam, which incurred increasing pressure from the press, government officials and the conservative wing of the civil rights movement.[247] Whether from the pulpit or in demonstrations, King spoke bluntly about the injustices perpetrated in the name of national interests, these events included headlining a Los Angeles rally which included four senatorial politicians, in addition to speaking at James Bevel's demonstration outside the UN building.[248] He also worked with Dr Spock in an anti-war demonstration in the Chicago March of 1967 which consisted of 5,000 people.[249] This was accompanied by a speech in Harlem's Riverside Church where he condemned the war for draining the US Treasury and subverting the war on poverty.[250] As a result, King was criticised by White House aide John Roche, President Johnson and Hoover, all of whom suggested that King had become enamoured with communism and was part of a subversive element seeking to distort core US values.[251]

King also condemned America as being the foremost imperial power and arguing that US imperialism was fuelled by economic greed and racial supremacy.[252] According to Fairclough,

King did not see America's involvement in Vietnam as an isolated aberration, but as part of a wider 'pattern of suppression' that embraced Africa and Latin America in addition to Southeast Asia. America bolstered the racist regimes in South Africa and Rhodesia; American arms and personnel helped to fight rebels and guerrillas in Venezuela, Guatemala, Columbia, and Peru. ... Ultimately, he believed, the answer lay ... in Western capitalism ...

multinational cartels stripped under-developed nations of their resources 'while turning over a small rebate to a few members of a corrupt aristocracy'. The historic freedom accorded to capital in the United States had made government the servant of private profit.[253]

Whereas Malcolm X's condemnation of US foreign policy could be dismissed as the conspiratorial views of a racial radical, Dr King was a world-renowned humanist who was widely respected amongst white and non-white people. In brief, the denunciation of war from a man awarded a Nobel Peace Prize and a man associated with the American dream was a major blow to President Johnson and America's political establishment.[254] In short, the pragmatic but tentative alliance between King and the executive branch had faltered as King felt that black people's economic interests required that they compel the federal government to promote egalitarian policies designed to redistribute America's wealth.

War on poverty

As part of his efforts to eradicate poverty, King launched the Poor People's Campaign (PPC) in 1967. The movement was multiracial and King intended to lead a second March on Washington that would take America's poor to the capital in view of the world and force Washington to act.[255]

Meanwhile, the impact of the anti-war movement was reflected in the fact that President Johnson informed Americans in March 1968 that he would not seek re-election, which was directly attributable to the political outcry against the war.[256] It was in this hostile climate that King made the fateful journey to Memphis to support the strike action of black refuse collectors.[257] In Memphis, King made his final speech (on 3 April) at the Bishop Charles Masonic Temple were he prophesied his death.[258] Like Malcolm, King realised that his activism had amassed a formidable array of enemies both in and outside the government and that his death was eminent hence he stated:

> I got into Memphis. And some began to say the threats, or talk about the threats that were out. What would happen to me from some of our sick White brothers? Well, I don't know what will happen now. We've got some difficult days ahead. But it doesn't matter with me now. Because I've been to the mountain top. And I don't mind. Like anybody, I would like to live a long life. Longevity has its place. But I'm not concerned about that now. I just want to do God's will. And he has allowed me to go up to the mountain top. And I've looked over. And I've seen the Promised Land. I may not get there with you. But I want you to know tonight, that we as a people will get to the Promised Land.[259]

The next day, on 4 April 1968, Dr King was assassinated,[260] and despite the arrest and conviction of known racist James Earl Ray,[261] as in the case of

Malcolm X, theories of a wider conspiracy abound. For example, in '1977–78 the US Congress House Select Committee on Assassinations concluded that "there is likelihood" that Ray did not plan the assassination alone'.[262] Indeed, William Pepper, a respected lawyer, has argued that 'King's assassination was part of a much wider conspiracy and a cover-up that "ultimately expose[s] the dark underbelly of the American government and the covert activities of its military and intelligence organizations and their fealty to corporate interests and organized crime"'.[263] Ling also acknowledges the possibility of a wider conspiracy involving government agencies, but he is less than convinced that the government would have planned the assassination of King.[264]

Alternatively, Gerald Posner maintains that James Earl Ray killed King, but it was government agencies' efforts to neutralise and destroy King that created the atmosphere which facilitated King's murder.[265] In general, African-Americans felt King had been murdered by the white power structure, an amorphous power bloc which protected white interests. King's death triggered a wave of riots[266] and increased the appeal of black power advocates determined to meet white violence head on.

In brief, the final years of King's life were marked by an increase in government animus towards him.[267] The evidence indicates that King was illegally pursued by Hoover and the FBI,[268] to the extent that FBI official William Sullivan concocted a plan to coerce him into committing suicide.[269] Furthermore, the Johnson administration tried to coerce King into abandoning his anti-war stance. Indeed, the government officials who labelled King a communist where trying to safeguard their preferred brand of US foreign policy.

Conclusion

In summary, this chapter indicates that King, Malcolm X and Elijah Muhammad where subjected to state repression which was both racially and politically motivated. In short, state agencies sanctioned schemes designed to splinter, co-opt and destroy the black movement. One must concur with Kenneth O'Reilly's thesis that from its inception the FBI has employed its most deadly tactics against African-Americans. A number of authors have correctly identified that African-Americans have been subjected to unprecedented and pernicious treatment by intelligence agencies and government officials and one would have to acknowledge the role of racism in shaping this reality.

Essentially both King and Malcolm were subjected to counter-intelligence measures akin to those employed against foreign nationals. However, while race was surely a factor one must be open to other explanations.

In regards to Malcolm, his fiery denunciations of the white devil and his call for *the end of white supremacy* clearly disturbed government officials and white America and generated hostility towards Malcolm. However, careful analysis of Malcolm's rhetoric suggests that his advocacy of revolutionary violence was not dissimilar to the precepts enshrined in the constitution and the US Bill of Rights. In short, Malcolm argued from a human rights perspective that the government's failure to protect African-Americans created the context for them to assert their human right to self-defence. Alternatively, one would think that King's unrelenting commitment to non-violence should have engendered a less bellicose response to King; nonetheless, the FBI subjected both King and Malcolm to counter-intelligence operations predicated on causing the death or harm to both leaders. The question is: why?

A holistic evaluation of the harsh treatment meted out to King and Malcolm conceives the government's actions within a broader context of domestic and international relations. Simply put, Euro-American's anxiety over African-American demands mirrored the West's anxiety towards the demands and actions of the colonised masses of the non-white world. That is to say, Du Bois' edict in 1900 regarding the colour-line becoming the major fault line in global politics rang true as from WWII through to the closing of the century:[270] race became a central facet in international relations.

Thus King's and Malcolm's activism should be viewed as part of a global struggle against European colonialism and white supremacy. Unfortunately, historians and civil rights scholars have under-acknowledged the symbiotic relationship between African-Americans' quest for racial equality and global forces attempting to narrow the (global) North–South divide. The failure to emphasise the transnational qualities of America's racial struggle is particularly perplexing as both men made reference to the external forces which helped define the African-American struggle. For example, Malcolm's attempt to move from civil to human rights reflected his awareness that segregation was a human rights issue comparable to ending apartheid in Southern Africa. In short, King and Malcolm recognised that human rights violations could form a pretext for soliciting UN support, especially since Bandung and decolonisation had facilitated the rise of non-white nations who might be persuaded to back African-Americans quest for racial equality.

Likewise, one could identify the executive branch's efforts to promote racial reforms as a response to a mass movement and as counter-measures designed to safeguard America's democratic image and to counteract Soviet, Chinese and Cuban ascendancy in the developing world, in addition to blocking the development of a coordinated transnational network between African-Americans, Africans and other non-white nations. King's forestalled engagement with foreign affairs reflects the gravitas of Cold War rivalries and his awareness that African-Americans who challenged US foreign policy would receive swift and decisive punishment from the white establishment. In brief, King's and Malcolm's relationships with the white establishment was predicated on their racial identity and their politics; however, their relative standing deteriorated relative to their efforts to influence US foreign policy.

Simply put, from Roosevelt through to LBJ the executive branch's engagement with racial issues was only partially in response to African-American activism. The Cold War played a major part in stimulating federal support for the racial realignment. Thus the legal interventions of the judicial and executive branch of the federal government were part of a self-interested reconstruction that had three primary objectives: to reduce the level of racial conflict within the domestic sphere; to neutralise Soviet and Cuban claims that America was plagued by racial supremacy; and finally, America's post-WWII presidents became increasingly aware that they could ill afford extended criticism from the international community especially since the emerging nations were peopled by non-whites, whose influence was on the increase at the UN.

It is within this context that the actions of Malcolm and Martin must be assessed as each man had a major impact on America's standing in world politics. Since the Cold War amplified both domestic and foreign affairs, the US state was exceedingly sensitive to any events that jeopardised her international objectives. In short, the civil rights agenda was less of a revolution and more akin to reforms predicated on advancing America's national interests at home and abroad. Indeed, Malcolm's advocacy of black nationalism, Pan-Africanism and his UN petition, in addition to his calls for African-Americans to control the politics and economy of their own community, was deemed antithetical to Euro-American interests as it would have revolutionised US race relations. In brief, Malcolm's fiery condemnation of American power provided ammunition and political leverage to the Soviets, Chinese, and Cubans and emerging African and Asian nations, whose minerals resources and political allegiances played a significant role in securing America's national security agenda. Again Malcolm's desire to form an African-American Mau Mau to counter white supremacist violence troubled the security apparatus of the United States as it broached the possibility of a race war within America's domestic confines.

Although King's foreign affairs engagement was more conservative than Malcolm's, his anti-war stance undermined the Johnson administration as did his depiction of America as an imperialist power whose capitalism was used to exploit the masses of the non-white world in a manner approximating the exploitation of the African-American ghetto. Equally, King's statements in support of socialism were problematic as they contravened the American dream and individualism and called for an overhaul of the US economy. That in itself was cause for concern as the communist bloc could have used King's rhetoric to validate their criticism of capitalism. It is noteworthy that Hoover's FBI directive to prevent the rise of a black messiah mentioned Malcolm X and King as potential candidates who could have formed a national movement which could have revolutionised America. Thus Malcolm's decision to aid King and Martin's desire to aid Malcolm's UN campaign would have represented a powerful blow to sections of the Euro-American establishment. In brief, a tactical alliance between King and Malcolm would have definitely challenged the socio-economic, political, cultural and international profile of the United States. To conclude, the premature death of both leaders was not an accident of history; it was provoked and assisted by parts of the establishment[271] who desired to win the Cold War, safeguard America's Euro-American identity and maintain the racial dynamics that characterised the global North–South divide.

Hence, the heresy of Martin and Malcolm was to assail the status quo and attempt to alter the racial, economic, political and international parameters of American power.

8 Conclusion

The objective of this chapter is to highlight and underscore the significant themes presented and to determine the overall implications derived from the evidence presented in this book. It will assess the strengths and weaknesses of the theoretical models utilised to explain the empirical data pertaining to AAFAN's activities whilst pinpointing the larger questions raised by this research including an analysis of the theoretical implications. The chapter will initially summarise Chapters 3 to 6 in order to illuminate the specific details of each one and lead to the construction of a sound conclusion. Second, it will provide a general assessment of the theories utilised in this book. Third, it will highlight the specific theoretical conclusions derived from the evaluation of the empirical data examined in this research. Chapters 7 and 8 will be utilised to provide additional clarity to the overall argument regarding the pervasive character of the colour-line and its continuing impact on domestic and foreign affairs during the formation and beyond the first decade of the Cold War.

The forging of the African-American Foreign Affairs Community

The evidence from Chapter 3 indicates that the US state sought to neutralise the foreign policy goals of AAFAN. Instead of incorporating the goals of the UNIA or W. E. B. Du Bois, state agencies, under the auspices of J. Edgar Hoover, crushed the Garvey movement despite the sizeable constituency that it represented. In short, the international goals of the black nationalist community, i.e., the political liberation of African people, clashed with the conventions and racialised worldview of white America as evidenced by their actions to maintain the racial status quo.[1] The actions of Hoover and the Justice Department point to their unwillingness to accept African-Americans' international and domestic challenge to WASP dominance, because the UNIA's 'race first' and Pan-Africanist ideals were antithetical to the maintenance of Anglo-Saxon hegemony. The evidence points to the Western nations' efforts (whether explicit or implicit) to maintain their racial and political dominance over the colonised world just as America maintained the politically constructed colour-line. Although the state's response to Du Bois' liberal Pan-Africanism was less hostile than its reaction to the UNIA, the US government rejected African-Americans' efforts to realign the domestic and international status quo irrespective of their radical or liberal ideals.

The Italo-Ethiopian War 1934–36

AAFAN's efforts to aid Ethiopia did nothing to encourage state support for that embattled African nation, as the US administration's alleged neutrality and trade with Italy undermined Ethiopian interests and Ethiopia received no aid, which, given Hunt's contention regarding the racialisation of US foreign policy, is hardly surprising. Arguably, US racial doctrines and practices barred them and other Western nations from going to war to save an African nation from Italian colonialism. The great powers' and Russia's tacit acceptance of Italy's imperialist designs;[2] in addition, African-Americans' inability to aid Ethiopia in contrast to Italian-Americans' aid to Italy must be viewed within the context of a domestic and international system of Western hegemony, which had politically and economically marginalised people of African descent. African-Americans' marginal status was intrinsically related to their racial designation, which limited their right to vote and effectively weakened their ability to punish or reward the state in regard to its policies. In truth, African-Americans' alienation from the state prompted them to launch a (largely) race-based campaign that assumed that white people domestically and internationally would not support Ethiopia. As a result, AAFAN took on a Pan-Africanist and nationalist orientation to its struggle to aid Ethiopia. State intervention in African-American endeavours halted their efforts to fight on behalf of Ethiopia. Clearly the state desired to hinder AAFAN's objectives (albeit for legal reasons) rather than support its foreign affairs goals. Evidently, America did not employ innovative means to save Ethiopia as it did in defence of Britain during WWII. Despite the fact that the issue of national sovereignty and totalitarian aggression were factors in the IEW, America's reaction was decisively different. Perhaps the complexion of the victims combined with US affinity with Britain and her strategic interests provide an explanation of why fascist aggression in Africa failed to ignite the US administration's and the Western nations' anti-fascist passions. Aside from African-Americans' fight[3] in defence of European sovereignty in WWII, and despite the great powers' indifference to the plight of Ethiopia, during the mid-1930s America's actions correlate with Hunt's contention that white Americans believed that 'above all places Africa invited white domination.'[4] Indeed, could British and French colonialists and the WASP elite, whose own nation practised a form of racial apartheid, be committed to an African nation that held no strategic importance for themselves, and risk alienating a white industrial nation. Essentially the IEW had divergent meanings; for people of African descent the war represented the white world's continuing war on Africans and an attack on one of the last bastions of African sovereignty. Ethiopia was doomed due to its reliance on the league and incompetent white advisors who failed to protect Ethiopian. Given white efforts to prevent black unity[5] and the racial conventions of the early twentieth century, the Ethiopian appeals to the League of Nations and Western nations was hopeless. Although some white people claimed that Haile Selassie and Ethiopians did not racially identify with African-Americans, Selassie did reinforce the bonds between both groups as he 'sent Malaku Bayen to the United states of America to co-ordinate efforts in favour of Ethiopia. ... Perhaps Bayen's greatest contribution to the Ethiopian cause was his attempt to improve Afro-American, African, and Ethiopian relations and to create greater racial bonds with his countrymen.'[6] For most white people in America, Ethiopia was a mysterious and faraway place for which it was not worth abandoning its isolationist policies. In reality, the war signalled the rise of the fascist aggression that Haile Selassie warned would eventually engulf Europe. Given the fact that the IEW was a 'gateway' to the events surrounding WWII, mainstream scholars should have researched this conflict more thoroughly in regard to international relations, the demise of the League of Nations (since the league was ineffective in executing its mandate to prevent international military conflicts) and racial polarisation that occurred in Italian and African-American communities.

From isolation to globalism

African-Americans' characterisation of the war in Europe as a white man's war was partially correct. European imperialism created the context for a struggle between the Allies and the Axis powers who sought to gain additional territories in Europe and throughout the globe.[7] However, whilst European nations vied for supremacy, their respective colonies were forced to fight in defence of their respective colonialists while Japan's attack on Pearl Harbour lead to American and African-American participation in WWII.

Due to the resentment derived from defeat of Ethiopia and centuries of white domination, some African-Americans felt that a European conflict could inadvertently aid the black cause by undermining Western dominance over people of colour. While prevailing logic might assume that Nazi racism would catapult African-Americans to the forefront of the war against the Axis powers, perhaps the role of the state in shaping public and African-American opinion has been underestimated. Given that Nazi racism was not unrelated to the racism espoused by European imperialists and white America, some black people were initially indifferent to the allied cause. The evidence suggests that state propaganda in support of the Allies in addition to the extreme nature of Nazi ideology became a decisive factor in African-Americans' conversion to the allied cause. In brief, patriotic fervour and the state's domestic reforms encouraged African-American support for US interventionism. The evidence reveals that African-Americans were encouraged to forget their domestic grievances and their disdain for European imperialism and fight on behalf of a government that accepted their second-class citizenship. The utilisation of African-American leaders to promote US intervention in the war was an example of the state and quasi-state organisations' strategy to put a 'black face' on state power and thereby convince black people they were part of the American political mainstream. The deployment of African-Americans in American wars dates back to the war of independence through the civil war and WWI and points to the power of the white elite to convince black people that their interests were identical or similar to those of the political elite.[8] Whilst one recognises the significance of African-American participation in US wars, it is equally noted that their sacrifices failed to win the political equality they desired despite some white encouragement to support America's national interests at critical junctures.[9] Consequently, some African-Americans' support of the Allies prior to Pearl Harbour was an attempt to demonstrate their commitment to America in the hope of being granted their civil rights. Critics have acknowledged that black support of mainstream causes had not necessarily been rewarded. Indeed, even the state acknowledged African-American indifference in relation to WWII as it identified black opposition to fighting for white America via RACON, the state-sponsored surveillance of the black community, which lead to the prosecution of African-American nationalists who refused to fight on behalf of the white world. Although RACON demonstrates the existence of a radical wing of black dissidents, the majority of African-Americans supported the allied cause despite America's previous record of exploitation. Nevertheless, African-Americans did secure domestic concessions by highlighting their service to America and the Allies but failed to influence US foreign policy or impact on allied colonialism. Thus AAFAN was moved by the state as opposed to affecting state policies (in this regard AAFAN was more successful in impacting the domestic arena). The state neutralised all opposition to their interventionist thrust, especially after the bombing of Pearl Harbour, and the AAFAN was never granted access to the decision-making process pertaining to foreign policy. In retrospect, the overtures to black people initiated by the WASP elite including the CFR were pragmatic and (mostly) self-serving as the WASP elite secured the support of African-Americans to the allied cause as opposed to correcting the racial imbalance regarding state actions, which they were doubtlessly aware of prior to 1941. For African-Americans, the period between 1939 and 1941 was significant as, irrespective of the establishment's foreign policy motives, African-Americans were granted access to state institutions in an unprecedented manner, which facilitated their direct involvement in the activities surrounding the formation of the UNO. In addition, the double-V campaign that sought victory at home and abroad encouraged the formation of MOWN, which highlighted the power of civil unrest in forcing state reforms, a lesson which was duly noted during the 1960s.

African-Americans and the formation of the United Nations

Chapter 6 validates the contention that WWII facilitated the forward momentum of AAFAN due to their mobilisation in defence of America in addition to their domestic campaign in pursuit of racial equality. However, AAFAN's increased interaction with government officials was also a by-product of African-Americans' organisational maturity, which resulted from their successes during the war. This suggests that African-Americans' defence of their interests affected their level of participation pertaining to US foreign policy. AAFAN'S status was not exclusively based on white racism as the degree of African-American resistance to the colour-line determined their political status and their ability to effect changes in US foreign policy. AAFAN's increased interaction with US officials did little to define or redefine the state's agenda pertaining to the US delegation's proposals for the UN charter. AAFAN's dissatisfaction with the Dumbarton Oaks accords and their attempts to re-orientate the state's foreign policy by lobbying the official delegation had a limited impact.

Although the activities of Du Bois, Walter White and Bethune highlighted the issue of colonialism and racial equality, the official delegation avoided committing themselves to the practical resolution of these issues despite appearing to be sympathetic to AAFAN's cause. Ironically, African-Americans who were directly affected by racial inequality were dependent on the white elite who were reluctant to challenge the racial status quo in America to compel white nations to ratify a racial equality clause within the UN charter. In brief, AAFAN could not effectively aid colonised continental or diasporean Africans because they lacked the necessary power or resources to define and direct the US delegation's foreign policy. Again, AAFAN was forced to accept the state's position and abandon its Pan-Africanist approach in favour of the conservative approach, which was more acceptable to whites, i.e., black non-engagement with foreign affairs except when required by the state for propaganda purposes. Subsequently African-American leaders' withdrew from foreign affairs due to pressure from white people who urged them to avoid providing the Soviet Union the opportunity to criticise America.' As a result, with the exception of Du Bois and Paul Robeson, most African-Americans abandoned the internationalism they had vigorously supported during the war and immersed themselves in the struggle to win domestic racial equality. While white America appeared to be less hostile to the African-American call for domestic reforms, as opposed to that of an international organisation intervening in US affairs, neither domestic nor international racial equality was a priority for white America, which was hostile to African-Americans call for domestic reforms and the prospective threat of an international organisation meddling in US affairs. America's racial reforms in the 1960s were assisted by the struggles of African-Americans during the 1940s and government recognition that racial reforms were essential if the United States desired to compete successfully in the Cold War.

The aim of this book was to investigate the activities of the AAFAN from the dawn of the twentieth century through to 1968. The evidence suggests that the period examined, in relation to African-Americans, was largely defined by the two world wars, the IEW and the Cold War. These historical episodes redefined the African-Americans' understanding of domestic and foreign affairs and in time led to significant changes in US race relations. This study confirms that African-Americans' interest in racial equality extended to the international arena, where they called for justice for all African people. This is significant given the claims that

> the Negro of the United States has lost even the remembrance of his country ... he abjured their religion and forgot their customs when he ceased to belong to Africa, without acquiring any claim to European privileges. But he remains half-way between two races; sold by the one, repulsed by the other; finding not a spot in the universe to call by the name of country.[10]

De Tocqueville mistakenly assumed that Europeans successfully destroyed Africans' identity, but he acknowledged white America's efforts to oppress African-Americans and the attendant power inequalities that resulted from their efforts. This is significant, as the evidence suggests AAFAN's attempts to mobilise the African-American community to pursue their international agenda were hampered by the pervasive nature of the US colour-line, i.e., institutionalised racism.

The centrality of race

That white America has politically and economically oppressed African-Americans is verified by US history as the capture and enslavement of African people (along with the cultural and biological devastation of the native American population), initiated by Euro-Americans, set the tone for US race relations. On reflection, the creation and existence of white political supremacy vis-à-vis the African-American population is as American as the democratic principles established by the founding fathers who codified the notion of racialised slavery and African inferiority within the American constitution. Consequently, despite numerous victories against white political and economic hegemony within the domestic sphere, African-Americans have been unable to establish political parity with the Euro-American population.[11] Thus, the period 1900–1968, which includes the three case studies and the three accompanying chapters, is consistent with the historical pattern of white political supremacy.[12]

In brief, Michael Hunt's contention regarding the racial orientation of US foreign policy should be extended to account for white people's successful domination and colonisation of state institutions[13] in order to maintain their control over the direction of foreign policy and politics in general. In the light of the prevalence of white institutional control, some authors maintain that African-Americans' domestic status is analogous to a colonised population, i.e., 'colonial subjects [with] their political decisions made for them by the colonial masters, and those decisions ... handed down directly or through a process of indirect rule. Politically decisions ... affect[ing] black lives have been made by white people – the "white power structure".'[14] The suggestion that AAFAN's racial status and the political hegemony of white America has affected black people's efforts to secure their interests in regard to domestic and international issues corresponds to the general thrust of American race relations.[15] Consequently, one cannot assess the causes of black marginalisation without accounting for the role of race. US racial conventions created the context for white domination by granting white people greater access to political and economic resources,[16] which ensured white and specifically WASP hegemony.[17] Irrespective of AAFAN's actions, US racism conditioned the American elite to negate black interests due to their inferior status. Racism and its core assumptions justified the exclusion of black people from the corridors of power and guaranteed the institutionalisation of white hegemony in government generally[18] and in relation to foreign policy. The absence of black people in the State Department and the executive branch points to the legitimacy of this argument. One could argue that African-Americans lacked the academic qualifications required to assume government positions. The question is, whether black people were incapable of fulfilling state requirements[19] or had the racial conventions of America conspired to ensure black people were prevented from receiving the necessary education and social status to facilitate their entry into the foreign policy establishment and other high-ranking positions. Given that black people were prevented from reading and writing during their enslavement and the organised efforts of white people inhibited black empowerment during and beyond reconstruction, the evidence suggests that if (generally) African-Americans were illequipped to engage in domestic and foreign affairs, it was primarily a result of the white people's social and political engineering not their inherent inferiority. The educational and organisational achievements of African-Americans such as Du Bois, who was part of the African-American intelligentsia that pioneered the Niagara Movement, the NAACP and the 1900 Pan-African Conference, point to the existence of black people who could have been trained to assume government posts in relation to foreign affairs. While the state and US society appeared to be indifferent to the early activities of AAFAN, it would ultimately attempt to derail its efforts to engage in foreign affairs.[20]

Race and power

One of the primary objectives of this study is to examine African-Americans' efforts to promote and define international relations in accordance with their interests in order to combat domestic and international white supremacy. Irrespective of AAFAN's foreign policy proposals, its domestic subordination in relation to the construction of US foreign policy was detrimental to achieving its goals. The relative political and economic distance between AAFAN and the framers of US foreign policy was undoubtedly connected to the dominance and subordination of their respective groups, which ensured white power over the black population in America.

The difficult question for political and social scientists is to establish the basis of the power inequalities that existed between the relevant parties. AAFAN's inability to orient US foreign policy towards its objectives was a result of its political powerlessness. An analysis of US history reveals that Western Europeans have dominated US politics especially in regard to 'blacks who have only been given a claim to political equality and economic opportunity since the 1960s'.[21] The basis of their dominance was derived from the following: their extermination and political domination of the native American population,[22] the capture and exploitation of the labour and energy resources of millions of Africans,[23] in addition to the Euro-Americans' efforts in constructing American society, combined with the immense dividends obtained from their exploitation and oppression of African-Americans.

That much of America's initial wealth was derived from enforced labour is beyond dispute, as according to Sterling Stuckey, slavery 'enabled the country to be built much faster than it would have been otherwise. blacks worked as bondsmen, and, in an overwhelming majority of cases, without ever receiving pay for their labour. They worked the principal crops ... [in America] ... cotton, tobacco, indigo, sugar cane, and rice.'[24] Slavery and the propaganda which justified white racism laid the basis for the colour-line and the assumption of white superiority over black people which was validated by its actual creation, whereby the

> Subordination of people of colour ... [became] functional to the operation of American society ... and the colour of one's skin ... [became] a primary determinant of people's position in the social [power] structure. ... [thus] Racism is a structural relationship based on the subordination of one racial group by another. Given this perspective, the determining feature of race relations is not prejudice towards blacks, but rather the superior position of whites and the institutions – ideological as well as structural – which maintain it.[25]

The legacy of white hegemony was responsible for AAFAN's marginal role in US foreign policy. While C. Wright Mills points to the existence of an interlocking power elite[26] that has inordinate power within US society and presides over the key decision-making institutions, he fails to systematically examine the racialised character of the ruling elite.[27] Although white Americans

> often disagreed on aspects of the 'Negro question', sometimes emotionally so, they nonetheless agreed almost universally on the fundamental issue of white Supremacy and black inferiority. By the beginning of the twentieth century the issue of the place of blacks in American society rested on the same foundation that it had three centuries earlier—the protean association of inferiority with darkness of skin colour.[28]

Mills fails to indicate that America's ruling class has being overwhelmingly WASP, dating back to the founding fathers. While wealth is a factor in the dominance of this class race and racism (which prohibited the black people's attempts to challenge white economic supremacy), was used as an additional determinant in regards to the assumed right to rule. Consequently, notwithstanding the existence of distinct interest groups vying for political hegemony irrespective of political ideology, historically white people have maintained their dominance over black people.[29] Indeed, Hacker argued America is inherently a "white" country: in character, in structure, in culture. Needless to say, black Americans create lives of their own. Yet, as a people, they face boundaries and restrictions set by the white majority. America's version of *apartheid*, while lacking overt legal sanction comes closest to the system even now being reformed in the land of its invention.'[30]

Hacker's thesis undermines the pluralist belief in a diffusion of power in relation to African and Euro-Americans, perhaps, pluralism provides better insight into the distribution of power among white interest groups. Given the historical legacy of white dominance regarding foreign policy formation, the AAFAN's marginal role reflects the realities of US politics. Hence Du Bois and African-Americans' efforts to influence US foreign policy were hampered by US racial conventions, which stifled black empowerment and undermined the status of black policy recommendations. Nevertheless, one must account for the empirical evidence derived from the second and third case studies that highlight government efforts to reform US race relations prior to and during WWII. According to Salama Layton, the racial reforms instituted during the 1940s and the Cold War era advanced state interests, as, 'what should be clear is that the United States government was not pushing for racial reforms because of moral reasons. Indeed, the government was ambivalent to civil rights issues on moral grounds.'[31] Layton maintains that

> the cold war and its attendant pressures on the United States government to find allies against the Soviet Union, improved the initial bargaining position of civil rights advocates in the United States. These advocates acted strategically to maintain that position and to achieve real social and political gains. It is the context and the strategic actions that explain the success that civil rights advocates enjoyed in the 1940s.[32]

Therefore the state's incorporation of African-Americans such as Ralph Bunche supported state interests as opposed to combating the evils of racial oppression. The foreign policy establishment did not advance African-Americans' interests or seriously consider incorporating their policy recommendations into the decision-making process.

Significantly, the state and foreign policy establishment's incorporation of African-Americans in 1941 was designed to encourage African-American leaders to support the state's interventionist policies in contrast to their former indifference to the war in Europe. During the post-war period, state anti-communism and white liberals such as Eleanor Roosevelt[33] successfully encouraged mainstream black leaders such as Walter White to forego their internationalist struggle (which championed UN intervention in member states' domestic affairs and decolonisation) for black liberation in favour of a domestic civil rights struggle. The evidence suggests that state liaisons with the AAFAN compelled it to align itself with state interests while racial and international issues were subordinated in favour of national solidarity. The ability of the state to steer the AAFAN's agenda validates the examination of the core assumptions of the racialised colony thesis.

Theoretical implications

The notion that white people have colonised the African-American population was essentially drawn from a comparison of the colonised status of continental and diasporean Africans. While this model is not fully compatible with the circumstances of African-Americans, it is helpful in highlighting the AAFAN's/ African-Americans' relationship to the foreign policy establishment. While Hunt highlights the racial worldview of the foreign policy establishment, the evidence suggests that the international objectives of AAFAN were incompatible with US foreign policy. One could argue that the efforts of the AAFAN and international black constituencies (that attended the Pan-African Congress in 1919) to resolve the issue of Germany's colonies and to erase the international colour-line were given little attention by European powers on the basis of their political incompatibility. Even America's efforts to prevent African-Americans from attending the Pan-African Congress, by refusing to issue passports to prospective attendees in addition to falsely declaring that the Congress would not be held, could be construed as race neutral political sabotage. Clearly the US state's actions can be interpreted in a number of ways. However, it would be naïve and politically inconsistent with European and Euro-American history to suggest that the maintenance of white hegemony was not part of the Western nations' political agenda. Indeed, the fact that the participants at the Versailles Peace Conference were almost exclusively white nations, whose actions supported the international status quo,[34] supports the view that the Western nations' global agenda was inherently racialised. Concisely, European and Euro-American early twentieth-century politics were determined by a complex web of political and economic factors, and the belief in the cultural and racial supremacy of Western nations.

Therefore European and Euro-American disregard for Marcus Garvey's UNIA during the 1920s is predictable, given the aforementioned desire to maintain the global status quo, which the UNIA sought to challenge. In brief, the federal government's and J. Edgar Hoover's assault on Marcus Garvey and the UNIA, via covert surveillance and politically directed charges, which was reinforced by racial propaganda, was intended to maintain the domestic racial hierarchy in addition to safeguarding European imperialism. Overall America's political sabotage and apparent indifference to the plight of Ethiopia, despite the latter's alleged neutrality, suggests that America was not sufficiently concerned with the international objectives of AAFAN or the colonised status of African people (diasporean or continental) to either promote or protect their interests. In addition, the US foreign policy establishment was not orientated towards recruiting African-Americans to engage in the construction of foreign policy and the US state's interests were not compatible with the interests of African-Americans. As a result, the state opted to curtail African-American activists from pursuing their international goals, suggesting that the ideological requirements of Western hegemony worked in tandem with the socio-political, economic and military actions of white nations to perpetuate the politically engineered colour-line in order to ensure Western hegemony.[35] The evidence suggests that the AAFAN's marginal role in foreign affairs resulted from white America's efforts to protect their privileged position by projecting the myth of black inferiority, which justified the absence of black people within government positions due to their inability to acquire the necessary intellectual competence or designated qualifications. In short, white racism not black disinterest in foreign affairs was the cause of African-American marginalisation.

The fact that the US foreign policy establishment's first important[36] contact with AAFAN occurred just prior to America's entry into WWII is significant, as it lends weight to the contention that the US foreign policy establishment's orientation towards AAFAN was primarily utilitarian. The domestic demands for African-American labour to aid the war effort, coupled with the Allies' efforts to deflect Axis propaganda regarding US racism, compelled the state to liaise with AAFAN and promote racial reforms. Significantly, the political establishment's overtures to black leaders such as A. Philip Randolph (who had previously defined the war in Europe as a white man's war) resulted in Randolph's support of the state's position.[37] The state secured AAFAN's support despite its failure to implement AAFAN's agenda of decolonisation and international racial equality. Although blacks received domestic concessions during the war, they fought to secure democratic freedoms for European imperialists despite being bereft of the four freedoms within the American political context.[38] In short, African-Americans were exploited by racially orientated white people 'while aghast at the racist teachings propagated by Germany, they could not forget the racism, which confronted them daily in the United States. They were also aware of the imperialism, which was practised by Britain and France.'[39] As a result, African-Americans were engaged in a battle with their domestic colonisers along with the fascist regimes, as were the colonised masses in Africa, the Caribbean and Asia. Significantly, the colonised masses in Africa, Asia and the Caribbean along with the AAFAN, were not greeted with a new world order based on the four freedoms and racial equality after the war. Rather, Europe and America ultimately attempted to maintain Western imperialism while failing to pursue racial equality within the international arena.

Far too often in discussions regarding US racism, the role of the state in the maintenance of white political hegemony is ignored, which implies that individuals and institutions that comprise the state have been insulated from US racial conventions and therefore have promoted the interests of all Americans. However, Omni and Winant argue that the state facilitated white people's efforts to monopolise access to the bulk of US resources in order to ensure their dominance.[40] While it is clear that the state has assisted the cause of African-Americans, its actions have often sought to promote the cause of US 'national interests' as opposed to politically liberating black people. For example, the Emancipation Proclamation is often viewed as a humanitarian effort to promote racial equality as opposed to part of Lincoln's strategy to save the union and win the civil war. Similarly, the state's advocacy of African-American civil rights during the Cold War was part of the state's efforts to counteract Soviet propaganda and African-American activists' criticism and actions against domestic racism.[41] Despite the state's domestic interventions, the historical evidence suggests that (major) state interventions have occurred at moments of national crisis that necessitated racial reforms for the good of national interests.[42] In contrast, the state appears to have invested more effort in the suppression of African-Americans and the tacit support of the individual states' legal and socio-political suppression of African-Americans under the cover of the state's rights. Thus it is erroneously assumed that US racism was predominantly a facet of the southern states while the federal government, the northern states and the Midwest were much less concerned with issues of race. However, the evidence suggests that the US state has been at the centre of US racial oppression and that it has consistently promoted overtly or covertly assisted the creation and maintenance of white privilege. In short, the notion that the US state inertly reflected American society's racial conventions in contrast to the virulent racism of the southern states is a myth, which is invalidated by the federal government's historical indifference to the recruitment of African-Americans to its various departments.[43] Essentially, if state officials sought to prevent African-American employment in government institutions within the national capital, then it would clearly have problems responding to African-American foreign policy objectives. The assertion that state officials (which needs to be thoroughly researched as it raises some searching questions) hampered black employment within government institutions suggests that African-American under-representation in the federal government and their marginal role in the construction of US foreign policy are inextricably linked to the state's historical attempts to secure and maintain white hegemony in America. The US state's role in the political and capitalist exploitation of the African-American population necessitated this book utilisation of the Marxist theory.

One of the major strengths of the Marxist theory is its critique of Western capitalism in regard to its tendency towards economic exploitation of the proletariat and the creation of stratified classes within society (despite the fact that communist regimes such as the Soviet Union, whose political doctrines drew largely from Marxism failed to eliminate the existence of a political and economic elite). The contention that economic relations are the motor force of human history is a compelling one; however, theories that suggest human relations are derived from singular causes are problematic. Hence neo-Marxists' attempts to provide adaptations to Marx's original theory. In relation to this study, there is no conclusive evidence to validate that a capitalist class controlled the formation and construction of US foreign policy between 1900 and 1945. The fact that this research has failed to validate the Marxist theory contention does not entirely preclude the Marxist contention, although it has been argued that the preconditions for a Marxist revolution did not exist within the American political system.[44] In relation to this research, the Marxist theory fails to explain how US racial conventions have assumed a specific character, which negated the entry or influence of AAFAN irrespective of class, as 'Racist discourses have multiple power functions (such as domination over non-Europeans) that are neither reducible nor intelligible in terms of class exploitation alone.' Essentially, the state's drive to recruit African-Americans into its interventionist constituency was dictated by domestic and international requirements. Clearly the state's domestic reforms were designed to validate US propaganda in support of democratic freedom and to secure the aid of the African-American population in the US war effort. Presumably American capitalists could have opted to maximise on trade with the European combatants in order to reap the maximum profits while remaining neutral as they did in the IEW. However, irrespective of Japan's attack on Pearl Harbour, US interventionists were mobilising to support Britain's war effort because the Anglo-American alliance was based on other factors such as cultural and political affinity and shared ancestry.[45] US entry into the war resulted from a complex interplay of political and economic factors, which were interconnected to the maintenance of US sovereignty and the maintenance of democracy in Europe. Capitalism in itself is not an all-pervading determinant of the US state's actions and the existence of a near omnipotent capitalist class clearly does not exist due to the fragmented nature of US political and economic identities.

This research also questions the notion that Marxist/socialist or communist doctrines enabled American or Americanised white people to transcend US racial conventions and thereby form an alliance with African-Americans based on racial equality. For example, the communist and African-American coalition during the IEW and beyond floundered due to the inability of white and black people to overcome their racial designations, because of the capitalist classes' ability to force black and white workers to compete for jobs (i.e. the split market theory). The African-American community's rejection of Marxism and communism also stems from the centrality of religion and liberation theology to the African-American liberation struggle, which contradicts the anti-religious doctrines of Marxism/communism. In addition, black nationalists, Pan-Africanists and mainstream black leaders have rejected the Marxist proposition of a inter-racial alliance between working-class white and black people. Indeed, African-Americans knew from experience that working-class whites were part of the white collective that had brutalised people of colour for centuries. In fact, even black converts to the Marxist doctrine questioned (in America) the strategy of forming an inter-racial movement. Finally, the political establishment's characterisation of Marxism/ communism as un-American, undoubtedly influenced black people who desired to integrate into the American mainstream to reject Marxism and communism.

Consequently, the Soviet Union's economic relations with Italy in 1935 reinforced the belief that, aside from their radical/revolutionary rhetoric, communists were as self-interested as capitalists (in this instance) and, along with other white nations, did nothing to protect Ethiopian sovereignty despite their anti-imperialist rhetoric. In short, black people referred to Marxist/communist's inability to solve the realties of US race relations and the inability of its proponents to effectively unite with the black community along with its fellow black cohorts, as proof of the theory's failure to advance the African-American struggle for racial equality.[46] Michael Hunt's assertion that US foreign policy is intrinsically linked to its racial worldview suggests that economics is not the definitive factor in human history. One recognises then that economics and race are significant factors in human relations relative to the state's perceived national interests and their specific circumstances will determine the state's actions. However, historical precedence, which forms the basis of the socio-political and economic configuration of a state, can be instrumental in shaping human relations.[47] Therefore the historical legacy of white privilege is central to the marginal status of black people in the construction of US foreign policy.

The pluralist theory argues that power within the American political system is dispersed between different interests. The canon of pluralism suggests no single group can monopolise[48] power within the US socio-political and economic spheres. While the classical pluralist model suggests power is dispersed in America, it acknowledges the existence of power inequalities between interest groups in America. For example, the pluralist's point to the relative inequalities that can exist between business interests in relation to other interest groups, which has been highlighted by a number of studies. Unfortunately, the pluralist theory does not account for the historical legacy of the privileged position of the WASP elite and white Americans in general in relation to African-Americans.[49] American history is clearly defined by the hierarchical demarcation between the descendants of enslaved Africans and the white population. While one cannot (and need not) prove that every person identified as white has accrued privileges denied to African-Americans, the evidence is incontrovertible regarding the collective privileges bestowed on Euro-Americans.[50] The fact that pluralists say little regarding race and its impact on group mobilisation is problematic since the US political system was designed to 'separate the powers of government into three branches – legislative, executive and judicial – each of which would have the constitutional weapons to check each other.'[51] American aversion to the centralisation of power suggests that US political culture purports to favour multiple power sources even amongst interest groups. However, in practice the racial conventions defied American political logic by assuring that the white majority accumulated a monopoly over the decision-making process within the domestic sphere. The fact that between 1900 and 1945 racism prevented large sections of the African-American population from voting deprived them of a vital resource to affect presidential policy, and which, when combined with the interest group method of organisation, arguably provides a more effective means of pursuing their interests. In short, African-American second-class citizenship indicated their importance domestically and, when weighed in the balance, contributed to their marginal position in the construction of foreign policy. The domestic reforms promoted during WWII resulted from US labour needs, in relation to the war, not the recognition that white people enjoyed a monopoly of power over black people. As a result, the state was willing to discuss AAFAN's views on international affairs while doing nothing to advance their international interests. Indeed, in 1919 the state also ignored the black activists' foreign policy goals knowing that a small cadre of black intellectuals could do nothing to compel the state to pursue their goals.

Certainly the peace conference delegates did not consult the Pan-African congress delegates to ascertain their views on the fate of Germany's colonies or the plight of colonised Africans, because the global black constituency lacked the legitimacy and power to warrant Western attention. Again during the IEW, America and Britain aided Mussolini's war effort via trade while watching Ethiopia's demise. However, 'after June 1940 ... Britain put into effect the offensive military plans prepared at the time of the IEW of 1935–36. In the battle to free Ethiopia from Fascist rule, Britain used South African, Indian, and African troops, thus partially fulfilling Marcus Garvey's prediction that Ethiopia should be liberated by black soldiers!'[52] Thus the evidence suggests that the threat posed by the Axis powers forced America[53] to address its domestic colour-line and dialogue with African-Americans about international relations. Unfortunately, the pluralist theory fails to correctly account for the structural impediments placed before the AAFAN due to its racial designation. The Nazi regime's views (many of which were shared by some Americans) prompted the state to undergo domestic reforms to ensure black participation in the war and to maximise on their propaganda efforts. Thus America's racial reforms were largely stimulated by international events as opposed to an innate desire to promote change by the state and by white people in general. On reflection, major racial reforms such as the emancipation proclamation and the Fourteenth amendment, the reforms occasioned by WWII and the civil rights struggle (while accounting for African-American efforts) were by-products of the state's efforts to protect/promote the national interest. One can argue that white people have shown little desire to promote real racial equality without external prompting, which is why the state has been the principal party (along with African-Americans) to ensure the reorientation of the racial colour-line for political reasons as opposed to humanitarian principles of racial equality. Some authors reject the pluralist proposition that 'the interest group system in the United states is open and accessible'[54] for African-Americans because white people have enjoyed a monopoly of power over the black population, which dates back to the founding fathers and has been maintained throughout American history. Consequently, the pluralist notion of diverse interest groups, afforded the opportunity to promote their interests in America, may more accurately reflect the competition among white people to win power[55] for their constituent group, while the colour-line curtailing African-Americans from utilising conventional means to promote their interests in America ultimately calls into question America's pre-1960s claims of democracy, because as Mouffe states 'for democracy to exist, no social agent[s] should be able to claim any mastery of the foundation of society'.[56]

A strong case has been made by some authors that white people have maintained a political fiefdom in America and slavery, institutional racism, Jim Crow, the negation of black voting rights and black people's marginal representation in government support their claims. However, some political scientists who maintain that 'the fundamental purpose of theory is ... to explain, comprehend and interpret reality'[57] ignore, or fail to devote primary attention to, theories of race in their research. One wonders why Dunleavy and O'Leary's 'Theories of the state' is silent regarding the state's role in the construction and maintenance of racial hierarchies, given the role of the state in the construction of apartheid in South Africa,[58] racial equality in the US and the European state's use of racial propaganda to facilitate their imperial conquest of Africa and Asia. Some political theorists may argue that liberal democracy is incompatible with state-sanctioned racial oppression; however, this claim needs to be examined more thoroughly in addition to pluralism's inability to explain African-American marginalisation (specifically) in relation to US foreign policy and more generally.

The evidence derived from this research points to the concerted efforts of African-Americans to examine international issues for themselves, in order to determine and facilitate their own interests. However, the case studies validate the contention that white America generally, and the state specifically, were averse to incorporating African-Americans into the foreign policy establishment except when it would facilitate the state's interests. As a result, the WWII prompted the state to enlist blacks in its interventionist coalition. In contrast, AAFAN's anti-colonialism (during the war) and its call for post-war de-colonialisation was ignored by the US government and the European colonialists. Overall, this research suggests that African-American attempts to transform international relations were antithetical to American and Western interests. Despite the fact that white nations used race to exclude black people from positions of authority and power, the 'race first' and Pan-Africanist doctrines adopted by people of African descent in America and internationally were rejected by white people. Ultimately Du Bois and Garvey's Pan-Africanist thrust to aid African people was rejected not because white people hate black people but because white people recognised that racial identity had provided them with a powerful means of group organisation, which if utilised by black people could threaten Western global hegemony. Therefore America and Britain helped to ensure the destruction of the UNIA during the 1920s. The fact that black nationalists spear-headed the African-Americans' campaign to aid Ethiopia is indicative of African-American recognition that international affairs were conducted on a racialised basis and that the League of Nations and the states it represented, which were over-whelmingly white, were not prepared to halt Italy's attack on Ethiopia. White hegemony was, if not always explicitly stated, a given fact during the 1930s, whilst black people's identification with their African heritage and their attempts to free the black world were incompatible with white Western hege-mony. As a result, black identification with Ethiopia was discouraged and white people pointed out that Ethiopians were not black Africans and did not consider themselves Negroes. Again the West, including America, allowed Italy's rape of Ethiopia but was apparently able to aid Ethiopian insurgents during the WWII when it suited their interests. Essentially this study suggests that racism in America was utilised to ensure the unequal distribution of power between white and black people. Indeed, even when African-Americans such as Ralph Bunche sought to influence foreign policy without adhering to a racialised worldview, he was confronted by state institutions that struggled to see beyond his racial identity.[59] In short, the notion that US foreign policy has managed to avoid operating on a racial basis, considering America's inability to do so domestically, is an example of political dissonance whereby the elite institutions' elevated status propagates the false assumption that they have transcended socio-political maladies such as racism. Nevertheless, scho-lars most avoid projecting racism as a monolithic edifice that explains all anomalies within the African-American community, in addition to recognising the power inequalities amongst the white population, still Roediger demon-strates how black oppression was used to assuage class antagonism amongst white Americans[60] and therefore ensure a high level of co-operation among white people. In essence, US foreign policy and the state officials that exe-cuted it (during the specified period of this research) appeared to reflect American racial conventions and consequently orientated themselves to people of colour domestically or internationally in a manner consistent with white hegemony. In short, Hunt's assessment of US foreign policy as reflecting the racially orientated democratic values established by the founding fathers is correct[61] as the evidence indicates that African-Americans' struggles to effect changes in the international arena were stifled as a direct result of their domestic marginalisation. However, their political activism coupled with the consequences of historical events enabled the AAFAN to win concessions from the state that created leverage for the liberalising forces in US society irrespective of their actual motives. In addition, the struggle to realign the international racial status quo allowed African-Americans to harness and refine their organisational skills and alert the state and Americans in general that a new social force was emerging that would ultimately reform US society and force the Western world to redefine its racial worldview. The racial colony theory provides the best explanation for African-Americans' increased participation in foreign affairs between 1900 and 1945, as the racial colony theory accounts for white political hegemony generally but recognises that historical events and black activism increased African-Americans status in relation to the construction of US foreign policy.

Chapter 6 illustrates how the ideological parameters of AAFAN where redefined to accord with state interests. That is, AAFAN's prior commitment to African independence was curtailed due to the narrow confines of McCarthyite politics, increased political repression and efforts to overturn Jim Crow without being labelled as communist agitators. To be plain, Chapter 7 indicates that AAFAN was decimated due to state repression. While African-American leaders such as Walter White still addressed international issues, their views were expressed via an anti-communist rationale designed to tally with mainstream views.

Furthermore, White and the cohort of conservative internationalists used a pragmatic blend of conformity, support and spin to win domestic concessions by backing state-sanctioned foreign policy. Significantly, White and the NAACP rejected the organic internationalism championed by Du Bois and Robeson (amongst others) which weakened and constrained AAFAN's efforts to secure their human rights. Moreover the repressive tactics of the state fractured and dismantled the pursuit of a radical movement that envisioned ending white supremacy at home and abroad. As a result, the politics of Dr King and a new generation of African-American leaders failed to appreciate or chose not to articulate (due to fear of repression) the symbiotic relationship between US and global white hegemony. Thus, a regional brand of civil rights took precedence over the creation of a transnational movement which addressed the national and international parameters of white hegemony. Still the petitions to the UN and the limited adherence to a modernised variant of Pan-Africanism fuelled African-American interest in the ANC's defiance campaign, the Mau Mau in Kenya, the Bandung conference and Ghanaian independence, all of which were accompanied by a renewed interest in international politics and their African identity. In contrast, the relative conservatism of mainstream black leaders was challenged by the pulsating undercurrent of black nationalism, and racial internationalism, extolled by Elijah Muhammad, Malcolm X and the apostles of a black power revolution. However, in the 1950s adherence to a state-centred approach to foreign affairs prevented the construction of a fluid transnational coalition between AAFAN and the anti-colonialist movement in the developing world.

Chapter 7 demonstrates continuity in regard to state repression. It suggests that the state increased its level of repression and was clearly concerned about the development of a transnational movement against white hegemony. Hence, the US intelligence network was used to neutralise perceived threats in a calculated and ruthless manner. Indeed, from African-American reformists to so-called revolutionaries the state engaged in intense surveillance and counter-intelligence schemes. Thus the treatment of King and Malcolm was not necessarily unique. Nonetheless, the prominence of Malcolm and King and their overt engagement with foreign affairs did elicit a special response from state agencies. One can see similarities between the treatment of Lumumba, King and Malcolm as US agents played an indirect role in neutralising or targeting all three, and ultimately all three men were assassinated amid allegations of the American government's involvement. In addition, their racial identity may have impacted on the severity of the counter-intelligence employed against them.

While Malcolm's vitriol against white racism was bound to provoke white America, his criticism was often based on historical and contemporary examples of racial supremacy. Even his calls for self-defence were grounded in US political culture. Significantly, King's evocations of racial brotherhood were insufficient to protect him from counter-intelligence schemes and the wrath of the Johnson administration.

While their domestic activism partially explains the state's malevolence towards King and Malcolm, their respective criticism of foreign affairs must be acknowledged as a key factor which increased relative to their intervention in foreign affairs. That is, Cold War politics and calls for the socio-economic and political restructuring of the USA and the fear of the emergence of a transnational movement geared to decolonisation and racial equality defined the state's response to King and Malcolm. The fact is King and Malcolm's actions were informed by both domestic and global factors which could have dramatically transformed the African-American struggle.

Chapter 7 suggests that the civil rights' struggle has not being placed in the broader international struggle whereby events in America, Africa and Asia created a transnational current of change in the lives of people of colour including President Obama. This is problematic as it undermines the transnational qualities of the nationalist movements in the developing world and the quest for racial equality in America. For example, Stokely Carmichael's use of the colonisation metaphor to describe black America was a consequence of his reading of nationalist literature in the developing world and his ideological tutelage under King and Malcolm who both saw black America as an impoverished colony of white America.

Indeed, the state's motive for racial reforms reflects the complexity of managing a mass movement, counteracting Soviet and Cuban and Chinese criticism and striving to project a liberal image to newly established non-white nations. Thus when King and Malcolm threatened to sully America's liberal image, they were treated in accordance with Cold War logic designed to neutralise foreign opposition. In brief, while state-sanctioned racial realignment was acceptable, activities designed to reformulate capitalism and redistribute American wealth or radically alter US politics were deemed as foreign and subversive.

In a sense, the death of Malcolm and King may have led to an unsustained radicalisation but it also left black America bereft of internationally recognised leaders whose stature could facilitate a transnational network which could lobby on behalf of African and non-white nations or mount a campaign to receive international assistance from the UN. Despite the conjecture, the prospect of an alliance between King and Malcolm would have posed major problems in regard to America's domestic and foreign policy. Indeed, their respective deaths precluded Hoover's fear of a black messiah[62] with both domestic and international standing. In fact, the respective deaths of both men arguably hampered the African-American struggle in the 1970s and 1980s.

Notes

1 Introduction

1 J. H. Carruthers, *The Irritated Genie: An Essay on the Haitian Revolution*, Chicago: Kemetic Institute, 1985, xviii; M. Karenga, *Introduction to Black Studies*, Los Angeles: University of Sankore Press, 1993, 135; Dr M. K. Asante, *African-American History: A Journey of Liberation*, Maywood: The Peoples Publishing Group, Inc., 1995, 118.

2 J. H. Clarke, *Notes for an African World Revolution: Africans at the Crossroads*, Trenton: Africa World Press, 1992, 185.

3 D. L. Lewis, *W. E. B. Du Bois: The Fight for Equality and the American Century 1919–1963*, New York: Henry Holt and Company, LLC, 2000, 59.

4 Lewis, *The Fight for Equality*, 502; A. S. Layton, *International Politics and Civil Rights Policies in the United States, 1941–1960*, Cambridge: Cambridge University Press, 2000, 48.

5 C. E. Lincoln, 'The Race Problem and International Relations,' in G. W. Shepherd Jr., ed., *Racial Influences on American Foreign Policy*, New York: Basic Books, 1970, 53.

6 B. P. Bowser, 'Race and US Foreign Policy: A Bibliography Essay,' *Sage Race Relations*, 1 February 1987, vol. 12, 5.

7 This book unlike existing academic research employs racial theories to systematically examine and evaluate US foreign policy.

8 H. Adi and M. Sherwood, *The 1945 Manchester Pan-African Congress Revisited*, London: New Beacon Books Ltd., 1995, 62.

9 G. W. Shepherd Jr., ed., *Racial Influences on American Foreign Policy*, London: Basic Books, 1970, 5.

10 Bowser, 'Race and US Foreign Policy,' 5.

11 Ibid., 5.

12 P. Seabury, 'Racial Problems in American Foreign Policy,' in Shepherd, *Racial Influences*, 61.

13 B. G. Plummer, *Rising Wind: Black Americans and U.S. Foreign Affairs, 1935–1960*, London: University of North Carolina Press, 1996, 1.

14 W. E. B. Du Bois, *The Soul of Black Folk*, New York: Alfred A. Knopf, Inc., 1993, 5.

15 Plummer, *Rising Wind*, 5.

16 M. H. Hunt, *Ideology and U. S. Foreign Policy*, London: Yale University Press, 1987, 16; M. L. Krenn, *The Color of Empire: Race and American Foreign Relations*, Washington, DC: Potomac Books, 2006, xiv; T. McCarthy, Race, Empire and the Idea of Human Development, Cambridge: Cambridge University Press, 2009, 69.

17 R. D. Roediger, *How Race Survived U.S. History: From Settlement and Slavery to the Obama Phenomenon*, London: Verso, 2008.

18 A. Hacker, *Two Nations: Black and White, Separate, Hostile, Unequal*, New York: Macmillan, 1992, 4.

19 M. K. Asante, *The Painful Demise of Eurocentrism*, Trenton: Africa World Press, Inc., 1999, 13.

20 Hunt, *Ideology and U.S.*, xii; S. E. Ambrose, *Rise to Globalism: American Foreign Policy Since 1938*, London: Penguin Books Ltd., 1993, xi; J. Dumbrell, *The Making of US Foreign Policy*, Manchester: Manchester University Press, 1990, 6.

21 Plummer, *Rising Wind*, 3; Bowser, 'Race and US Foreign Policy,' 4; G. Shepperson, 'Notes on Negro American Influences on the Emergence of African Nationalism,' *Journal of African History*, 1960, vol. 1, no. 2, 306; J. L. Roark, 'American Black Leaders: The Response of Colonialism and the Cold War,' *African Historical Studies*, 1971, vol. 4, no. 2, 253.

22 A. Sbacchi, *Legacy of Bitterness: Ethiopia and Fascist Italy, 1935–1941*, Trenton: The Red Sea Press, 1997, 17.

23 Plummer, *Rising Wind*, 2; Clarke, *Notes for an African World*, 183.

24 Plummer, *Rising Wind*, 3; Bowser, 'Race and US Foreign Policy,' 4; Shepperson, 'Notes on Negro American Influences,' 306; Roark, 'American Black Leaders,' 253.

25 Clarke, *Notes for an African World*, 187.

26 Plummer, *Rising Wind*, 13.

27 K. Verney, *Black Civil Rights in America*, London: Routledge, 2004, 13.

28 Clarke, *Notes for an African World*, 190.

29 M. Karenga, *Introduction to Black Studies*.

30 The Niagara Movement, which was formed in 1905 and preceded the National Association for the Advancement of Colored People, was dedicated to black liberation both domestically and internationally, as was the UNIA which was formed in 1916. Chapter 3 will demonstrate that Du Bois was instrumental in involving the NAACP in international issues despite its original remit.

31 G. Padmore, *Pan-Africanism or Communism? The Coming Struggle for Africa*, London: Dennis Dobson, 1956, 25.

32 T. Cross, *The Black Power Imperative: Racial Inequality and the Politics of Non-Violence*, New York: Faulkner Books, 1987, 396.

33 J. H. Clarke, *Critical Lessons: In Slavery and the Slave Trade*, Richmond: Native Sun Publishers, 1996, 7.

34 H. Zinn, *A People's History of the United States: From 1492 to the Present*, London, Addison Wesley Longman Limited, 1996, 23.

35 I. Parmar, 'Resurgent Academic Interest in the Council on Foreign Relations,' *Politics: Surveys, Debates and Controversies in Politics*, February 2001, vol. 21, no. 1, 32.

36 The use of AAFAN establishes an ideological boundary in order to present the findings derived from the empirical evidence in a comprehensive manner.

37 B. G. Plummer, 'Evolution of the Black Foreign Policy Constituency,' in M. L. Krenn, ed., *The African-American Voice in U.S. Foreign Policy Since World War II*, London: Garland Publishing, Inc., 1999, 91.

38 The term 'network' does not imply that AAFAN was ideologically homogeneous; rather, it indicates that the active participates were all engaged in constructing foreign policies.

39 Karenga, *Introduction to Black Studies*.

40 H. Adi, and M. Sherwood, *Pan-African History: Political Figures from Africa and the Diaspora since 1787*, London: Routledge, 2003.

41 Adi and Sherwood, *Pan-African History*.

42 Plummer, 'Evolution of the Black,' 91.

43 The term 'talented tenth' referred to the African-American educated elite who Du Bois argued should lead the black struggle. D. L. Lewis, *W. E. B. Du Bois: Biography of A Race 1868–1919*, New York: Henry Holt and Company, 1994, 441.

44 Plummer, 'Evolution of the Black,' 19.
45 C. Anderson, *Eyes Off the Prize: African Americans, the United Nations, and the Struggle for Human Rights, 1944–55*, Cambridge: Cambridge University Press, 2003; K. R. Janken, *White: The Biography of Walter White, Mr. NAACP*, New York: The New Press, 2003.
46 Karenga, *Introduction to Black Studies*, 169.
47 Shepperson, 'Notes on Negro American Influences,' 306; Adi and Sherwood, *The 1945 Manchester*, 54; R. A. Hill, *Pan-African Biography*, Los Angeles: Crossroads Press, 1987, 98.
48 Roediger, *How Race Survived U.S. History*; M. Keita, *Race and the Writing of History: Riddling the Sphinx*, Oxford: Oxford University Press, 2000.
49 T. Martin, *Marcus Garvey, Hero: A First Biography*, Dover: Majority Press, 1983, 61.
50 H. Campbell, *Rasta and Resistance: From Marcus Garvey to Walter Rodney*, London, Hansib Publishing Limited, 1985, 54.
51 Clarke, *Notes for an African World Revolution*, 199.
52 Janken, *White*.
53 J. H. Cone, *Martin and Malcolm and America: A Dream or a Nightmare*, London: Fount Paperbacks, 1993, 4.
54 J. M. Washington, ed., *A Testament of Hope: The Essential Writings and Speeches of Martin Luther King, Jr.*, New York: HarperCollins Publishers, 1991, 321.
55 Broderick, F. L., Meier, A., Rudwick, E., eds., *Black Protest in the Twentieth Century*, London: Collier Macmillan Publishers, 1986, 102.
56 Ledwidge, M., Miller, L. B. and Parmar, I., ed., *New Directions in US Foreign Policy*, New York: Routledge, 2009, 155.
57 C. W. Cheng, 'The Cold War: Its Impact on the Black Liberation Struggle Within the United States,' in Krenn, *The African-American Voice*, 129.
58 Ledwidge *et al.*, *New Directions*.
59 Hunt, *Ideology and U.S.*, 60.
60 Shepherd, *Racial Influences*, 3.
61 McCarthy, *Race, Empire and the Idea*, 72.
62 Krenn, *The Color of Empire*.
63 Clarke, *Notes for an African World Revolution*.
64 I. Parmar, 'The Issue of State Power: The Council on Foreign Relations as a Case Study,' *Journal of American Studies*, Apr. 1995, 84.
65 Ibid., 79.
66 Bowser, 'Race and US Foreign Policy,' 6.
67 Clarke, *Notes for an African World Revolution*, 248.
68 D. L. Lewis, ed., *W. E. B. Du Bois: A Reader*, New York: Henry Holt and Company Inc., 1995, 42.
69 Adi and Sherwood, *Pan-African History*.
70 Bowser, 'Race and US Foreign Policy,' 5.
71 Ibid., 10; Plummer, *Rising Wind*, 1.
72 T. J. R. Kornweibel, *'Seeing Red' Federal Campaigns Against Black Militancy, 1919–25*, Indianapolis: Indiana University Press, 1998; B. Z. A. Kondo, *Conspiracys: Unravelling the Assassination of Malcolm X*, Washington, DC: Nubia Press, 1993.
73 Jones notes the racial bias of the FBI. R. Jeffreys-Jones, *The FBI: A History*, London: Yale University Press, 2007, 6.
74 K. O'Reilly, *'Racial Matters': The FBI's Secret File on Black America, 1960–1972*, London: The Free Press, 1991, 12.
75 R. K. Yin, *Case Study Research: Design and Methods*, 3rd edition, London: Sage Publications, 2003, xiii.
76 Yin, *Case Study Research*, 1.

77 W. R. Scott, 'Malaku E Bayen: Ethiopian Emissary to Black America, 1936–41,' *Ethiopian Observer*, 1972, 132; R. Ross, 'Black Americans and Italo-Ethiopian Relief, 1935–36,' *Ethiopian Observer*, 1972, vol. 15, no. 2, 122.
78 Seabury, 'Racial Problems,' 53.
79 Karenga, *Introduction to Black Studies*, 11; J. H. Carruthers, *Intellectual Warfare*, Chicago: Third World Press, 1999, 81.
80 S. M. Lipset, *American Exceptionalism: A Double-Edged Sword*, London: W. W. Norton & Company, 1997, 113; Cross, *The Black Power Imperative*, ix.
81 Campbell, *Rasta and Resistance*, 73.
82 Plummer, *Rising Wind*, 37.
83 Ibid., 43.
84 Sbacchi, *Legacy of Bitterness*, 6.
85 M. Naison, *Communists in Harlem during the Depression*, Chicago: University of Illinois Press, 1983, 138.
86 P. M. Von Eschen, *Race Against Empire Black Americans and Anti-Colonialism, 1937–1957*, London: Cornell University Press, 1997, 34.
87 Roark, 'American Black Leaders,' 37.
88 J. Woodland, 'How did Participation in America's wars affect Black Americans,' *American Studies Today*, Liverpool: American Studies Resource Centre, 2001, 20.
89 Layton, *International Politics*, 39.
90 Miroff, B., Seidelman, R., Swanstrom, T., *The Democratic Debate: An Introduction to American Politics*, New York: Houghton Mifflin Company, 1998, 547; Ambrose, *Rise to Globalism*, xii; Dumbrell, *The Making of U.S.*, 69, Layton, *International Politics*, 12.
91 D. E. Shi and G. Tindal, *America: A Narrative History*, London: W. W. Norton & Company, 1993, 763.
92 Von Eschen, *Race Against Empire*.
93 Zinn, *A People's History*, 410.
94 Lewis, *The Fight for Equality*, 462.
95 J. S. Nye, *Understanding International Conflict: An Introduction to Theory and History*, New York: HarperCollins College Publishers, 1993, 87.
96 G. Breitman, C. L. R. James and E. Keemer, *Fighting Racism in World War II*, London, Pathfinder, 1991, 31.
97 Ibid., 31.
98 J. H. Clarke, *Marcus Garvey and the Vision of Africa*, New York: Vintage Books, 1974, 270.
99 Lewis, *The Fight for Equality*, 467.
100 M. Soloman, 'Black Critics of Colonialism and the Cold War,' in Krenn, *The African-American Voice*, 36.
101 Layton, *International Politics*, 39.
102 African-Americans demands for racial equality were replicated during the 1960s at the height of the Cold War, which similarly provided a favourable context that enabled black people to secure their interests due to the pressures stemming from international politics.
103 H. W. Van Loon, *The Story of Mankind*, London: W. W. Norton & Company Ltd., 2000, 552.
104 Nye, *Understanding International Conflict*, 99.
105 Lewis, *The Fight for Equality*, 502; Kondo, *Conspiracies*, 11; Shi and Tindal, *America*, 809.
106 M. L. Dudziak, 'Josephine Baker, Racial Protest, and the Cold War,' in Krenn, *The African-American*, 136.
107 Loon, *The Story*, 536.
108 C. Beckner, *100 African-Americans Who Shaped American History*, San Francisco: Bluewood Books, 1995, 59; H. Aptheker, *A Documentary History of*

the *People in the United States*, Volume 5, New York: Carol Publishing Group, 1993, 55.

109 Soloman, 'Black Critics,' 53.

110 Ibid., 53.

111 R. Harris, 'Ralph Bunche and Afro-American Participation in Decolonization,' in Krenn, *The African-American Voice*, 173; H. Aptheker, 'W. E. B. Du Bois and Africa,' in R. A. Hill, ed., *Pan-African Biography*, Los Angeles: African Studies Center, 1987, 112; Von Eschen, *Race Against Empire*, 83; G. Horne, *Black and Red: W. E. B. Du Bois and Afro-American Response to the Cold War, 1944–1963* New York: University of New York, 1986, 36.

112 Von Eshen, *Race Against Empire*, 79, Roark, 'American Black Leaders,' 257.

113 C. Anderson, 'From Hope to Disillusion,' in Krenn, M. L., ed., *The African American Voice in US Foreign Policy Since World War II*, London: Garland Publishing Inc., 1999, 184.

114 Ibid., 184.

115 Harris, 'Ralph Bunche,' 172.

116 Ledwidge *et al.*, *New Directions*.

117 Hunt, *Ideology and U.S*, 52; Ledwidge *et al.*, *New Directions*, 152; T. Borstelmann, *The Cold War and the Color Line*, Cambridge: Harvard University Press, 2001, 6.

118 Shepherd, *Racial Influences*, 6.

119 Plummer, *Rising Wind*, 1

120 Ibid. 1.

121 B. W. Jentleson, *American Foreign Policy: The Dynamics of Choice in the 21st Century*, London: W. W. Norton & Company, 2007.

122 R. Miliband, *The State in Capitalist Society*, London, André Deutsch, 1968, 4.

123 Singh, R., ed., *Governing America: The Politics of a Divided Democracy*, Oxford: Oxford University Press, 2003, 36.

124 P. Hirst, *Representative Democracy and its Limits*, Oxford: Polity Press, 1990, 40.

125 Singh, *Governing America*; R. Maidment, 'Democracy in the USA since 1945,' in D. Goldblatt, M. Kiloh, P. Lewis, and D. Potter, eds., *Democratization* Cambridge: Polity Press, 1997, 122.

126 R. A. Dahl, *Pluralist Democracy in the United States*, Chicago: Rand McNally, 1967, 24.

127 M. Smith, 'Pluralism,' in G. Marsh and G. Stoker, eds., *Theory and Methods in Political Science*, New York: Palgrave, 1995, 212.

128 Ibid., 216.

129 Ibid., 215.

130 R. Polenberg, *One Nation Divisible: Class, Race, and Ethnicity in the United States since 1938*, Middlesex: Penguin Books, 1983, 25.

131 B. Blauner, 'Talking Past Each Other: Black and White Languauges of Race,' in F. L. Pincus and H. J. Ehlich, eds., *Race and Ethnic Conflict: Contending Views on Prejudice, Discrimination and Ethnoviolence*, Oxford: Westview Press, 1994, 25.

132 Blauner, 'Talking Past Each Other,' 25.

133 Ibid., 25.

134 Miroff, *The Democratic Debate*, A-32.

135 I. Parmar, 'The Issue of State Power, The Council on Foreign Relations as a Case Study,' *Journal of American Studies*, Apr. 1995, 13.

136 Miliband, *The State*, 4. In this regard Des Kings' analysis within *Separate and Unequal* of the state's poor employment record (during the period studied) in relation to African-Americans highlights the government's failure to protect the political and economic welfare of blacks within state institutions. According to Des King 'the U.S. Administration constituted a powerful institution upholding arrangements privileging Whites and discriminating against Blacks. In the eight decades before 1964, the Federal government used its power and authority to

support segregated race relations. Historically, the segregation of Black American citizens in the federal bureaucracy is a major but neglected aspect of the U.S. federal government, with implications for both the position of these citizens in the United States and the character of the state.' D. King, *Separate and Unequal: Black Americans and the US Federal Government*, Oxford: Clarendon Press 1995, vii.

137 A. H. Birch, *Concept and Theories of Modern Democracy*, London: Routledge, 2002, 200.

138 Birch, *Concept and Theories*, 200.

139 Parmar, 'The Issue of State Power,' 76.

140 C. W. Mills, *The Power Elite*, New York: Oxford University Press, 1956, 292.

141 Ibid., 19.

142 L. Back and J. Solomos, *Theories of Race and Racism*, London: Routledge Press, 2001, 395.

143 Christie, K., ed., United States Foreign Policy and National Identity in the Twenty-First Century, London: Routledge, 2008, xiv.

144 D. Merrill and T. G. Paterson, eds., *Major Problems in American Foreign Relations, Volume II: Since 1914*, New York: Houghton Mifflin Company, 2000, 19.

145 King, *Separate and Unequal*, 16.

146 K. Verney, *Black Civil Rights in America*, London: Routledge, 2004, 1; D. Goldblatt, M. Kiloh, P. Lewis, and D. Potter, eds., *Democratization*, Cambridge: Polity Press, 1997, 34; Roediger, *How Race Survived U.S. History*, 197.

147 Parmar, 'The Issue of State Power,' 75.

148 Krenn, *The Color of Empire*.

149 Ledwidge *et al.*, *New Directions*; D. King, 'The Racial Bureaucracy: African-Americans and the Federal Government in the Era of Segregated Race Relations,' *Governance: An International Journal of Policy and Administration*, October 1999, vol. 12, no. 4, 345.

150 Ibid.,156.

151 T. Skocpol, *States and Social Revolutions*, Cambridge: Cambridge University Press, 1979, 30; S. Krasner, *Defending the National Interest*, Princeton: Princeton University Press, 1978, 11; P. Evans, D. Rueschemeyer and T. Skocpol, eds., *Bringing the State Back In*, Cambridge: Cambridge University Press, 1985, 9.

152 F. L. Bender, ed., *Karl Marx The Communist Manifesto*, London: Norton, 1988, 24.

153 I. Parmar, *Special Interests, The State and the Anglo-American Alliance, 1939–1945*, London: Frank Cass, 1995, 11.

154 J. Lively and A. Reeve, eds., *Modern Political Theory from Hobbes to Marx Key Debates*, London: Routledge, 1991, 284; P. Dunleavy and B. O'Leary, *Theories of the State: Politics of Liberal Democracy*, London: MacMillan, 1987, 206.

155 It is, however, conceivable in the contemporary times race/ethnicity may predominate over class formations.

156 Bender, *Karl Marx*, 24.

157 I. Hampsher-Monk, *A History of Modern Political Thought: Major Political Thinkers from Hobbes to Marx*, Cambridge: Blackwell, 1995, 529.

158 G. Taylor, 'Marxism,' in G. Marsh, and G. Stoker, eds., *Theory and Methods in Political Science*, New York: Palgrave, 1995, 249.

159 F. Engels, *The Origins of the Family, Private Property and the State*, Peking: Foreign Language Press, 1978, 208.

160 D. Held, *Models of Democracy*, Cambridge: Polity Press, 1987, 119.

161 D. Marsh, 'Convergence between Theories of the state,' in Marsh and Stoker, *Theory and Methods*, 281.

162 Robinson, C. J., *Black Marxism: The Making of the Black Radical Tradition*, London: The North Carolina Press, 1983, xiii.

163 Bender, *Karl Marx*, 57.

164 Cross, *The Black Power Imperative*, 4; D. H. Swinton, 'The Economic Status of African-Americans: Limited Ownership and Persistent Inequality,' in B. Tidwell, ed., *The State of Black America*, New York: National Urban League, 1992, 74; A. Hacker, *Two Nations: Black and White, Separate, Hostile, Unequal*, New York: Macmillan, 1992, 4.
165 Singh, *Governing America*.
166 K. Christie, ed., *United States Foreign Policy and National Identity in the Twenty-First Century*, London: Routledge, 2008.
167 Ledwidge *et al.*, *New Directions*.
168 A. M. Schlesinger, Jr., *The Disuniting of America Reflections on a Multicultural Society*, London: W. W. Norton & Company, 1998, 20.
169 Lipset, *American Exceptionism*, 195; I. Parmar, 'Resurgent Academic Interest in the Council on Foreign Relations,' *Politics: Surveys, Debates and Controversies in Politics*, February 2001, vol. 21, no. 1, 34.
170 Shepherd, *Racial Influences*, 6.
171 McCarthy, *Race, Empire and the Idea*, 122.
172 Jentleson, *American Foreign Policy*, 73.
173 A. Wilson, *Blueprint for Black Power: A Moral, Political and Economic Imperative for the Twenty-First Century*, New York: Afrikan World Infosystems, 1998, 142.
174 Ibid., 144.
175 C. V. Hamilton and K. Ture, *Black Power: The Politics of Liberation*, New York: Vintage Books, 1992, 7.
176 Wilson, *Blueprint for Black Power*, 503.
177 Ibid., 504.
178 Karenga, *Introduction to Black Studies*, 422.
179 Ibid., 422.
180 Hamilton and Ture, *Black Power*, 6.
181 Ibid., 10.
182 Ibid., 10.
183 D. T. Wellman, *Portraits of White Racism*, New York: Cambridge University Press, 1977, 35.
184 Omi, M. and Winant, H., *Racial Formation in the United States from the 1960s to 1990s*, London: Routledge, 1994, 65.
185 Hamilton and Ture., *Black Power*, 6. The fact that 'Until the middle of the twentieth century Black Americans were employed in relatively few numbers by the Federal government' King, *Separate and Unequal*, 80, is indicative of white hegemony within and over the state.
186 Omi and Winant, *Racial Formation*, 81; Wilson, *Blueprint for Black Power*, 141; King, *Separate and Unequal*, 12.
187 Hacker, *Two Nations*, 15.
188 Wilson, *Blueprint for Black Power*, 249.
189 Ibid., 141.
190 Kondo, *Conspiracies*, 11.
191 Keita, *Race and the Writing of History*; Carruthers, *Intellectual Warfare*.
192 Carruthers, *Intellectual Warfare*, 74.
193 K. C. Minion Morrison, 'Reflections of Senior Scholar on the Profession of International Studies,' *International Studies Perspective*, Vol. 9, No. 4, November 2008.
194 Ledwidge, *et al.*, *New Directions*, 165.

2 The forging of the African-American Foreign Affairs Community

1 H. Aptheker, 'W. E. B. Du Bois and Africa,' in R. A. Hill, ed., *Pan-African Biography*, Los Angeles: Crossroads Press, 1987, 101.

2 I. S. Cohen and R. W. Logan, *The American Negro: Old World Background and New World Background*, Boston: Houghton Mifflin Company, 1970, 138.
3 Cohen and Logan, *The American Negro*, 151.
4 T. Martin, *Pan-African Connection: From Slavery to Garvey and Beyond*, Dover: Majority Press, 1985, vii.
5 C. West, *Prophesy Deliverance! An Afro-American Revolutionary Christianity*, Philadelphia: Westminster Press, 1988, 41.
6 S. Stuckey, *'I want to be an African:' Paul Robeson and the ends of nationalist theory and practice, 1919–1945*, Los Angeles: Center for Afro-American Studies, 1976, 1.
7 J. H. Clarke, *Notes for an African World Revolution Africans at the Crossroads*, New Jersey: African World Press, Inc., 1992, 21.
8 A. M. Schlesinger, Jr., *The Disuniting of America: Reflections on a Multicultural Society*, London: W. W. Norton & Company, 1998, 87; B. G. Plummer, *Rising Wind: Black Americans and US Foreign Affairs, 1935–1960*, London: The University of North Carolina Press, 1996, 23.
9 P. Henry, 'Pan-Africanism: A Dream Come True,' *Foreign Affairs*, Apr. 1959, 450.
10 C. A. Diop, *Civilization or Barbarism: An Authentic Anthropology*, New York: Lawrence Hill Books, 1991, 219.
11 G. Padmore, *Africanism and Communism? The Coming Struggle for Africa*, London: Dennis Dobson, 1956, 115.
12 H. Campbell, *Rasta and Resistance: From Marcus Garvey to Walter Rodney*, London: Hansib Publishing Limited, 1985, 51.
13 Clarke, *Notes for and African World*, 391.
14 Martin, *Pan-African Connection*, 12.
15 I. Parmar, 'The Issue of State Power: The Council on Foreign Relations as a Case Study,' *Journal of American Studies*, Apr. 1995, 84.
16 Ibid., 79.
17 B. P. Bowser, 'Race and US Foreign Policy: A Bibliography Essay,' *Sage Race Relations*, 1 February 1987, vol., 6.
18 M. H. Hunt, *Ideology and U.S. Foreign Policy*, London: Yale University Press, 1987, 91.
19 *Report of The Pan-African Conference*. Held on the 23, 24 and 25 July, 1900 at Westminster Town Hall, Westminster, S.W.1, *The Papers of W. E. B. Du Bois, 1803 (1877–1963) 1965, Special Collection*, Sanford, NC: Microfilming Corp. of America, 1980, microfilm reel 2, frame 1136: 3.
20 *Report of The Pan-African Conference*, July, 1900, 3.
21 Ibid., 4.
22 Ibid., 4.
23 H. Adi and M. Sherwood, *The 1945 Manchester Pan-African Congress Revisited*, London: New Beacon Books Ltd., 1995, 62.
24 Plummer, *Rising Wind*, 14.
25 R. Lewis, *Marcus Garvey: Anti-Colonial Champion*, Trenton: Africa World Press, Inc., 1998, 30.
26 R. A. Hill, ed., *Marcus Garvey: Life and Lessons: A Centennial Companion to the Marcus Garvey and Universal Negro Improvement Association Papers*, London: University of California Press, 1987, 99.
27 W. E. B. Du Bois, *The Autobiography of W. E. B. Du Bois*, New York: International Publishers Co., Inc., 1997, 289.
28 A. N. Wilson, *Afrikan-Centred Consciousness Versus The New World Order: Garveyism in the Age of Globalism*, New York: Afrikan World InfoSystems, 1999, 25.
29 Adi and Sherwood, *The 1945 Manchester*, 62.
30 Hill, *Marcus Garvey*, 101.
31 P. M. Von Eschen, *Race Against Empire: Black Americans and Anticolonialism, 1937–1957*, New York: Cornell University Press, 1997, 9.

32 *Report of The Pan-African Conference*, July, 1900, 7.
33 D. L. Lewis, *W. E. B. Du Bois: Biography of a Race, 1868–1919*, New York, Henry Holt and Company, 1994, 249.
34 Martin, *Pan-African Connection*, 207. In addition to delegates from: Liberia: Hon F. R, Johnson, ex-attorney general; Gold Coast: A. F. Ribero, Lawyer; Sierra Leone: G. W. Dove, lawyer; Ivory Coast: Dr. R. K. Savage of Edinburgh University; Jamaica: A. R. Hamilton; Antigua: Rev. Joseph Mason, pastor of a London parish; Prof. J. Love; Trinidad: H. Sylvester Williams; R. E. Phipps, lawyer; A. Pierre; St. Lucia: C. W. French; John E. Quinland surveyor; Dominica: George Christian; Canada: Rev. Henry Brown; Scotland: Dr. Mayer; Ireland: Mr. and Mrs. J. F. Loudin; Miss Adams; Cuba: Dr. John Alcindor; Haiti and Ethiopia: Benito. Martin, *Pan-African Connection*, 207.
35 Martin, *Pan-African Connection*, 206.
36 Ibid., 208.
37 R. Lewis, and P. Bryan, eds., *Garvey His Work and Impact*, Trenton: Africa World Press, Inc., 1991, 202.
38 Ibid., 202.
39 *Report of The Pan-African Conference*, July, 1900, 2.
40 Ibid., 15.
41 Ibid., 15.
42 Ibid., 11.
43 Ibid., 15.
44 Ibid., 16.
45 Ibid., 11.
46 Ibid., 12.
47 Ibid., 13.
48 Ibid., 13.
49 Ibid., 14.
50 D. Agbeyebiawo, *The Life and Works of W. E. B. Du Bois*, Accra: Stephil Printing Press & Co. Ltd., 1998, 82.
51 Clarke, *Notes for and African World*, 183.
52 *Constitution and By-Laws of the Niagara Movement*, 839+.
53 Aptheker, 'W. E. B. Du Bois,' 101. The Niagara movement was organised to promote racial equality in America. *Constitution and By-Laws of the Niagara Movement*, 839+.
54 Padmore, *Africanism and Communism*, 113.
55 *The Niagara Movement: A circular for the 1905 meeting, 13 September 1905, The Papers of W. E. B. Du Bois*, microfilm reel 2, frame 839+.
56 Hill, *Marcus Garvey*, 101.
57 Ibid., 100.
58 Ibid., 102.
59 Ibid., 101.
60 F. L. Broderick, A. Meier and E. Rudwick, eds., *Black Protest Thought in the Twentieth Century*, London: Collier Macmillan Publishers, 1986, xxvi.
61 Padmore, *Africanism and Communism*, 115.
62 Broderick *et al.*, *Black Protest*, xxvi.
63 Padmore, *Africanism and Communism*, 115; Du Bois, *The Autobiography*, 138.
64 Cohen and Logan, *The American Negro*, 164.
65 Padmore, *Africanism and Communism*, 115.
66 Cohen and Logan, *The American Negro*, 7.
67 Du Bois, *The Autobiography*, 254; W. James, *Holding Aloft the Banner of Ethiopia Caribbean Radicalism in Early Twentieth Century America*, London: Verso, 2000, 188.
68 H. Zinn, *A People's History of the United States: From 1492 to the Present*, London, Addison Wesley Longman Limited, 1996, 340.

69 D. L. Lewis, *Biography of a Race, 1868–1919,* New York: Henry Holt and Company, 1994, 391.

70 Ibid., 397.

71 'Du Bois fought Booker T. Washington tooth and nail for advocating this very same view and yet consented to be Villard's NAACP underling – for years'. O. G. Villiard, 'The Negro and the Domestic Problem,' *Alexanderaq's Magazine,* 15 November 1905, 8–9.

72 Clarke, *Notes for and African World,* 68.

73 Padmore, *Africanism and Communism,* 115.

74 Ibid., 115.

75 J. L. Roark, 'American Black Leaders: The Response of Colonialism and the Cold War,' *African Historical Studies 4,* 1971, no. 2: 254.

76 Ibid., 254.

77 Padmore, *Africanism and Communism,* 125.

78 Wilson, *Afrikan-Centred Consciousness,* 15.

79 Ibid., 22.

80 Clarke, *Notes for and African World,* 137.

81 C. E. Lincoln, 'The Race Problem and International Relations,' in G. W. Shepherd, Jr., ed., *Racial Influences on American Foreign Policy* London: Basic Books Inc., Publishers, 1970, 46.

82 Wilson, *Afrikan-Centred Consciousness,* 23.

83 Lewis, *Garvey His Work,* 215.

84 T. Martin, *Marcus Garvey, Hero: A First Biography,* Dover: Majority Press, 1983, 50.

85 Ibid., 319.

86 Ibid., 320.

87 Wilson, *Afrikan-Centred Consciousness,* 24.

88 Martin, *Marcus Garvey, Hero,* 101.

89 Ibid., 102.

90 Ibid., 101.

91 Lincoln, 'The Race Problem,' 46.

92 Hill, *Marcus Garvey,* 37.

93 Letter from W. E. B. Du Bois to His Excellency, Georges S. Clemenceau, Premier of France, 14 January 1918, *The Papers of W. E. B. Du Bois,* microfilm reel 6, frame 402.

94 *Letter from W. E. B. Du Bois to Mr. George Foster Peabody, 28 August 1918,* 2.

95 Memorandum to the Labor Party of England on the American Negro, 21 February 1918, *The Papers of W. E. B. Du Bois,* microfilm reel 6, frame 724.

96 *Letter from W. E. B. Du Bois to Mr. George Foster Peabody, 28 August* 1918, 2.

97 T. J. R. Kornweibel, *'Seeing Red' Federal Campaigns Against Black Militancy, 1919–1925,* Indianapolis: Indiana University Press, 1998, 101.

98 Letter from Franklin Polk the Acting Secretary of State to W. E. B. Du Bois, 2 January 1919, *The Papers of W. E. B. Du Bois,* microfilm reel 8, frame 305.

99 D. L. Lewis, *W. E. B Du Bois: The Fight for Equality and the American Century, 1919–1963,* New York: Henry Holt and Company, 2000, 60.

100 Ibid., 60.

101 Martin, *Marcus Garvey, Hero,* 65.

102 Memorandum from National Assoc. of Loyal Negroes to Dr W. E. B. Du Bois and Dr R. R. Moton, 15 January 1919, *The Papers of W. E. B. Du Bois,* microfilm reel 7, frame 1136.

103 *Memorandum from National Assoc. of Loyal Negroes to Dr. W. E. B. Du Bois and Dr. R. R. Moton, 15 January 1919,* 1136.

104 W. E. B. Du Bois, 'Letters from Dr. Du Bois,' *The Crisis,* February 1919, vol. 17, no. 4, 163.

105 Ibid., 163.

106 W. E. B. Du Bois, 'Editorial: The Peace Conference,' *The Crisis*, January 1919, vol. 17, no. 3, 111.
107 Ibid., 120.
108 W. E. B. Du Bois, 'National Association for the Advancement of Colored People,' *The Crisis*, January 1919, vol. 17, no. 3, 120.
109 W. E. B. Du Bois, 'Africa and the World Democracy,' *The Crisis*, February 1919, vol. 17, no. 4, 173–76.
110 Ibid., 176.
111 Cablegram mass meeting, Monday evening, 6 January, 1919, Carnegie Hall, New York.
112 Clarke, *Notes for and African World*, 178; Plummer, *Rising Wind*, 17; P. G. Lauren, *Power and Prejudice: The Politics and Diplomacy of Racial Discrimination*, Boulder: Westview Press, 1988, 77; Henry, 'Pan-Africanism,' 443.
113 Plummer, *Rising Wind*, 17.
114 J. H. Clarke, *Marcus Garvey and the Vision of Africa*, New York: Vintage Books, 1974, 12.
115 Plummer, *Rising Wind*, 17.
116 W. E. B. Du Bois, 'Opinion of W. E. B. Du Bois: My Mission,' *The Crisis*, May 1919, vol. 18, no. 1, 8.
117 Plummer, *Rising Wind*, 17.
118 Lewis, *Biography of a Race*, 567.
119 Martin, *Marcus Garvey, Hero*, 64.
120 Hill, *Marcus Garvey*, 39.
121 Ibid., 40.
122 Wilson, *Afrikan-Centred Consciousness*, 26.
123 Hill, *Marcus Garvey*, 43.
124 Kornweibel, *Seeing Red*, 100.
125 Martin, *Marcus Garvey, Hero*, 102.
126 W. Churchill and J. V. Wall, *The Cointelpro Papers: Documents from the FBI's Secret Wars against Dissent in the United States*, Boston: South End Press, 1990, 91.
127 Lincoln, 'The Race Problem,' 47.
128 A. Sbacchi, *Legacy of Bitterness: Ethiopia and Fascist Italy, 1935–1941*, Trenton: The Red Sea Press, 1997, 4.
129 K. O'Reilly, *Racial Matters: the FBI's Secret file on Black America, 1960–1972*, New York: The Free Press, 1991, 13.
130 Wilson, *Afrikan-Centred Consciousness*, 25.
131 Churchill, *The Cointelpro Papers*, 94.
132 Lincoln, 'The Race Problem,' 47.
133 Du Bois, 'Africa and the World,' 173.
134 Letter from N. A. A. C. P. to Dr. W. E. B. Du Bois, 11 February 1919, *The Papers of W. E. B. Du Bois*, microfilm reel 7, frame 1179.
135 A statement from Du Bois to the Board of Directors (not sent) concerning its attitude towards his French trip, Apr. 14, 1919, *The Papers of W. E. B. Du Bois*, microfilm reel 7, frame 1179, 1.
136 Du Bois,*The Autobiography*, 298.
137 Lewis, *The Fight for Equality*, 554.

3 A case study of the Italo-Ethiopian War 1934–36

1 D. Burley, 'Learned They Had A True, Great History,' *The Chicago Defender*, 4 January 1936, 24.
2 J. A. Rogers, *The Real Facts about Ethiopia*, Baltimore: Black Classic Press, 1982, 13.
3 Rogers, *The Real Facts*, 10.

4 G. Salvemini, *Italian Fascist Activities in the United States*, New York: Center for Migration Studies, 1977, viii.

5 L. G. Halden, 'The Diplomacy of the Ethiopian Crisis,' *Journal of Negro History*, Apr. 1937, vol. 22 (2), 167.

6 A. J. Barker, *The Civilising Mission, A History of the Italo Ethiopian War of 1935–1936*, New York: The Dial Press, Inc., 1968, 107.

7 D. W. Wainhouse, *International Peace Observation: A History and Forecast*, Baltimore: Johns Hopkins Press, 1966, 68.

8 J. S. Nye, Jr., *Understanding International Conflicts*, Boston: HarperCollins College Publishers, 1993, 78.

9 M. S. Means, *Ethiopia And the Missing Link in African History*, Pennsylvania: The Atlantis Publishing Company, 1945, v.

10 J. G. Jackson, *Ages Of Gold and Silver*, Texas: American Atheist Press, 1990, 70. Indeed 'Herodotus says, that there were two Ethiopian nations, one in India, the other in Egypt'. G. Higgins, *Anacalypsis*, New York: A&B Books Publishers, 1992, 54. George Rawlinson Professor of Ancient History at Oxford University stated 'that a Cushite or Ethiopian race did in the earliest times extend itself along the shores of the Southern ocean from Abyssinia to India. The whole peninsula of India was peopled by a race of this character before the influx of the Aryans'. R. Rashidi, 'Africans in Early Asian Civilsations: An Overview,' R. Rashidi, ed., *African Presence in Early Asia*, London: Transaction Publishers, 1999, 39. Walker claims that the 'Asiatic Ethiopians are generally thought to have been the Dravidians, the first inhabitants of India, they were the founders of the ancient civilisation in the Indus valley Pakistan and western India … [Walker states] … There are a 100 million Dravidian speakers in southern India today. Many are of very black complexions with straight wavy or curly hair. Some are indistinguishable from Africans, but the vast majority resemble the indigenous Australians'. R. Walker, *Classical Splendour: Roots of Black History*, London: Bogle-L'Overture Press, 1999, 110.

11 H. Campbell, *Rasta and Resistance: From Marcus Garvey to Walter Rodney*, London: Hansib Publishing Limited, 1985, 48.

12 T. Martin, *Marcus Garvey, Hero A First Biography*, Dover: Majority Press, 1983, 142.

13 Burley, 'Learned They Had,' 24; W. E. B. Du Bois, 'Inter-racial Implications of the Ethiopian Crisis: A Negro View,' *Journal of Foreign Affairs*, 1935, 84.

14 O. T'Shaka, *Return to the African Mother Principle of Male and Female Equality*, Oakland: Pan Afrikan Publishers and Distributors, 1995, 167.

15 Ross, R., 'Black Americans and Italo-Ethiopian Relief, 1935–36,' *Ethiopia Observer*, 1972, vol. 15, no. 2: 122; W. R. Scott, 'Malaku E Bayen: Ethiopian Emissary to Black America, 1936–41,' *Ethiopian Observer*, 1972, vol. xv: no.2: 132; B. Plummer, *Rising Wind: Black Americans and US Foreign Affairs, 1935–1960*, London: University of North Carolina Press, 1996, 37; M. Naison, *Communists in Harlem during the Depression* Chicago: The University of Illinois Press, 1983, 138.

16 Ross, 'Black Americans and Italo-Ethiopian Relief,' 122.

17 Plummer, *Rising Wind*, 39.

18 Ibid., 39.

19 Ibid., 39.

20 J. H. Franklin, *From Slavery to Freedom*, New York: Vintage Books, 1969, 574.

21 N. Venturni, 'Over the Years People Don't Know: Italian Americans and African Americans in Harlem in the 1930's,' in D. R. Gabbacia and F. M. Ottanelli, *Italian Workers of the World: Labour Migration and the formation of Multiethnic States*, Chicago: University of Illinois, 2001, 202.

22 J. H. Clarke, *Notes for an African World Revolution Africans at the Crossroads*, Trenton: African World Press, Inc., 1992, 240.

23 S. K. B. Asante, 'The Afro-American and the Italo-Ethiopian Crisis 1934–36,' *Journal of Negro History*, 1973, 172.
24 Plummer, *Rising Wind*, 40.
25 Ibid., 40.
26 Author not stated, 'Halt Italians Petition Asks,' *The New York Amsterdam Star News*, 20 July 1935, 2.
27 A. Sbacchi, *Legacy of Bitterness: Ethiopia and Fascist Italy, 1935–1941*, Trenton: The Red Sea Press, 1997, xviii; *The New York Amsterdam Star News*, 1 June 1935, 11; Wainhouse, *International Peace Observation*, 70.
28 Author not stated, 'League Council Will Attempt to Prevent African War,' *The New York Amsterdam Star News*, 13 July 1935, 13.
29 R. A. Hill, *The FBI's RACON Racial Conditions in the United States During World War II*, Boston: Northeastern University Press, 1995, 509.
30 Sbacchi, *Legacy of Bitterness*, 13.
31 Asante, 'The Afro-American and the Italo-Ethiopian Crisis,' 173.
32 Venturni, 'Over the Years People Don't Know,' 201.
33 Asante, 'The Afro-American and the Italo-Ethiopian Crisis,' 171.
34 Ibid., 172.
35 Scott, 'Malaku E Bayen,' 133.
36 Ibid., 133.
37 W. R. Scott, 'Black Nationalism and the Italo-Ethiopian Conflict, 1934–36,' *Journal of Negro History*, Apr. 1978, vol. 63, 125.
38 Scott, 'Black Nationalism and the Italo-Ethiopian Conflict,' 125.
39 Ibid., 125.
40 Sbacchi, *Legacy of Bitterness*, 14.
41 Asante, 'The Afro-American and the Italo-Ethiopian Crisis,' 174.
42 Plummer, *Rising Wind*, 40.
43 Ibid., 40.
44 Ibid., 41.
45 Asante, 'The Afro-American and the Italo-Ethiopian Crisis,' 171.
46 Ibid., 171.
47 I. Parmar, 'Resurgent Academic Interest in the Council on Foreign Relations,' *Politics*, 2001, vol. 21 (1), 33.
48 I. Parmar, 'Anglo-American Elites in the Interwar Years: Idealism and Power in the Intellectual Roots of Chatham House and the Council on Foreign Relations' *International Relations*, 2002, vol. 16 (1), 64.
49 Ross, 'Black Americans and Italo-Ethiopian Relief,' 122–31.
50 Asante, 'The Afro-American and the Italo-Ethiopian Crisis,' 171.
51 Scott, 'Black Nationalism and the Italo-Ethiopian Conflict,' 125.
52 Plummer, *Rising Wind*, 41.
53 Ross, 'Black Americans and Italo-Ethiopian Relief,' 129.
54 Plummer, *Rising Wind*, 47.
55 Venturni, 'Over the Years People Don't Know,' 198.
56 Asante, 'The Afro-American and the Italo-Ethiopian Crisis,' 171; Naison, *Communists in Harlem*, 155.
57 Author not stated, 'Chicago Aroused Prof. Cook Back from War Threats On Normandy,' *The New York Amsterdam Star News*, 13 July 1935, 3; Author not stated, 'Attack 10,000 Anti-fascists,' *The New York Amsterdam Star News*, 7 September 1935, 3.
58 Plummer, *Rising Wind*, 47.
59 Ibid., 47.
60 Ibid., 41.
61 Nye, *Understanding International*, 79.
62 Plummer, *Rising Wind*, 47.

63 Asante, 'The Afro-American and the Italo-Ethiopian Crisis,' 174.
64 Author not stated, 'Seeks 5,000 Troops Here,' *The New York Amsterdam Star News*, 13 July 1935, 3. Ev.
65 Asante, 'The Afro-American and the Italo-Ethiopian Crisis,' 174.
66 Ibid., 174; Author not stated, 'Close Ranks, Says Leader,' *The New York Amsterdam Star News*, 9 November 1935, 2.
67 Scott, 'Black Nationalism and the Italo-Ethiopian Conflict,' 128.
68 Ibid., 128.
69 Asante, 'The Afro-American and the Italo-Ethiopian Crisis,' 175.
70 Ibid., 175.
71 Ibid., 175.
72 Naison, *Communists in Harlem*, 156.
73 Asante, 'The Afro-American and the Italo-Ethiopian Crisis,' 122. These publications show that support for Ethiopia was not confined to the Black Nationalist and Pan-Africanist groups.
74 Asante, 'The Afro-American and the Italo-Ethiopian Crisis,' 176.
75 Clarke, *Notes for and African World*, 106.
76 Plummer, *Rising Wind*, 52.
77 Ibid., 52.
78 Scott, 'Black Nationalism and the Italo-Ethiopian Conflict,' 128.
79 Sbacchi, *Legacy of Bitterness*, 14.
80 Scott, 'Malaku E Bayen,' 120.
81 Plummer, *Rising Wind*, 42.
82 Venturni, 'Over the Years People Don't Know,' 208.
83 Author not stated, 'Ethiopia's War, Mitchell States,' *The New York Amsterdam Star News*, 12 October 1935, 1.
84 Scott, 'Black Nationalism and the Italo-Ethiopian Conflict,' 130.
85 Venturni, 'Over the Years People Don't Know,' 204.
86 Naison, *Communists in Harlem*, 138
87 Ibid., 129.
88 Asante, 'The Afro-American and the Italo-Ethiopian Crisis,' 124.
89 Scott, 'Black Nationalism and the Italo-Ethiopian Conflict,' 124.
90 Plummer, *Rising Wind*, 41.
91 Scott, 'Black Nationalism and the Italo-Ethiopian Conflict,' 130.
92 Plummer, *Rising Wind*, 50.
93 Ross, 'Black Americans and Italo-Ethiopian Relief,' 129.
94 Plummer, *Rising Wind*, 50.
95 Ibid., 121.
96 Ibid., 121.
97 Ibid., 121.
98 Salvemini, *Italian Fascist Activities*, xvi.
99 Plummer, *Rising Wind*, 122.
100 Scott, 'Black Nationalism and the Italo-Ethiopian Conflict,' 122.
101 Ibid., 123.
102 Ibid., 123.
103 Scott, 'Malaku E Bayen,' 128.
104 Sbacchi, *Legacy of Bitterness*, xx.
105 Scott, 'Black Nationalism and the Italo-Ethiopian Conflict,' 128. 'The war enthusiasm resulted in at least two additional ends: the growth of pan-African sentiment and the building of black pride'. Ross, 'Black Americans and Italo-Ethiopian Relief,' 129.
106 Asante, 'The Afro-American and the Italo-Ethiopian Crisis,' 179.
107 Sbacchi, *Legacy of Bitterness*, xx.
108 Scott, 'Black Nationalism and the Italo-Ethiopian Conflict,' 126.

109 Ibid., 126.
110 Plummer, *Rising Wind*, 52.
111 Sbacchi, *Legacy of Bitterness*, 8; Salvemini, *Italian Fascist Activities*, xxx.
112 Plummer, *Rising Wind*, 45. Gaetano Salvemini contends 'if anyone should gather all the utterances of American cardinals and bishops about Mussolini, all the sermons, all the articles and essays of Catholic priests and monks … one would have the most impressive and astounding anthology of Fascist glorification'. Salvemini, *Italian Fascist Activities*, 146. Indeed, During the Italian invasion of Ethiopia, consular and priestly cooperation reached its apex. Scalabrini Provincial Franch offered Consul General Carosi $100 for the Italian Red Cross in December 1935 and the three Servite pastors on the North Side contributed $25 each to the cause. On 19 January 1926, a mass was held for Italian soldiers in Africa at the Scalabrini church, Our Lady of Pompeii, as part of an Italian Red Cross Benefit Program. Consul General Carosi, who took 'the place of the Duce in the reception, was present to collect the gold wedding bands and jewellery of the many mothers and sweethearts who follow[ed] the example of their kin in Italy and contribute[d] rings and others golden articles … to Italy to help the cause of the Mother Country … over 600 Pompeii parishioners attended the reception where Consul General Carosi collected $344.62 and an unspecified quantity of gold articles. The collections of gold rings was also made at St. Anthony, another Scalabrini parish'. P. R. D'Agostino, *Missionaries in Babylon: The Adaptation of Italian Priests to Chicago's Church, 1870–1940*, Volume 1, Chicago: University of Chicago Divinity School, 1993, 356.
113 A. Murray, 'White Norms, Black Deviation,' in J. A. Ladner, ed., *The Death of White Sociology: Essays on Race and Culture*, Baltimore: Black Classic Press, 1998, 97.
114 B. Harris, Jr., *The United States and the Italo-Ethiopian Crisis*, Palo Alto: Stanford University Press, 1964, 21.
115 US State Department, *Peace and War: United States Foreign Relations 1931–1941*, Washington: United States Government Printing Office, 1943, 21.
116 Author not stated, 'Halt Italians,' 2.
117 Harris, *The United States*, 20.
118 US State Department, *Peace and War*, 25. Italian-Americans 'circumvent[ed] … [Americas] … moral embargo and the League[s] … sanctions by sending copper postcards to Italy … [and] … donat[ing] gold to their homeland … thousands of Italian American women contributed rings and other jewellery. In May 1936, Italian American communities everywhere sponsored collective remarriage ceremonies, where priests blessed replacement iron wedding rings, which had been sent for this purpose by fascist authorities in Rome'. Venturni, 'Over the Years People Don't Know,' 202.
119 US State Department, *Peace and War*, 24.
120 Ibid., 29.
121 Ibid., 30.
122 Ibid., 32.
123 Ibid., 31.
124 Ibid., 31.
125 Plummer, *Rising Wind*, 44.
126 Asante, 'The Afro-American and the Italo-Ethiopian Crisis,' 175.
127 Scott, 'Black Nationalism and the Italo-Ethiopian Conflict,' 129.
128 Ibid., 129.
129 Plummer, *Rising Wind*, 43.
130 The Federal Bureau of Investigation (FBI), investigated individuals and organisations campaigning for Ethiopia. However, its racist exclusion of African-Americans from its organisation forced the FBI to use black police officers to gather intelligence regarding black organisations. Plummer, *Rising Wind*, 43.

131 The evidence suggests that AAFAC did not launch an extensive campaign to directly lobby the government to aid Ethiopia although the *Amsterdam News* called for American intervention on Ethiopia's behalf. Author not stated, 'Seek to Halt Duce's March: See Italian Aggression As Peril to Western Civilization,' *The New York Amsterdam Star News*, 28 September 1935, 3.

132 As the state 'brought [black] military recruitment to a halt'. Plummer, *Rising Wind*, 43.

133 Scott, 'Black Nationalism and the Italo-Ethiopian Conflict,' 129.

134 I. Parmar, 'The Issue of State Power: The Council On Foreign Relations as a case Study,' *Journal of American Studies*, 1995, 73.

135 M. H. Hunt, *Ideology and US Foreign Policy*, London: Yale University Press, 1987, 12

136 J. H. Clarke, *Marcus Garvey and the Vision of Africa*, New York: Vintage Books, 1974, 357.

137 Plummer, *Rising Wind*, 48.

138 Ibid., 49.

139 Author not stated, 'Group Protests US Arms Ban: Roosevelt Telegram Flays "Aloofness by Government",' *The New York Amsterdam Star News*, 12 October 1935, 3.

140 Plummer, *Rising Wind*, 49; Wainhouse, *International Peace Observation*, 76.

141 Halden, 'The Diplomacy,' 169.

142 Plummer, *Rising Wind*, 51.

143 Clarke, *Marcus Garvey*, 357.

144 Hunt, *Ideology and US,* 12; B. P. Bowser, 'Race and US Foreign Policy: A Bibliography Essay,' *Sage Race Relations*, 1 February 1987, vol. 12, 4.

145 P. Seabury, 'Racial Problems in American Foreign Policy,' in G. W. Shepherd, Jr., *Racial Influences on American Foreign Policy*, New York: Basic Books, Inc., Publishers, 1970, 67.

146 Clarke, *Marcus Garvey*, 357.

147 Clarke, *Marcus Garvey*, 357.

148 Salvemini, *Italian Fascist Activities*, iii.

149 Ibid., iii; F. M. Ottanelli, '"If Fascism Comes to America We Will Push It Back into the Ocean": Italian American Antifacism in the 1920s and 1930s,' in Gabbacia and Ottanelli, *Italian Workers of the World*, 185.

150 Salvemini, *Italian Fascist Activities*, xvi.

151 Venturni, 'Over the Years People Don't Know,' 202.

152 Salvemini, *Italian Fascist Activities*, 52.

153 Ottanelli, 'If Facism Comes to America', 190.

154 Venturni, 'Over the Years People Don't Know,' 206.

155 Salvemini, *Italian Fascist Activities*, 202.

156 Ibid., 204.

157 Ibid., 205.

158 Ibid., 208.

159 P. Cobianchi, 'Carnival-Banquet Given to Rev. Teofilo Zutta: A Few Words to Mr Nicholas Mona,' *L'Indipendente*, 25 July 1936, 18; M. E. Brown, *The Scalabrinians in North America 1887–1934*, New York: CMS, 1996, 320.

160 Venturni, 'Over the Years People Don't Know,' 210.

161 Naison, *Communists in Harlem*, 139.

162 Venturni, 'Over the Years People Don't Know,' 197.

163 Plummer, *Rising Wind*, 50.

164 Ibid., 50.

165 Ibid., 53.

166 Salvemini, *Italian Fascist Activities*, 30.

167 Clarke, *Marcus Garvey*, 357.

168 Salvemini, *Italian Fascist Activities*, 64.
169 Ibid., 197.
170 D'Agostino, *Missionaries in Babylon*, 355.
171 Venturni, 'Over the Years People Don't Know,' 197.
172 P. M. Von Eschen, *Race Against Empire Black Americans and Anti-Colonialism, 1937–1957*, London: Connell University Press, 1997, 10.
173 Plummer, *Rising Wind*, 41.
174 Venturni, 'Over the Years People Don't Know,' 204.
175 Von Eschen, *Race Against Empire*, 11.
176 G. Breitman, C. L. R. James and E. Keemer, *Fighting Racism in World War II, A Week-By-Week Account of the Struggle Against Racism and Discrimination in the United States During 1939–45*, London: Pathfinder, 1991, 30.
177 Author not stated, 'Russian Exports to Italy Expand,' *The New York Amsterdam Star News*, 7 September 1940, 1.
178 Plummer, *Rising Wind*, 49.
179 Ibid., 43.
180 Asante, 'The Afro-American and the Italo-Ethiopian Crisis,' 176.
181 Ibid., 176.
182 Naison, *Communists in Harlem*, 156; Asante, 'The Afro-American and the Italo-Ethiopian Crisis,' 176.
183 Naison, *Communists in Harlem*, 173.
184 H. R. Issacs, 'Race and Color,' in G. W. Shepherd, Jr., *Racial Influences on American Foreign Policy*, New York: Basic Books, Inc., Publishers, 1970, 22.
185 Naison, *Communists in Harlem*, 174.
186 Scott, 'Black Nationalism and the Italo-Ethiopian Conflict,' 123.
187 The point being 'that Russians also share other varieties of "white" attitudes and behaviour patterns toward non-whites'. Issacs, 'Race and Color,' 31.
188 Naison, *Communists in Harlem*, 195.
189 C. E. Lincoln, 'The Race Problem and International Relations,' in G. W. Shepherd, Jr., ed., *Racial Influences on American Foreign Policy*, 50.
190 Plummer, *Rising Wind*, 49.
191 Ibid., 49.
192 Ibid., 49.
193 Wainhouse, *International Peace Observation*, 70.
194 Ibid., 69.
195 As the league had reportedly 'sworn to defend' Ethiopia. Breitman *et al*, *Fighting Racism in World War II*, 29.
196 Breitman *et al.*, *Fighting Racism in World War II*, 29.
197 Du Bois, 'Inter-racial Implications,' 85.
198 Nye, *Understanding International*, 79.
199 Clarke, *Marcus Garvey*, 13/17.
200 Breitman *et al.*, *Fighting Racism in World War II*, 30; Author not stated, 'Seek to Halt Duce's March,' 3.
201 US State Department, *Peace and War*, 29.
202 Plummer, *Rising Wind*, 12; A. S. Layton, *International Policies and Civil Rights Policies in the United States*, Cambridge: Cambridge University Press, 2000, 23.
203 M. T. P. Lochard, 'Black Races Profit from the Italian-Ethiopian Conflict,' *The Chicago Defender*, 4 January 1936, 23.
204 Sbacchi, *Legacy of Bitterness*, 8.
205 Ibid., 15.
206 Ibid., xx.
207 Scott, 'Malaku E Bayen,' 132.
208 Sbacchi, *Legacy of Bitterness*, xvi.

209 Clarke, *Notes for and African World*, 11; A. Wilson, *Blueprint for Black Power: A Moral, Political and Economic Imperative for the Twenty-First Century*, New York: Afrikan World Infosystems, 1998, 504. Indeed, even Du Bois became an advocate of black separation in his article *A Negro Nation within the Nation.* D. L. Lewis, ed., *W. E. B. Du Bois: A Reader*, New York: Henry Holt and Company, 1995, 569.
210 B. Miroff, R. Seidelman, T. Swanstrom, *The Democratic Debate: An Introduction to American Politics*, New York: Houghton Mifflin Company, 1995, A–32.
211 Parmar 'Anglo-American Elites,' 57.
212 K. O' Reilly, *'Racial Matters': The FBI's Secret File on Black America, 1960–1972*, London: The Free Press, 1991, 10.
213 Hunt, *Ideology and US*, 12
214 Ibid., 12
215 Salvemini, *Italian Fascist Activities*, 223.
216 Asante, 'The Afro-American and the Italo-Ethiopian Crisis,' 129.
217 While Des King highlights the racialised character of the state generally, additional research pertaining to the racial orientation of the foreign policy establishment needs to be conducted.
218 Wilson, *Blueprint for Black Power*, 146.
219 E. F. Frazier, *Black Bourgeosie*, London: MacMillan Publishing, 1962, 95; H. Cruse, *The Crisis of the Negro Intellectual*, New York: Quill, 1984, 90; Wilson, *Blueprint for Black Power*, 233.
220 Lochard, 'Black Races Profit,' 23.
221 Plummer, *Rising Wind*, 37.
222 Ibid., 37.
223 Venturni, 'Over the Years People Don't Know,' 208.

4 From isolationism to globalism: African-Americans' response to US entry into the Second World War 1939–41

1 G. Padmore, 'The Second World War and the Darker Races,' *The Crisis*, November 1939, vol. 46, no 11, 327.
2 This case study is unique because AAFAC's orientation to WWII was arguably determined by external interests as opposed to being a reflection of African-Americans' own movement. Indeed, African-Americans' response to WWII is arguably fuelled by the interventionist bloc's propaganda; consequently, the centrality of the interventionists bloc's involvement in AAFAC's actions is reflected in its presence within this chapter.
3 K. Verney, *Black Civil Rights in America*, London: Routledge, 2004, 35.
4 The first is freedom of speech and expression everywhere in the world. The second is freedom of every person to worship God in his own way everywhere in the world. The third is freedom from want – which, translated into world terms, means economic understandings which will secure to every nation a healthy peacetime life for its inhabitants – everywhere in the world. The fourth is freedom from fear – which, translated into world terms, means a world-wide reduction of armaments to such a point and in such a thorough fashion that no nation will be in a position to commit an act of physical aggression against any neighbor – anywhere in the world. Department of State Publication, *United States Foreign Policy 1931–1941*, Washington DC, Administration Printing Office, 1983, 99.
5 P. Kennedy, *The Rise and Fall of the Great Powers: Economic Change and Military Conflict from 1500 to 2000*, London: Fontana Press, 1988, 433.
6 Ibid., 434.
7 J. S. Nye, Jr., *Understanding International Conflicts*, New York: HarperCollins College Publishers, 1993, 82.

8 H. Bull, *The Anarchical Society, A Study of Order in World Politics*, London: Macmillan Press Ltd., 1995, 231. Rev. S. M. Means, *Ethiopia And the Missing Link in African History*, Pennsylvania: The Atlantis Publishing Company, 1980, 116.

9 Article by W. E. B. Du Bois in the Amsterdam Star News, 11 November 1939, 'As the Crow Flies,' *The Papers of W. E. B. Du Bois, 1803, 1877–1963 1965, Special Collection*, Sanford, N. C.: Microfilming Corp. of America, 1980, microfilm reel 84, frame 258.

10 S. E. Ambrose, *Rise to Globalism: American Foreign Policy Since 1938*, London: Penguin Books Ltd., 1993, xi.

11 Nye, *Understanding International*, 88.

12 Department of State Publication, *United States Foreign*, 76.

13 Ibid., 100.

14 M. H. Hunt, *Ideology and U. S. Foreign Policy*, London: Yale University Press, 1987, 49.

15 Ibid., 147.

16 Ibid., 148.

17 P. Seabury, 'Racial Problems in American Foreign Policy,' in G. W. Shepherd, Jr., *Racial Influences on American Foreign Policy*, New York: Basic Books, Inc., Publishers, 1970, 64.

18 Indeed 'American society on the eve of World War II was sharply divided along class, racial, and ethnic lines'. R. Polenberg, *One Nation Divisible: Class, Race, and Ethnicity in the United State's Since* 1938, Middlesex: Penguin Books, 1983, 25.

19 Polenberg, *One Nation Divisible*, 39.

20 H. Zinn, *A People's History of the United State's: From 1492 to the Present*, London: Addison Wesley Longman Limited, 1996, 399.

21 E. Hobsbawn, *Age of Extremes: The Short Twentieth Century 1914–1991*, London: Abacus, 2000, 40.

22 E. J. Hobsbawn, *Nations and Nationalism since 1780 Programmer, Myth, Reality*, Cambridge: Cambridge University Press, 1995, 40.

23 Zinn, *A People's History*, 402; Department of State Publication, *United States Foreign*, 95.

24 Hobsbawn, *Nations and Nationalism*, 41.

25 Zinn, *A People's History*, 401.

26 Address delivered by Paul Robeson at the New York Herald Tribune on Current Problems, New York: 16 November 1943, 'American Negroes in the War,' *Paul Robeson Collection, 1925–1956*, New York: Schomberg Center for Research, 1978, microfilm reel 2, box 2, folder 1, 2.

27 Plummer, *Rising Wind: Black Americans and U.S. Foreign Affairs, 1935–1960*, London: The University of North Carolina Press, 1996, 64.

28 Padmore, 'The Second World War,' 327.

29 Author not stated, 'Along the NAACP Battlefront: 30th Annual Conference in Richmond, VA,' *The Crisis*, September 1939, vol. 46, no. 9, whole no. 345, 281.

30 Guest editorials, 'No Time for Hypocrisy,' *The New York Amsterdam Star News*, 27 July 1935, 20.

31 H. R. Issacs, 'Race and Color in World Affairs,' in G. W. Shepherd, Jr., *Racial Influences on American Foreign Policy*, New York: Basic Books, Inc., Publishers, 1970, 19.

32 G. F. McCray, 'The Labor Front,' *The Chicago Defender*, 20 December 1941, 1.

33 Letter from Max Yergan to W. E. B. Du Bois, 18 November 1939, *The Papers of W. E. B. Du Bois*, microfilm reel 50, frame 343.

34 R. A. Hill, ed., *The FBI's Racon: Racial Conditions in the United States during World War II*, Boston, Northeastern University Press, 1995, 2.

35 C. A. Clegg III, *An Original Man: The Life and Times of Elijah Muhammad*, New York: St Martin's Press, 1997, 82.

36 Articles and Speeches by Frank R. Crosswaith, 24 July 1940, 'For Immediate Release,' *Frank R. Crosswaith Papers, 1917–1965*, New York: Schomberg Center for Research, 1993, box 6, folder 4, 2.
37 Articles and Speeches by Frank R. Crosswaith, 24 July, 1940, 'For Immediate Release,' 2
38 *The Chicago Defender*, 12 July 1941, 14.
39 Author not stated, 'Japan and the Negro,' *The Chicago Defender*, 9 August 1941, 14.
40 Author not stated, 'Says Japan May Defend Ethiopia: Boston Group Hears Organizer Speak,' *The New York Amsterdam Star News*, 27 July 1935, 20.
41 Letter from Waldo Mcnutt to W. E. B. Du Bois, 13 February 1939, *The Papers of W. E. B. Du Bois*, microfilm reel 50, frame 494. Letter to Waldo Mcnutt 25 February 1939, 494.
42 Polenberg, *One Nation Divisible*, 71.
43 G. Breitman *et al.*, *Fighting Racism in World War II: A Week-by-Week Account of the Struggle against Racism and Discrimination in the United States during 1939–45*, London: Pathfinder, 1991, 91.
44 P. M. Von Eschen, *Race Against Empire Black Americans and Anti-Colonialism, 1937–1957*, London: Cornell University Press, 1997, 26.
45 F. L. Broderick *et al.*, eds., *Black Protest Thought in the Twentieth Century*, London: MacMillan, 1986, 220.
46 Author not stated, 'The Negro Faces the Future,' *The New York Amsterdam Star News*, 4 January 1941, 1.
47 I. S. Cohen and R. W. Logan, *The American Negro: Old World Background and New World Experience*, Boston: Houghton Mifflin Company, 1970, 200.
48 Von Eschen, *Race Against Empire*, 22.
49 Article by Frank R. Crosswaith, 17 July 1941, 'British Struggle Against Hitlerism,' *Frank R. Crosswaith Papers*, box 6, folder 2, 2. Clearly Crosswaith sought to engage the black population's support by linking the war of liberation in Europe with African-American efforts to win civil rights at home.
50 Author not stated., 'Freedom of Negro Press,' *The Chicago Defender*, 20 December 1941, 3.
51 Polenberg, *One Nation Divisible*, 70.
52 Author not stated, 'NAACP Conference Resolutions: National Defense,' *The Crisis*, September 1941, vol. 48, no. 9, 296.
53 Author not stated, 'Five Years Too Late,' *Amsterdam News*, 15 June 1941, 10.
54 Robert S. Abbott, 'Looking at the Future,' *The Chicago Defender*, 27 December 1941, 18.
55 Clegg III, *An Original Man*, 73.
56 R. A. Hill, ed., *Pan-African Biography*, Los Angeles: African Studies Center, 1987, 683.
57 Ibid., 34.
58 I. Parmar, 'Another important group that needs more cultivation', The Council on Foreign Relations and the Mobilisation of Black Americans for Interventionism, 1939–41, *Ethnic and Racial Studies*, September 2004, 23.
59 Hill, *Pan-African*, 4.
60 Article by W. E. B. Du Bois in the Amsterdam Star News, 29 November 1941, 'As the Crow Flies,' *The Papers of W. E. B. Du Bois*, microfilm reel 84, frame 381, 1.
61 Address delivered by Paul Robeson at the New York Herald Tribune on Current Problems, New York, 16 November 1943, 'American Negroes in the War,' 2. R. Wilkins, 'Watchtower,' *The New York Amsterdam Star News*, 7 Jun. 1941, 10.
62 Zinn, *A People's History*, 398.
63 Wilkins, 'Watchtower,' 22 February 1941, 14.
64 C. G. Woodson and C. H. Wesley, *The Negro in Our History*, Gainesville: The Associated Publishers, Inc., 1972, 628.

65 'Black Heritage' Episode 7–70 by St. Clair Drake, 'The Desegregation Decade – World War II Experience,' *John Henrik Clarke Papers, 1937–1996*, New York, Schomberg Center for Research, 1994, box 28, folder 24, 3; author not stated, 'Leaders of Race Pledge Support as war Comes,' *The Chicago Defender*, 13 December 1941, 1.

66 Verney, *Black Civil Rights*, 33.

67 Parmar, 'Another important group,' 23.

68 Author not stated, 'NAACP Conference Resolutions,' 296.

69 'Black Heritage' Episode 7–70 by St. Clair Drake, 'The Desegregation Decade – World War II Experience,' *John Henrik Clarke Papers*, box 28, folder 24, 1.

70 Verney, *Black Civil Rights*, 34.

71 Similarly African-Americans successfully obtained additional civil rights during the Cold War period especially in the 1950s and 1960s, which was due in part to the colour-line's adverse effect on US foreign policy.

72 C. V. Hamilton and K. Ture, *Black Power: The Politics of Liberation*, New York, Vintage Books, 1992, 27.

73 D. L. Lewis, *W. E. B Du Bois: The Fight for Equality and The American Century, 1919–1963*, New York: Henry Holt, 2000, 466.

74 Articles and Speeches by Frank R. Crosswaith, 5 July 1941, 'Negro Labor Spurns Hitlarism and Stalism,' *Frank R. Crosswaith Papers,* box 5, folder 11, 2. African-Americans such as M. H. Davis, Bishop of the Second Episcopal Church, felt that the MOWM was unpatriotic. M. H. Davis, 'Against Job Marchers,' *The Chicago Defender*, 5 July 1941, 14.

75 'Black Heritage' Episode 6–69 by St Clair Drake, 'The Demand for a Double 'V',' *John Henrik Clarke Papers*, box 28, folder 24, 13.

76 Articles and Speeches by Frank R. Crosswaith, 5 July 1941, 'Negro Labor Spurns Hitlarism and Stalism,' *Frank R. Crosswaith Papers*, box 5, folder 11, 4., 'Black Heritage' Episode 6–69 by St Clair Drake, 'The Demand for a Double 'V',' 12.

77 Staff Correspondent, 'Roosevelt Won't Address Marchers to Washington: Creates Sub-Committee,' *The New York Amsterdam Star News*, 28 Jun. 1941, 5.

78 Hill, *Pan-African*, 4.

79 'Black Heritage' Episode 7–70 by St Clair Drake, 'The Desegregation Decade – World War II Experience,' 6.

80 J. Woodland, 'How did Participation in America's wars affect Black Americans,' *American Studies Today*, Liverpool, American Studies Resource Centre, 2001, 20; 'Black Heritage' Episode 7–70 by St Clair Drake, 'The Desegregation Decade – World War II Experience,' 3; Author not stated, 'NAACP Conference Resolutions,' 296; Author not stated, 'Roosevelt's Executive Order,' *The Chicago Defender*, 5 July 1941, 14.

81 Author not stated, 'Another Victory For Us,' *The Chicago Defender*, 26 July 1941, 14. The fact 'that the executive order was regarded as a genuine breakthrough showed ... how accustomed most Americans were to ... [racism] ... and how unaccustomed they were to federal efforts to erase it'. Polenberg, *One Nation Divisible*, 39.

82 Polenberg, *One Nation Divisible*, 33; Woodson and Wesley, *The Negro*, 628.

83 Author not stated, 'Capital March To Go On As Planned,' *The New York Amsterdam Star News*, 28 June 1941, 15.

84 R. A. Hill, ed., *The FBI's Racon: Racial Conditions in the United State's during World War II*, Boston, Northeastern University Press, 1995, 3.

85 Broderick *et al.*, *Black Protest*, 220.

86 D. E. Shi, and G. Tindal, *America: A Narrative History*, London, W. W. Norton & Company, 1993, 758; Microsoft ® Encarta, 'Isolationism,' *Encarta 98 Deluxe Edition Encyclopedia*, Seattle, Microsoft Corp., 1997.

87 Shi and Tindal, *America*, 767.

88 Department of State Publication, *United States Foreign*, 105.
89 Microsoft ® Encarta, 'Isolationism,'.
90 Ambrose, *Rise to Globalism*, 7.
91 Department of State Publication, *United States Foreign*, 76.
92 Shi and Tindal, *America*, 769.
93 Ambrose, *Rise to Globalism*, 3.
94 Ibid., 3.
95 Not all black people supported lend-lease which is exemplified by the *'Thumbs down on Lend Lease'*. Author not stated, 'Negro Congress Votes Against Bundles For Britain Campaign Too,' *The New York Amsterdam Star News*, 1 Mar. 1941, 9. Alternatively the National Negro Congress felt that lend-lease should be extended to Ethiopia. Author not stated, 'Urges President Roosevelt to Grant Lend-Lease Aid to Ethiopia,' *The New York Amsterdam Star News*, 30 August 1941, 3.
96 Shi and Tindal, *America*, 773.
97 Department of State Publication, *United States Foreign*, 77.
98 Microsoft ® Encarta, 'Roosevelt, Franklin Delano,' 4.
99 Author not stated, 'Fall of France,' *The Weekly Newsmagazine: 1940s Highlights*, 27 May 1940.
100 Although America had commenced a re-armament programme prior to Japan's attack on Pearl Harbour. Department of State Publication, *United States Foreign*, 80.
101 Letter from Henry Stimson to W. E. B. Du Bois, January 24, 1940, *The Papers of W. E. B. Du Bois*, microfilm reel 51, frame 92.
102 Shi and Tindal, *America*, 769.
103 Ibid., 775.
104 *The Papers of W. E. B. Du Bois*, microfilm reel 51, frame 92.
105 Article by W. E. B. Du Bois in the *Amsterdam Star News*, 11 November 1939, 'As the Crow Flies,' 258.
106 Department of State Publication, *United States Foreign*, 106.
107 Parmar, 'Another important group', 713.
108 Article by Frank R. Crosswaith, 17 July 1941, 'British Struggle Against Hitlerism,' 1.
109 Article by Frank R. Crosswaith, 17 July 1941, 'British Struggle Against Hitlerism,' 2.
110 A. S. Layton, *International Politics and Civil Rights Policies in the United State's: 1941–1960*, Cambridge: Cambridge University Press, 2000, 42.
111 R. Wilkins, 'Editorials: "Defending Democracy",' *The Crisis*, October 1939, vol. 46, no. 10, 305.
112 Parmar, 'Another important group,' 16.
113 Ibid., 16.
114 Statement from Frank R. Crosswaith, 2 November 1940, 'Colored People Have a Stake in the War,' *Frank R. Crosswaith Papers*, box 5, folder 18, 1–2.
115 L. Finkle, *Forum for Protest. The Black Press During World War II*, London: Associated University Press, 1975, 199. The WASP elite recruited specific African-Americans as the CDAAA and FFF only wanted black leaders of the right 'sort of intelligence' who would 'respond to the sound program of the Committee'. (Letter from Edwin R. Embree, Julyius Rosenwald Fund) to Roger S. Green, 12 July 1940, *CDAAA Papers*, Princeton, Seeley G. Mudd Manuscript Library, Princeton University, 1993, Box 8.
116 Author not stated, 'A. Philip Randolph, Leader,' *The New York Amsterdam Star News*, 12 June 1941, 14.
117 Parmar, 'Another important group,' 21.
118 R. Wilkins, 'For the Right to Exploit Dark Peoples,' *The Crisis*, November 1939, vol. 46, no. 11, 337.
119 Article to the editor from Frank R. Crosswaith, 5 July 1941, 'Negro Labor Spurns Hitlarism and Stalism,' *Frank R. Crosswaith Papers*, box 6, folder 4, 2. Article by Frank R. Crosswaith, 17 July 1941, 'British Struggle Against Hitlerism,' 2.

120 Letter, Greene, CDAAA to Donald C. Blaisdell, June 27, 1941, *CDAAA Papers*, Princeton, Seeley G. Mudd Manuscript Library, Princeton University Press, 1993, Box 8. The following organisations were also represented: the Council for Democracy, Friends of Democracy, Student Defenders of Democracy and Union for Democratic Action.

121 Parmar, 'Another important group,' 18.

122 Memorandum, Jun. 5, 1941, 'Outline of a Project,' *CDAAA Papers*, Princeton: Seeley G. Mudd Manuscript Library, Princeton University, 1993, Box 8.

123 However there is no evidence that the CFR conferred with African-Americans during the IEW.

124 'Why Not Ethiopia, Too?' *The New York Amsterdam Star News*, 5 Apr. 1941, 16.

125 Article by W. E. B. Du Bois in the *Amsterdam Star News*, 29 November 1941, 'As the Crow Flies,' 2.

126 Author not stated, 'Our Democracy,' *The Chicago Defender*, 19 July 1941, 16.

127 Author not stated, 'Opinion in Harlem Favors Roosevelt Foreign Policy,' *The New York Amsterdam Star News*, 31 May 1941, 1.

128 P. Grose, *Continuing the Inquiry: The Council on Foreign Relations from 1921 to 1996*, New York, CFR, 1996, 18; H. L. Stimson, and B. McGeorge, *On Active Service in Peace and War*, New York: Harper and Brothers, 1947, 461.

129 Letter, Roscoe Dungee (editor, *Black Dispatch*) to Edward white (FFF, Harlem branch), 12 November 1941, *FFF Papers*, Princeton, Seeley G. Mudd Manuscript Library, Princeton University, 1993, Box 29. Carter Glass was US Senator for Virginia, a conservative Democrat; he was considered as a man of 'the most unimpeachable moral and patriotic character'. M. L. Chadwin, *The Hawks of World War II*, Chapel Hill: University of North Carolina Press, 1968, 164.

130 Chadwin, *The Hawks*, 164.

131 Memorandum sent by Mrs Thomas to Mr. Greene, June 10, 1941, 'Literature for Mr. Lewis,' *CDAAA Papers*, Princeton, Seeley G. Mudd Manuscript Library, Princeton University, 1993, Box 8. Chadwin, *The Hawks*, 185.

132 Hunt, *Ideology and U. S.*, 147.

133 Shi and Tindal, *America*, 772.

134 Hunt, *Ideology and U. S.*, 147.

135 Parmar, 'Another important group,' 23. Letter, Edward White to Ulric Bell, August 4, 1941, *FFF Papers*, Box 29.

136 Author not stated, 'Fight for Freedom Growing,' *The New York Amsterdam Star News*, 23 August 1941, 5.

137 Lewis, *The Fight for Equality*, 401.

138 Hunt, *Ideology and U. S.*, 148.

139 Parmar, 'Another important group,' 23.

140 Hunt, *Ideology and U. S.*, 150.

141 Department of State Publication, *United States Foreign*, 83.

142 Nye, *Understanding International*, 80.

143 The US government's support of the Allies was also geared to protect US trade. Department of State Publication, *United States Foreign*, 114.

144 African-Americans' presence in administrative posts is not necessarily indicative of the incorporation of African-American views. Ture maintains regarding America 'there ... [is] ... an entire class of "captive leaders" in the black communities. These are black people with certain technical and administrative skills who could provide useful leadership ... in the black communities but do not because they have become beholden to the white power structure'. Hamilton and Ture, *Black Power*, 13.

145 Additional research is needed to validate or invalidate this point.

146 W. E. B. Du Bois, 'As the Crows Flies,' *The New York Amsterdam Star News*, 30 August 1941, 14.

147 The recruitment of A. Phillip Randolph by the foreign affairs establishment was significant given that during the 1940s he was the leader of African-Americans mass movement fighting for civil rights 'Black Heritage' Episode 7–70 by St Clair Drake, 'The Desegregation Decade – World War II Experience,' 15 which made Randolph a valuable asset in their efforts to influence the Black community.

148 From the Amsterdam News Readers, 'Views on Many Questions: A white man's war,' *The New York Amsterdam Star News*, 7 June 1941, 10.

149 Hill, *The FBI's Racon*, 93

150 Author not stated, 'Betrayers of the Race,' *The Chicago Defender*, 11 October 1941, 14.

151 Author not stated, 'Harlem Fight For Freedom Committee Plans Parade, Mass Meeting Sunday,' *The New York Amsterdam News*, 21 June 1941, 2.

152 Author not stated, 'Fight for Freedom,' *The New York Amsterdam Star News*, 14 June 1941, 10.

153 The 'Double V' campaign originated with 'one Afro-American newspaper, the Pittsburgh Courier ... [who] ... popularised the slogan'; 'Black Heritage' Episode 6–69 by St Clair Drake, 'The Demand for a Double 'V',' 1. *The Chicago Defender*, 12 July 1941, 14.

154 The evidence suggests the WASP elite insulated the foreign policy establishment from the arena of popular democracy and executed its own agenda while influencing the US public to support its mobilisation for war. If it could be validated that the US electorate were compelled to accept the dictates of WASP foreign policy, then the partially represented African-American electorate would, by extension, be even more marginal than their white counterparts. Undoubtedly these contentions need to be more thoroughly researched.

155 Author not stated, 'NAACP Delegates Told America Must Believe in "All Men" or Give Up Deals,' *The New York Amsterdam Star News*, 28 Jun. 1941, 3.

5 African-Americans and the formation of the United Nations Organisation 1944–47

1 Article in *New Africa, Council on African Affairs Monthly Bulletin*, 'College Faculties Point to International Responsibility for Future of Colonies,' edition April 1944, *The Papers of W. E. B. Du Bois, 1803, (1877–1963) 1965, Special Collection*, Sanford: NC, Microfilming Corp. of America, 1980, microfilm reel 55, frame 1130.

2 M. L. Dudziak, 'Josephine Baker, Racial Protest, and the Cold war,' in M. L. Krenn, ed., *The African-American Voice in US Foreign Policy since World War II*, London: Garland Publishing, Inc., 1999, 135.

3 P. M. Von Eschen, *Race Against Empire: Black Americans and Anticolonialism, 1937–1957*, London: Cornell University Press, 1997, 78.

4 Author not stated, 'Dumbarton Oaks: Washington Conversations on International Peace and Security Organisation, 7 October 1944' (www.ibiblio.org/pha/policy/1944/441007a.html), 1.

5 A. Herbert, *A Documentary History of the Negro People in the United States*, Volume 5, New York: Carol Publishing Book, 1993, 55.

6 A. S. Layton, *International Politics and Civil Rights Policies in the United States, 1941–1960*, Cambridge: Cambridge University Press, 2000, 47; C. Anderson, 'From Hope to Disillusion: African-Americans, the United Nations, and the Struggle for Human Rights, 1944–47,' in M. L. Krenn, ed., *The African-American Voice in US Foreign Policy Since World War II*, London: Garland Publishing Inc., 1999, 181.

7 B. G. Plummer, 'Evolution of the Black Foreign Policy Constituency,' in M. L. Krenn, ed., *The African-American Voice in US Foreign Policy Since World War II*, London: Garland Publishing Inc., 1999, 91.

8 B. Kingsbury and A. Roberts, 'Introduction: The UN's Roles in International Society since 1945,' in B. Kingsbury, *et al.*, eds, *United Nations Divided World: The UN's Roles in International Relations*, Second Edition, Oxford: Clarendon Press, 1993, 6.

9 Staff of the Senate Committee in Foreign Relations and the Department of State, 'The Avalon Project at Yale Law School: The Yalta Conference, February 1945' (www.yale.edu/lawweb/avalon/wwii/yalta.htm), 1.

10 US State Department, *Foreign Relations of the United States: Diplomatic Papers*, Washington: United States Government Printing Office, 1967, pl viii.

11 D. E. Shi and G. Tindal, *America: A Narrative History*, London: W. W. Norton & Company, 1993, 802.

12 The desire to extend the bounds of democracy and political freedom to all nations and remove the spectre of totalitarianism.

13 Kingsbury and Roberts, 'Introduction: The UN's Roles,' 28. An alternative perspective on the UN points to the tendency to maintain western hegemony within the organisation. Kingsbury and Roberts, 'Introduction: The UN's Roles,' 121.

14 B. G. Plummer, *Rising Wind: Black Americans and US Foreign Affairs, 1935–1960*, London: The University of North Carolina Press, 1996, 83.

15 Shi and Tindal, *America*, 804.

16 J. L. Roark, 'American Black Leaders: The Response to Colonialism and the Cold war, 1943–53,' in M. L. Krenn, ed., *The African-American Voice in US Foreign Policy since World War II*, London: Garland Publishing, Inc., 1971, 37.

17 T. J. Farer and F. Gaer, 'The UN and Human Rights: At the End of the Beginning,' in B. Kingsbury and A. Roberts, *United Nations, Divided World: The UN's Roles in International Relations*, Oxford: Clarendon Press, 1995, 245.

18 Ibid., 245.

19 J. Woodland, 'How did Participations in America's wars affect black Americans,' *American Studies Today*, Winter 2001, nos. 9–10, 19.

20 Roark, 'American Black Leaders,' 39.

21 Anderson, 'From Hope to Disillusion,' 181; Layton, *International Politics*, 63.

22 Letter from W. E. B. Du Bois to Mr. Hamilton Fish Armstrong, 4 January 1943, *The Papers of W. E. B. Du Bois*, microfilm reel 55, frame 282.

23 Roark, 'American Black Leaders,' 39. Indeed, Mark Solomon states that during WWII, African-Americans' demonstrated an increasing interest in Africa. M. Soloman, 'Black Critics of Colonialism and the Cold War,' in M. L. Krenn, ed., *The African American Voice in US Foreign Policy since World War II*, London: Garland Publishing Inc., 1999, 55.

24 Von Eschen, *Race Against Empire*, 74.

25 R. L. Harris, Jr., 'Racial Equality and the United Nations Charter,' A. L. Robinson and P. Sullivan, eds., *New Directions in Civil Rights Studies*, London: University Press of Virginia, 1991, 126.

26 Layton, *International Politics*, 50. The following African-American organisations: the NAACP, CAA and the 'Communist-dominated National Negro Congress' sought to realign domestic and international race relations. Anderson, 'From Hope to Disillusion,' 181.

27 Letter from Walter White, Secretary of the NAACP to W. E. B. Du Bois, 19 June 1943, *The Papers of W. E. B. Du Bois*, microfilm reel 55, frame 525.

28 Letter from Amy Jacques Garvey to Prof. W. E. B. Du Bois, 31 January 1944, *The Papers of W. E. B. Du Bois*, microfilm reel 56, frame 104.

29 H. Aptheker, ed., *Autobiography of W. E. B. Du Bois*, United States of America, International Publishers, 1997, 298.

30 S. Graham, 'Why was Du Bois Fired? 1948,' in H. Aptheker, *A Documentary History of the Negro People in the United States*, Volume 5, New York, Carol Publishing Group, 1993, 360. Aptheker, *Autobiography of W. E. B.*, 326.

31 Anderson, 'From Hope to Disillusion,' 183.
32 Which Du Bois joined in 1948 on invitation from Robeson after his dismissal from the NAACP. Aptheker, *Autobiography of W. E. B. Du Bois*, 344.
33 According to Mark Solomon, Max Yergan's political development was influenced by Kwame Nkrumah, Jomo Kenyatta and Nmandi Azikwe while in London, which validates the existence of a Pan-African network. Solomon, 'Black Critics,' 56.
34 Letter from Henry S. Villard (Chief, Division of African Affairs) to Mr. Robeson, 4 January 1945, *The Papers of W. E. B. Du Bois*, microfilm reel 56, frame 1376.
35 Roark, 'American Black Leaders,' 39.
36 Von Eschen, *Race Against Empire*, 69.
37 Article in *New Africa*, Council on African Affairs Monthly Bulletin, 'Editorial,' edition August 1943, *The Papers of W. E. B. Du Bois*, microfilm reel 55, frame 172.
38 Letter from Rev. J. H. Horace to Friends and Co-Workers, 1945, *The Papers of W. E. B. Du Bois*, microfilm reel 56, frame 1195.
39 Plummer, *Rising Wind*, 132.
40 The San Francisco Conference and the Colonial Issue, Statement of the Council on African Affairs, 1945, *The Papers of W. E. B. Du Bois*, microfilm reel 56, frame 1376.
41 Article in New Africa, Council on African Affairs Monthly Bulletin, 'Editorial,' edition November 1944, *The Papers of W. E. B. Du Bois*, microfilm reel 55, frame 1130.
42 In contrast to the separatist tactics adopted and advanced by black nationalists during the Italo-Ethiopian War.
43 Plummer, *Rising Wind*, 117.
44 The San Francisco Conference and the Colonial Issue, Statement of the Council on African Affairs, 1945, 1.
45 The remit of the AUN is not specified within the cited document.
46 Harris, 'Racial Equality,' 130.
47 Ibid., 130.
48 US State Department, *Foreign Relations*, 526.
49 D. L. Lewis, *W. E. B. Du Bois: The Fight for Equality and the American Century, 1919–1963*, New York: Henry Holt and Company, 2000, 504; Anderson, 'From Hope to Disillusion,' 183.
50 Randolph was particularly disappointed that the Allies were only applying the Atlantic Charter to Europe. Harris, 'Racial Equality,' 130/132.
51 Ibid., 132.
52 By preventing '750 million colored and black people [from possessing a] voice in the proposed world forum'. Ibid., 131.
53 Therefore avoiding the complication of involvement in domestic disputes.
54 They maintained that a black agenda or 'a black quest for separate black representation at the United Nations Conference on International Organization (UNCIO) would be divisive'. Plummer, *Rising Wind*, 126.
55 Indeed, the State Department felt the Dumbarton Oaks accords should not aim to court public support. US State Department, *Foreign Relations*, 71.
56 'IV An Analysis of the Proposals – Plus and Minus,' *The Papers of W. E. B. Du Bois*, microfilm reel 57, frame 1343, 4. The Department of State said the UN would be committed to the 'maintenance of good relations between the great powers'. US State Department, *Foreign Relations*, 71.
57 P. G. Lauren, *Power and Prejudice: The Politics and Diplomacy of Racial Discrimination*, Boulder, Westview Press, 1988, 147–50. Plummer, *Rising Wind*, 118. Harris, 'Racial Equality,' 133. Von Eschen, *Race Against Empire*, 74.
58 'We know the Dumbarton Oaks proposal is substantially the American plan'. Association for the United Nations, Inc., Pamphlet, 13 February 1945, *The Papers of W. E. B. Du Bois*, microfilm reel 56, frame 1035, 3.

59 Dumbarton Oaks and San Francisco, An analysis of the Proposals together with suggestions for improvements to be made in the drafting of the Charter of a World Security Organization, 'IV An Analysis of the Proposals – Plus and Minus,' 6.
60 The AUN wrote to Secretary of State Edward Stettinius detailing the short-comings of the Dumbarton Oaks accords. Letter from the Association for the United Nations, Inc., to the Honorable Edward R. Stettinius, Jr., 1945, *The Papers of W. E. B. Du Bois,* microfilm reel 56, frame 1035.
61 Von Eschen, *Race Against Empire*, 78.
62 Ibid., 79.
63 Ibid., 79.
64 Solomon, 'Black Critics,' 55.
65 Plummer, 'Evolution of the Black,' 92.
66 Shi and Tindal, *America*, 774.
67 Plummer, *Rising Wind*, 125.
68 The *Pittsburgh Courier* called for black representation at the Peace Conference. Von Eschen, *Race Against Empire*, 75. Plummer, *Rising Wind*, 125. Harris suggested that 'Afro-American leaders took two major issues to the conference ... they sought racial equality at home and self determination for colonized people abroad'. Harris, 'Racial Equality,' 130.
69 Harris, 'Racial Equality,' 131.
70 Plummer, *Rising Wind*, 125.
71 Ibid., 126. Letter from Paul Robeson (Chairman) and Max Yergan (Executive Director) to Walter white, 29 November 1944, *The Papers of W. E. B. Du Bois,* microfilm reel 55, frame 1130.
72 Du Bois wrote to Ralph Bunche regarding the conference and outlined recommendations regarding its the format in his letter of 31 January 1945 from the Department of State. Letter from W. E. B. Du Bois to Ralph Bunche, Mar. 17, 1945, *The Papers of W. E. B. Du Bois,* microfilm reel 56, frame 1251. Bunche maintained links with black leaders who he was prepared to advise, although he declined the invitation to attend the conference due to 'preparations for the forthcoming United Nations Conference'. Letter from Ralph Bunche to W. E. B. Du Bois, 31 January 1945, *The Papers of W. E. B. Du Bois,* microfilm reel 56, frame 1251.
73 Plummer, *Rising Wind*, 133. Interestingly both Henry Villard, chief-of-staff of the State Department's Division of African Affairs, and Ralph Bunche failed to attend the Colonial Conference despite their invitations. Von Eschen, *Race Against Empire*, 76.
74 The convening of the conference indicated AAFAN's desire to obtain direct insight into international issues from the perspective of individuals residing in diverse geographic regions.
75 Plummer, *Rising Wind*, 125.
76 Ibid., 125.
77 In addition to Bunche, whose 'role as an insider in 1944–46 ... made him inaccessible to black American leaders', Von Eschen, *Race Against Empire*, 76, proving that the inclusion of black people within powerful white institutions could dilute their effectiveness in pursuing black interests.
78 Article in *New Africa*, Council on African Affairs Monthly Bulletin, 'Resolution, Adopted Unanimously at Conference, 14 April 1944,' edition May, 1944, *The Papers of W. E. B. Du Bois,* microfilm reel 55, frame 1130.
79 Plummer, *Rising Wind*, 134.
80 Ibid., 134.
81 Von Eschen, *Race Against Empire*, 79.
82 African-Americans' political marginality and Washington's adherence to the colour-line, which is substantiated by King [D. King, *Separate And Unequal:*

Black Americans and the US Federal Government, Oxford, Clarendon Press 1995, 9], damaged their chances of selection to the US delegation. Plummer, *Rising Wind*, 131.

83 Ibid., 132.

84 Aptheker, *Autobiography of W. E. B.*, 329. R. Harris, 'Ralph Bunche and Afro-American Participation in Decolonization,' in R. A. Hill, ed., *Pan-African Biography*, Los Angeles: African Studies Center, 1987, 128.

85 Plummer, *Rising Wind*, 139. Du Bois established a tactical liaison with Bunche 'one of the strategically positioned members of the United states delegation, to do what he could, Du Bois transmitted precise language that he hoped to see inserted in the UN Charter [to Bunche]'. Lewis, *The Fight for Equality*, 1.

86 Plummer, *Rising Wind*, 131.

87 Telegram from Mary McLeod Bethune on behalf of the NCNW declaring their support for Walter White and the NAACP status as official observers. Telegram from Mary McLeod Bethune to Walter White, 16 April 1945, *The Papers of W. E. B. Du Bois*, microfilm reel 56, frame 1190. Consequently, the NAACP could induce the UNCIO participants to 'face what is one of the most serious problems of the twentieth century – the question of race and color'.

88 US State Department, *Foreign Relations*, 149. Plummer, *Rising Wind*, 132. Anderson, 'From Hope to Disillusion,' 186. Black participation at the UN conference was ensured due to the extensive lobbying of the NAACP and the black community. Harris, 'Racial Equality,' 134. Harris maintains that 'the NAACP consultants' two major demands ... [were] ... decolonization and the call for a world bill of rights'. Ibid., 137.

89 Formerly The League of Nations Association, Inc.

90 Letter from Mrs Charlotte B. Mahon to the organisation representatives of the Association for the United Nations, Inc., 5 April 1945, *The Papers of W. E. B. Du Bois*, microfilm reel 56, frame 1035. Harris, 'Racial Equality,' 133. Clearly Du Bois was considered important by individuals and organisations involved in foreign affairs.

91 This is verified by Rev. J. L. Horace's (head of the federated organisations of colored peoples) letter to Du Bois on 20 September 1945.

92 Telegram from Mrs A. M. P. Strong (President) to Walter White (Secretary of the NAACP), 16 April 1945, *The Papers of W. E. B. Du Bois*, microfilm reel 56, frame 1342.

93 Significantly the three black consultants were high-ranking officials of the NAACP. Plummer, *Rising Wind*, 151.

94 Note the NAACP was led by white people exclusively until the mid-1970s.

95 Von Eschen, *Race Against Empire*, 80.

96 Harris, 'Racial Equality,' 136.

97 Plummer, *Rising Wind*, 139.

98 Ibid., 132. The MOW movement also campaigned for the UN Charter to include a bill of rights. Harris, 'Racial Equality,' 130.

99 This is validated by the creation of the Coalition of National Negro Organisations of America for World Security and Equality wich lobbied on behalf of minority rights. Plummer, *Rising Wind*, 134.

100 Davidson argues that many 'black intellectuals ... [have been] ... engulfed in a sea of whiteness and some of them ultimately ... [came] ... to identify with the colonizer'. J. Ladner, ed., *The Death of White Sociology: Essays on Race and Culture*, Baltimore: Black Classic Press, 1988, 45, which suggests black incorporation within predominantly white institutions does not necessarily led to the promotion of black interests.

101 Plummer, *Rising Wind*, 135.

102 Significantly the state utilised the services of an organisation that mirrored American racial conventions, as white people exclusively led the NAACP until 1975.

103 S. F. Yette, *The Choice: The Issue of Black Survival in America*, Maryland, Cottage Books, 1971, 43.
104 Harris, 'Racial Equality,' 136. The colonialists attempted to utilise select individuals from the oppressed group to sanction their policies to their people. Hence on 'Thursday, 26 April, at the Third Baptist Church in San Francisco Perry Howard, a Washington DC, Attorney, opened the meeting [attended by the NAACP consultants] by declaring that the masses of the people were ... the real spokesmen [at the UN] rather than an organization that the State Department handpicked to advise the American delegation'. Harris, 'Racial Equality,' 138.
105 Plummer, *Rising Wind*, 138.
106 Harris maintains that Haiti did 'make racial discrimination a major issue'. Harris, 'Racial Equality,' 141.
107 Harris, 'Racial Equality,' 141.
108 Plummer, *Rising Wind*, 139. However, Bunche was instrumental in promoting and defending the interests of the colonialised masses whilst maintaining a strategic relationship with Du Bois to secure black interests. Lewis, *The Fight for Equality*, 509.
109 Solomon, 'Black Critics,' 54.
110 Roark, 'American Black Leaders,' 51.
111 Harris, 'Racial Equality,' 142, Harris, 'Ralph Bunche,' 130.
112 Layton, *International Politics*, 46.
113 Harris, 'Ralph Bunche,' 133. Bunche's support of AAFAN's agenda's indicated that he was not completely divorced from AAFAN's international agenda.
114 US State Department, *Foreign Relations*, 546. Harris, 'Racial Equality,' 142.
115 Von Eschen, *Race Against Empire*, 81. Farer and Gaer, 'The UN and Human Rights,' 248.
116 US State Department, *Foreign Relations*, 793
117 G. Breitman, ed., *Malcolm X Speaks: Selected Speeches and Statements*, New York, Pathfinder., 1989, 57. B. Kingsbury and A. Roberts, eds., *United Nations, Divided World: The UN's Roles in International Relations*, second edition, Oxford: Clarendon Press, 1995, 28.
118 Du Bois 'prepared the petition the NAACP presented to the United Nations in 1947 which outlined the history of the denial of human rights to minorities in the United states and appealed to the United Nations for redress ... [in addition] in 1951 Du Bois, Paul Robeson, Benjamin Davis, and other black leaders on the left again brought America's treatment of colored people before the United Nations. In *We Charge Genocide* they accused the United states of mass murder. They argued that "white supremacy at home makes for colored massacres abroad," and that the "lyncher and the atom bomber are related"'. Roark, 'American Black Leaders,' 47.
119 Z. A. Kondo, *Conspiracies: Unravelling the Assassination of Malcolm X*, Washington: Nubia Press, 1993, 45.
120 H. Aptheker, 'W. E. B. Du Bois and Africa,' in R. A. Hill, ed., *Pan-African Biography*, Los Angeles: African Studies Center, 1987, 113.
121 Solomon, 'Black Critics,' 72.
122 Roark maintains that the US administration was clearly anti-colonialist during the war. Roark, 'American Black Leaders,' 40.
123 J. S. Nye, Jr., *Understanding International Conflicts An Introduction to Theory and History*, New York: HarperCollins College Publishers, 1993, 99.
124 S. E. Ambrose, *Rise to Globalism American Foreign Policy since 1938*, London, Penguin Books, 1993, 30. Von Eschen, *Race Against Empire*, 70.
125 'What's Past is Prologue,' *The Papers of W. E. B. Du Bois*, microfilm reel 57, frame 1343.
126 Harris, 'Racial Equality,' 127. The Phelps-Stokes report suggested that the US State Department create 'an African affairs Division', which it subsequently did. Harris, 'Racial Equality,' 127.

127 US State Department, *Foreign Relations*, 124. Von Eschen claims that the Roosevelt's administration was divided over colonialism which promoted a civil war among its staff. Von Eschen, *Race Against Empire*, 70

128 Harris, 'Racial Equality,' 129.

129 P. Kennedy, *The Rise and Fall of the Great Powers*, London: Fontana Press, 1989, 474

130 US State Department, *Foreign Relations*, 140.

131 Ibid., 141.

132 Ibid., 142.

133 This appeared to be consistent with US foreign policy. US State Department, *Foreign Relations*, 20.

134 Von Eschen, *Race Against Empire*, 73.

135 Letter from E. R. Stettinius, Jr. to Mr. Robeson, 5 January 1944, *The Papers of W. E. B. Du Bois*, microfilm reel 56, frame 1376.

136 Letter from Henry S. Villard (Chief, Division of African Affairs) to Mr. Robeson, 4 January 1945, 1376. Anderson, 'From Hope to Disillusion,' 184.

137 Solomon, 'Black Critics,' 74.

138 'IV An Analysis of the Proposals – Plus and Minus,' 5. Consequently anti-colonialism was largely ignored by the US delegation and the state as was the issue of self-government in the colonies. Solomon, 'Black Critics,' 62.

139 Von Eschen, *Race Against Empire*, 82.

140 Solomon, 'Black Critics,' 73.

141 D. Goldblatt *et al.*, eds., *Democratization*, Cambridge: Polity Press, 1997, 310. Solomon, 'Black Critics,' 75. P. Cammack *et al.*, *Third World Politics: A Comparative Introduction*, Houndsmill: The Macmillan Press Ltd., 1993, 251.

142 Letter from Clark M. Eichelberger to the organisation representatives of the Association for the United Nations, Inc., 20 February 1945, *The Papers of W. E. B. Du Bois*, microfilm reel 56, frame 1035.

143 In relation to the UN being utilised to aid oppressed groups such as African-Americans, the State Department and Stettinius were 'adamant that his job in San Francisco was to create a charter … not to take up subject like the Negro's question'. Anderson, 'From Hope to Disillusion,' 186.

144 Dumbarton Oaks and San Francisco, An analysis of the Proposals together with suggestions for improvements to be made in the drafting of the Charter of a World Security Organization, 'III The Dumbarton Oaks Proposals, What They Are,' *The Papers of W. E. B. Du Bois*, microfilm reel 57, frame 1343, 2.

145 D. M. Barrett, 'Presidential Foreign Policy,' in J. Dumbrell, *The Making of US Foreign Policy*, Manchester: Manchester University Press, 1990, 68.

146 C. E. Lincoln, 'The Race Problem and International Relations,' in G. W. Shepherd Jr., *Racial Influences on American Foreign Policy*, New York: Basic Books, Inc., Publishers, 1970, 57.

147 African-American participation at San Francisco was a reversal of fortune given their exclusion (except Robert Moton who declined to address the conference on behalf of black people) from the 1919 Peace Conference, where they were denied passports to ensure they could not attend. The NAACP's request that the government employ African-Americans' as 'representatives to the conference' [Harris, 'Racial Equality,' 131] was adhered to by the government. Du Bois succeeded in lobbying Stettinius to select him as one of the US delegations consultants 'however, it … became evident that the consultants were to be nothing more than "window dressing".' Anderson, 'From Hope to Disillusion,' 185.

148 Letter from Sidney Hertzberg to W. E. B. Du Bois, Mar. 28, 1945, *The Papers of W. E. B. Du Bois*, microfilm reel 56, frame 1319. The US delegation consisted of the following individuals, 'Secretary of State Stettinius, Chairman; the Honourable Cordell Hull; Senator Connally; Senator Vandenburg; Representative Bloom;

Representative Eaton; Commander Harold Stassen; Dean Virginia Gildersleeve.'
US State Department, *Foreign Relations*, 70.

149 E. Hobsawn, *Age of Extremes The Short Twentieth Century 1914–1991*, London: Abacus, 2000, 216.

150 US State Department, *Foreign Relations*, 484.

151 Harris, 'Racial Equality,' 139.

152 Ibid., 140.

153 Solomon, 'Black Critics,' 73, 76.

154 This explains the US administration's extensive involvement of its armed forces, specifically the military and navy. US State Department, *Foreign Relations*, 94.

155 Ibid., 123.

156 Secretary Stimson stated that 'the basis of Presidents Roosevelt's ... [foreign policy had opposed US territorial expansion while advocating the establishment of US military] bases'. Ibid., 313.

157 Although the observers/consultants received 'democratic concessions from the official delegations at UNCIO', US foreign policy rejected the principles of the Atlantic Charter and elected to defend their own interests. Plummer, *Rising Wind*, 132. Solomon, 'Black Critics,' 63.

158 Von Eschen, *Race Against Empire*, 82.

159 US State Department, *Foreign Relations*, 793.

160 Ibid., 491.

161 Text of speech to Foreign Policy Association by Colonel Oliver Stanley, printed by British Information Services, An Agency of the British Government, 19 January 1945, *The Papers of W. E. B. Du Bois*, microfilm reel 57, frame 270, 2.

162 US State Department, *Foreign Relations*, 794. Anderson, 'From Hope to Disillusion,' 188.

163 Roark, 'American Black Leaders,' 41.

164 The reversal of American foreign policy was both recognised and criticised by African-Americans and the black press, as *The Chicago Defender*, 26 May 1945, made 'Sweeping demands that the United States delegation end its opposition to freedom for colonial peoples'. Von Eschen, *Race Against Empire*, 83.

165 Anderson, 'From Hope to Disillusion,' 188. In brief US domestic race relations determined US foreign policy in this instance.

166 US State Department, *Foreign Relations*, 527

167 Plummer, *Rising Wind*, 141.

168 Kondo, *Conspiracies: Unravelling the Assassination*, 53.

169 Anderson, 'From Hope to Disillusion,' 187.

170 Plummer, *Rising Wind*, 132, As the 'consultants ... forced the US delegation to agree to a human rights commission'. Anderson, 'From Hope to Disillusion,' 190.

171 Ibid., 213.

172 Ibid., 213.

173 US State Department, *Foreign Relations*, 599.

174 Von Eschen, *Race Against Empire*, 83.

175 Plummer, 'Evolution of the Black,' 99.

176 Du Bois' letter addressed to Mr. Lawrence E. Spivak. Letter from Mr. Lawrence E. Spivak to W. E. B. Du Bois, 22 May 1945, *The Papers of W. E. B. Du Bois*, microfilm reel 56, frame 1084. Von Eschen, *Race Against Empire*, 78.

177 Roark, 'American Black Leaders,' 39.

178 Although Plummer claims that the adoption of UN human rights principles resulted from non-governmental organisation's (including African-Americans') pressure tactics at San Francisco. Plummer, *Rising Wind*, 152.

179 African-American desire for a racial equality clause was a domestic and foreign affairs issue because the US delegation's proposals 'prevented the UN from doing anything to stop the human rights abuses that blacks suffered in the United

States ... [in addition] ... the American proposal side stepped the issue of independence'. Anderson, 'From Hope to Disillusion,' 186.

180 C. W. Cheng, 'The Cold War: Its Impact on the Black Liberation Struggle within
the United States,' in M. L. Krenn, ed., *The African-American Voice in US Foreign Policy since World war II*, London: Garland Publishing, Inc., 1971, 105.

181 H. Arkes, *Bureaucracy, the Marshall Plan and the National Interest*, Cambridge:
Cambridge University Press, 1972, 50.

182 The Secretary of War, Secretary of the Navy. US State Department, *Foreign
Relations*, 350.

183 Cheng, 'The Cold War,' 105, 107.

184 B. Miroff, R. Seidelman and T. Swanstrom, *The Democratic Debate: An Introduction to American Politics*, New York: Houghton Mifflin Company, 1998, 500.

185 US State Department, *Foreign Papers*, 797.

186 Ibid., 546. Anderson, 'From Hope to Disillusion,' 193.

187 King, *Separate and Unequal*, 17.

188 Indeed, *The Crisis* maintained that the US betrayed her revolutionary history.
Roark, 'American Black Leaders,' 39.

189 The US delegation stifled anti-colonialism. Roark, 'American Black Leaders,' 39.

190 'Black Heritage' Episode 7–70 by St. Clair Drake, 'The Desegregation Decade –
World war II Experience,' *John Hendrik Clarke Papers, 1937–1996*, New York:
Schomberg Center for Research, 1994, box 28, folder 24, 8.

191 Plummer, 'Evolution of the Black,' 99.

192 US State Department, *Foreign Relations*, 1209.

193 Indeed, the allied nation's rivalry stemmed from which white nation or nations would
assume the leading role in the West's control and exploitation of the rest of the world.

194 Cheng, 'The Cold War,' 129.

195 US State Department, *Foreign Relations*, 560.

196 Statism is silent regarding the racial orientation of the state, which engineered and
sanctioned the disparities between white and black people.

197 US State Department, *Foreign Relations*, 1355.

198 Ibid., 1431.

199 Cheng, 'The Cold War,' 105.

200 Plummer, 'Evolution of the Black,' 76.

201 M. Karenga, *Introduction to Black Studies*, third edition, Los Angeles: University
of Sankore Press, 2002, 304.

202 African-American absence from the delegation does not provide definitive evidence of institutional racism although Des King's study of the US state highlights
its tendency to exclude black people from governmental roles. Indeed, 'Federal
support of segregated race relations shaped black Americans' relations with the
government. As the black leader A. Philip Randolph pointed out in 1943, black
Americans occupied a position different from that of another section of the
population of this country'. Black Americans found themselves compelled to
struggle against the state: 'The Negroes are in the position of having to fight their
own government ... because the Government today is the primary factor, major
factor, in this country in propagating discrimination against Negroes. It is perpe-
tuating and freezing an inferior status of second-class citizenship for Negroes in
America's state'. King, *Separate and Unequal*, 4.

203 Aptheker, *Autobiography of W. E. B.*, 330.

204 Letter from Mrs Frances M. Pollak, Secretary, Speaker's Bureau, Americans
United for World Organization, Inc. to W. E. B. Du Bois, 8 May 1945, *The
Papers of W. E. B. Du Bois*, microfilm reel 56, frame 1112.

205 US State Department, *Foreign Relations*, 1208.

206 Letter from Mr Lawrence E. Spivak to W. E. B. Du Bois, 22 May 1945, 1084.

207 US State Department, *Foreign Relations*, 332.

208 Dudziak, 'Josephine Baker, Racial Protest,' 136.
209 Harris, 'Racial Equality,' 137.
210 Letter from W. E. B. Du Bois to Mr Armstrong, 9 July 1945, *The Papers of W. E. B. Du Bois,* microfilm reel 57, frame 187.
211 Harris, 'Racial Equality,' 144.
212 US State Department, *Foreign Relations,* 599. In short, the sponsoring states agreed to limit the protection of the weak by making the assembly a talking shop without power to enforce its recommendations.
213 US State Department, *Foreign Relations,* 652.
214 Dudziak, 'Josephine Baker, Racial Protest,' 159.
215 Letter from W. E. B. Du Bois to the Editor of the New York Times, 1 November 1946, *The Papers of W. E. B. Du Bois,* microfilm reel 59, frame 120.
216 Solomon, 'Black Critics,' 221.
217 Dudziak, 'Josephine Baker, Racial Protest,' 160.
218 Cheng, 'The Cold War,' 112.
219 Ibid., 138.
220 Ibid., 131.
221 Ibid., 104–19, 121–33, Layton, *International Politics,* 63, Von Eschen, *Race Against Empire,* 77. In addition to Plummer's contention that AAFAN used the UN to win domestic concessions. Plummer, *Rising Wind,* 46.
222 Roark, 'American Black Leaders,' 52.
223 Harris, 'Racial Equality,' 145.

6 Human rights, racial reconstruction and the Cold War 1950–60

1 J. H. Clarke, *Notes for an African World Revolution: Africans at the Crossroads,* Trenton: Africa World Press, 1992.
2 K. K. Gaines, *Black Expatriates and the Civil Rights Era: American Africans in Ghana,* The University of North Carolina Press: Chapel Hill, 2006.
3 P. E. Joseph, *Waiting 'Til the Midnight Hour: A Narrative History of Black Power in America',* New York: Henry Holt & Company, 2006.
4 B. W. Jentleson, *American Foreign Policy: The Dynamics of Choice in the Twenty-first Century,* London: W. W. Norton & Company, 2007, 98; D. L. Lewis, *W. E. B. Du Bois: The Fight for Equality and the American Century 1919–1963,* New York: Henry Holt and Company, LLC, 2000, 525.
5 In short, 'To obtain the economic and military resources to carry out an aggressive foreign policy, Truman had to convince Americans of the reality of the Soviet threat', S. E. Ambrose, *Rise to Globalism: American Foreign Policy Since 1938,* London: Penguin Books Ltd., 1993, 78.
6 E. Foner, *Give Me Liberty! An American History,* London: W. W. Norton and Company, 2009, 843; T. Borstelmann, *Apartheid's Reluctant Uncle: The United States and Southern Africa in Early Cold War,* Oxford: Oxford University Press, 1993, 56.
7 Jentleson, *American Foreign Policy,* 101.
8 Ibid., 100. Indeed, at '1:00 P.M. on 12 March 1947, Truman … asked for aid for immediate aid for Greece and Turkey … in a single sentence Truman … defined American policy for the next generation and beyond', Ambrose, *Rise to Globalism,* 82.
9 Ambrose, *Rise to Globalism,* 84; Jentleson, *American Foreign Policy,* 102.
10 Foner, *Give Me Liberty,* 847.
11 Jentleson, *American Foreign Policy,* 102.
12 NSC68 called for 'a global ring of overseas military bases, military alliances beyond NATO, and a substantial increase in defence spending,' Jentleson, *American Foreign Policy,* 104.
13 M. Ledwidge, 'American Power and Racial Dimensions of U. S. Foreign Policy,' *International Politics* (forthcoming).

14 Ambrose, *Rise to Globalism*; M. Isserman and Kazin, *America Divided: The Civil War of the 1960s*, Oxford: Oxford University Press, 2008; K. Christie, ed., *United States Foreign Policy and National Identity in the Twenty-First Century*, London: Routledge, 2008.

15 Borstelmann, *Apartheid's Reluctant Uncle*; A. S. Layton, *International Politics and Civil Rights Policies in the United states 1941–1960*, Cambridge: Cambridge University Press, 2000; P. G. Lauren, *Power and Prejudice: The Politics and Diplomacy of Racial Discrimination*, Boulder: Westview Press, 1996.

16 C. Anderson, *Eyes Off the Prize: African Americans, the United Nations, and the Struggle for Human Rights, 1944–1955*, Cambridge: Cambridge University Press, 2006; Lauren, *Power and Prejudice*, 1996; P. M. Von Eschen, *Race Against Empire Black Americans and Anti-Colonialism, 1937–1957*, London: Connell University Press, 1997.

17 J. L. Roark, 'American Black Leaders: The Response of Colonialism and the Cold War,' *African Historical Studies*, 1971, 253–70.

18 Foner, *Give Me Liberty*.

19 Von Eschen, *Race Against Empire*.

20 B. G. Plummer, *Rising Wind: Black Americans and U.S. Foreign Affairs, 1935–1960*, London: The University of North Carolina Press, 1996; M. Marqusee, *Redemption Song: Muhammad Ali and the Spirit of the Sixties*, London: Verso, 1999.

21 Foner, *Give Me Liberty*.

22 R. W. Logan, *The American Negro: Old World Background and New World Background*, Boston: Houghton Mifflin Company, 1970, 209; M. L. Krenn, *The Color of Empire: Race and American Foreign Relations*, Washington, DC: Potomac Books, 2006, 75.

23 Roark, 'American Black Leaders,' 258.

24 R. F. Williams, *Negroes with Guns*, Detroit: Wayne State University Press, 1998; T. B. Tyson, *Radio Free Dixie: Robert F. Williams & the Roots of Black Power*, London: The University of North Carolina Press, 1999; A. Fairclough, *Better Day Coming: Blacks and Equality, 1890–2000*, London: Penguin Books, 2002.

25 Lewis, *W. E. B. Du Bois*, 522; K. R. Janken, *White: The Biography of Walter White, Mr. NAACP*, New York: The New Press, 2003, 303.

26 Anderson, *Eyes Off the Prize*; M. L. Dudziak, *Cold War Civil Rights: Race and the Image of American Democracy*, Oxford: Princeton University Press, 2000.

27 K. Verney, *Black Civil Rights in America*, London: Routledge, 2004, 35; Joseph, *Waiting Til the Midnight Hour*, 5; P. J. Ling, *Martin Luther King, Jr.*, London: Routledge, 2006, 20.

28 Dudziak, *Cold War*.

29 G. Lewis, *Massive Resistance: The White Response to the Civil Rights Movement*, London: Hodder Education, 2006.

30 F. N. Nesbitt, *Race for Sanctions: African Americans against Apartheid 1946–1994*, Indianaolis: Indiana University Press, 2004.

31 Lewis, *Massive Resistance*.

32 Anderson, *Eyes Off the Prize*.

33 Nesbitt, *Race for Sanctions*.

34 M. L. Krenn, ed., *The African American Voice in US Foreign Policy Since World War II*, London: Garland Publishing Inc., 1999.

35 Von Eschen, *Race Against Empire*.

36 P. Robeson, *Here I Stand*, London: Dobson Books, 1958.

37 Layton, *International Politics*, 50.

38 Anderson, *Eyes Off the Prize*, 20.

39 Ibid., 20.

40 Layton, *International Politics*, 50; Von Eschen, *Race Against Empire*, 19.

41 Anderson, *Eyes Off the Prize*, 78.

42 Ibid.
43 Dudziak, *Cold War*, 2002.
44 Krenn, *The African American Voice.*
45 Layton, *International Politics,* 50.
46 Ibid., 51.
47 Ibid., 51. All of which would become their respective countries' Heads of State.
48 Ibid., 51.
49 Anderson, *Eyes Off the Prize*, 81.
50 Ibid., 81.
51 Ibid., 81.
52 Ibid., 81.
53 Ibid., 81.
54 Ibid., 86; Nesbitt, *Race for Sanctions.*
55 Roark, 'American Black Leaders,' 261.
56 Janken, *White: The Biography of Walter White.*
57 Roark, 'American Black Leaders,' 262.
58 For example, in the domestic context, 'less than a month before Truman's speech, an epileptic Willie Earle had been dragged out of a South Carolina Jail, mutilated, and then virtually decapitated by a series of shotgun blasts and then, despite detailed confessions, his murderers were found "not guilty" by a jury of their peers,' Anderson, *Eyes Off the Prize*, 100.
59 Roark, 'American Black Leaders,' 262.
60 Ibid., 262.
61 Anderson, *Eyes Off the Prize*, 103.
62 Roark, 'American Black Leaders,' 261–62.
63 D. Long and B.C. Schmidt, *Imperialism and Internationalism in the Discipline of International Relations,* New York: State University of New York, 2005.
64 Roark, 'American Black Leaders,' 262.
65 Janken, *White: The Biography of Walter White.*
66 J. H. Meriwether, *Proudly We Can Be Africans: Black Americans and Africa, 1935–1961,* London: The University of North Carolina Press, 2002, 83.
67 Ibid., 83.
68 Anderson, *Eyes Off the Prize.*
69 Janken, *White: The Biography of Walter White.*
70 Von Eschen, *Race Against Empire.*
71 Foner, *Give Me Liberty.*
72 T. Borstelmann, *The Cold War and the Color Line,* Cambridge: Harvard University Press, 2001, 49.
73 Logan, *The American Negro*, 210; S.A. Shull, *American Civil Right Policy from Truman to Clinton: The Role Presidential Leadership,* New York: M. E. Sharpe, 2000, 36.
74 Foner, *Give Me Liberty.*
75 Plummer, *Rising Wind.*
76 Ibid.
77 Meriwether, *Proudly We Can Be Africans*, 76.
78 Nesbitt, *Race for Sanctions.*
79 Meriwether, *Proudly We Can Be Africans*, 77–78.
80 Foner, *Give Me Liberty.*
81 Meriwether, *Proudly We Can Be Africans*, 84; Foner, *Give me Liberty*, 869; Fairclough, *Better Day Coming*, 212.
82 Plummer, *Rising Wind.*
83 Janken, *White: The Biography of Walter White.*
84 Meriwether, *Proudly We Can Be Africans*, 89.
85 Borstelmann, *Apartheid's Reluctant Uncle.*

86 Nesbitt, *Race for Sanctions*.
87 Borstelmann, *Apartheid's Reluctant Uncle*, 4.
88 Nesbitt, *Race for Sanctions*; Borstelmann, *Apartheid's Reluctant Uncle*.
89 Nesbitt, *Race for Sanctions*.
90 Ibid.
91 Meriwether, *Proudly We Can Be Africans*, 92.
92 Borstelmann, *Apartheid's Reluctant Uncle*.
93 Nesbitt, *Race for Sanctions*.
94 Meriwether, *Proudly We Can Be Africans*, 100.
95 For example in 'May 1953 the United States, Britain and South Africa jointly opened a Uranium plant in South Africa', Meriwether, *Proudly We Can Be Africans*, 110.
96 Von Eschen, *Race Against Empire*, 154.
97 Meriwether, *Proudly We Can Be Africans*.
98 Nesbitt, *Race for Sanctions*.
99 Plummer, *Rising Wind*, 226.
100 B. Karim, ed., *The End of White World Supremacy Four Speeches by Malcolm X*, New York: Arcade Publishing, 1971, 15; Clarke, *Notes for an African*, 378.
101 Gaines, *Black Expatriates*.
102 Foner, *Give Me Liberty*.
103 Plummer, *Rising Wind*.
104 Nesbitt, *Race for Sanctions*.
105 Meriwether, *Proudly We Can Be Africans*, 112.
106 Ibid., 113.
107 Ibid., 115.
108 Ibid., 117.
109 Ibid., 118.
110 Nesbitt, *Race for Sanctions*.
111 Meriwether, *Proudly We Can Be Africans*, 122.
112 Borstelmann, *Apartheid's Reluctant Uncle*, 129; Dudziak, *Cold War*, 57.
113 Meriwether, *Proudly We Can Be Africans*, 121.
114 Joseph, *Waiting 'Til the Midnight Hour*.
115 Clarke, *Notes for an African*, 162, Chinweizu, *The West and the Rest of Us: White Predators, Black Slavers and the African Elite*, Lagos: Pero Press, 1987, 130.
116 Meriwether, *Proudly We Can Be Africans*, 127.
117 Ibid., 135.
118 Ibid., 135.
119 www.timesonline.co.uk/tol/news/world/africa/article3694930.ece
120 Karim, *The End of White*; Tyson, *Radio Free Dixie*.
121 Ling, *Martin Luther*; J. A. Kirk, ed., *Martin Luther King, Jr and the Civil Rights Movement: Controversies and Debates*, New York: Palgrave Macmillan, 2007; F. L. Broderick *et al.*, eds., *Black Protest in the Twentieth Century*, London: Collier Macmillan Publishers, 1986.
122 Meriwether, *Proudly We Can Be Africans*, 143.
123 Nesbitt, *Race for Sanctions*, 28.
124 Plummer, *Rising Wind*, 213.
125 Meriwether, *Proudly We Can Be Africans*, 124.
126 Plummer, *Rising Wind*.
127 Ibid.; Meriwether, *Proudly We Can Be Africans*.
128 Chinweizu, *The West and the Rest of Us*.
129 Meriwether, *Proudly We Can Be Africans*, 128.
130 Ibid., 128; Plummer, *Rising Wind*, 244.
131 Nesbitt, *Race for Sanctions*.
132 Meriwether, *Proudly We Can Be Africans*; Borstelmann, *The Cold War*.

133 Meriwether, *Proudly We Can Be Africans.*
134 Ibid.
135 Ibid.
136 Borstelmann, *Apartheid's Reluctant Uncle.*
137 Ibid.
138 Meriwether, *Proudly We Can Be Africans.*
139 Ibid., 133.
140 Ibid., 135.
141 Ibid., 135.
142 Plummer, *Rising Wind*, 213.
143 Ibid., 243.
144 Meriwether, *Proudly We Can Be Africans*, 139.
145 Ibid., 139.
146 Ibid., 140.
147 Ibid., 141.
148 Ibid., 142.
149 Nesbitt, *Race for Sanctions.*
150 Meriwether, *Proudly We Can Be Africans*, 146.
151 C. Pedersen, *Obama's America*, Edinburgh: Edinburgh University Press, 2009, 121.
152 J. H. Cone, *Martin and Malcolm and America: A Dream or a Nightmare*, London: Fount Paperbacks, 1993, 115; Meriwether, *Proudly We Can Be Africans*, 148.
153 Fairclough, *Better Day Coming*, 213.
154 Anderson, *Eyes Off the Prize*, 171.
155 Janken, *White: The Biography of Walter White*, 322; Fairclough, *Better Day Coming*, 213.
156 H. Adi and M. Sherwood, *The 1945 Manchester Pan-African Congress Revisited*, London: New Beacon Books Ltd., 1995, 51.
157 Anderson, *Eyes Off the Prize*, 175.
158 Janken, *White: The Biography of Walter White.*
159 It is of note that the CRC was backed by the Communist USA which added an additional layer to the Truman administration's response to the organisation.
160 Layton, *International Politics*, 65.
161 Ibid., 67.
162 Anderson, *Eyes Off the Prize*, 191.
163 Layton, *International Politics*, 68.
164 Evanzz, K., *The Messenger: The Rise and Fall of Elijah Muhammad*, New York: Pantheon Books, 1999, 167.
165 Janken, *White: The Biography of Walter White*, 320.
166 Anderson, *Eyes Off the Prize.*
167 Layton, *International Politics*, 67.
168 Anderson, *Eyes Off the Prize*, 209.
169 Von Eschen, *Race Against Empire.*
170 Borstelmann, *Apartheid's Reluctant Uncle.*
171 Dudziak, *Cold War.*
172 R. Singh, ed., *Governing America: The Politics of a Divided Democracy*, Oxford: Oxford University Press, 2003.
173 Dudziak, *Cold War*; Isserman and Kazin, *America Divided.*
174 Singh, *Governing America.*
175 Verney, *Black Civil Rights in America*, 5.
176 L. Sartain and K. Verney, *Long is the Way and Hard: One Hundred Years of the NAACP*, Fayetteville: The University of Arkansas Press, 2009, 4.
177 D. E. Shi and G. Tindal, *America: A Narrative History*, London: W. W. Norton & Company, 1993.

178 Borstelmann, *The Cold War*, 93.
179 M. Cox and I. Parmar, ed., *Soft Power and US Foreign Policy: Theoretical, Historical and Contemporary Perspective,* London: Routledge, 2010.
180 Lauren, *Power and Prejudice*, 220; Borstelmann, *The Cold War*, 93.
181 Borstelmann, *The Cold War*, 94; Dudziak, *Cold War*, 109.
182 Borstelmann, *The Cold War*, 94.
183 Dudziak, *Cold War*, 2002.
184 Krenn, The Color of Empire, 83.
185 Von Eschen, *Race Against Empire*; Krenn, *The Color of Empire*; Lauren, *Power and Prejudice.*
186 M. X, *Malcolm X on Afro-American History,* New York: Pathfinder, 1988, 158; Gaines, *Black Expatriates*, 71.
187 Borstelmann, *The Cold War*, 95.
188 Ibid., 96.
189 Ibid., 96.
190 Meriwether, *Proudly We Can Be Africans.*
191 Von Eschen, *Race Against Empire*, 168.
192 Ibid., 171.
193 Ibid., 172.
194 Ibid., 171.
195 Plummer, *Rising Wind.*
196 Ibid., 250.
197 Borstelmann, *The Cold War.*
198 Von Eschen, *Race Against Empire*, 170.
199 Ibid., 171.
200 Ibid., 171.
201 Ibid., 171.
202 Gaines, *Black Expatriates.*
203 Layton, *International Politics.*
204 Von Eschen, *Race Against Empire*, 173.
205 K. Evanzz, *The Judas Factor: The Plot to Kill Malcolm X*, New York: Thunder's Mouth Press, 1992, 50.
206 Pedersen, *Obama's America*, 47.
207 Fairclough, *Better Day Coming*, 227.
208 Note there 'had been a boycott in Baton Rouge, Louisiana, two years before hand, which had ended after a week because both sides agreed to a compromise,' Fairclough, *Better Day Coming*, 227.
209 Fairclough, *Better Day Coming*, 227.
210 Ling, *Martin Luther.*
211 Fairclough, *Better Day Coming.*
212 M. Ledwidge, 'Race, African-American and US foreign policy,' in M. Ledwidge *et al, New Directions in US Foreign Policy*, New York: Routledge, 2009, 153.
213 Ling, *Martin Luther*, 42.
214 Ibid., 42.
215 Foner, *Give Me Liberty.*
216 Lewis, *Massive Resistance.*
217 Borstelmann, *Apartheid's Reluctant Uncle*, 99.
218 Lewis, *Massive Resistance.*
219 Ibid., 48.
220 Ibid., 48.
221 Dudziak, *Cold War*, 116.
222 Ibid., 115.
223 Borstelmann, *Apartheid's Reluctant Uncle*, 103.

224 Layton, *International Politics*, 122.
225 Ibid., 122.
226 Dudziak, *Cold War*.
227 Foner, *Give Me Liberty*, 908.
228 Isserman and Kazin, *America Divided*, 32.
229 Dudziak, *Cold War*, 117.
230 Layton, *International Politics*, 123.
231 Ibid., 126.
232 Ibid., 125.
233 Dudziak, *Cold War*, 118.
234 Layton, *International Politics*, 127.
235 Borstelmann, *The Cold War*, 104.
236 Ibid., 104; Dudziak, *Cold War*, 133
237 Borstelmann, *The Cold War*, 104.
238 Ibid., 105.
239 Ibid., 106.
240 M. Keita, *Race and the Writing of History: Riddling the Sphinx*, Oxford: Oxford University Press, 2000; Clarke, *Notes for an African*, 1992; X, *Malcolm X*.
241 According to Albert Van Dantzig that 'within three centuries (Europeans built) more than sixty castles, forts and lodges ... along a stretch of coast less than 300 miles long' in order to facilitate their extract of Ghana's human and mineral resources Van Dantzig.
242 A. Boahen, *Topics in West African History*, London: Longman Group, 1971;, E. K. Agorsah, ed., *Maroon Heritage: Arcaeological Ethnographic and Historical Perspectives,* Kingston: Canoe Press, 1994; Gaines, *Black Expatriates*.
243 Adi and M. Sherwood, *The 1945 Manchester Pan-African*.
244 Ibid.
245 Ibid., 143.
246 Clarke, *Notes for an African*, 105.
247 Ibid., 103.
248 Adi and Sherwood, *The 1945 Manchester Pan-African Congress*.
249 Clarke, *Notes for an African*, 1992.
250 Ledwidge, 'American Power'; B. Obama, *Dreams From My Father: A Story of Race and Inheritance,* Edinburgh: Canongate Books, 2009.
251 Ibid.
252 Adi and Sherwood, *The 1945 Manchester Pan-African Congress*.
253 Ibid., 144.
254 Meriwether, *Proudly We Can Be Africans*, 153.
255 Ibid.
256 Clarke, *Notes for an African*, 1992.
257 Gaines, *Black Expatriates*.
258 Meriwether, *Proudly We Can Be Africans*.
259 Ledwidge, 'American Power'.
260 Gaines, *Black Expatriates*.
261 Meriwether, *Proudly We Can Be Africans*.
262 Ibid.
263 Nesbitt, *Race for Sanctions*.
264 Von Eschen, *Race Against Empire*, 181.
265 Meriwether, *Proudly We Can Be Africans*.
266 Von Eschen, *Race Against Empire*, 182.
267 Gaines, *Black Expatriates*.
268 Meriwether, *Proudly We Can Be Africans*, 160.
269 Borstelmann, *The Cold War*.
270 Ibid.

271 Gaines, *Black Expatriates*; Dudziak, *Cold War*.
272 Nesbitt, *Race for Sanctions*, 31; Meriwether, *Proudly We Can Be Africans*, 164.
273 Borstelmann, *Apartheid's Reluctant Uncle*, 121.
274 Gaines, *Black Expatriates*.
275 Borstelmann, *The Cold War*, 123.
276 Cox and Parmar, *Soft Power*.
277 Borstelmann, *The Cold War*.
278 Gaines, *Black Expatriates*.
279 Ibid.
280 Meriwether, *Proudly We Can Be Africans*, 163.
281 Krenn, *The African American Voice*.
282 Janken, *White: The Biography of Walter White*, Anderson, *Eyes Off the Prize*.

7 Malcolm and Martin and the shadow of US foreign policy

1 J. H. Cone, *Martin and Malcolm and America: A Dream or a Nightmare*, London: Fount Paperbacks, 1993.
2 M. Karenga, *Introduction to Black Studies*, Los Angeles: The University of Sankore Press, 1993.
3 Cone, *Martin and Malcolm*.
4 K. K. Gaines, *Black Expatriates and the Civil Rights Era: American Africans in Ghana*, The University of North Carolina Press: Chapel Hill, 2006.
5 J. H. Meriwether, *Proudly We Can Be Africans: Black Americans and Africa, 1935–1961*, London: University of North Carolina Press, 2002, 181.
6 T. Borstelmann, *The Cold War and the Color Line*, Cambridge: Harvard University Press, 2001, 139.
7 M. Isserman and M. Kazin, *America Divided: The Civil War of the 1960s*, Oxford: Oxford University Press, 2008.
8 P. E. Joseph, *Waiting 'Til the Midnight Hour: A Narrative History of Black Power in America*, New York: Henry Holt & Company, 2006.
9 A. Fairclough, *Better Day Coming: Blacks and Equality, 1890–2000*, London: Penguin Books, 2002.
10 S. F. Yette, *The Choice: The Issue of Black Survival in America*, Silver Spring: Cottage Books, 1971, 22.
11 R. J. Rickford, *Betty Shabazz: Surviving Malcolm X*, Illinois: Sourcebooks, 2003. D. Howard-Pitney, *Martin Luther King Jr., Malcolm X, and the Civil Rights Struggle of the 1950s and 1960s: A Brief History with Documents*, Boston: Bedford St. Martins, 2004.
12 A. Haley, *The Autobiography of Malcolm X*, New York: Grove Press, 1986.
13 W. Strickland, ed., *Malcolm X Make it Plain*, London: Penguin Books, 1995, 11.
14 Ibid., 23.
15 Ibid., 12.
16 R. P. Collins, *Seventh Child*, New Jersey: Birch Lane Press Book, 1998, 13.
17 A. Rashad, ed., *Elijah Muhammad & the Ideological Foundation of The Nation of Islam*, Virginia: U.B. & U.S. Communications Systems, 1994, 185.
18 Collins, *Seventh Child*.
19 R. A. Hill, *The FBI's RACON: Racial Conditions in the United States During World War II*, Boston: Northeastern University Press, 1995, 1.
20 C. E. Marsh, 'Malolm X – From Detroit Red to Mecca: The Evolution of a Black Leader's Vision from Separation to Third World Liberation,' in I. Van Sertima, ed., *Great Black Leaders: Ancient and Modern*, New York: Journal of African Civilisation Ltd., 1993, 78.
21 W. W. Sales, Jr., *From Civil Rights to Black Liberation: Malcolm X and the Organization of Afro-American Unity*, Massachusetts: South End Press, 1994, 33.

22 Haley, *Malcolm X*, 36.
23 Ibid., 159.
24 Sales, *From Civil Rights*, 33; J. H. Clarke, *Malcolm X: The Man and His Times*, Trenton: Africa World Press, 1992.
25 C. E. Lincoln, *The Black Muslims in America*, New Jersey: Africa World Press, 1994, 15.
26 Cone, *Martin and Malcolm*, 161.
27 C. A. Clegg, III, *An Original Man: The Life and Times of Elijah Muhammad*, New York: St. Martin's Press, 1997.
28 M. A. Gomez, *Black Crescent: The Experience and Legacy of African Muslims in the Americas*, Cambridge: Cambridge University Press, 2005, 277.
29 Hill, *The FBI's RACON*, 544; K. Evanzz, *The Judas Factor: The Plot to Kill Malcolm X*, New York: Thunder's Mouth Press, 1992, 25.
30 Cone, *Martin and Malcolm*, 49.
31 Clegg, *An Orginal Man*, 1997.
32 Evanzz, *The Judas Factor*, 15.
33 Ibid.
34 W. Churchill and J. V. Wall, *Agents of Repression: The FBI's Secret Wars Against the Black Panther Party and the American Indian Movement*, Cambridge: South End Press, 2002, 55; C. Carson, ed., *Malcolm X: The FBI File*, New York: Carroll and Graf Publishers, 1993, 26; R. Jeffreys-Jones, *The FBI: A History*, London: Yale University Press, 2007.
35 Gomez, *Black Crescent*, 339.
36 Ibid., 344.
37 Rickford, *Betty Shabazz*.
38 Gomez, *Black Crescent*, 339.
39 Collins, *Seventh Child*.
40 Clarke, *Malcolm X*.
41 Gomez, *Black Crescent*, 348.
42 Haley, *Malcolm X*.
43 Strickland, *Malcolm X*, 70; Evanzz, *The Judas Factor*, 164.
44 J. H. Clarke, *Notes for an African World Revolution: Africans at the Crossroads*, Trenton: Africa World Press, 1992.
45 Evanzz, *The Judas Factor*.
46 Gomez, *Black Crescent*, 349.
47 Clegg, *An Original Man*.
48 Ibid.
49 K. Evanzz, *The Messenger: The Rise and Fall of Elijah Muhammad*, New York: Pantheon Books, 2006, 193.
50 Evanzz, *The Judas Factor*.
51 Evanzz, *The Messenger*.
52 Ibid.
53 Ibid.
54 Clegg, *An Orginal Man*.
55 Evanzz, *The Judas Factor*, 199.
56 Gomez, *Black Crescent*, 350.
57 Clegg, *An Original Man*, 138.
58 Ibid., 140.
59 Clegg, *An Original Man*, 144.
60 Evanzz, *The Messenger*.
61 Gomez, *Black Crescent*, 350.
62 Clegg, *An Original Man*, 144.
63 Borstelmann, *The Cold War*, 126.
64 Ibid., 126.

65 Ibid.
66 Ibid., 126.
67 Meriwether, *Proudly We Can Be Africans.*
68 Evanzz, *The Judas Factor*, 81.
69 Carson, *Malcolm X*; Joseph, *Waiting 'Til the Midnight Hour*; B. Z. A. Kondo, *Conspiracys: Unravelling the Assassination of Malcolm X*, Washington, DC: Nubia Press, 1993.
70 Evanzz, *The Judas Factor*, 83; Kondo, *Conspiracys.*
71 T. B. Tyson, *Radio Free Dixie: Robert F. Williams & the Roots of Black Power*, London: The University of North Carolina Press, 1999, 205.
72 Ibid., 220.
73 Evanzz, *The Judas Factor*, 84.
74 Ibid., 84.
75 Ibid., 84.
76 Strickland, *Malcolm X.*
77 Evanzz, *The Judas Factor*, 84.
78 Ibid., 85.
79 Strickland, *Malcolm X.*
80 Evanzz, *The Judas Factor*, 84.
81 Gomez, *Black Crescent*, 350.
82 F. N. Nesbitt, *Race for Sanctions: African Americans against Apartheid 1946–1994*, Indianaolis: Indiana University Press, 2004, 42.
83 Gomez, *Black Crescent*, 350.
84 Ibid., 350; Nesbitt, *Race for Sanctions*, 41.
85 Borstalmann, *The Cold War*, 129.
86 Kondo, *Conspiracies*, 17.
87 Gomez, *Black Crescent*, 351.
88 Borstalmann, *The Cold War*, 130.
89 F. Fanon, *Black Skin, White Masks*, London: Pluto Press, 1993.
90 Gomez, *Black Crescent*, 351.
91 Joseph, *Waiting 'Til the Midnight Hour.*
92 M. L. Dudziak, *Cold War Civil Rights: Race and the Image of American Democracy*, Oxford: Princeton University Press, 2000.
93 Nesbitt, *Race for Sanctions.*
94 Dudziak, *Cold War Civil Rights.*
95 Borstalmann, *The Cold War*, 139.
96 Ibid., 141.
97 Dudziak, *Cold War Civil Rights.*
98 Borstalmann, *The Cold War*, 156.
99 Carson, *Malcolm X.*
100 K. O'Reilly, '*Racial Matters*': The FBI's Secret File on Black America, 1960–1972*, London: The Free Press, 1991.
101 Borstalmann, *The Cold War*, 158.
102 Joseph, *Waiting 'Til the Midnight Hour*, 77.
103 Dudziak, *Cold War Civil Rights.*
104 Borstalmann, *The Cold War*, 160.
105 Ibid., 168.
106 Ibid., 170.
107 Clegg, *An Original Man*; Evanzz, *The Judas Factor.*
108 Strickland, *Malcolm X.*
109 Ibid.
110 Rickford, *Betty Shabazz.*
111 Clegg, *An Original Man*; K. K. Gaines, *Black Expatriates.*
112 Collins, *Seventh Child*, 157.

113 Joseph, *Waiting 'Til the Midnight Hour*, 92.
114 Clegg, *An Original Man*.
115 Evanzz, *The Judas Factor*, 1992.
116 Kondo, *Conspiracies*, 41; Joseph, *Waiting 'Til the Midnight Hour*, 92.
117 Rickford, *Betty Shabazz*.
118 Clegg, *An Original Man*, 205; Gaines, *Black Expatriates*, 184.
119 Kondo, *Conspiracies*, 1993.
120 Rickford, *Betty Shabazz*, 2003.
121 Gomez, *Black Crescent*.
122 Sales, *From Civil Rights*.
123 Collins, *Seventh Child*.
124 Clarke, *Malcolm X*.
125 Kondo, *Conspiracies*, 41.
126 Ibid., 41.
127 Ibid., 41.
128 Strickland, *Malcolm X*.
129 Rashad, *Elijah Muhammad*, 18; Sales, *From Civil Rights*, 122.
130 Kondo, *Conspiracies*, 42.
131 Gomez, *Black Crescent*, 352; Collins, *Seventh Child*, 170. Given Saudi Arabia's strategic importance in regards to American oil supplies, Malcolm's popularity there was not necessarily in line with US interests.
132 Kondo, *Conspiracies*.
133 Rashad, *Elijah Muhammad*, 12; Gomez, *Black Crescent*, 363.
134 Gaines, *Black Expatriates*, 200; H. Adi *et al.*, *Pan-African History: Political Figures from Africa and the Diaspora since 1787*, London: Routledge, 2003, 125.
135 Gaines, *Black Expatriates*, 200; Adi, *Pan-African History*.
136 Sales, *From Civil Rights*.
137 Kondo, *Conspiracies*, 43.
138 Evanzz, *The Judas Factor*.
139 Nesbitt, *Race for Sanctions*, 57.
140 Evanzz, *The Judas Factor*.
141 Kondo, *Conspiracies*, 44.
142 Ibid., 44.
143 Rickford, *Betty Shabazz*, 213.
144 Kondo, *Conspiracies*, 46.
145 Rashad, *Elijah Muhammad*, 19; O. T'Shaka, *The Political Legacy of Malcolm X*, California: Pan Afrikan Publications, 1983, 229.
146 Sales, *From Civil Rights*, 122.
147 Nesbitt, *Race for Sanctions*, 58.
148 Sales, *From Civil Rights*, 124.
149 Kondo, *Conspiracies*.
150 Ibid.
151 Gaines, *Black Expatriates*, 197.
152 Carson, *Malcolm X*, 323.
153 Evanzz, *The Judas Factor*.
154 Kondo, *Conspiracies*, 49.
155 Ibid., 49.
156 Ibid., 49.
157 Note Kondo maintains the CIA had a file on Malcolm as early as 1959 due to his trips abroad and had noted his meeting with Castro and his UN campaign; Kondo, *Conspiracies*, 50.
158 Kondo, *Conspiracies*, 50.
159 Ibid., 50.
160 Ibid.; Evanzz, *The Judas Factor*; Carson, *Malcolm X*.

161 Kondo, *Conspiracies*, 51.
162 Ibid., 51.
163 Joseph, *Waiting 'Til the Midnight Hour*.
164 Sales, *From Civil Rights*.
165 Collins, *Seventh Child*; Carson, *Malcolm X*.
166 Kondo, *Conspiracies*, 52.
167 Nesbitt, *Race for Sanctions*, 58.
168 Sales, *From Civil Rights*, 77.
169 Kondo, *Conspiracies*, 53.
170 Adi, *Pan-African History*, 127.
171 Ibid., 127.
172 A. Epps, *Malcolm X: Speeches at Harvard*, New York: Paragon House, 1991.
173 Evanzz, *The Judas Factor*, 267.
174 Kondo, *Conspiracies*, 55.
175 Evanzz, *The Judas Factor*.
176 Kondo, *Conspiracies*, 55.
177 Ibid., 55.
178 Gomez, *Black Crescent*, 354.
179 Clegg, *An Original Man*, 215.
180 Cone, *Martin and Malcolm*, 207; Evanzz, *The Judas Factor*.
181 Evanzz, *The Judas Factor*, 159.
182 Churchill, *Agents of Repression*, 97.
183 Howard-Pitney, *Martin Luther King*, 1; Van Sertima, *Great Black Leaders*, 1993.
184 Evanzz, *The Judas Factor*.
185 Note that the CIA's Domestic Operations Division requested FBI files on Malcolm on the 27 March, 1964, Evanzz, *The Judas Factor*, 229.
186 Ibid., 229.
187 Ibid., 229.
188 Ibid., 234.
189 Ibid., 236.
190 Ibid., 240; Cone, *Martin and Malcolm*, 207.
191 Evanzz, *The Judas Factor*, 266.
192 Ibid., 274.
193 Howard-Pitney, *Martin Luther King*, 188.
194 M. Marqusee, *Redemption Song: Muhammad Ali and the Spirit of the Sixties*, London: Verso, 1999.
195 Joseph, *Waiting 'Til the Midnight Hour*, 115; Kondo provides biographical data on the alleged assassins who are listed as, Albert BenJamin Thomas, Leon Davis, Talmadge Hayer, William Bradley and Wilbur Mckinley; Kondo, *Conspiracies*, 203–5.
196 Evanzz, *The Judas Factor*; Kondo, *Conspiracies*; T'Shaka, *The Political Legacy*; Collins, *Seventh Child*; Rickford, *Betty Shabazz*.
197 Strickland, *Malcolm X*, 202.
198 Kondo, *Conspiracies*; Evanzz, *The Judas Factor*.
199 Clegg, *An Original Man*, 229.
200 Strickland, *Malcolm X*; Rickford, *Betty Shabazz*.
201 Rickford, *Betty Shabazz*.
202 Clegg, *An Original Man*.
203 Note it is still currently believed by the uninformed that Minister Louis Farrakhan was directly involved with the murder of Malcolm X.
204 Rickford, *Betty Shabazz*, 242.
205 E. Foner, *Give Me Liberty! An American History*, London: W. W. Norton and Company, 2009, 929.
206 J. A. Kirk, ed., *Martin Luther King, Jr and the Civil Rights Movement: Controversies and Debates*, New York: Palgrave Macmillan, 2007, 177.

207 K. Verney, *Black Civil Rights in America*, London: Routledge, 2004, 61.
208 P. J. Ling, *Martin Luther King, Jr.*, London: Routledge, 2006.
209 Adi, *Pan-African History*, 107.
210 Howard-Pitney, *Martin Luther King*.
211 Clegg, *An Original Man*, 238.
212 Ling, *Martin Luther*.
213 Marqusee, *Redemption Song*, 164.
214 Fairclough, *Better Day Coming*, 314.
215 Marqusee, *Redemption Song*.
216 Fairclough, *Better Day Coming*, 315.
217 Marqusee, *Redemption Song*, 179.
218 Ibid.; M. L. Krenn, *The Color of Empire: Race and American Foreign Relations*, Washington, DC: Potomac Books, 2006.
219 Yette, *The Choice*.
220 J. A. Colaiaco, *Martin Luther King, Jr.: Apostle of Militant Nonviolence*, New York: St. Martin's Press, 1988, 181.
221 Marqusee, *Redemption Song*.
222 Joseph, *Waiting 'Til the Midnight Hour*; Tyson, *Radio Free Dixie*.
223 C. Pedersen, *Obama's America*, Edinburgh: Edinburgh University Press, 2009, 66.
224 Colaiaco, *Martin Luther King*, 152.
225 Ling, *Martin Luther*, 212.
226 Clegg, *An Original Man*, 237.
227 Ling, *Martin Luther*, 219.
228 Ibid., 230.
229 Kirk, *Martin Luther King*, 174.
230 Ibid., 175.
231 Ling, *Martin Luther*, 259.
232 Ibid., 253.
233 I. S. Cohen and R. W.Logan, *The American Negro: Old World Background and New World Experience*, Boston: Houghton Mifflin Company, 1970, 261.
234 Joseph, *Waiting 'Til the Midnight Hour*.
235 Ibid., 136.
236 Colaiaco, *Martin Luther King*, 162.
237 J. M. Washington, ed., *A Testament of Hope: The Essential Writings and Speeches of Martin Luther King, Jr.*, New York: HarperCollins Publishers, 1991.
238 Joseph, *Waiting 'Til the Midnight Hour*.
239 Karenga, *Introduction to Black Studies*.
240 Ling, *Martin Luther*.
241 Ibid.
242 Kirk, *Martin Luther King*, 243.
243 Ibid.
244 Ibid., 179.
245 Ibid., 187.
246 Ibid., 187.
247 Ling, *Martin Luther*.
248 Ibid., 264.
249 Ibid., 265.
250 Ibid., 265.
251 Ibid., 267.
252 Colaiaco, *Martin Luther King*, 180.
253 Kirk, *Martin Luther King*, 188.
254 Ibid., 188.
255 Foner, *Give Me Liberty*, 953.
256 Ibid., 953.

257 Ling, *Martin Luther.*
258 Washington, *A Testament of Hope*, 286.
259 Washington, *A Testament of Hope*, 286.
260 Joseph, *Waiting 'Til the Midnight Hour*, 227.
261 Kirk, *Martin Luther King*, 195.
262 Ibid., 195.
263 Ibid., 196.
264 Ibid.
265 Kirk, *Martin Luther King.*
266 Marqusee, *Redemption Song*, 241.
267 Kondo, *Conspiracies*, 150.
268 Kirk, *Martin Luther King.*
269 Ibid.
270 Pedersen, *Obama's America*, 40.
271 Kondo, *Conspiracies*, 151.

8 Conclusion

1 Like the British colonialists who rankled at Garvey's challenge to their colonial domination of continental and diasporean Africans.
2 Nevertheless, African-Americans were not the only people of African descent to rally behind Ethiopia. 'The Ethiopian crisis also affected people of African ancestry in other parts of the world. In Jamaica the disbanded West Indian Regiment volunteered for service to Ethiopia. The Rastafarians, who worshipped Haile Selassie, Ras Tafari Makkonen was the Emperor's name before he became Haile Selassie, joined the Ethiopian World Federation. In Cuba 2,000 were reported mobilized to aid Ethiopia in the war against Italy'. A. Sbacchi, *Legacy of Bitterness: Ethiopia and Fascist Italy, 1935–1941*, Trenton: The Red Sea Press, 1997, 17.
3 Significantly, during the IEW, African-Americans correctly argued that Italian aggression would lead to further international conflicts.
4 M. H. Hunt, *Ideology and U.S. Foreign Policy*, London: Yale University Press, 1987, 79.
5 Sbacchi, *Legacy of Bitterness*, 7.
6 Ibid., 16.
7 W. E. B. Du Bois, 'African Roots of War,' *Atlantic Monthly*, 1915, vol. 115, 707–14.
8 J. Woodland, 'How did Participation in America's Wars affect black Americans?', *American Studies Today*, Issue 9/10, Winter 2001, 18.
9 Woodland, 'How did Participation,' 18.
10 A. De Tocqueville, *Democracy in America: Vol. I and II*, New York: Alfred A. Knopf, Inc., 1994, 3, J. H. Carruthers, *Intellectual Warfare*, Chicago, Third World Press, 1999, 81. Clearly de Tocqueville failed to distinguish between loss and the systematic application of psycho-cultural and physical violence employed by Europeans in order to perfect the making of the slave.
11 G. W. Jr., *Racial Influences on American Foreign Policy*, New York: Basic Books, Inc., Publishers, 1970, 8.
12 H. Cruse, *The Crisis of the Negro Intellectual*, New York, Quill, 1984, 394.
13 D. King, *Separate and Unequal: black Americans and the U.S. Federal government*, Oxford: Oxford University Press, 1995, 9
14 K. Ture, *et al. Black Power the Politics of Liberation*, New York: Vintage Books, 1992, 7. Clearly the colonial analogy is not perfect but it does illuminate some aspects of black oppression in America.
15 H. R. Isaacs, 'Race and Color in World Affairs,' in G. W. Shepherd Jr., *Racial Influences on American Foreign Policy*, New York: Basic Books, Inc., Publishers, 1970, 49.

16 T. Cross, *The Black Power Imperative: Racial Inequality and the Politics of Non-Violence*, New York, Faulkner Books, 1987, 109.

17 Cruse, *Crisis of the Negro*, 395.

18 King, *Separate and Unequal*, 12.

19 Of course one recognises that 'the group in power is always likely to use every means at its disposal to create the impression that it deserves to be where it is. And it is not above suggesting that those who have been excluded have only themselves to blame', which is incidentally what many white theorists argued. J. A. Ladner, *The Death of White Sociology, Essays on Race and Culture*, Baltimore: Black Classic Press, 1998, 112.

20 C. E. Lincoln, 'The Race Problem and International Relations,' G. W. Shepherd Jr., *Racial Influences on American Foreign Policy*, New York, Basic Books, Inc., Publishers, 1970, 50.

21 S. M. Lipset, *American Exceptionism: A Double-Edged Sword*, London: W. W. Norton & Company, 1997, 115.

22 D. Brown, *Bury My Heart at Wounded Knee*, London: Vintage, 1991, 8.

23 J. H. Franklin, *From Slavery to Freedom*, New York: Vintage Books, 1957, 47.

24 S. Sterling, 'Slavery and the Building of America', in J. H. Clarke, *Critical Lessons in Slavery and the Slavetrade*, Richmond: Native Sun Publishers, 1996, 113.

25 D. T. Wellman, *Portrait of White Racism*, New York: Cambridge University Press, 1977, 35–36.

26 C. W. Mills, *The Power Elite*, New York: Oxford University Press, 292.

27 M. Ledwidge, 'Race, African-Americans and US foreign Policy,' in Ledwidge *et al*, eds., *New Directions in US Foreign Policy*, London: Routledge, 2009, 151.

28 Hunt, *Ideology and U.S.*, 51.

29 A. Wilson, *Blueprint for Black Power: A Moral, Political and Economic Imperative for the Twenty-First Century*, New York: Afrikan World Infosystems, 1998, 141.

30 A. Hacker, *Two Nations: Black and White, Separate, Hostile, Unequal*, New York, Macmillan, 1992, 4.

31 A. S. Layton, *International Politics and Civil Rights Policies in the United States 1941–1960*, Cambridge, University of Cambridge, 2000, 63.

32 Layton, *International Politics*, 63.

33 C. Anderson, 'From Hope to Disillusion: African-Americans', the United Nations, and the Struggle for Human Rights, 1944–47,' in M. L. Krenn, *The African-American Voice in U.S. Foreign Policy since World War Two*, London: Garland Publishing, Inc., 1999, 203.

34 Who, evidently, were committed to Western dominance as they failed to champion the cause of the colonised masses of the world who were overwhelmingly people of colour, in addition to rejecting Baron Makino's unsuccessful attempts to guarantee the League Covenant supported the Equality of Nations and racial equality. R. A. Hill, *The FBI's Racon: Racial Conditions in the United States during World War II*, Boston: Northeastern University Press, 1995, 509.

35 Chinweizu, *The West and the Rest of Us: White Predators Black Slavers and the African Elite*, Lagos, Pero Press, 1987, 41 points to the function of the Berlin Conference in securing Western dominance. In addition, the League of Nations' failure to propose or execute colonial reform and racial equality supports the notion that it was dedicated to preserving the status quo.

36 Whereby US state officials and African-Americans met to facilitate the common goal of defeating the Axis powers.

37 Although this doesn't negate the existence of other factors that encouraged black participation in the war effort.

38 Despite the fact that the Allies depicted themselves as being the champions of freedom and humanity.

39 N. Coombs, 'The Black Experience in America, Chapter 10: Fighting Racism at Home and Abroad,' (http://cti.itc.virginia.edu/~ybf2u/Thomas-Hill/library/Coombs/10.html), 5.

40 M. Omi and H. Winant, *Racial Formation in the United States from the 1960s to 1990s*, London: Routledge, 1994, 85.

41 Layton, *International Politics*, 63.

42 M. Omi and Winant, *Racial Formation*, London: Routledge, 1994, 85.

43 King, *Separate and Unequal*, 5.

44 Lipset, *American Exceptionism*, 79.

45 In addition, if Britain fell to Germany, then Germany would ultimately be in a position to attack America and American interests.

46 Indeed, Robinson maintains that Marxism, a derivative of Western thought, is itself infused with the notion of white Western supremacy. C. J. Robinson, *Black Marxism: The Making of the Black Radical Tradition*, London, North Carolina Press, 1983, xxix.

47 Hunt, *Ideology and U.S.*, 48. In essence, the hierarchical character of US race relations was formulated by the institutionalisation of race-based slavery that formed the basis for the future generation's adherence to a racialised code of white supremacy, which became an institutional reality in US society.

48 It is not always clear whether interest group monopoly is defined as a time period whereby a group cannot dominate a sphere of activity indefinitely or whether group dominance is confined to a limited number of issues.

49 A. Murray, 'White Norms, Black Deviation,' in J. A. Ladner, *The Death of White Sociology*, 96.

50 Cross, *The Black Power Imperative*, 201; M. Ledwidge, 'American Power and Racial Dimensions of U. S. Foreign Policy,' *International Politics*, 2011, forthcoming.

51 B. Miroff, R. Seidelman, T. Swanstrom, *The Democratic Debate: An Introduction to American Politics*, New York: Houghton Mifflin Company 1998, 36.

52 Sbacchi, *Legacy of Bitterness*, xxviii.

53 And the allied nations to reassess their overt commitment to white political supremacy.

54 Miroff, *The Democratic Debate*, 232.

55 As 'in coming to terms with pluralism, what is really at stake is power and antagonism'. M. Chantal, 'Democracy, Power, and the Political,' in B. Seyla, *Democracy and Difference Contesting the Boundaries of the Political*, Princeton: Princeton University Press, 1996, 247.

56 Chantal, 'Democracy, Power,' 248.

57 G. Marsh and G. Stoker, eds., *Theory and Methods in Political Science*, New York, Palgrave, 1995, 16.

58 While some scholars might maintain that the remit of Dunleavy and O'Leary was to study theories of the state in relation to liberal democracies, the pervasiveness and importance of race in Western democracies merits its discussion and examination in theories of the state.

59 Ledwidge *et al*, *New Directions*.

60 D. R. Roediger, *The Wages of Whiteness*, London: Verso, 1995, 13.

61 These values were tainted and formulated by state-sanctioned racialised enslavement, which created a colour-line that placed inordinate power in the hands of the white majority.

62 P. E. Joseph, *Waiting 'Til the Midnight Hour: A Narrative History of Black*, New York: Henry Holt & Company, 2006.

Bibliography

Books

Achcar, G. and Chomsky, N., *Perilous Power: The Middle East and U.S. Foreign Policy*, London: Paradigm Publishers, 2007.

Adi, H. and Sherwood, M., *The 1945 Manchester Pan-African Congress Revisited*, London: New Beacon Books Ltd, 1995.

——, *Pan-African History: Political Figures from Africa and the Diaspora since 1787*, London: Routledge, 2003.

Agbeyebiawo, D., *The Life and Works of W. E. B. Du Bois*, Accra, Ghana: Stephil Printing Press & Co. Ltd, 1998.

Agorsah, E. K., ed., *Maroon Heritage: Arcaeological Ethnographic and Historical Perspectives*, Kingston: Canoe Press, 1994.

Ajami, F., Bartley, R. L., Binyan, L., Huntington, S. P., Kirkpatrick, J. J., Mahbubani, K., Piel, G. and Weeks, A. L., *Samuel P. Huntington's The Clash of Civilizations? The Debate*, New York: Council on Foreign Relations, 1996.

Ambrose, S. E., *Rise to Globalism: American Foreign Policy Since 1938*, London: Penguin Books Ltd, 1993.

Anderson, C., 'From Hope to Disillusion,' in Krenn, M. L., ed., *The African American Voice in US Foreign Policy Since World War II*, London: Garland Publishing Inc., 1999.

——, *Eyes Off the Prize: African Americans, the United Nations, and the Struggle for Human Rights, 1944–1955*, Cambridge: Cambridge University Press, 2003.

Andrew, C. and Jeffrey-Jones, R., ed., *Eternal Vigilance? 50 Years of the CIA*, London: Frank Cass & Company, 1997.

Aptheker, H., *A Documentary History of the People in the United States*, Volume 5, New York: Carol Publishing Group, 1993.

——, ed., *Autobiography of W. E. B. Du Bois*, New York: International Publishers, 1997.

Arkes, H. *Bureaucracy, the Marshall Plan and the National Interest*, Cambridge: Cambridge University Press, 1972.

Arnove, R. F., ed., *Philanthropy and Cultural Imperialism*, Boston: GK Hall, 1980.

Asante, Dr. M. K., *African American History: A Journey of Liberation*, Maywood: The Peoples Publishing Group, Inc., 1995.

——, *Afrocentricity*, New Jersey: Africa World Press, 1989.

——, *The Painful Demise of Eurocentrism*, Trenton: Africa World Press, Inc., 1999.

Back, L. and Solomos, J., *Theories of Race and Racism*, London: Routledge Press, 2001.

Baldwin, J., *The Fire Next Time*, London: Penguin Groups, 1964.

Barker, A. J., *The Civilising Mission, A History of the Italo Ethiopian War of 1935–1936*, New York: The Dial Press, Inc., 1968.

Barker, E., Johnston, H. H., Lankester, Murray, G. and Wells, H. G., *The Outline of History: Being a Plain History of Life and Mankind*, London: George Newnes Limited, 1998.

Barry, N. P., *An Introduction to Modern Political Theory*, Basingstoke: Macmillan, 2000.

Beckner, C., *100 African-Americans Who Shaped American History*, San Francisco: Bluewood Books, 1995.

Beetham, D., *The Legitimation of Power and the Free Society*, Atlantic Highlands: Humanities Press International, 1991.

Bender, F.L., ed., *Karl Marx The Communist Manifesto*, London: Norton, 1988.

Bentley, A., *The Process of Government*, Chicago: University of Chicago Press, 1967.

Bernal, M., *Black Athena The Afroasiatic Roots of Classical Civilization*, London: Vintage, 1991.

Beynon, E. D. *Master Fard Muhammad: Detroit History*, Georgia: The Universal Truth, 1990.

Birch, A. H., *Concept and Theories of Modern Democracy*, London: Routledge, 2002.

Boahen, A., *Topics in West African History*, London: Longman Group, 1971.

Borstelmann, T., *Apartheid's Reluctant Uncle: The United States and Southern Africa in Early Cold War*, Oxford: Oxford University Press, 1993.

——, *The Cold War and the Color Line*, Cambridge: Harvard University Press, 2001.

Breitman, G., ed., *By Any Means Necessary: Speeches, Interviews and a Letter by Malcolm X*, London: Pathfinder Press, 1987.

——, *Malcolm X Speaks: Selected Speeches and Statements*, New York: Pathfinder, 1989.

Breitman, G., James, C. L. R. and Keemer, E., *Fighting Racism in World War II, A Week-By-Week Account of the Struggle Against Racism and Discrimination in the United States During 1939–45*, London: Pathfinder, 1991.

Broderick, F. L., Meier, A. and Rudwick, E., eds., *Black Protest in the Twentieth Century*, London: Collier Macmillan Publishers, 1986.

Brown, D., *Bury My Heart at Wounded Knee*, London: Vintage, 1991.

Brown. M. E., *The Scalabrinians in North America 1887–1934*, New York: CMS, 1996.

Bull, H., *The Anarchical Society: A Study of Order in World Politics*, London: Macmillan, 1995.

Cameron, F., *US Foreign Policy after the Cold War: Global Hegemon or Reluctant Sheriff?* London: Routledge, 2005.

Cammack, P., Poole, D. and Tordoff, W. *Third World Politics: A Comparative Introduction*, London: The Macmillan Press Ltd, 1993.

Campbell, H., *Rasta and Resistance: From Marcus Garvey to Walter Rodney*, London: Hansib Publishing Limited, 1985.

Carnoy, M., *The State and Political Theory*, Princeton: Princeton University Press, 1984.

Carruthers, J. H., *Intellectual Warfare*, Chicago: Third World Press, 1999.

——, *The Irritated Genie: an essay on the Haitian Revolution*, Chicago: Kemetic Institute, 1985.

Carson, C., ed., *Malcolm X: The FBI File*, New York: Carroll and Graf Publishers, 1993.

Chadwin, M. L., *The Hawks of World War II*, Chapel Hill: University of North Carolina Press, 1968.

Chinweizu, *The West and the Rest of Us: White Predators, Black Slavers and the African Elite*, Lagos: Pero Press, 1987.

Chowdhry, G. and Nair, S., ed., *Power Postcolonialism and International Relations: Reading Race, Gender and Class*, London: Routledge, 2004.

Christie, K., ed., *United States Foreign Policy and National Identity in the Twenty-First Century*, London: Routledge, 2008.

Churchill, W. and Wall, J. V., *Agents of Repression: The FBI's Secret Wars Against the Black Panther Party and the American Indian Movement*, Cambridge: South End Press, 2002.

——, *The Cointelpro Papers: Documents from the FBI's Secret Wars Against Dissent in the United States*, Boston: South End Press, 1990.

Clark, S., ed., *Malcolm X: February 1965, The Final Speeches*, London: Pathfinder, 1997.

——, *Malcolm X Talks to Young People: Speeches in the US Britain and Africa*, London: Pathfinder, 1991.

Clarke, J. H., *Christopher Columbus and the Afrikan Holocaust: Slavery and the Rise of European Capitalism*, New York: A & B Publishers Group, 1998.

——, *Critical Lessons: In Slavery and the Slave Trade*, Richmond: Native Sun Publishers, 1996.

——, *Malcolm X: The Man and His Times*, Trenton: Africa World Press, 1992.

——, *Marcus Garvey and the Vision of Africa*, New York: Vintage Books, 1974.

——, *Notes for an African World Revolution: Africans at the Crossroads*, Trenton: Africa World Press, 1992.

Clegg, III, C. A., *An Original Man: The Life and Times of Elijah Muhammad*, New York: St Martin's Press, 1997.

Cohen, I. S. and Logan, R. W., *The American Negro: Old World Background and New World Experience*, Boston: Houghton Mifflin Company, 1970.

Colaiaco, J. A., *Martin Luther King, Jr.: Apostle of Militant Nonviolence*, New York: St Martin's Press, 1988.

Collins, B. and Jeffrey-Jones, R., ed., *The Growth of Federal Power in American History*, Illinois: Northern Illinois University Press, 1983.

Collins, R. P., *Seventh Child*, New Jersey: Birch Lane Press Book, 1998.

Cone, J. H., *Martin and Malcolm and America: A Dream or a Nightmare*, London: Fount Paperbacks, 1993.

Cox, A., *Power in Capitalist Societies*, Brighton: Wheatsheaf Books, 1985.

Cox, M. and Parmar, I., ed., *Soft Power and US Foreign Policy: Theoretical, Historical and Contemporary Perspectives*, London: Routledge, 2010.

Cross, T., *The Black Power Imperative: Racial Inequality and the Politics of Non-Violence*, New York: Faulkner Books, 1987.

Cruse, H., *The Crisis of the Negro Intellectual: A Historical Analysis of the Failure of Black Leadership*, New York: Quill, 1984.

D'Agostino, P. R., *Missionaries in Babylon: The Adaptation of Italian Priests to Chicago's Church, 1870–1940*, Volume 1, Chicago: University of Chicago Divinity School, 1993.

Dahl, R. A., *A Preface to Democratic Theory*, Chicago: University of Chicago Press, 1956.

——, *Pluralist Democracy in the United States*, Chicago: Rand McNally, 1967.

——, *Who Governs?* New Haven: Yale University Press, 1961.

Dantzig, A. V., *Forts and Castles of Ghana*, Accra: Sedco Publishing, 1980.

De Tocqueville, A., *Democracy in America. Vol. I and II*, New York: Alfred A. Knopf, Inc., 1994.

Diop, C. A., *Civilisation or Barbarism: An Authentic Anthropology*, New York: Lawrence Hill Books, 1991.

——, *The African Origin of Civilization: Myth or Reality*, Illinois: Lawrence Hill Books, 1974.

Du Bois, W. E. B., *The Autobiography of W. E. B. Du Bois*, New York: International Publishers Co., Inc., 1997.

——, *The Soul of Black Folk*, New York: Alfred A. Knopf, Inc., 1993.

Dudziak, M. L., *Cold War Civil Rights: Race and the Image of American Democracy*, Oxford: Princeton University Press, 2000.

Dumbrell, J., *The Making of US Foreign Policy*, Manchester: Manchester University Press, 1990.

Dunleavy, P. and O'Leary, B., *Theories of the State: Politics of Liberal Democracy*, London: MacMillan, 1987.

Dye, T. R., *Power and Society: An Introduction to the Social Sciences*, 5th ed., Pacific Grove: Brooks-Cole, 1983.

Engels, F., *The Origins of the Family, Private Property and the State*, Peking: Foreign Language Press, 1978.

Engels, F. and Marx, K., *The German Ideology*, New York: International Publishers, 1970.

Epps, A., *Malcolm X: Speeches at Harvard*, New York: Paragon House, 1991.

Essien-Udom, E. U., *Black Nationalism: A Search for an Identity in America*, London: The University of Chicago Press, 1971.

Evans, P., Rueschemeyer, D. and Skocpol, T., eds., *Bringing the State Back In*, Cambridge: Cambridge University Press, 1985.

Evans, E. J., *The Forging of the Foreign State*, New York: Longman, 1996.

Evanzz, K., *The Judas Factor: The Plot to Kill Malcolm X*, New York: Thunder's Mouth Press, 1992.

——, *The Messenger: The Rise and Fall of Elijah Muhammad*, New York: Pantheon Books, 1999.

Fairclough, A., *Better Day Coming: Blacks and Equality, 1890–2000*, London: Penguin Books, 2002.

Fanon, F., *Black Skin, White Masks*, London, Pluto Press, 1993.

Femia, J., *Gramsci's Political Thought*, Oxford: Clarendon, 1987.

Finer, S. E., *Anonymous Empire*, London: Pall Mall, 1966.

Finkle, L., *Forum for Protest. The Black Press During World War II*, London: Associated University Press, 1975.

Foner, E., *Give Me Liberty! An American History*, London: W. W. Norton and Company, 2009.

Franklin, J. H., *From Slavery to Freedom*, New York: Vintage Books, 1969.

Frazier, E. F., *Black Bourgeoisie*, London: MacMillan Publishing, 1962.

Fried, A., *McCarthyism The Great American Red Scare: A Documentary History*, Oxford: Oxford University Press, 1997.

Gabbacia, D. R. and Ottanelli, F. M., *Italian Workers of the World: Labour Migration and the formation of Multiethnic States*, Chicago: University of Illinois, 2001.

Gaines, K. K., *Black Expatriates and the Civil Rights Era: American Africans in Ghana*, The University of North Carolina Press: Chapel Hill, 2006.

Gallcchio, M. *The African American Encounter with Japan and China: Black Internationalism in Asia, 1895–1945*, London: University of North Carolina Press, 2000.

Gallen, D., ed., *Malcolm X As They Knew Him*, New York: Ballantine Books, 1992.

Gallen, D., Karim, B. and Skutches, P., *Remembering Malcolm*, New York: Ballantine Books, 1996.

Gardell, M., *Countdown to Armageddon: Louis Farrakhan and the Nation of Islam*, London: Hurst and Company, 1996.

Goldblatt, D., Kiloh, M., Lewis, P. and Potter, D., eds., *Democratization*, Cambridge: Polity Press, 1997.

Goldstein, R. J., *Political Repression in Modern America From 1870 to 1976*, Chicago: University of Illinois Press, 2001.

Goldwyn, R. and Schambra, W., eds., *How Capitalist is the Constitution?* Washington DC: American Enterprise Institute, 1982.

Gomez. M. A., *Black Crescent: The Experience and Legacy of African Muslims in the Americas*, Cambridge: Cambridge University Press, 2005.

Greene, C. Y., ed., *Malcolm X Make it Plain*, London: Penguin Books, 1995.

Grose, P., *Continuing the Inquiry: The Council on Foreign Relations from 1921 to 1996*, New York: CFR, 1996.

Gurtov, M., *Superpower on Crusade: The Bush Doctrine in US Foreign Policy*, London: Lynne Rienner Publishers, 2006.

Hacker, A., *Two Nations: Black and White, Separate, Hostile, Unequal*, New York: Macmillan, 1992.

Haley, A., *The Autobiography of Malcolm X*, New York: Grove Press, 1986.

Hamilton, A., *et al, The Federalist*, New York: The Colonial Press, 1901.

Hamilton, C. V. and Ture, K., *Black Power: The Politics of Liberation*, New York: Vintage Books, 1992.

Hampsher-Monk, I., *A History of Modern Political Thought: Major Political Thinkers from Hobbes to Marx*, Cambridge: Blackwell, 1995.

Haralambos, M. and Holborn, M., *Sociology Themes and Perspectives*, London: Collins Educational, 1995.

Harris, Jr., B., *The United States and the Italo-Ethiopian Crisis*, Palo Alto: Stanford University Press, 1964.

Harris, J. E., *African America Reactions to War in Ethiopia, 1936–1941*, London: Louisana State University, 1994.

Hart, C., *Doing a Literature Review: Releasing the Social Science Research Imagination*, London, Sage Publications, 1998.

Haskins, J., *Louis Farrakhan and the Nation of Islam*, New York: Walker and Company, 1996.

Heale, M. J., *American Anticommunism: Combating the Enemy Within, 1830–1970*, London: The Johns Hopkins University Press, 1990.

Held, D., *Models of Democracy*, Cambridge: Polity Press, 1987.

Henry, C. P., *Ralph Bunche: Model Negro or American Other?* New York: New York University Press, 1999.

Henslin, J. M., *Down to Earth Sociology*, New York: The Free Press, 1985.

Herbert, A., *A Documentary History of the Negro People in the United States*: Volume 5, New York: Carol Publishing Book, 1993.

Higgins, G., *Anacalypsis*, New York: A & B Books Publishers, 1992.

Hill, R. A., ed., *Marcus Garvey: Life and Lessons: A Centennial Companion to the Marcus Garvey and Universal Negro Improvement Association Papers*, London: University of California Press, 1987.

——, *Pan-African Biography*, Los Angeles: African Studies Center, 1987.

——, *The FBI's RACON: Racial Conditions in the United States During World War II*, Boston: Northeastern University Press, 1995.

Hilliard III, A. G., *SBA: The Reawakening of the African Mind*, Gainesville: Makare Publishing Company, 1997.

Hirst, P., *Representative Democracy and its Limits*, Oxford: Polity Press, 1990.

Hoare, Q. and Nowell-Smith, G., eds., *Selections from the Prison Notebooks of Antonia Gramsci*, London: Lawrence Wishart, 1971.

Hobsbawn, E., *Age of Extremes: The Short Twentieth Century 1914–1991*, London: Abacus, 2000.

——, *Nations and Nationalism since 1780 Programmer, Myth, Reality*, Cambridge: Cambridge University Press, 1995.

Horne, G., *Black and Red: W. E. B. Du Bois and Afro-American Response to the Cold War, 1944–1963*, New York: University of New York, 1986.

Howard-Pitney, D., *Martin Luther King Jr., Malcolm X, and the Civil Rights Struggle of the 1950s and 1960s: A Brief History with Documents*, Boston: Bedford St Martins, 2004.

Hunt, M. H., *Ideology and U. S. Foreign Policy*, London: Yale University Press, 1987.

Isserman, M. and Kazin, M., *America Divided: The Civil War of the 1960s*, Oxford: Oxford University Press, 2008.

Jackson, J. G., *Ages Of Gold and Silver*, Austin: American Atheist Press, 1990.

Jackson, R., *Writing the War on Terrorism: Language, Politics and Counter-Terrorism*, Manchester: Manchester University Press, 2005.

James, W., *Holding Aloft the Banner of Ethiopia Caribbean Radicalism in Early Twentieth Century America*, London: Verso, 2000.

Janken, K. R., *White: The Biography of Walter White, Mr. NAACP*, New York: The New Press, 2003.

Jeffreys-Jones, R., *The FBI: A History*, London: Yale University Press, 2007.

Jentleson, B. W. *American Foreign Policy: The Dynamics of Choice in the 21st Century*, London: W. W. Norton & Company, 2007.

Jessop, B., *The Capitalist State*, Oxford: Blackwell, 1982.

Jones, B., Kavanagh, D., Moran, M., Norton, P., *Politics UK*, 4th edition, London: Longman, 2001.

Jones, B. G., ed., *Decolonizing International Relations*, Plymouth: Rowman & Littlefield Publishers, 2006.

Joseph, P. E., *Waiting 'Til the Midnight Hour: A Narrative History of Black Power in America*, New York: Henry Holt & Company, 2006.

Kambon, K. K. K., *African/Black Psychology in the American Context: An African-Centered Approach*, Tallahassee: Nubian Nation Publication, 1998.

Karenga, M., *Introduction to Black Studies*, Los Angeles: The University of Sankore Press, 2002.

Karim, B., ed., *The End of White World Supremacy Four Speeches by Malcolm X*, New York: Arcade Publishing, 1971.

Keita, M., *Race and the Writing of History: Riddling the Sphinx*, Oxford: Oxford University Press, 2000.

Kennedy, P., *The Rise and Fall of the Great Powers: Economic Change and Military Conflict from 1500 to 2000*, London: Fontana Press, 1988.

King, D., *Separate and Unequal: Black Americans and the U.S. Federal Government*, Oxford: Oxford University Press, 1995.

Kingsbury, B. and Roberts, A., eds., *United Nations Divided World: The UN's Roles in International Relations*, 2nd edition, Oxford: Clarendon Press, 1993.

Kirk, J. A., *Martin Luther King Jr.: Profiles in Power*, Harlow: Pearson Education, 2005.
——, ed., *Martin Luther King, Jr and the Civil Rights Movement: Controversies and Debates*, New York: Palgrave Macmillan, 2007.
Kondo, B. Z. A., *Conspiracies: Unravelling the Assassination of Malcolm X*, Washington, DC: Nubia Press, 1993.
Kornweibel, T. J. R., *'Seeing Red' Federal Campaigns Against Black Militancy, 1919–1925*, Indianapolis: Indiana University Press, 1998.
Krasner, S., *Defending the National Interest*, Princeton: Princeton University Press, 1978.
Krenn, M. L., *The Color of Empire: Race and American Foreign Relations*, Washington, DC: Potomac Books, 2006.
——, ed., *The African American Voice in US Foreign Policy Since World War II*, London: Garland Publishing Inc., 1999.
Kush, I. K., *What They Never Told You in History Class*, New York: A & B Publishers Group, 1999.
Ladner, J., ed., *The Death of White Sociology: Essays on Race and Culture*, Baltimore: Black Classic Press, 1988.
Lai, D., ed., *Global Perspectives: International Relation, U.S. Foreign Policy, and the View from Abroad*, London: Lynne Rienner Publishers, 1997.
Lasch, C., *The Agony of the American Left: One Hundred Years of Radicalism*, Middlesex: Penguin Books, 1973.
Latham, E., *The Group Basis of Politics*, New York: Octagon Books, 1965.
Lauren, P. G., *Power and Prejudice: The Politics and Diplomacy of Racial Discrimination*, Boulder: Westview Press, 1996.
Layton, A. S., *International Politics and Civil Rights Policies in the United States 1941–1960*, Cambridge: Cambridge University Press, 2000.
Ledwidge, M., Miller, L. B. and Parmar, I., ed., *New Directions in US Foreign Policy*, New York: Routledge, 2009.
Lewis, D. L., *Biography of a Race, 1868–1919*, New York: Henry Holt and Company, 1994.
——, ed., *W. E. B. Du Bois: A Reader*, New York: Henry Holt and Company Inc., 1995.
——, *W. E. B. Du Bois: The Fight for Equality and the American Century 1919–1963*, New York: Henry Holt and Company, LLC, 2000.
Lewis, G., *Massive Resistance: The White Response to the Civil Rights Movement*, London: Hodder Education, 2006.
Lewis, R., *Marcus Garvey: Anti-Colonial Champion*, Trenton: Africa World Press, Inc., 1998.
—— and Bryan, P., eds., *Garvey His Work and Impact*, Trenton: Africa World Press, Inc., 1991.
Lincoln, C. E., *The Black Muslims in America*, New Jersey: Africa World Press, 1994.
Ling, P. J., *Martin Luther King, Jr.*, London: Routledge, 2006.
Lipset, S. M., *American Exceptionalism: A Double-Edged Sword*, London: W. W. Norton & Company, 1997.
Lively, J. and Reeve, A., eds., *Modern Political Theory from Hobbes to Marx Key Debates*, London: Routledge, 1991.
Locke, A., ed., *The New Negro: Voices of the Harlem Renaissance*, New York: Macmillan Publishing Company, 1992.
Logan, R. W., *The American Negro: Old World Background and New World Background*, Boston: Houghton Mifflin Company, 1970.
——, *The Betrayal of the Negro: From Rutherford B. Hayes to Woodrow Wilson*, New York: Da Capo Press, 1997.

Lomax, L. C., *When the Word is Given*, New York: The World Publishing Company, Ohio, 1963.

Long, D. and Schmidt, B. C., *Imperialism and Internationalism in the Discipline of International Relations*, New York: State University of New York, 2005.

Lukes, S., *Power: A Radical View*, London: MacMillan, 1974.

——, ed., *Readings In Social and Political Theory: Power*, Oxford: Basil Blackwell Ltd, 1986.

Mackie, L., *The Great Marcus Garvey*, London: Hansib Publications, 2001.

Mann, M., *The Sources of Social Power, Volume 2: The Rise of Classes and Nation-states, 1760–1914*, Los Angeles: Cambridge University Press, 1993.

Marable, M., *How Capitalism Underdeveloped Black America: Problems in Race, Political Economy, and Society*, Boston: South End Press, 1983.

Marcuse, H., *Reason and Revolution: Hegel and the Rise of Social Theory*, London: Routledge and Kegan Paul Ltd., 1977.

Marqusee, M., *Redemption Song: Muhammad Ali and the Spirit of the Sixties*, London: Verso, 1999.

Martin, T., *Marcus Garvey, Hero: A First Biography*, Dover: Majority Press, 1983.

——, *Pan-African Connection: From Slavery to Garvey and Beyond*, Dover: Majority Press, 1985.

——, *Race First: The Ideological and Organisational Struggles of Marcus Garvey and the Universal Negro Improvement Association*, Dover: Majority Press, 1986.

Marsh, G. and Stoker, G., eds., *Theory and Methods in Political Science*, New York: Palgrave, 1995.

Marx, K., *Selected Writings*, Oxford: Oxford University Press, 1977.

Mauk, D. and Oakland, J., *American Civilization*, London: Routledge, 1995.

McCarthy, T., *Race, Empire and the Idea of Human Development*, Cambridge: Cambridge University Press, 2009.

Means, Rev. M. S., *Ethiopia And the Missing Link in African History*, Pennsylvania: The Atlantis Publishing Company, 1945.

Meriwether, J. H., *Proudly We Can Be Africans: Black Americans and Africa, 1935–1961*, London: The University of North Carolina Press, 2002.

Merrill, D. and Paterson, T. G., eds., *Major Problems in American Foreign Relations, Volume II: Since 1914*, New York: Houghton Mifflin Company, 2000.

Miliband, R., *The State in Capitalist Society*, London: André Deutsch, 1968.

Mills, C. W., *The Power Elite*, New York: Oxford University Press, 1956.

Miroff, B., Seidelman, R. and Swanstrom, T., *The Democratic Debate: An Introduction to American Politics*, New York: Houghton Mifflin Company, 1998.

Morris, P., *Power: A Philosophical Analysis*, Manchester: Manchester University Press, 1987.

Myrdal, G., *An American Dilemma: The Negro Problem and Modern Democracy*, New York: Harper and Bow Publishers, 1962.

Naison, M., *Communists in Harlem during the Depression*, Chicago: The University of Illinois Press, 1983.

Nesbitt, F. N., *Race for Sanctions: African Americans against Apartheid 1946–1994*, Indianaolis: Indiana University Press, 2004.

Nye, J. S., *Understanding International Conflict: An Introduction to Theory and History*, New York: HarperCollins College Publishers, 1993.

Obama, B., *Dreams From My Father: A Story of Race and Inheritance*, Edinburgh: Canongate Books, 2009.

Omi, M. and Winant, H., *Racial Formation in the United States from the 1960s to 1990s*, London: Routledge, 1994.

O'Reilly, K., '*Racial Matters': The FBI's Secret File on Black America, 1960–1972*, London: The Free Press, 1991.

Padmore, G., *Pan-Africanism or Communism? The Coming Struggle for Africa*, London: Dennis Dobson, 1956.

Parmar, I., *Special Interests, The State And Anglo-American Alliance, 1939–1945*, London: Frank Cass, 1995.

Pedersen, C., *Obama's America*, Edinburgh: Edinburgh University Press, 2009.

Perry, B., *Malcolm: The Life of a Man Who Changed Black America*, New York: Station Hill Press, 1992.

Pfeffer, P. F., *A. Philip Randolph, Pioneer of the Civil Rights Movement*, Baton Rouge: Louisiana State University Press, 1990.

Pincus, F. L. and Ehlich, H. J., eds., *Race and and Ethnic Conflict: Contending Views on Prejudice, Discrimination and Ethnoviolence*, Oxford: Westview Press, 1994.

Plummer, B. G., *Rising Wind: Black Americans and U.S. Foreign Affairs, 1935–1960*, London: The University of North Carolina Press, 1996.

Polenberg, R., *One Nation Divisible: Class, Race, and Ethnicity in the United States Since 1938*, Middlesex: Penguin Books, 1983.

Polsby, N., *Community Power and Democratic Theory*, New Haven: Yale University Press, 1963.

Poulantzas, N., *State, Power, Socialism*, London: New Left Book, 1978.

Powers, R. G., *Secrecy and Power: The Life of J. Edgar Hoover*, London: Hutchinson, 1987.

Rashad, A., ed., *Elijah Muhammad & the Ideological Foundation of The Nation of Islam*, Virginia: UB & US Communications Systems, 1994.

Rashidi, R., ed., *African Presence in Early Asia*, London: Transaction Publishers, 1999.

Rickford, R. J., *Betty Shabazz: Surviving Malcolm X*, Illinois: Sourcebooks, 2003.

Robeson, P., *Here I Stand*, London: Dobson Books, 1958.

Robinson, C. J., *Black Marxism: The Making of the Black Radical Tradition*, London: The North Carolina Press, 1983.

Robinson, A. L. and Sullivan, P., eds., *New Directions in Civil Rights Studies*, London: University Press of Virginia, 1991.

Roediger, D. R., *How Race Survived U.S. History: From Settlement and Slavery to the Obama Phenomenon*, London: Verso, 2008.

——, *The Wages of Whiteness: Races and the Making of the American Working Class*, London: Verso, 1995.

Rogers, J. A., *The Real Facts about Ethiopia*, Baltimore: Black Classic Press, 1982.

Sales, Jr., W. W., *From Civil Rights to Black Liberation: Malcolm X and the Organization of Afro-American Unity*, Massachusetts: South End Press, 1994.

Salvemini, G., *Italian Fascist Activities in the United States*, New York: Center for Migration Studies, 1977.

Sartain, L. and Verney, K., *Long is the Way and Hard: One Hundred Years of the NAACP*, Fayetteville: The University of Arkansas Press, 2009.

Sbacchi, A., *Legacy of Bitterness: Ethiopia and Fascist Italy, 1935–1941*, Trenton: The Red Sea Press, 1997.

Schlesinger, Jr., A. M., *The Disuniting of America Reflections on a Multicultural Society*, London: W. W. Norton & Company 1998.

Scott, W. R. *The Sons of Sheba's Race: African-Americans and the Italo-Ethiopian War, 1935–1941*, Bloomington: Indiana University Press, 1993.

Seyla, B., *Democracy and Difference Contesting the Boundaries of the Political*, Princeton: Princeton University Press, 1996.

Shepherd Jr., G. W., ed., *Racial Influences on American Foreign Policy*, London: Basic Books, Inc, Publishers, 1970.

Shi, D. E. and Tindal, G., *America: A Narrative History*, London: W. W. Norton & Company, 1993.

Shull, S. A., *American Civil Right Policy from Truman to Clinton: The Role Presidential Leadership*, New York: M. E. Sharpe, 2000.

Singh, R., ed., *Governing America: The Politics of a Divided Democracy*, Oxford: Oxford University Press, 2003.

———, *The Farrakhan Phenomenon: Race, Reaction, and the Paranoid Style in American Politics*, Washington, DC: Georgetown University Press, 1997.

Skocpol, T., *States and Social Revolutions*, Cambridge: Cambridge University Press, 1979.

Smedley, A., *Place in North America, Origin and Evolution of World View*, Oxford: West View Press, 1993.

Solomos, J., *Race and Racism in Britain*, London: MacMillan, 1993.

Stimson, H. L. and McGeorge, B., *On Active Service in Peace and War*, New York: Harper and Brothers, 1947.

Strickland, W., ed., *Malcolm X Make it Plain*, London: Penguin Books, 1995.

Stuckey, S., *'I want to be an African:' Paul Robeson and the ends of nationalist theory and practice, 1919–1945*, Los Angeles: Center for Afro-American Studies, 1976.

Tidwell, B., ed., *The State of Black America*, New York: National Urban League, 1992.

T'Shaka, O., *The Political Legacy of Malcolm X*, California: Pan Afrikan Publications, 1983.

———, *Return to the African Mother Principle of Male and Female Equality*, Oakland: Pan Afrikan Publishers and Distributors, 1995.

Tucker, D. F. B., *Marxism and Individualism*, Oxford: Basil Blackwell, 1978.

Tyson, T. B., *Radio Free Dixie: Robert F. Williams & the Roots of Black Power*, London: The University of North Carolina Press, 1999.

Urquhart, B. *An American Life*, London: W. W. Norton & Company Ltd, 1993.

Van Loon, H. W., *The Story of Mankind*, London: W. W. Norton & Company Ltd, 2000.

Van Sertima, I., *Egypt Child of Africa*, New Brunswick: Transaction Publishers, 2002.

———, ed., *Great Black Leaders: Ancient and Modern*, New York: Journal of African Civilisation Ltd, 1993.

Verney, K., *The Debate on Black Civil Rights in America*, Manchester: Manchester University Press, 2006.

———, *Black Civil Rights in America*, London: Routledge, 2004.

Vincent, T. G., *Black Power and the Garvey Movement*, Berkeley: Ramparts Publishers, 1973.

Von Eschen, P. M., *Race Against Empire Black Americans and Anti-Colonialism, 1937–1957*, London: Connell University Press, 1997.

Wainhouse, D. W., *International Peace Observation: A History and Forecast*, Baltimore: Johns Hopkins Press, 1966.

Walker, R., *Classical Splendour: Roots OF Black History*, London: Bogle-L'Overture Press. 1999.

Wandor, M., ed., *The Body Politic, Writings from the Women's Liberation Movement in Britain 1969–72*, London: Stage 1, 1972.

Wartenberg, T. E., *The Forms of Power: From Domination to Transformation*, Philadelphia: Temple University Press, 1990.

Washington, J. M., ed., *A Testament of Hope: The Essential Writings and Speeches of Martin Luther King, Jr.*, New York: HarperCollins Publishers, 1991.

Wellman, D. T., *Portraits of White Racism*, New York: Cambridge University Press, 1977.

West, C., *Prophesy Deliverance! An Afro-American Revolutionary Christianity*, Philadelphia: Westminster Press, 1988.

——, *Prophetic Fragments*, Trenton: Africa World Press, 1988.

White Jr., V. L., *Inside the Nation of Islam: A Historical and Personal Testimony by a Black Muslim*, Florida: University Press of Florida, 2001.

Wilford, H., *The Mighty Wurlitzer*, London: Harvard University Press, 2008.

William, K., *Tabb, The Political Economy of the Black Ghetto*, New York: W. W. Norton, 1970.

Williams, E., *Capitalism & Slavery*, Chapel Hill: The University of North Carolina Press, 1994.

Williams, R. F., *Negroes with Guns*, Detroit: Wayne State University Press, 1998.

Wilson, A. N., *Afrikan-Centred Consciousness Versus The New World Order: Garveyism in the Age of Globalism*, New York: Afrikan World InfoSystems, 1999.

——, *Blueprint for Black Power: A Moral, Political and Economic Imperative for the Twenty-First Century*, New York: Afrikan World Infosystems, 1998.

Wilson, G., *Interest Groups*, Oxford: Basil Blackwell, 1990.

Wilson, W. J., *The Declining Significance of Race*, London: University of Chicago Press, 1978.

Woodson, C. G. and Wesley, C. H., *The Negro in Our History*, Gainesville: The Associated Publishers, Inc., 1972.

X, M., *Malcolm X on Afro-American History*, New York: Pathfinder, 1988.

Yette, S. F., *The Choice: The Issue Of Black Survival In America*, Silver Spring: Cottage Books, 1971.

Yin, R. K., *Case Study Research: Design and Methods*, 3rd edition, London: Sage Publications, 2003, xiii.

Zimmer, H., *Philosophies of India*, Princeton: Princeton University Press, 1989.

Zinn, H., *A People's History of the United States: From 1492 to the Present*, London: Addison Wesley Longman Limited, 1996.

Articles

Asante, M. K., 'On the Wings of Nonsense,' *Black Books Bulletin: Wordswork*, 1993–94, 37–42.

Asante, S. K. B., 'The Afro-American and the Italo-Ethiopian Crisis 1934–36,' *Journal of Negro History*, 1973, 167–84.

Bachrach, P. and Baratz, M. S., 'The Two Faces of Power,' *American Science Review*, 1962, 947–52.

Blumer, H., 'Race Prejudice as a Sense of Group Position,' *The Pacific Sociological Review*, Spring 1958, 3–7.

Bowser, B. P., 'Race and US Foreign Policy: A Bibliography Essay,' *Sage Race Relations*, 1 Feb. 1987, 4–31.

Dahl, R., 'The Concept of Power,' *Behavioral Science*, 1957, 202–3.

Drake, St C., 'Black Studies and Global Perspectives: An Essay,' *Journal of Negro Education*, 1984, vol. 53, no. 3, 226–42.

Du Bois, W. E. B., 'African Roots of War,' *Atlantic Monthly 115*, 1915, 707–14.

Du Bois, W. E. B., 'Inter-racial Implications of the Ethiopian Crisis: A Negro View,' *Journal of Foreign Affairs*, 1935, 82–92.

Fraser, C., 'Understanding American Policy Towards the Decolonization of European Empires, 1945–64,' *Diplomacy & Statecraft*, 1992, vol. 3, no. 1, 105–25.

Halden, L. G., 'The Diplomacy of the Ethiopian Crisis,' *Journal of Negro History*, Apr. 1937, 163–99.

Henry, P., 'Pan-Africanism: A Dream Come True,' *Foreign Affairs*, Apr. 1959, 443–52.

King, D., 'The Racial Bureaucracy: African Americans and the Federal Government in the Era of Segregated Race Relations,' *Governance: An International Journal of Policy and Administration*, Oct. 1999, 345–78.

Ledwidge, M., 'American Power and Racial Dimensions of U. S. Foreign Policy,' *International Politics*, 2011, forthcoming.

Minion K. C. Morrison, 'Reflections of Senior Scholar on the Profession of International Studies,' *International Studies Perspective*, Nov. 2008, vol. 9, no. 4, 459–63.

Parmar, I., 'Anglo-American Elites in the Interwar Years: Idealism and Power in the Intellectual Roots of Chatham House and the Council on Foreign Relations,' *International Relations*, 2002, vol. 16, no. 1, 53–75.

——, '"Another important group that needs more cultivation": The Council on Foreign Relations and the Mobilisation of Black Americans for Interventionism, 1939–41,' *Ethnic and Racial Studies*, Sept. 2004, 710–31.

——, 'Resurgent Academic Interest in the Council on Foreign Relations,' *Politics: Surveys, Debates and Controversies in Politics*, Feb. 2001, vol. 21, 31–39.

——, 'The Issue of State Power: The Council on Foreign Relations as a Case Study,' *Journal of American Studies*, Apr. 1995, 73–95.

Roark, J. L., 'American Black Leaders: The Response of Colonialism and the Cold War,' *African Historical Studies*, 1971, 253–70.

Ross, R., 'Black Americans and Italo-Ethiopian Relief, 1935–36,' *Ethiopia Observer*, 1972, 122–31.

Shepperson, G., 'Notes on Negro American Influences on the Emergence of African Nationalism,' *Journal of African History*, 1960, 299–312.

Scott, W. R., 'Black Nationalism and the Italo-Ethiopian Conflict 1934–36,' *Journal of Negro History*, Apr. 1978, 125.

——, 'Malaku E Bayen: Ethiopian Emissary to Black America, 1936–41,' *Ethiopian Observer*, 1972, 132–38.

Smith, R. M., 'Beyond Tocqueville, Myrdal and Hartz: The Multiple Traditions in America,' *American Political Science Review*, 1993, 547–63.

Smith, M. J., 'Pluralism, Reformed Pluralism and Neo-Pluralism,' *Political Studies*, 1990, 210–22.

Villiard, O. G., 'The Negro and the Domestic Problem,' *Alexanderaq's Magazine*, 15 Nov. 1905, 8–15.

Woodland, J., 'How did Participation in America's wars affect Black Americans,' *American Studies Today*, Liverpool: American Studies Resource Centre, 2001, 18–22.

CD

Author not stated, *The Weekly Newsmagazine: 1940s Highlights*, 27 May 1940.

Websites

Author not stated, 'Dumbarton Oaks: Washington Conversations on International Peace and Security Organisation, Oct. 7, 1944,' http://www.ibiblio.org/pha/policy/1944/441007a.html.

Coombs, N., 'The Black Experience in America, Chapter 10: Fighting Racism at Home and Abroad,' http://cti.itc.virginia.edu/~ybf2u/Thomas-Hill/library/Coombs/10.html.

Staff of the Senate Committee on Foreign Relations and the Department of State, 'The Avalon Project at Yale Law School: The Yalta Conference, February 1945,' http://www.yale.edu/lawweb/avalon/wwii/yalta.htm.

Archives

The Papers of W. E. B. Du Bois, 1803, 1877–1963 1965, Special Collection, Sanford, NC: Microfilm Corp. of America, 1980.

CDAAA Papers, Princeton: Seeley G. Mudd Manuscript Library, Princeton University, 1993.

FFF Papers, Princeton: Seeley G. Mudd Manuscript Library, Princeton University, 1993.

Frank R. Crosswaith Papers, 1917–1965, New York: Schomberg Center for Research, 1993.

John Henrik Clarke Papers, 1937–1996, New York: Schomberg Center for Research, 1994.

Paul Robeson Collection, 1925–1956, New York: Schomberg Center for Research, 1978.

Government Documents

U.S. State Department, *United States Foreign Policy 1931–1941*, Washington DC: Government Printing Office, 1983.

U.S. State Department, *Peace and War: United States Foreign Relations 1931–1941*, Washington DC: United States Government Printing Office, 1943.

Newspapers

The Crisis, 1919, 1939, 1941
The Chicago Defender, Chicago: 1936, 1941, 1945
The New York Amsterdam Star News, New York: 1935, 1940, 1941

Index